Lecture Notes of the Institute for Computer Sciences, Social Informatics and Telecommunications Engineering   125

T0226329

Dirk Pesch   Andreas Timm-Giel
Ramón Agüero Calvo   Bernd-Ludwig Wenning
Kostas Pentikousis (Eds.)

Mobile Networks and Management

5th International Conference, MONAMI 2013
Cork, Ireland, September 23-25, 2013
Revised Selected Papers

 Springer

Volume Editors

Dirk Pesch
Cork Institute of Technology, Ireland
E-mail: dirk.pesch@cit.ie

Andreas Timm-Giel
Hamburg University of Technology, Germany
E-mail: timm-giel@tuhh.de

Ramón Agüero Calvo
University of Cantabria, Santander, Spain
E-mail: ramon@tlmat.unican.es

Bernd-Ludwig Wenning
Cork Institute of Technology, Ireland
E-mail: berndludwig.wenning@cit.ie

Kostas Pentikousis
EICT GmbH, Berlin, Germany
E-mail: k.pentikousis@eict.de

ISSN 1867-8211   e-ISSN 1867-822X
ISBN 978-3-319-04276-3   e-ISBN 978-3-319-04277-0
DOI 10.1007/978-3-319-04277-0
Springer Cham Heidelberg New York Dordrecht London

Library of Congress Control Number: 2013956560

CR Subject Classification (1998): C.2, H.4, D.2

Typesetting: Camera-ready by author, data conversion by Scientific Publishing Services, Chennai, India

Printed on acid-free paper

Springer is part of Springer Science+Business Media (www.springer.com)

Preface

This volume is the result of the 5th International ICST Conference on Mobile Networks and Management (MONAMI), which was held in Cork, Ireland, during on September 23–25 2013, hosted by the Cork Institute of Technology (CIT).

The MONAMI conference series aims at closing the gap between hitherto considered separate and isolated research areas, namely, multi-access and resource management, mobility and network management, and network virtualization. Although these have emerged as core aspects in the design, deployment, and operation of current and future networks, there is still little interaction between the experts in these fields. MONAMI enables cross-pollination between these areas by bringing together top researchers, academics, and practitioners specializing in the field of mobile network and service management.

The conference opened with two half-day tutorials: "ZigBee Wireless Sensor and Control Network," addressing one of the key scientific aspects of the MONAMI conference, presented by Ataollah Elahi of Southern Connecticut State University. In parallel, Paul Sutton, of CTVR, the Telecommunications Research Centre, Trinity College Dublin, presented the Iris system in his tutorial entitled "Building Software Radio Systems with Iris," which also featured some demonstrations of cognitive radio applications. Prof. Mischa Dohler, from King's College London, UK, opened the second day with his vision on "Machine-to-Machine in Smart Cities and Smart Grids: Vision, Technologies and Applications." Finally, Prof. Linda Doyle, from Trinity College Dublin, Ireland, opened the last day of the conference with her keynote on "Management of Cognitive Radio Systems," which provided a very interesting view on the future of this technological area.

After a thorough peer review process, 18 papers were selected for inclusion in the main track of the technical program. Each paper was reviewed by at least three competent researchers, including at least one Technical Program Committee member. In addition, MONAMI 2013 hosted a well-received special session on Future Research Directions, which featured four papers. All in all, 22 peer-reviewed papers were orally presented at the conference. This volume includes the revised versions of all papers that were presented at MONAMI 2013 in a single-track format. Attendance increased in MONAMI 2013 and all newcomers acknowledged the collegial atmosphere that characterizes the conference making it an excellent venue, not only to present novel research work, but also to foster stimulating discussions between the attendees.

This volume is organized thematically in five parts, starting with "TCP, Multi-Path and Coding" in Part I. "Mobile Networks" aspects are discussed in Part II. Part III presents new approaches related to "Wireless Sensor and Vehicular Networks." Part IV addresses "Wireless Communications and

Traffic." Finally, Part V includes papers presenting avant-garde research directions, including cloud connectivity, orchestration, and SDN.

We close this short preface to the volume by acknowledging the vital role that the Technical Program Committee members and additional referees played during the review process. Their efforts ensured that all submitted papers received a proper evaluation. We thank EAI and ICST for assisting with organization matters, and CREATE-NET and Cork Institute of Technology for hosting MONAMI 2013. The team that put together this year's event is large and required the sincere commitment of many folks. Although too many to recognize here by name, their effort should be highlighted. We particularly thank Elisa Mendini for her administrative support on behalf of EAI, and Prof. Imrich Chlamtac of CREATE-NET for his continuous support of the conference. Finally, we thank all delegates for attending MONAMI 2013 and making it such a vibrant conference!

November 2013   Dirk Pesch
                                                  Andreas Timm-Giel
                                                       Ramón Agüero
                                              Bernd-Ludwig Wenning
                                                 Kostas Pentikousis

Organization

General Chairs

Dirk Pesch   Cork Institute of Technology, Ireland
Andreas Timm-Giel   Hamburg University of Technology, Germany

Technical Program Committee Chairs

Sven van der Meer   Ericsson, Ireland
Ramon Aguero   University of Cantabria, Spain

Keynotes Chair

John Strassner   Huawei, USA

Tutorials Chair

Susana Sargento   University of Aveiro, Portugal

Publicity Chair

Bernd-Ludwig Wenning   Cork Institute of Technology, Ireland

Publications Chair

Kostas Pentikousis   EICT GmbH, Germany

Financial Chair

Maciej Muehleisen   Hamburg University of Technology, Germany

Web Chair

Jarno Pinola   VTT Technical Research Centre of Finland,
                             Finland

Table of Contents

Wireless Communications and Traffic

Future Research Directions

Trade-Off between Cost and Goodput in Wireless: Replacing Transmitters with Coding

MinJi Kim[1], Thierry Klein[2], Emina Soljanin[2],
João Barros[3], and Muriel Médard[1]

[1] Research Laboratory of Electronics (RLE), MIT
Cambridge, MA USA 02139
{minjikim,medard}@mit.edu
[2] Alcatel-Lucent Bell Laboratories
Murray Hill, NJ USA 07974
thierry.klein@alcatel-lucent.com, emina@research.bell-labs.com
[3] Department of Electrical and Computer Engineering, University of Porto
Porto, Portugal
jbarros@fe.up.pt

Abstract. We study the cost of improving the *goodput*, or the useful data rate, to user in a wireless network. We measure the cost in terms of number of base stations, which is highly correlated to the energy cost as well as capital and operational costs of a network provider. We show that increasing the available bandwidth, or throughput, may not necessarily lead to increase in goodput, particularly in lossy wireless networks in which TCP does not perform well. As a result, much of the resources dedicated to the user may not translate to high goodput, resulting in an inefficient use of the network resources. We show that using protocols such as TCP/NC, which are more resilient to erasures and failures in the network, may lead to a goodput commensurate with the throughput dedicated to each user. By increasing goodput, users' transactions are completed faster; thus, the resources dedicated to these users can be released to serve other requests or transactions. Consequently, we show that translating efficiently throughput to goodput may bring forth better connection to users while reducing the cost for the network providers.

1 Introduction

Mobile data traffic has been growing at an alarming rate with some estimating that it will increase more than 25-folds in the next five years [1]. In order to meet such growth, there has been an increasing effort to install and upgrade the current networks. As shown in Figure 1, mobile service providers often install more infrastructure (e.g. more base stations) in areas which already have full coverage. The new infrastructure is to provide more bandwidth, which would lead to higher quality of experience to users. However, this increase in bandwidth comes at a significant energy cost as each base station has been shown to use 2-3 kilowatts (kW) [2]. The sustainability and the feasibility of such rapid development have been brought to question as several trends indicate that the technology efficiency improvements may not be able to keep pace with the traffic growth [2].

D. Pesch et al. (Eds.): MONAMI 2013, LNICST 125, pp. 1–14, 2013.
© Institute for Computer Sciences, Social Informatics and Telecommunications Engineering 2013

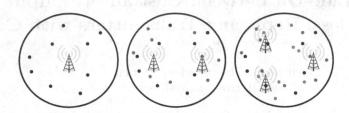

Fig. 1. As number of users in a given area grows, a service provider may add additional base stations not for coverage but for bandwidth. As red users join the network, a second base station may be necessary; as green users join the network, a third base station may become necessary in order to maintain a certain level of quality of service.

We show that maintaining or even improving users' quality of experience may be achieved without installing more base stations. In some cases, we show that the users' quality of experience may be improved while reducing the number of base stations. We measure users' quality of experience using the throughput perceived by the user or the application, i.e. *goodput*. We make a clear distinction between the terms goodput and *throughput*, where goodput is the number of *useful* bits over unit time received by the user and throughput is the number of bits transmitted by the base station per unit time. In essence, throughput is indicative of the bandwidth/resources provisioned by the service providers; while goodput is indicative of the user's quality of experience. For example, the base station, after accounting for the FEC overhead, may be transmitting bits at 10 megabits per second (Mbps), i.e. throughput is 10 Mbps. However, the user may only receive useful information at 5 Mbps, i.e. goodput is 5 Mbps.

There can be a significant disparity between throughput and goodput, particularly in lossy networks using TCP. TCP often mistakes random erasures as congestion [3, 4]. For example, 1-3% packet loss rate is sufficient to harm TCP's performance [3–6]. This performance degradation can lead to inefficient use of network resources and incur substantially higher cost to maintain the same goodput. There has been extensive research to combat these harmful effects of erasures and failures; however, TCP even with modifications does not achieve significant improvement. References [4, 7] give an overview of various TCP versions over wireless links.

This disparity between throughput and goodput can be reduced by using a transport protocol that is more resilient to losses. One method is to use multiple base stations simultaneously (using multiple TCP connections [8] or multipath TCP [9]). However, the management of the multiple streams or paths may be difficult, especially in lossy networks. Furthermore, each path or TCP stream still suffer from performance degradation in lossy environments [8, 9].

We propose TCP/NC [5, 10] as an alternative transport protocol. We provide an overview of TCP/NC in Section 1.1 TCP/NC may not be the only viable solution, and other transport protocols that can combat erasures may be used.

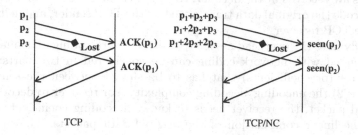

Fig. 2. Example of TCP and TCP/NC. In the case of TCP, the TCP sender receives duplicate ACKs for packet p_1, which may wrongly indicate congestion. However, for TCP/NC, the TCP sender receives ACKs for packets p_1 and p_2; thus, the TCP sender perceives a longer RTT but does not mistake the loss to be congestion.

We use TCP/NC for its effectiveness and simplicity. TCP/NC allows a better use of the base stations installed, and can improve the goodput without any additional base stations. Improving the goodput with the same or a fewer number of base stations implies reduction in energy cost, operational expenses, capital expenses, and maintenance cost for the network provider. The results in this paper can also be understood as being able to serve more users or traffic growth with the same number of base stations. This may lead to significant cost savings, and may be of interest for further investigation.

We note that, to prevent TCP's performance degradation, cellular systems such as LTE have implemented various mechanisms (e.g. HARQ [11] and lower layer retransmissions) with stringent bit-error rates to reduce packet loss rate. Using a transport protocol that can combat erasures, e.g. TCP/NC, may relieve the lower layers from such stringent performance requirements. It would be interesting to study the effect of using erasure-resilient transport protocols on the lower layers' performance requirements, and the cross-layer optimization to improve the throughput and the energy cost of cellular systems.

1.1 Overview of TCP/NC

Reference [10] introduces a new *network coding* layer between the TCP and IP in the protocol stack. The network coding layer intercepts and modifies TCP's acknowledgment (ACK) scheme such that random erasures do not affect the transport layer's performance. To do so, the *encoder*, the network coding unit under the sender TCP, transmits R random linear combinations of the buffered packets for every transmitted packet from TCP sender. The parameter R is the *redundancy factor*. Redundancy factor helps TCP/NC to recover from random losses; however, it cannot mask correlated losses, which are usually due to congestion. The *decoder*, the network coding unit under the receiver TCP, acknowledges *degrees of freedom* instead of individual packets, as shown in Figure 2. Once enough degrees of freedoms are received at the decoder, the decoder solves the set of linear equations to decode the original data transmitted by the TCP sender, and delivers the data to the TCP receiver.

We briefly note the overhead associated with network coding. The main overhead associated with network coding can be considered in two parts: 1) the coding vector (or coefficients) that has to be shared between the sender and the receiver; 2) the encoding/decoding complexity. For receiver to decode a network coded packet, the receiver needs to know the coding coefficients used to generate the linear combination of the original data packets. The first overhead can be minimized with the sender including a seed for a pseudo-random number generator which allows the receiver to generate the coding coefficients in each coded packet. The second overhead associated with network coding is the encoding and decoding complexity, and the delay associated with the coding operations. Note that to affect TCP's performance, the decoding/encoding operations must take substantial amount of time to affect the round-trip time estimate of the TCP sender and receiver. However, we note that the delay caused the coding operations is negligible compared to the network round-trip time. For example, the network round-trip time is often in milliseconds (if not in hundreds of milliseconds), while encoding/decoding operations involve a matrix multiplication/inversion in a field (e.g. $\mathbf{F}_{256}$), which can be performed in a few microseconds.

In [10], the authors present two versions of TCP/NC – one that adheres to the end-to-end philosophy of TCP, in which coding operations are only performed at the source and destination; another that takes advantage of network coding even further by allowing any subset of intermediate nodes to re-encode. Note that re-encoding at the intermediate nodes is an optional feature, and is not required for TCP/NC to work. Here, we focus on TCP/NC with end-to-end network coding. However, a similar analysis applies to TCP/NC with re-encoding.

2   Model

Consider a network with n users. We assume that these n users are in an area such that a single base station can cover them as shown in Figure 1. If the users are far apart enough that a single base station cannot cover the area, then more base stations are necessary; however, we do not consider the problem of coverage.

The network provider's goal is to provide a *fair* service to any user that wishes to start a transaction. Here, by fair, we mean that *every user receives the same average throughput*, denoted as r_t Mbps. It would be interesting to extend and analyze TCP/NC or other alternative protocols under different notions of fairness as well as in networks with priority-based scheduling. However, in this paper, we use a simple definition of *fairness* in which all users receive the same throughput.

The network provider wishes to have enough network resources, measured in number of base stations, so that any user that wishes to start a transaction is able to join the network immediately and achieve an average throughput of r_t Mbps. We denote r_g to be the goodput experienced by the user. Note that $r_g \leq r_t$.

We denote n_{bs} to be the number of base stations needed to meet the network provider's goal. We assume that every base station can support at most $R_{\max}$ Mbps (in throughput) and at most $N_{\max}$ active users simultaneously. In this paper, we assume that $R_{\max} = 300$ Mbps and $N_{\max} = 200$.

A user is *active* if the user is currently downloading a file; *idle* otherwise. A user decides to initiate a transaction with probability p at each time slot. Once a user decides to initiate a transaction, a file size of f bits is chosen according to a probability distribution P_f. We denote μ_f to be the expected file size, and the expected duration of the transaction to be $\Delta = \mu_f/r_g$ seconds. If the user is already active, then the new transaction is added to the user's queue. If the user has initiated k transactions, the model of adding the jobs into the user's queue is equivalent to splitting the goodput r_g to k transactions (each transaction achieves a rate of r_g/k Mbps).

We denote p_p to be the probability of packet loss in the network, and RTT to be the round-trip time. In a wireless, p_p and RTT may vary widely. For example, wireless connection over WiFi may have RTT ranging from tens of milliseconds to hundreds of milliseconds with loss rates typically ranging from 0-10%. In a more managed network (such as cellular networks), RTT are typically higher than that of a WiFi network but lower in loss rates.

3   Analysis of the Number of Base Stations

We analyze the number of base stations n_{bs} needed to support n users given throughput r_t and goodput r_g. We first analyze $P(\Delta, p)$, the probability that a user is active at any given point in time. Given $P(\Delta, p)$, we compute the expected number of active users at any given point in time and n_{bs} needed to support these active users.

Consider a user u at time t. There are many scenarios in which u would be active at t. User u may initiate a transaction at precisely time t with probability p. Otherwise, u is still in the middle of a transaction initiated previously.

To derive $P(\Delta, p)$, we use the Little's Law. For a stable system, the Little's Law states that the average number of jobs (or transactions in our case) in the user's queue is equal to the product of the arrival rate p and the average transaction time Δ. When $\Delta p \geq 1$, we expect the user's queue to have on average at least one transaction in the long run. This implies that the user is expected to be active at all times. When $\Delta p < 1$, we can interpret the result from Little's Law to represent the probability that a user is active. For example, if $\Delta p = 0.3$, the user's queue is expected to have 0.3 transactions at any given point in time. This can be understood as the user being active for 0.3 fraction of the time. Note that when the system is unstable, the long term average number of uncompleted jobs in the user's queue may grow unboundedly. In an unstable system, we assume that in the long term, a user is active with probability equal to one.

Therefore, we can state the following result for $P(\Delta, p)$.

$$P(\Delta, p) = \min\{1, \Delta p\} = \min\left\{1, \frac{\mu_f}{r_g} \cdot p\right\}. \tag{1}$$

Given $P(\Delta, p)$, the expected number of active users is $nP(\Delta, p)$. We can now characterize the expected number of base stations needed as

$$n_{bs} = nP(\Delta, p) \cdot \max\left\{\frac{r_t}{R_{\max}}, \frac{1}{N_{\max}}\right\}. \tag{2}$$

In Equation (2), $\max\left\{\frac{r_t}{R_{\max}}, \frac{1}{N_{\max}}\right\}$ represents the amount of base stations' resources (the maximum load $R_{\max}$ or the amount of activity $N_{\max}$) each active user consumes. The value of n_{bs} from Equation (2) may be fractional, indicating that actually $\lceil n_{bs} \rceil$ base stations are needed.

Note the effect of r_t and r_g. As shown in Equation (2), increasing r_t incurs higher cost while increasing r_g reduces the cost. Therefore, when a network provider dedicates resources to increase r_t, the goal of the network provider is to increase r_g proportional to r_t.

4 Best Case Scenario

In an ideal scenario, the user should see a goodput $r_g = r_t$. In this section, we analyze this best case scenario with $r = r_t = r_g$. Once we understand the optimal scenario, we then consider the behavior of TCP and TCP/NC in Section 5 where generally $r_g \leq r_t$.

4.1 Analytical Results

In Figures 3a and 3b, we plot Equation (2) with $\mu_f = 3.2$ MB and $\mu_f = 5.08$ MB for varying values of p. As r increases, it does not necessarily lead to increase in n_{bs}. Higher r results in users finishing their transactions faster, which in turn allows the resources dedicated to these users to be released to serve other requests or transactions. As a result, counter-intuitively, we may be able to maintain a higher r with *the same or a fewer* number of base stations than we would have needed for a lower r. For example, in Figure 3a, when $r < 1$ Mbps, the rate of new requests exceeds the rate at which the requests are handled; resulting in an unstable system. As a result, most users are active all the time, and the system needs $\frac{n}{N_{\max}} = \frac{1000}{200} = 5$ base stations.

There are many cases where n_{bs} is relatively constant regardless of r. For instance, consider $p = 0.03$ in Figure 3b. The value of n_{bs} is approximately 4-5 throughout. However, there is a significant difference in the way the resources are used. When r is low, all users have slow connections; therefore, the base stations are fully occupied not in throughput but in the number of active users. On the other hand, when r is high, the base stations are being used at full-capacity in terms of throughput. As a result, although the system requires the same number

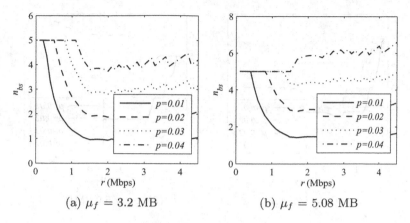

(a) $\mu_f = 3.2$ MB   (b) $\mu_f = 5.08$ MB

Fig. 3. The values of n_{bs} from Equation (2) with $n = 1000$ and varying p and r

of base stations, users experience better quality of service and users' requests are completed quickly.

When p and r are high enough, it is necessary to increase n_{bs}. As demand exceeds the network capacity, it becomes necessary to add more infrastructure to meet the growth in demand. For example, consider $p = 0.04$ in Figure 3b. In this case, as r increases n_{bs} increases.

4.2 Simulation Results

We present MATLAB simulation results to verify our analysis results in Section 4.1. We assume that at every 0.1 second, a user may start a new transaction with probability $\frac{p}{10}$. This was done to give a finer granularity in the simulations; the results from this setup is equivalent to having users start a new transaction with probability p every second. We assume that there are $n = 1000$ users. For each iteration, we simulate the network for 1000 seconds. Each plot is averaged over 100 iterations.

Once a user decides to start a transaction, a file size is chosen randomly in the following manner. We assume there are four types of files: $f_{doc} = 8$KB (a document), $f_{image} = 1$MB (an image), $f_{mp3} = 3$ MB (a mp3 file), $f_{video} = 20$ MB (a small video), and are chosen with probability p_{doc}, p_{image}, p_{mp3}, and p_{video}, respectively. In Figure 4a, we set $[p_{doc}, p_{image}, p_{mp3}, p_{video}] = [0.3, 0.3, 0.3, 0.1]$. This results in $\mu_f = 3.2$ MB as in Figure 3a. In Figure 4b, we set $[p_{doc}, p_{image}, p_{mp3}, p_{video}] = [0.26, 0.27, 0.27, 0.2]$, which gives $\mu_f = 5.08$ MB as in Figure 3b.

The simulation results show close concordance to our analysis. Note that the values in Figures 4a and 4b are slightly greater than that of Figures 3a and 3b. This is because, in the simulation, we round-up any fractional n_{bs}'s since the number of base stations needs to be integral.

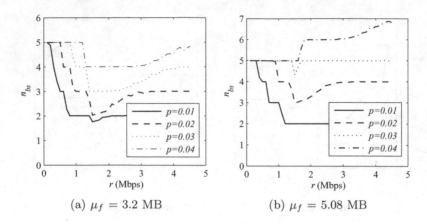

(a) $\mu_f = 3.2$ MB   (b) $\mu_f = 5.08$ MB

Fig. 4. Average value of n_{bs} over 100 iterations with $n = 1000$ and varying p and r

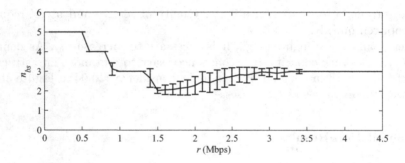

Fig. 5. Average and standard deviation of n_{bs} over 100 iterations with $\mu_f = 3.2$ MB and $p = 0.02$

In Figure 5, we show the average value of n_{bs} and its standard deviation δ for $\mu_f = 3.2$ MB and $p = 0.02$. A plot similar to that of Figure 5 can be obtained for different values of μ_f and p; however, we omit them for want of space. When $r < 0.5$ Mbps, $n_{bs} = 5$ and $\delta = 0$. This is because all users' connections are slow and all users are active; thus, $\frac{n}{N_{max}} = 5$ base stations are always needed (resulting in $\delta = 0$).

Understanding the effect of the standard deviation δ is important. For example, when $r = 2$ Mbps, we have $n_{bs} = 2.28$ and $\delta = 0.2036$. Therefore, when $r = 2$ Mbps, we needed two base stations in most iterations, only occasionally three. This indicates that the third base station is needed to serve the occasional bursts of activities. Thus, to ensure a certain level of throughput to users, it is important to over-provision, e.g. install $\geq n_{bs} + 2\delta$ base stations to overcome the stochastic variations in activities. However, as r increases further (> 3 Mbps),

δ approaches zero. When $r > 3$ Mbps, bursty user activities do not lead to variations in n_{bs}; all user requests are completed quickly enough that bursty activities have negligible effect on n_{bs}. Therefore, when we consider the stochastic nature of user activities, it may be even more desirable to have large r.

5   Analysis for TCP/NC and TCP

We now study the effect of TCP and TCP/NC's behavior. We use the model and analysis from [5] to model the relationship between r_g and p_p for TCP and TCP/NC. We denote r_{g-nc} to be the goodput when using TCP/NC, and r_{g-tcp} to be that for TCP. We set the maximum congestion window, $W_{\max}$, of TCP and TCP/NC to be 50 packets (with each packet being 1000 bytes long), and their initial window size to be 1. We consider $RTT = 100$ ms and varying p_p from 0% to 5%. We note that, given r_t and p_p, $r_g \le r_t(1 - p_p)$ regardless of the protocol used.

In [5, 10], TCP/NC has been shown to be robust against erasures; thus, allowing it to maintain a high throughput despite random losses. For example, if the network allows for 2 Mbps per user and there is 10% loss rate, then the user should see approximately $2 \cdot (1 - 0.1) = 1.8$ Mbps. Reference [5] has shown, both analytically and with simulations, that TCP/NC indeed is able to achieve goodput close to 1.8 Mbps in such a scenario while TCP fails to do so.

5.1   Behavior of r_{g-nc} with Varying p_p

Equation (20) from [5] provides the goodput behavior of TCP/NC, which we provide below in Equation (3).

$$r_{g-nc} = \frac{1}{tSRTT}\left(tW_{\max} - \frac{(W_{\max} - 1)^2 + (W_{\max} - 1)}{2}\right), \tag{3}$$

where $SRTT$ is the effective RTT observed by TCP/NC and increases with p_p and t represents the duration of the connection (in number of RTTs). Equation (3) shows the effect of network coding. The goodput of TCP/NC decreases with p_p; however, the effect is indirect. As p_p increases, the perceived RTT increases, which leads to TCP/NC reducing its rate.

Combining Equation (3) and $r_{g-nc} \le r_t(1 - p_p)$, we obtain the values of r_{g-nc} for various r_t, RTT, and p_p. In Figure 6a, the values of r_{g-nc} plateaus once r_t exceeds some value. This is caused by $W_{\max}$. Given $W_{\max}$ and RTT, TCP/NC and TCP both have a maximal goodput it can achieve. In the case with RTT = 100 ms, the maximal goodput is approximately 4 Mbps. Note that regardless of p_p, all TCP/NC flows achieve the maximal achievable rate. This shows that TCP/NC can overcome effectively the erasures or errors in the network, and provide a goodput that closely matches the throughput r_t.

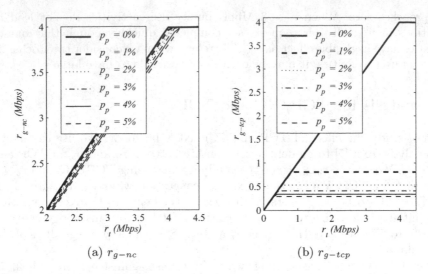

(a) r_{g-nc} (b) r_{g-tcp}

Fig. 6. The value of r_{g-nc} and r_{g-tcp} against r_t for varying values of p_p. We set $RTT = 100$ ms.

5.2 Behavior of r_{g-tcp} with Varying p_p

Equation (16) from [5] provides the goodput behavior of TCP, which we provide below in Equation (4).

$$r_{g-tcp} \approx \min\left(\frac{W_{\max}}{RTT}, \frac{1-p_p}{p_p} \frac{1}{RTT\left(\frac{5}{3} + \sqrt{\frac{2}{3}\frac{1-p_p}{p_p}}\right)} \right). \tag{4}$$

Note that unlike TCP/NC, TCP performance degrades proportionally to $\sqrt{\frac{1}{p}}$.

Combining Equation (4) and $r_{g-tcp} \leq r_t(1 - p_p)$, we obtain the values of r_{g-tcp} for various r_t, RTT, and p_p as shown in Figure 6b. As in Figure 6a, the values of r_{g-tcp} are also restricted by $W_{\max}$. However, TCP achieves this maximal goodput only when $p_p = 0\%$. This is because, when there are losses in the network, TCP is unable to recover effectively from the erasures and fails to use the bandwidth dedicated to it. For $p_p > 0\%$, r_{g-tcp} is not limited by $W_{\max}$ but by TCP's performance limitations in lossy wireless networks.

5.3 The Number of Base Stations for TCP/NC and TCP

We use the values of r_{g-nc} and r_{g-tcp} from Sections 5.1 and 5.2 to compare the number of base stations for TCP/NC and TCP using Equation (2). We assume that $SRTT = RTT$. In general, $SRTT$ is slightly larger than RTT.

Figures 7 and 8 show n_{bs} predicted by Equation (2) when $RTT = 100$ ms. TCP suffers performance degradation as p_p increases; thus, n_{bs} increases rapidly with p_p. Note that increasing r_t without being able to increase r_g leads to inefficient

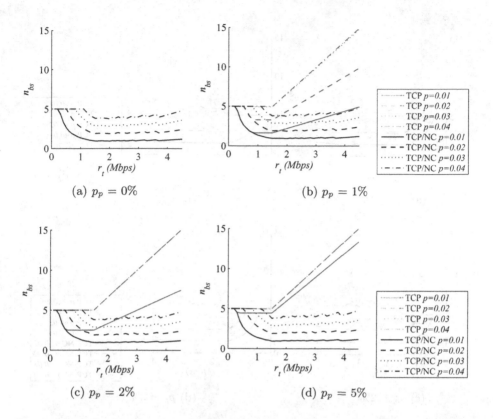

Fig. 7. The value of n_{bs} from Equation (2) for TCP and TCP/NC with varying p_p and p. Here, $RTT = 100$ ms, $W_{\max} = 50$, $n = 1000$, and $\mu_f = 3.2$ MB. In (a), $p_p = 0$ and both TCP and TCP/NC behaves the same; thus, the curves overlap. Note that this result is the same as that of Figure 3a. In (b), the value of n_{bs} with TCP for $p = 0.03$ and 0.04 coincide (upper most red curve). In (c) and (d), the values of n_{bs} with TCP for $p > 0.01$ overlap.

use of the network, and this is clearly shown by the performance of TCP as r_t increases with $p_p > 0\%$.

However, for TCP/NC, n_{bs} does not increase significantly (if any at all) when p_p increases. As discussed in Section 3, TCP/NC is able to translate better r_t into r_{g-nc} despite $p_p > 0\%$, i.e. $r_t \approx r_{g-nc}$. As a result, this leads to a significant reduction in n_{bs} for TCP/NC compared to TCP. Note that n_{bs} for TCP/NC is approximately equal to the values of n_{bs} in Section 3 regardless of the value of p_p. Since TCP/NC is resilient to losses, the behavior of r_{g-nc} does not change as dramatically against p_p as that of r_{g-tcp} does. As a result, we observe n_{bs} for TCP/NC to reflect closely the values of n_{bs} seen in Section 3, which is the best case with $r_t = r_g$.

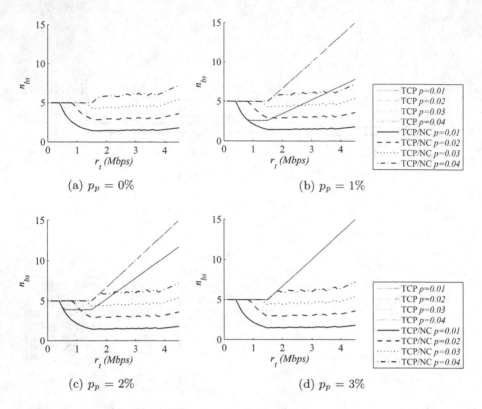

Fig. 8. The value of n_{bs} from Equation (2) for TCP and TCP/NC with varying p_p and p. Here, $RTT = 100$ ms, $W_{max} = 50$, $n = 1000$, and $\mu_f = 5.08$ MB. In (a), the results for TCP and TCP/NC are the same. Note that this result is the same as that of Figure 3b. In (b) and (c), the value of n_{bs} with TCP for $p > 0.01$ coincide (upper red curve). In (d), the values of n_{bs} with TCP for any p all overlap. We do not show results for $p_p = 4\%$ or 5% as they are similar to that of (d).

As shown in Figure 9, we observe a similar behavior for other values of RTT as we did for $RTT = 100$ ms. The key effect of the value of RTT in the maximal achievable goodput. For example, if W_{max} is limited to 50, the maximal achievable goodput is approximately 0.8 Mbps when $RTT = 500$ ms, which is much less than the 4 Mbps achievable with $RTT = 100$ ms. As a result, for $RTT = 500$ ms, neither r_{g-nc} nor r_{g-tcp} can benefit from the increase in r_t beyond 0.8 Mbps. Despite this limitation, TCP/NC still performs better than TCP when losses occur. When demand exceeds the maximal achievable goodput, n_{bs} increases for both TCP/NC and TCP in the same manner.

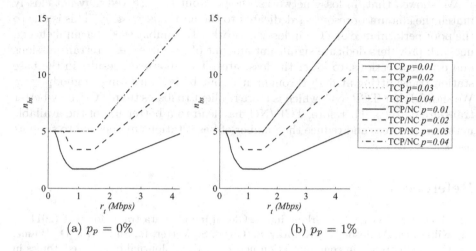

Fig. 9. The value of n_{bs} from Equation (2) for TCP and TCP/NC with varying p_p and p. Here, $RTT = 500$ ms, $W_{max} = 50$, $n = 1000$, and $\mu_f = 3.2$ MB. In (a), the results for TCP and TCP/NC are the same. The curves for $p = 0.03$ and $p = 0.04$ are the same both for TCP and TCP/NC. In (b), the value of n_{bs} with TCP for any p all overlap, while the TCP/NC curves are the same as in (a). We do not show results for $p_p > 1\%$ as they are similar to that of (b).

6   Conclusions

In wireless networks, the solution to higher demand is often to add more infrastructure. This is indeed necessary if all the base stations are at capacity (in terms of throughput). However, in many cases, the base stations are "at capacity" either because they are transmitting redundant data to recover from losses; or because they cannot effectively serve more than a few hundred active users. This may be costly as base stations are expensive to operate. One way to make sure that wireless networks are efficient is to ensure that, whenever base stations are added, they are added to effectively increase the goodput of the network.

We studied the number of base stations n_{bs} needed to improve the goodput r_g to the users. It may seem that higher r_g necessarily increases n_{bs}. Indeed, if there are enough demand (i.e. r_g, p, or μ_f are high enough), we eventually need to increase n_{bs}. However, we show that this relationship is not necessarily true. When r_g is low, each transaction takes more time to complete and each user stays in the system longer. This degrades the user experience and delays the release of network resources dedicated to the user. This is particularly important as the number of active users each base station can support is limited to the low hundreds. We observed that, given r_t, achieving low r_g may lead to a significant increase in n_{bs} and an ineffective use of the network resources; while achieving high r_g may lead to reduction in n_{bs}.

We showed that, in lossy networks, the goodput r_g observed may not closely match the amount of resources dedicated to the user, e.g. $r_g \ll r_t$. This is due to the poor performance of TCP in lossy networks. To combat these harmful effects, network providers dedicate significant amount of resources, e.g. retransmissions and error corrections, to lower the loss rates. This, however, results in the base station transmitting at high throughput r_t but little translating to goodput r_g. We showed that TCP/NC, which is more resilient to losses than TCP, may better translate r_t to r_g. Therefore, TCP/NC may lead to a better use of the available network resources and reduce the number of base stations n_{bs} needed to support users at a given r_g.

References

1. Cisco, Cisco visual networking index: Global mobile data traffic forecast (2011)
2. Kilper, D., Atkinson, G., Korotky, S., Goyal, S., Vetter, P., Suvakovic, D., Blume, O.: Power trends in communication networks. IEEE Journal of Selected Topics in Quantum Electronics 17(2), 275–284 (2011)
3. Padhye, J., Firoiu, V., Towsley, D., Kurose, J.: Modeling TCP throughput: A simple model and its empirical validation. In: Proceedings of the ACM SIGCOMM (1998)
4. Balakrishnan, H., Padmanabhan, V.N., Seshan, S., Katz, R.H.: A comparison of mechanisms for improving TCP performance over wireless links. IEEE/ACM Transactions on Networking 5 (December 1997)
5. Kim, M., Médard, M., Barros, J.: Modeling network coded TCP throughput: A simple model and its validation. In: Proceedings of ICST/ACM Valuetools (May 2011)
6. Cáceres, R., Iftode, L.: Improving the performance of reliable transport protocols in mobile computing environments. IEEE Journal on Selected Areas in Communications 13(5) (June 1995)
7. Tian, Y., Xu, K., Ansari, N.: TCP in wireless environments: Problems and solutions. IEEE Comm. Magazine 43, 27–32 (2005)
8. Hacker, T.J., Athey, B.D., Noble, B.: The end-to-end performance effects of parallel TCP sockets on a lossy wire-area network. In: Proceedings of the IEEE IPDPS (2002)
9. Ford, A., Raiciu, C., Handley, M., Barre, S., Iyengar, J.: Architectural guidelines for multipath tcp development. IETF, Request for Comments, no. 6182 (March 2011)
10. Sundararajan, J.K., Shah, D., Médard, M., Jakubczak, S., Mitzenmacher, M., Barros, J.: Network coding meets tcp: Theory and implementation. Proceedings of IEEE 99, 490–512 (2011)
11. Lott, C., Milenkovic, O., Soljanin, E.: Hybrid ARQ: Theory, state of the art and future directions. In: Proceedgins of IEEE Information Theory Workshop (ITW), Bergen, Norway (July 2007)

Multipath Algorithms and Strategies to Improve TCP Performance over Wireless Mesh Networks

David Gómez, Carlos Rabadán, Pablo Garrido, and Ramón Agüero

Universidad de Cantabria, Santander, Spain
dgomez,ramon@tlmat.unican.es
{carlos.rabadan,pablo.garrido}@alumnos.unican.es

Abstract. The remarkable growth at the worldwide wireless device sales, together with the cost reduction of the subjacent technologies, has lead to a situation in which most of this type of terminals carry more than one interface to access the network, through potentially different radio access technologies. This fact has fostered the interest of the research community to address new solutions to exploit the possibility of launching multiple simultaneous transmissions through multiple interfaces. In this work we evaluate three different routing algorithms (*link*, *node* and *zone* disjoint) that aim to discover the optimal route configuration of disjoint paths over a wireless mesh network. We use the obtained results to evaluate, by means of simulation, the performance of the MultiPath TCP (MPTCP) protocol, which allows the simultaneous delivery of traffic across multiple paths, showing that the aggregated performance is significatively higher than the one achieved by the traditional single-path and single-flow TCP.

Keywords: Wireless Mesh Networks, Multipath Routing Algorithms, MPTCP, Multi-homed devices.

1 Introduction

Wireless technologies are probably one of the most relevant elements in the current communication realm. Besides the legacy wireless devices (e.g. cellphones, laptops, etc.), a new batch of increasingly popular equipment is looming, such as smartphones or tablets, which shows the huge potential of this type of communications. In absolute terms and at the time of writing, the number of wireless devices sales easily surpass 10^9 units; in fact, it is more and more usual that an average user owns several gadgets/devices. This trend is likely to continue during the near future, and designers and manufacturers will develop new ways to use these technologies, easing the end users' life.

Some of these devices will be able to get interconnected amongst themselves, leading to the so-called Wireless Mesh Networks (WMNs). In this sort of topologies, it will be (most of the times) necessary using several hops to reach the destination, by means of intermediate relay nodes. In order to establish one (or more) paths, the routing algorithm shall provide the set of appropriate paths

D. Pesch et al. (Eds.): MONAMI 2013, LNICST 125, pp. 15–28, 2013.

to communicate two nodes (unicast transmissions). On the other hand, there are two main mechanisms and protocols using such algorithm, *reactive* (or "on-demand") and *proactive*. Those which belong to the first group only exchange discovery or maintenance messages when needed, whilst the second group periodically updates the routing tables, thus causing a higher overhead.

Likewise, the manufacturers tendency to include multiple interfaces into their devices has become a reality. This phenomenon calls the design and implementation of novel protocols to allow the simultaneous usage of all the available resources at the different "access elements". Although there are various solutions dealing with this functionality, MPTCP has deservedly become one of the most relevant ones, heavily supported by its own IETF working group, exclusively devoted to the accurate development of this protocol, as well as a set of extensions that were conceived to complement its basic features and performance. MPTCP is in fact an evolution of the legacy TCP, and it shares most of its architecture. MPTCP allows to divide the load between different interfaces (provided that at least one of the nodes has more than one active IP address), thus boosting the traditional TCP performance.

This work is structured in two clearly differentiated stages: first, we evaluate the behavior of three different routing algorithms (namely, *link*, *node* and *zone* disjoint) so as to find the optimal set of disjoint paths over a WMN; afterwards, using the results of the first phase, we assess, based on an extensive simulation campaign over the ns-3 simulator, the MPTCP performance over this type of topologies, showing the enhancement compared to a traditional single-path TCP scheme.

The structure of this document is organized as follows: Section 2 briefly outlines the main related works, highlighting the novel aspects addressed in our work. Section 3 introduces the three routing algorithms that will be exploited for the MPTCP characterization; the operation of this protocol will discussed in Section 4. Section 5 depicts the most relevant results and discusses the potential benefits and drawbacks of multipath strategies. Finally, Section 6 concludes the paper and advocates some research lines that will be tackled in the future.

2   Related Work

In this work we exploit different routing algorithms to be used by multi-path strategies, assessing their potential benefits over WMNs. The use of multi-path communications might lead to a greater performance; moreover, they will bring about a more resilient connections, dynamically adjusting the load over the various paths, according to the particular network conditions.

As mentioned earlier, the classification of routing protocols for wireless multi-hop networks embraces two main groups. Both of them are based on mechanisms to discover and maintain routes over multi-hop networks. The *proactive* protocols (represented by *Optimized Link State Routing - OLSR* [5]), update the routing information by periodically flooding the network with topological information, thus introducing a remarkable overhead. On the other hand, the *reactive* or *on-demand* protocols (for instance, *Ad hoc On-demand Distance Vector routing - AODV* [14]) reduce, as much as possible, the exchange of control messages, triggering them only if needed.

The first generation of routing protocols was thought to operate with *single-path* strategies, where in case of a route break, the source node would need to start a new discovery process, in order to find alternative paths to reach the destination. The increasing interest on multi-path solutions during the last years opens new possibilities, and the implementation of new protocols is required. Most of the existing solutions are modifications of single-path protocols and can be classified according to how they select the alternative paths to the shortest one: *Link Disjoint (LD)*, which only excludes the links of the previously calculated routes (e.g. *Ad hoc On-demand Multipath Distance Vector - AODVM*), *Node Disjoint (ND)*, which does not allow any intermediate node to be active in two different routes (e.g. *Geographic Multipath routing Protocol - GMP*) and, finally, *Zone Disjoint (ZD)*, which inhibits the redundant participation of both the previously used nodes as well as their corresponding neighbors (e.g. *Zone Disjoint Multipath extension of the Dynamic Source Routing - ZD-MPDSR*).

Some of the most relevant works within this research line were carried out by Meghanathan [11,12], who, by means of graph theory, realizes a complete performance analysis of the link, node and zone disjoint algorithms over mobile ad hoc networks, where he thoroughly studies, through different simulation campaigns, different performance metrics that characterize the behavior of different routing schemes (e.g. number of routes found, average number of hops, average time between single/multipath route discoveries, etc.) Moreover, Waharte et al. [19] carry out another analysis that focused on LD and ND, paying special attention to the potential interferences between the different subflows (since they share the same channel), and estimate the resulting throughput as a function of the nodes' coverage area and their position within the scenario. Unlike Meghanathan's contribution, which only addresses the fundamental analysis of the routing algorithms, Waharte et al. apply end-user traffic (over UDP) to compare the performance of the different routing multipath solutions to that shown by a single-path scheme.

After finding the set of disjoint paths between a source node and a destination, we need to develop a solution to split a single connection into multiple subflows. Some proposals, based on the modifications of the legacy TCP operation have been already made (e.g. *mTCP* [22], *R-MTP* [10], *pTCP* [8]). The relevance of this type of communications is supported by the presence of standardization bodies, such as IETF, in the development of new protocols and techniques. In this sense, there are two working groups exclusively devoted to the design and implementation of the most relevant multi-path solutions: Stream Control Transmission Protocol (SCTP) [18] and MPTCP [7]. The former one uses multiple routes in order to provide some redundancy against failures, or to ease the mobility between different networks without breaking a session (at the transport level), but it does not support (yet) the simultaneous transmission over different paths; on the other hand, MPTCP focuses on the improvement of the TCP performance by multiplexing traffic load over different resources.

Regarding the analysis of MPTCP over wireless scenarios, we can highlight [9,15,13], all of them following complementary approaches, ranging from real scenarios (with emulated channels) over a Linux Kernel implementation [1], which shows a great improvement over the traditional TCP operation. On the other hand, the authors of [13] identify an important drawback if the physical attributes are rather different (e.g. IEEE 802.11 and 3G), due to the impact of the packet reordering algorithms. A common element of all these works is that they are based on rather simple topologies, consisting on one, or two hops.

Finally, it is worth highlighting the contribution of Chihani et al. [4], who implemented a fully-fledged MPTCP framework implementation for the ns-3 simulator, which served as the basis for the work developed herein, since we ported it to a newer version of the simulator, adapting its operation so as to use it over wireless technologies. Chihani et al. analyzed the performance of different congestion control algorithms [16], and compared the behavior of the congestion window at each subflow, using an FTP transmission over a simple wired topology, encompassing two terminals which were directly connected through point-to-point links.

3   Multipath Strategies Routing Algorithms

The main goal of the different multipath routing algorithms consists in finding an optimal set of disjoint paths to simultaneously carry the traffic load using multiple subflows, over a WMN scenario.

In order to describe the operation of each of the algorithms (*link*, *node* and *zone disjoint*), we will employ a traditional graph theory notation, as shown below.

Let G(V,E) be the graph representing the scenario over which we want to get the set of paths (using the LD, ND or *ZD* algorithms)[1] between the source and the destination nodes (s and d, respectively). The set V represents the group of vertices (nodes) deployed within the scenario, and E (edges) is the set of existing links. We will establish a link between two nodes if the distance between them is shorter than the corresponding range of transmission. In this work we will use homogeneous nodes, and all of them will share the same coverage.

The first step to get the set of paths is the same for the three algorithms: the Dijkstra's algorithm is used to find the shortest path between s and d. If there is, at least, one route in G, it is stored in the corresponding set (P_L, P_N o P_Z, for the LD, ND or ZD algorithms, respectively). After that, the graph ($G \rightarrow G'$) is updated with the constraints imposed by each of the algorithms. Below we show the procedure followed by each of the solutions:

---

[1] In this work, since the nodes do not move, the subjacent topology will stay static during the simulation time; therefore, we only need to calculate the routes once.

– **Link Disjoint.** We will remove from G all the links that were found with the Dijkstra's algorithm, thus building a new graph G'(V, E^L). The procedure is repeated as many times as there is a route $s - d$ (Dijkstra's algorithm is used again), incorporating the resulting path to P_L. When the algorithm is finished, P_L contains the set of link disjoint paths of the original graph G.
– **Node disjoint.** In this case, the graph is modified by deleting the nodes belonging to the previously selected path. Therefore, after each iteration a new route is added to P_N and a modified graph G'(V^N, E^N) is built. The procedure is executed as long as s can discover a route to d.
– **Zone disjoint.** This is the most restrictive algorithm, since it severely limits the graph between successive iterations, deleting the nodes belonging to the previous route, as well as their neighbors; as a result, the original graph G is modified to G'(V^Z, E^Z). When it becomes impossible finding new routes, the algorithm returns the set of routes P_Z.

In this work the routing tasks have been performed on an external framework, outside the MPTCP implementation, using a proprietary tool developed in C++, which generates a random scenario to establish the graph G (V,E). Afterwards, the route selection procedure was performed by means of a single process.

Since the main objective of this work is to analyze the performance of MPTCP, which simultaneously delivers the information over multiple (disjoint) paths, we will only consider as valid those sets (P_L, P_N or P_Z) with more than one path between s and d.

4   MPTCP as a Multipath Transport Level Solution

MPTCP was conceived as an evolution of the TCP protocol, the most relevant transport level solution, although its performance over wireless links has been questioned. Its appearance is tightly linked with growing availability of devices with multiple interfaces[2].

The basic principle of MPTCP is rather simple: if a terminal has multiple points of connection (interfaces) this can be exploited, simultaneously dividing the traffic between different subconnections. Thanks to these multipath strategies, the overall performance is improved, as well as the robustness of the communication. In MPTCP, for instance, the traffic can be drifted from one subflow to another one after a link (or node) fault.

In order to ease the migration from legacy protocols, ensuring the backward compatibility with TCP, RFC 6824 [7] establishes that any MPTCP implementation must be able to support any non-MPTCP-aware application; in such cases, the services will not be able to differentiate between MPTCP and TCP transport level connections. In this sense, MPTCP can be seen as a modified TCP version, sharing most of its architecture and adding different extensions to cope with the most relevant features.

---

[2] They are usually referred to as "multi-homed" devices.

Application	
MPTCP	
Subflow (TCP)	**Subflow (TCP)**
IP	IP

Fig. 1. MPTCP architecture

Another requirement to be fulfilled, according to the aforementioned RFC, is that at least one of the edge nodes must have more than one IP address for the correct establishment of a multi-path session.

Once the core operation of MPTCP has been outlined in [7], its main challenge can be mapped onto the accomplishment of the following three goals:

1. *Improve throughput*: The performance of a multipath connection should be, at least, alike the one shown by legacy TCP (assuming the best available path is used).
2. *Do not harm*: An MPTCP subflow should not take more resources than the ones consumed by the traditional TCP using the same path.
3. *Balance congestion*: Upon a congestion situation, MPTCP should offload as much traffic as possible from the most congested paths.

Once we have described the most relevant functionalities of the MPTCP protocol and its main goals, Figure 1 depicts its architecture within the TCP/IP model. As can be seen, it is placed at the transport level and, at the same time, it includes two different sublayers: the first one handles the application-oriented issues (e.g. session initialization/finalization, subflow discovery/establishment, etc.); on the other hand, the lower level will embrace one instance per subflow established during the TCP initialization phase. Additionally, each of these instances will be associated to a different IP entity, to which they will send the outgoing packets down.

One of the major challenges that MPTCP has to face is the need to ensure an efficient "resource pooling" [20]). In order to accomplish this goal and, at the same time, fulfill the three previously described objectives, a congestion control algorithm needs to be used so as to provide a coupled operation of the various congestion windows. Although the protocol supports a number of solutions, in this work we will assume that there is an independent congestion window per subflow[3]. A congestion controller will monitor (congestion windows sizes) the aggregated throughput of the transmission, paying special attention to the fulfillment of the MPTCP three goals: provide a higher throughput than TCP (**Goal 1**), without taking more resources than necessary (**Goal 2**) and taking as much load as possible from the most congested paths (**Goal 3**). In order to estimate the load of a simple TCP flow, the control entity measures the packet

---

[3] It is worth mentioning that, while the (additive) increase congestion windows expressions are specific to MPTCP, it does not modify the legacy TCP operation upon a packet loss, which will lead to a (multiplicative) decrease of the congestion window.

loss rate and the Round Trip Time (RTT), providing a new congestion window value for each subflow. The relevance of this mechanism has made IETF to develop a recommendation just to address it [17].

5 Simulation Platform and Results

In this section we will depict the most relevant features of the different simulation campaigns and we will discuss the most outstanding results. These have been divided into two clearly different groups: first, we study and compare the behavior of the three different routing algorithms presented in Section 3; on the other hand, and using the paths found by those algorithms, a characterization of the MPTCP performance is carried out, showing that it can actually improve the behavior of the legacy TCP.

5.1 Multipath Routing Algorithms Behavior

As a previous step to carrying out the performance analysis of the MPTCP protocol, we used a proprietary software to analyze the operation of different multipath routing approaches. In particular, the tool takes the following steps: (1) deploy the nodes within the scenario, (2) execute the three multipath routing algorithms and (3) generate the output files that will be afterwards used on ns-3 to perform the corresponding simulation campaign. We have established a set of aspects to be considered:

- The nodes will be deployed within a 100x100 meters squared area.
- Initially, disconnected graphs are discarded; i.e. only scenarios in which there is, at least, one path between any pair of nodes.
- In this work we do not consider node mobility, so nodes stay static during the simulation time.
- The coverage area of the nodes (disk radius model) is 20 meters.
- The source-destination nodes are selected so as to ensure same consistency to the multipath routes; by taking two points $(20, 50)$ and $(80, 50)$ as references (as shown in Figure 2); we select the source as the closest one to the first point and the receiver the closest to the latter reference point.

As an illustrative example, Figure 2 shows a random deployment of 16 nodes. In this particular topology we see that node 8 will take the transmitter role and node 3 will be the receiver. With regard to the selected routes, the three algorithms will provide the same result: the shortest path is $8 \rightarrow 13 \rightarrow 15 \rightarrow 3$, while the second option would be, for the three algorithms, $8 \rightarrow 11 \rightarrow 10 \rightarrow 12 \rightarrow 3$.

Figure 3 shows the percentage of multipath "feasible" topologies (those which there were two or more disjoint paths divided by the total number of runs)[4] as a function of the number of nodes. We can appreciate that LD always exhibits

---

[4] The experiment consisted in 1000 independent runs.

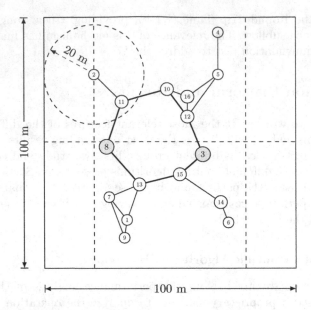

Fig. 2. Illustrative topology (16 nodes)

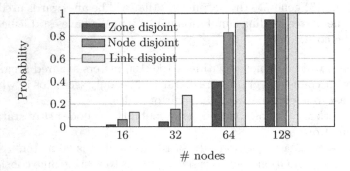

Fig. 3. Probability of finding a multipath strategy using the different routing algorithms

the best behavior, closely followed by *ND*; on the other hand, *ZD* appears as the most restrictive alternative.

After the first comparison, a new constraint was added. Only those topologies with, at least, two different routes (for the three routing algorithms) were considered. We used 32 nodes (all of them fulfilling the previous constraints) and generated 1000 scenarios. It is worth mentioning that, to get such a high number of deployments, many other scenarios were discarded, since, as shown in Figure 3, only 4.2% of the 32-node scenarios were multipath for the ZD algorithm (i.e. ZD found two or more paths between the two edge nodes).

First, Figure 4 shows the cumulative distribution function (cdf) of the total number of routes found by each of the studied schemes. As could have been

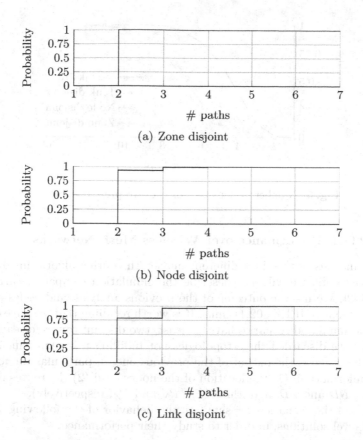

Fig. 4. *cdf* of the number of found routes for the different algorithms

expected, *LD* is the algorithm which provides the higher number of alternative paths, since it is the scheme which makes fewer changes to the graph between successive iterations. *ND* appears the intermediate solution, showing a non-negligible probability to discover three disjoint paths. On the other hand, the strong constraints imposed by *ZP* avoids finding more than two simultaneous routes.

Another insightful metric is the *cdf* of the number of hops of the two preferred routes, shown in Figure 5. As we can infer from the discussion given in Section 3, the shortest path (1st iteration) is the same for all the schemes, since all of them use the Dijkstra's algorithm to find it. However, the second alternate route length shows the same behavior as the previous statistic: *LD* finds, in the second iteration, the shortest path to reach the destination; *ND* appears again as the solution with the second shortest route, being *ZD* the scheme providing the longest paths. This is of outer relevance, since the number of hops will have a remarkable influence on the aggregated performance, since the greater the length of these paths the lower the throughput of the corresponding subflow.

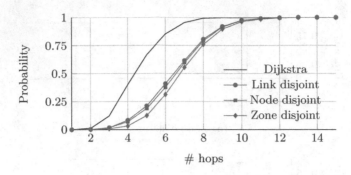

Fig. 5. Number of hops *cdf* for the two preferred routes

5.2   MPTCP Performance over Wireless Mesh Networks

After the analysis of the three different multipath routing algorithms over random deployments, we will now describe the simulation campaign, carried out over ns-3 [2]. We use the outcome of the previous analysis, and nodes are connected by means of IEEE 802.11 links. It is worth recalling that we have ensured that all the simulated scenarios have, at least, two disjoint routes for each of the algorithms (we discarded these topologies not fulfilling this requirement). The input of this stage is the output of the previous one, in particular the following pieces of information: (1) the location of the nodes, and (2) the routes returned by the *LD*, *ND* and *ZD* algorithms (P_L, P_N and P_Z, respectively).

For each of the scenarios, we simulate the behavior of the following different transport level solutions, in order to study their performance:

1. **Single-path TCP.** It corresponds to the legacy behavior, and the path used (recall that we are using static routes) is the shortest one, which is alike for the three algorithms.
2. **Single interface MPTCP.** In this case, we configure two different IP addresses sharing the same interface. In this sense, the overall performance might get damaged, since both subflows share the same wireless channel, increasing the number of contending stations and the probability of suffering collisions.
3. **Multi-interface MPTCP.** This last configuration is expected to yield the highest performance, since we use different channels (non-overlapping) for the two subflows and, therefore, there will not be any interference between them. For this, both the transmitter and the receiver must have two different interfaces, each of them associated to a particular subflow.

To carry out the analysis, we have ported the MPTCP implementation provided by Chihani et al. [4], to a newer version of ns-3 (ns-3.13 instead of ns-3.6). This framework follows the IETF recommendations [7,6,17]. For this particular work, we have selected *Linked Increases* and *DSACK* as the congestion control and reordering schemes, respectively (for further information about them, the reader might refer to [4]). The MPTCP layer will be added at each node according to the corresponding configuration (1 or 2 interfaces), distributing the load between the two different subflows.

Besides, it is worth mentioning some additional aspects about the simulation setup:

1. The source node sends a 20 MB file to the destination (*unicast* traffic). Since the objective is to assess the upper bound performance for each of the configurations, we ensure that there is always a packet waiting to be delivered at the transmitter's buffer. In this saturated scenario, the wireless medium acts as the real bottleneck.
2. The subjacent technology is IEEE 802.11b (at 11 Mbps), setting a maximum number of transmissions per frame of four.
3. Since an external process is used to obtain the routes with the three algorithms, the routing scheme is based on static routes.
4. There is a single cause of packet losses: the collisions between simultaneous node transmissions. We will consider ideal channels, where the frame losses rate due to the wireless propagation effect is null.

Due to space constraints, we only report the results achieved with the routes provided by the LD algorithm, which correspond to highest performances.

Figure 6 shows the overall performance[5] for the three schemes. It represents the average, maximum and minimum values of throughput as a function of the number of hops used by the shortest path. We can clearly appreciate the improvement brought about by using the two channel scenario, achieving a higher aggregated throughput (e.g. 50% for the 2-hop scenario), compared to the traditional single-path TCP. However, we can find few cases with a lower performance, corresponding to these situations in which the second path needs many

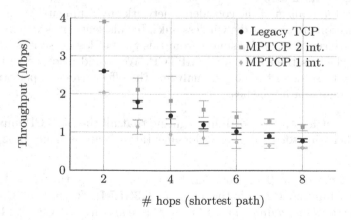

Fig. 6. Average throughput as a function of the number of hops of the first route

---

[5] In terms of throughput at the application level.

more hops than the first one. On the other hand, we can appreciate the limitation shown by the multipath strategy over a single channel WMN, since the contention caused by the high number of nodes contending for the channel leads to long idle times and a high probability of collision. The consequence is that the overall performance is quite lower than the one observed by the legacy TCP.

6 Conclussions and Future Work

In this work we have presented three different algorithms (link, node and zone disjoint) which were used to obtain the best set of disjoint paths over generic WMN topologies. We have focused on the use of multipath strategies over WMNs. We have compared their performance, in terms of feasibility (probability that there are two or more paths in a scenario), number of discovered paths and route length required to reach the destination node in such paths. According to the achieved results, the *ZD* algorithm seems too restrictive for the search of multiple disjoint paths.

Afterwards, using the outcomes of this first stage (the node deployment and the different routes between the source and the destination nodes), we compared the performance offered by the *MPTCP* protocol to the one exhibited by the legacy TCP, by means of a thorough simulation campaign carried out over the ns-3 platform, leading to improvements of about $\sim 50\%$ in some of the cases.

The work undertaken so far opens a broad rante of aspects to be tackled in our future research. Below we briefly descuss the most relevant ones.

– Analyze different routing schemes, exploiting the presence of multi-channel devices by means of appropriate graph-theory models, as the one proposed by Yang *et al.* in [21].
– Increase the realism of the considered network environments, by introducing transmission errors over the wireless links. In this sense, it is well known that TCP performance heavily suffers from this type of losses, so it is interesting to see which is their effect over MPTCP. We would also like to introduce mobility to some of the nodes, analyzing the effect over the performance of various multi-path schemes.

Last, but not least, it is worth highlighting that all the MPTCP implementation, together with some additional documentation, can be found in [3].

Acknowledgements. This work has been supported by the Spanish Government by its funding through the projects **C3SEM**, *"Cognitive, Cooperative Communications and autonomous SErvice Management"* (TEC2009-14598-C02-01), and **COSAIF**, *"Connectivity as a Service: Access for the Internet of the Future"* (TEC2012-38754-C02-02).

References

1. MPTCP - Linux Kernel implementation,
   http://mptcp.info.ucl.ac.be/pmwiki.php?n=Main.HomePage
2. The ns-3 network simulator, http://www.nsnam.org/
3. Source code and documentation of the MPTCP implementation (ns-3.13),
   https://github.com/dgomezunican/multipath-ns3.13
4. Chihani, B., Collange, D.: A multipath TCP model for ns-3 simulator. CoRR
   abs/1112.1932 (2011)
5. Clausen, T., Jacquet, P.: Optimized Link State Routing Protocol (OLSR). RFC
   3626 (Experimental) (October 2003), http://www.ietf.org/rfc/rfc3626.txt
6. Ford, A., Raiciu, C., Handley, M., Barre, S., Iyengar, J.: Architectural Guidelines for Multipath TCP Development. RFC 6182 (Informational) (March 2011),
   http://www.ietf.org/rfc/rfc6182.txt
7. Ford, A., Raiciu, C., Handley, M., Bonaventure, O.: TCP Extensions for
   Multipath Operation with Multiple Addresses. RFC (6824) (January 2013),
   http://www.ietf.org/rfc/rfc6824.txt
8. Hsieh, H.Y., Sivakumar, R.: A transport layer approach for achieving aggregate
   bandwidths on multi-homed mobile hosts. In: Proceedings of the 8th Annual International Conference on Mobile Computing and Networking, MobiCom 2002, pp.
   83–94. ACM, New York (2002), http://doi.acm.org/10.1145/570645.570656
9. Lim, M., Valdez, J.: MPTCP Wireless performance,
   http://reproducingnetworkresearch.wordpress.com/2012/06/06/
   mptcp-wireless-performance-draft/
10. Magalhaes, L., Kravets, R.H.: Transport level mechanisms for bandwidth aggre-
    gation on mobile hosts. In: Ninth International Conference on Network Protocols,
    pp. 165–171 (November 2001)
11. Meghanathan, N.: Stability and hop count of node-disjoint and link-disjoint multi-
    path routes in ad hoc networks. In: Third IEEE International Conference on Wire-
    less and Mobile Computing, Networking and Communications, WiMOB 2007, pp.
    42–42 (2007)
12. Meghanathan, N.: Performance comparison of link, node and zone disjoint multi-
    path routing strategies and minimum hop single path routing for mobile ad hoc
    networks. CoRR abs/1011.5021 (2010)
13. Nguyen, S.C., Nguyen, T.M.T.: Evaluation of multipath TCP load sharing with
    coupled congestion control option in heterogeneous networks. In: Global Informa-
    tion Infrastructure Symposium (GIIS), pp. 1–5 (2011)
14. Perkins, C., Belding-Royer, E., Das, S.: Ad hoc On-Demand Distance Vector
    (AODV) Routing. RFC 3561 (Experimental) (July 2003),
    http://www.ietf.org/rfc/rfc3561.txt
15. Raiciu, C., Paasch, C., Barre, S., Ford, A., Honda, M., Duchene, F., Bonaventure,
    O., Handley, M.: How hard can it be? designing and implementing a deployable
    multipath TCP. In: Proceedings of the 9th USENIX Conference on Networked
    Systems Design and Implementation, NSDI 2012, pp. 29–29. USENIX Association,
    Berkeley (2012), http://dl.acm.org/citation.cfm?id=2228298.2228338
16. Raiciu, C., Wischik, D., Handley, M.: Practical congestion control for multipath
    transport protocols. UCL Technical Report (6824) (January 2009)
17. Raiciu, C., Wischik, M.H.D.: Coupled Congestion Control for Multipath Transport
    Protocols. RFC (6356) (January 2011), http://www.ietf.org/rfc/rfc6356.txt

18. Stewart, R.: Stream Control Transmission Protocol. RFC 4960 (Proposed Standard) (September 2007), (updated by RFC 6096)
    http://www.ietf.org/rfc/rfc4960.txt
19. Waharte, S., Boutaba, R.: Totally disjoint multipath routing in multihop wireless networks. In: IEEE International Conference on Communications, ICC 2006, vol. 12, pp. 5576–5581 (2006)
20. Wischik, D., Handley, M., Braun, M.B.: The resource pooling principle. SIGCOMM Comput. Commun. Rev. 38(5), 47–52 (2008),
    http://doi.acm.org/10.1145/1452335.1452342
21. Yang, Y., Wang, J., Kravets, R.: Interference-aware load balancing for multihop wireless networks. Technical Report (2005)
22. Zhang, M., Lai, J., Krishnamurthy, A., Peterson, L., Wang, R.: A transport layer approach for improving end-to-end performance and robustness using redundant paths. In: Proceedings of the Annual Conference on USENIX Annual Technical Conference, ATEC 2004, p. 8. USENIX Association, Berkeley (2004),
    http://dl.acm.org/citation.cfm?id=1247415.1247423

Adaptation and Evaluation of Widely Used TCP Flavours in CCN

Asanga Udugama, Jinglu Cai, and Carmelita Göerg

University of Bremen, Germany
{adu,jlc,cg}@comnets.uni-bremen.de

Abstract. Content Centric Networking (CCN) is a paradigm shift from the way how networks of today work. The focus of networking in CCN is on the content and not on the hosts that are involved in a communication. One of the key cornerstones of today's communication model is the use of flow and congestion control to pipeline data and take appropriate action when congestion is perceived to exist in a network. TCP of the Internet protocol suite has shown us how application performance is enhanced in different communication situations. An interesting area of research is how TCP-like flow and congestion control can be adapted for CCN. The work presented here adapts the most widely used TCP flavours of NewReno, Compound and Cubic to operate in CCN. Due to the architectural differences that CCN has over IP based networks, this work identifies a number of additional algorithms to cater to the issues associated with these differences. Finally, the performance of these adapted TCP flavours and the algorithms are evaluated in an OPNET based simulator.

Keywords: Future Internet, Content Centric Networking, Flow and Congestion Control, Simulations.

1 Introduction

Network use has evolved to be dominated by content distribution and retrieval, while networking technology still speaks only of connections between hosts. Accessing content and services requires mapping from the "what" that users care about to the network's "where". Content Centric Networking (CCN) is a new paradigm in networking which treats content as a primitive - decoupling location from identity, security and access, and retrieving content by name. Using new approaches to routing named content, derived heavily from TCP/IP, CCN achieves simultaneous scalability, security and performance [1,2].

CCN retrieves content using interests that propagate all throughout the network. This is unlike networks of today, which are mainly based on TCP/IP. These networks have made TCP as the main transport protocol to communicate data between producers and consumers of content. One of the key advantages of TCP is its algorithms to handle reliable delivery of data, end-to-end. CCN on the other hand has a hop-by-hop content delivery mechanism and a receiver oriented communication architecture where delivery of content cannot be guaranteed by the

D. Pesch et al. (Eds.): MONAMI 2013, LNICST 125, pp. 29–44, 2013.

sender. Flow and Congestion Control (FC-CC) algorithms in TCP have worked well in current networks. There are a number of different TCP flavours in use today. The most widely used flavours are *NewReno*, *Compound* and *Cubic* [3,4,5]. These flavours which are based on the original TCP [6], attempt at addressing the issues associated with different network conditions. The work presented in [1] explains that the architecture of CCN has FC-CC built into it, mainly through the concept of flow balance, i.e., one *Interest* packet retrieves at most only one *Data* packet. It further states that the segment numbers in *Interest* packets act as the sequence number of TCP, CCN *Interest* packets acts as the TCP ACK [6] that acknowledges receipt of data and that TCP SACK is intrinsic due to *Interest* packets being re-sent for unreceived data.

There is research being done currently to introduce TCP-like FC-CC for CCN [7,8,9]. All of these efforts focus on developing new algorithms to perform FC-CC in CCN. One area that has lacked concentration is how the algorithms that currently exist in TCP would operate in CCN when they are adapted to operate in CCN. The work presented here adapts the algorithms of the 3 most widely used TCP flavours (*NewReno*, *Compound* and *Cubic*) to operate in CCN. Since there are a number of architectural differences that CCN has, compared to TCP/IP based networks, a couple of new algorithms have been identified to operate together with these adaptations. The rest of this paper describes our work as follows. The Section 2 details similar work done by others in the area of FC-CC together with a comparison of the work done by us. The Section 3 provides a description of the adaptation and the new algorithms we have identified for the selected TCP flavours to operate in CCN. The Section 4 details the OPNET based simulator we have built to evaluate our work, the performance results and the analysis of the results. Finally, Section 5 provides a summary of the work, conclusions and future work to be considered.

2   Related Work

Flow and Congestion Control (FC-CC) has been a topic of interest in CCN since the seminal work presented in [1]. The way in which FC-CC can be operated in CCN is fundamentally different from the way it is operated in current TCP/IP based networks. Therefore, a number of aspects must be addressed in order to make FC-CC possible in CCN. These aspects fall into 4 categories.

End-System Congestion Control Algorithm - There are multiple ways to manage the FC-CC congestion window (referred to as window hereafter) used to decide the amount of *Interest* packets that have to be sent at any given time. This window may be increased in size for successful receipts of *Data* packets or decreased when perceived packet losses or congestion is detected in the network.

Packet Loss Detection - FC-CC requires the knowledge of whether a requested *Interest* packet has been replied to with the corresponding *Data* packet. If a packet is lost or a *Data* packet arrives out-of-order, this is an indication of losses or congestion in the network.

Fairness Realisation - The architecture of CCN does not posses the end-to-end notion as in current TCP/IP based networks. This means that packets travel hop-by-hop and each hop determines how the CCN packets are forwarded. Since each hop has limited resources, there is a necessity to adopt specific fairness controls at each hop to give a faire share to each of the content flows that travel through that hop.

Flow Identification - As indicated above, fairness requires the identification of content flows to provide fair sharing of resources. In CCN, requests for content may originate from many different sources and a hop in the middle is unaware of the originator of the requests. Therefore, a flow identification method has to be adopted to assign resources fairly for the competing flows.

The authors of [7] investigates the performance of FC-CC using algorithms based on Additive Increase/Muliplicative Decrease (AIMD), constant and Constant Bit Rate (CBR) based window management. They utilise the Retransmission Timeout (RTO) and 3 out-of-order *Data* packet receipts to detect packet losses. Fairness is realised by maintaining per-flow queues in the internal buffer. When a buffer overflows, the packets in the longest queue are dropped based on Deficit Round Robin (DRR).

The authors of [8] based their window management using a CBR window. Fairness is realised by introducing a hop-by-hop *Interest* shaping algorithm that anticipates the drop of *Data* through buffer overflows. The *Interest* shaping rate is calculated using the delay from the *Interest* to the corresponding *Data*, the buffer size, the available bandwidth to send the *Interest* and *Data* packets, the number of queued *Data* packets for each flow and the number of conversations flowing through the same CCN node. In this work, the *Interest* shaping ensures that the buffer is equally distributed to each conversation.

The authors of [9] utilise an AIMD and a CBR based window management algorithm. The packet losses are detected using RTO. Fairness control is applied to the *Interest* flows. Each bottlenecked *Interest* flow maintains a queue for fair distribution of the buffer. The bandwidth distributed to the bottlenecked *Interest* flows is considered as the fair rate.

Flow identification in all these works [7,8,9] are done using the content name.

In contrast to these works, the work done by us focus on utilising the window management algorithms used in the most widely used TCP/IP flavours, viz., *NewReno*, *Cubic* and *Compound*. A further aspect considered is the handling of out-of-order packets. In CCN, packets may be out-of-order, not only due to losses or delays but also due to arrivals from different caches. Therefore, it is important to distinguish this difference before making window adjustments to avoid inappropriate adjustments that may result in performance degradations. Therefore, we have considered this aspect as an important factor in FC-CC and introduced an algorithm to handle this situation.

In all the above mentioned works [7,8,9], the focus has been on fairness controls that consider the flow of *Interest* packets. Our work too, considers fairness in the same manner, but goes beyond by also considering the *Data* packet flow, in addition to the *Interest* packets. In CCN, the payload of each data segment is carried in the *Data* packets. Since *Interest* packets do not carry this information, assigning a fair share of bandwidth must also consider the *Data* packets.

In CCN, the same content can be requested by multiple CCN nodes and due to the nature of CCN, intermediate nodes are unable to distinguish between different flows. Since the identification of a flow is quite important to handle fair sharing, we identify a flow by not only the Content Name and segment number (as in the other works [7,8,9]) but also by introducing a random nonce at the originator of *Interests* for every independent flow.

3   Adaptations

The architecture of CCN essentially uses a multicast or broadcast based mechanism to propagate *Interest* packets for content and the content (i.e., *Data* packets) flow over the paths that were created due to the propagation of the *Interest* packets. It is somewhat of a new way of communicating for mainstream communications of today, considering that unicast is the norm of current networks. The draft CCN specifications [1,10] discuss how CCN is architecturally close to TCP (flow balance, SACK, etc.). But when considered from a TCP point of view, we see that there are a number of issues that make FC-CC for CCN different from TCP FC-CC. Therefore, adaptation of the *NewReno*, *Compound* and *Cubic* flavours of TCP require considering the following aspects.

Control/Communication Orientation - In TCP, the sender of data in a communication session is in control of the session rather than the receiver. This means that the sender continually sends data to the receiver based on the senders view on how the network performs. On the other hand, no data will traverse the network unless the data has been requested for in CCN and therefore, in CCN, the receiver is in control. This means that the receiver is in charge of the data flow by controlling how *Interest* packets are sent.

Data Acknowledgment - In TCP, data are acknowledged by a message that travels in the opposite direction, to the sender. This acknowledgement (ACK) system is one of the fundamental pillars of TCP, used by the sender to make a number of decisions on how the rest of the data must be transmitted. But in CCN, there is no concept of content ACKs. Therefore, the receipt of *Data* itself is considered as the acknowledgement in CCN.

Congestion Window Management - One of the key aspects of TCP is the use of congestion windows to control the flow of data between the sender and the receiver. In TCP, this is maintained at the sender due to the sender orientation of TCP. On the other hand, since CCN is receiver oriented and the *Interest* sending is considered as the means by which the flow of data is controlled, the congestion windows must be maintained at the receiver.

Congestion (Packet Loss) Detection - TCP uses the RTO and the receipt of 3 duplicate ACKs as the basis for considering congestion in the network [6]. In the case of CCN, the RTO can be built in the same way as in TCP by considering the RTT associated with the *Interest-Data* cycle. But, CCN does not have the concept of 3 duplicate ACKs and further, unlike TCP, CCN has the additional problem of determining whether any out-of-order *Data* receipts are due to congestion (or packet loss) in the network or due to *Data* arriving from multiple sources.

Therefore, the work presented here identifies an algorithm called **Pre-Recovery** that addresses the issue associated with multi-source arrivals.

Recovery Algorithm - TCP uses the *Fast Recovery* and *Fast Retransmit* algorithms to resend data which are considered to be lost. Since CCN does not have the concept of duplicate ACKs, the work presented here identifies a CCN based **Fast Recovery** algorithm and **Selective Fast Retransmit** algorithm to handle the resending of *Interest* packets.

Resource Sharing Fairness - Due to the reasons explained in Section 2 on *Fairness Realisation*, the work presented here identifies a **Hop-by-hop Fairness Control** algorithm to provide fairness in sharing bandwidth.

The following sections describe the TCP flavour adaptations and the new algorithms identified for these adaptations to operate successfully.

3.1   Flow and Congestion Control Adaptation

The TCP flavours considered in the work presented here utilise the same algorithm during the *slow start* phase after establishing a connection or when an RTO occurs, i.e., it starts with $cwnd = 1$ and performs a $cwnd = cwnd+1$ for every non-duplicate ACK received until slow start threshold ($ssthresh$) is reached. In the case of CCN, the same operation is performed but considering the *Data* receipt as the ACK of a successful delivery of data for the corresponding *Interest* sent previously.

The differences of these flavours occur in the *congestion avoidance* phase of operation. They are as follows,

NewReno [3] - The increase of $cwnd$ is performed using $cwnd = cwnd + 1/cwnd$ on each non-duplicate ACK arrival.

Compound [4] - Compound uses a congestion window that is computed based on combining the loss based window ($cwnd$) similar to New Reno and the delay based window ($dwnd$) that is updated at the end of every RTT. If no early congestion is detected, $dwnd$ is increased and if early congestion is detected, the $dwnd$ is decreased.

Cubic [5] - Cubic uses a congestion window based on real time unlike the RTT used in *NewReno* and updates the current window based on $W(t) = C \cdot (t - K)^3 \cdot + W_{max}$ where t is the elapsed time since the last window reduction time, $K = \sqrt[3]{\frac{W_{max}\beta}{C \cdot}}$, W_{max} is the window size before the last reduction and $\beta = 0.2$.

We adopt the same differences in our adaptations (including the variables) considering *Data* receipt as the ACK, RTT computation from the *Interest-Data* cycle and 3 out-of-order *Data* packets as the rigger for the recovery process (described in Section 3.2). We term these adapted flavours as *CCN-NewReno*, *CCN-Compound* and *CCN-Cubic*.

3.2   *Pre-Recovery* Algorithm

TCP/IP always assumes a point-to-point communication basis where data arrives from one source. In CCN, on the other hand, requests for content may be served from multiple sources due to caches. Therefore, out-of-order *Data* receipts may be due to a (a) loss or a delay of *Interest* or *Data*, or (b) due to arrivals from multiple sources that could also be multi-path transmissions.

An algorithm is identified in this work (called the *Pre-Recovery* algorithm) to detect whether out-of-order *Data* receipts are due to (a) or (b). A summery of the operation of this algorithm is presented in the Table 1.

Table 1. Operation Summary of the *Pre-Recovery* Algorithm

Pre-Recovery	Operation
Entry	3 out-of-order *Data* receipts (3 is the FRT value used in TCP)
During	Congestion Window updated based on FC-CC flavour used
Exit	A loss detection and *Fast Recovery* entry or, total number of out-of-order *Data* $< FRT$, when $FRT = 3$ or, the occurrence of RTO

The fundamental idea behind this algorithm is to prevent the unnecessary changes that is made to the congestion window when a false packet loss is detected (disregarding the multi-source arrival issue). Figure 1 shows how multi-source arrivals or *Data* loss detections are made, respectively.

This algorithm utilises 3 variables in its process (Figure 1(a)). The FRT (similar as in TCP), maintains the amount of out-of-order *Data* packets that are considered for the algorithm to commence operation. Pre_FRT initially starts with the same FRT and is continuously checked to see if the contiguous receipts of out-of-order *Data* packets exceed the $FRT + Pre\_FRT$. As soon as an in-order *Data* packet arrives, the Pre_FRT is set to the $max(cnt, Pre\_FRT)$. A receipt of an in-order *Data* packet at this instance indicates a multi-source arrival and hence this algorithm will prevent the FC-CC moving into *Fast Recovery and Selective Fast Retransmit*. Thereby, *Pre-Recovery* prevents the ping-pong effect that the congestion window may display due to multi-source arrivals.

If the number of contiguous out-of-order *Data* receipts continue to grow beyond $FRT + Pre\_FRT$, FC-CC is moved into *Fast Recovery and Selective Fast Retransmit* (Figure 1(b)).

3.3   *Selective Fast Retransmit* Algorithm

Once the *Pre-Recovery* (Section 3.2) algorithm determines that a packet loss has occurred ($cnt = FRT + Pre\_FRT$), FC-CC moves into *Fast Recovery*. The *Fast Recovery* algorithm operates in a similar manner to TCP but with adaptations to operate in a CCN context.

On entry into *Fast Recovery*, the *cwnd* is reduced to $ssthresh + n$. In TCP, n is the 3 duplicate ACKs received. But in CCN, since the *Pre-Recovery* process would have received a number of out-of-order *Data* packets, n refers to these out-of-order packets. During the *Fast Recovery*, a receipt of an out-of-order *Data* packet results in the *cwnd* being increased in the same manner as TCP would

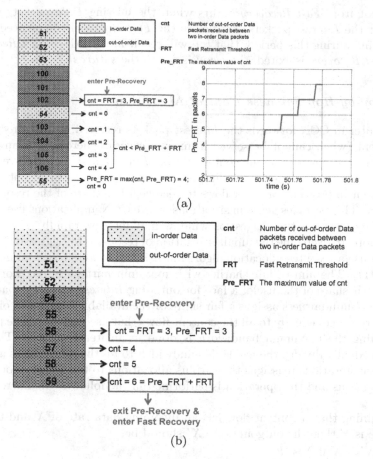

(a)

(b)

Fig. 1. Detection of Multi-source Arrivals and Lost *Data* in Pre-Recovery

perform in the case of a receipt of a duplicate ACK. Further, *cwnd* is decreased during this period when an in-order *Data* packet is received. This is done due to the consideration that *Interest* packets sent before the *Fast Recovery* for *Data* are not yet received. TCP has a similar behaviour (i.e., decrease of *cwnd*) when a partial ACK (i.e., an ACK that does not acknowledge all previous data) is received.

The recovery during *Fast Recovery* is performed by requesting for the missing data. TCP uses the *Fast Retransmit* algorithm. For CCN, we identify the *Selective Fast Retransmit* algorithm (also called "hole filling" in CCN in [1]) that requests for the missing *Data* packets. In TCP, even though there could be a number of missing data packets, the ACKs will only be sent for the last received in-order data until the next in-order data is received. CCN, on the other hand is in a better position as CCN is able to specifically request for the missing *Data* packets by resending the corresponding *Interest* packets. This process is identified as *Selective Fast Retransmit* in our work.

The exit from *Fast Recovery* occurs when the missing *Data* packets are received for the *Interest* packets sent before the *Fast Recovery* commenced. If an RTO occurs during this period, that too will result in the exit of *Fast Recovery*. Once *Fast Recovery* is exited, the *cwnd* is set to the *ssthresh*.

3.4 *Hop-by-Hop Fairness Control* Algorithm

Every router in CCN forwards the *Interest* packets received, in the direction of the content (when cannot be served from own cache). Therefore, at any given time, there are many different content flows (*Interest* and *Data*) traversing a CCN router. Since the router has limited resources, an aggressive content flow may make it impossible for other flows to receive a fair share of the resources of the router. This becomes acute in situations where CCN applications use FC-CC to retrieve content as the congestion window may increase rapidly.

Therefore, to overcome the unfair utilisation of resources by aggressive content flows, we use a resource allocation algorithm in CCN routers based on max-min fairness [11]. The aim of fair sharing with max-min fairness in our work is to assign a fair share of the use of a face for outgoing *Interest* and *Data* packets.

The max-min fairness assigns a fair share of the available bandwidth of a face (i.e., the resource) equally to all the content flows that use that face. The process of assigning the maximum bandwidth is done in an iterative basis. The first iteration equally divides the available bandwidth to all the active flows and the subsequent iterations reassigns the surplus allocations to the deficit allocations. The allocations and the operation is performed in the following manner.

* Assuming that a content flow has an incoming data rate of X and the fair share is F then the outgoing rate X' should be,
  * $X' = X$ if $X < F$;
  * $X' = F$ if $X \geq F$
* The data rate X is computed by $X = chunksize/\Delta t$ where *chunksize* is the size of the payload in the *Data* packet and Δt is the time interval between 2 sequentially arriving packets (*Interest* or *Data*)
* Fairness is applied to both *Interest* and *Data* flows associated with each content flow
* Since, only the *Data* packets carry a payload, information of the payload size (i.e., *chunksize*) is used to also determine the fair sharing for the corresponding *Interest* flows
* Flows that have *Interest* or *Data* arrivals above the assigned fair share (aggressive flows) are delayed based on the allocated bandwidth
* A flow is identified using the content name, sequence number and a nonce that is generated and assigned to the *Interests* a flow by the originator of those *Interests*
* The fairness assignment is considered for,
  * *Interest* packets that are forwarded after consulting the Forwarding Information Base (FIB)

- *Data* packets that are forwarded after consuming the corresponding Pending Interest Table (PIT) entry
- *Data* packets that are originated from the router itself due to the availability in the Content Store (CS)

4   Performance Results and Analysis

The validation of the adapted TCP flavours and the new algorithms is done using a packet level CCN simulator built in OPNET. The node model consists of 3 protocol layers (Figure 2(a)). The *Application Layer* implements the 3 FC-CC enabled applications (*CCN-NewReno*, *CCN-Compound* and *CCN-Cubic*) that perform *Interest* generation and *Data* consumption functionality. These applications also implement the *Pre-Recovery* and the *Selective Fast Retransmit* algorithms. The *CCN Layer* implements the forwarding mechanisms and the related management functionalities of CCN including the *Hop-by-hop Fairness Control* algorithm. In this simulator, CCN is made to operate over TCP/IP. Therefore, the lowest layer, which we term as the *Underlay Layer* consist of the 4 sub-layers; *Adaptation Layer*, *Transport Layer*, *Network Layer* and the the underlying *Link Layer*. The simulator uses UDP and Ethernet, and the *Adaptation Layer* handles the conversions between UDP and CCN.

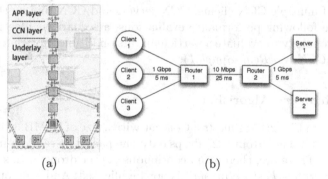

(a)   (b)

Fig. 2. CCN Node Architecture and Considered Network Topology in the Simulator

There are a number of other capabilities that are built into the simulator. Some of the relevant capabilities are explained below.

CS Policies - There are different *Cache Replacement* policies that can be used by a CS. Among them, Least Recently Used (LRU) is most commonly used in the context of CCN [12,13] and therefore, we have implemented the LRU *Cache Replacement* policy.

PIT Expiration Policy - The PIT registers the *Interests* with a timeout [1]. Since the *Interest* expiration in applications (with FC-CC) may clash with the PIT expirations (e.g., *Interest* packets re-sent by application may not be forwarded by *CCN Layer* due to unexpired PIT entry), we use a 2-level (*soft-hard*) timeout mechanism for PIT. An *Interest* packet received before *soft* timeout results in that *Interest* being only registered in PIT while any *Interest* after, results in it being forwarded as well. A *hard* timeout is considered as in [1].

Forwarding Strategies - [1] proposes 2 forwarding strategies. The *standard* strategy broadcasts received *Interest* packets to all the faces while the *best-face* strategy selects a face based on previous experiences and uses this face to send *Interest* packets out.

The evaluation considers a number of FC-CC enabled application versions that are configured with differing combinations (Table 2) of the algorithms discussed in Section 3 (settings). Therefore, in the following sections, when a reference is made to a performance graph such as *CCN-NewReno-Smart*, it indicates that the graph shows the performance of the *CCN-NewReno* implementation together with the *Fast Recovery, Selective Fast Retransmit* and *Pre-Recovery* enabled.

Table 2. Algorithms and Features enabled in Different Settings

Version	Simple1	Simple2	Simple3	Smart
Slow Start	√	√	√	√
Congestion Avoidance	√	√	√	√
Fast Recovery		√	√	√
Selective Fast Retransmit			√	√
Pre-Recovery				√

To evaluate these different FC-CC versions, a network topology is identified that consist of multiple CCN clients, CCN servers and CCN routers (Fig. 2(b)). In each of the following performance evaluations, a scenario is identified using parts of this topology to evaluate a particular version (Table 2) with a particular flavour (e.g., *CCN-NewReno-Simple1*).

4.1 *Fast Recovery* Algorithm

The "Client 1" in Fig. 2(b) requests a Content with a size of 20 MB, which resides on the "Server 1". The "Router 2" drops only one packet at random intervals at different rates. Therefore, there is no continuous packet drops in this setup and the effect of *Selective Fast Retransmit* is not highlighted. And also, out-of-order packets do not occur due to CCN *Data* packets coming from multiple sources since both routers are configured not to cache. CCN *Data* come only from the "Server 1" and thus the effect of *Pre-Recovery* is also not highlighted. These settings are used only to evaluate the effect of *Fast Recovery*. The 3 variants of *CCN-NewReno*, *CCN-Cubic* and *CCN-Compound* without *Fast Recovery*, i.e., "Simple1" and with *Fast Recovery*, i.e., "Smart" is analysed in this section.

Fig. 3 shows *cwnd* variations of *CCN-NewReno*, *CCN-Cubic* and *CCN-Compound*, respectively. Without *Fast Recovery* (i.e., "Simple1"), the receiver ("Client 1") enters *Slow Start* when detecting a packet loss through a retransmission timeout. When using *Fast Recovery* (i.e., "Smart"), a receiver reacts to a packet loss first with *Pre-Recovery* and then enters *Fast Recovery*. As explained in Section 3.3, it continues to increase *cwnd* until the *Pre-Recovery* threshold ($Pre\_FRT + FRT$) is reached and then enters *Fast Recovery*, in which *cwnd*

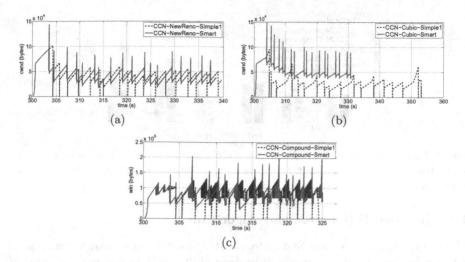

Fig. 3. *cwnd* variations : CCN-NewReno, CCN-Cubic and CCN-Compound with "Simple1" and "Smart" Settings

increases exponentially for receipts of each out-of-order *Data* packet (refers to the spikes between two consecutive *Congestion Avoidance* phases in Fig. 3 with "Smart" version) until it receives an in-order *Data* packet.

The difference between the three adapted variations are how *cwnd* updates during the *Congestion Avoidance* phase. The *CCN-NewReno cwnd* increases linearly during the *Congestion Avoidance* (Fig. 3(a)). *CCN-Cubic* increases in a linear manner immediately after entering the *Congestion Avoidance*, because *CCN-Cubic* emulates regular TCP *cwnd* when it is in the TCP-friendly region [5] (Fig. 3(b)). *Fast Recovery* reduces the download time (Fig. 4) for both *CCN-NewReno* and *CCN-Cubic*. *CCN-Cubic* shows a higher gain with *Fast Recovery* with the increase of the packet loss rates, compared to *CCN-NewReno*.

In contrast to the performance of *CCN-NewReno* and *CCN-Cubic*, *CCN-Compound* shows better performance without *Fast Recovery* (Fig. 3(c). This is due to the consideration of the delay-based window (*dwnd*) in addition to the *win* as determined by *CCN-NewReno*. The *dwnd* of *CCN-Compound* with "Simple1" grows more aggressively than *CCN-Compound* with "Smart". *dwnd* is only effective during the *Congestion Avoidance*. When a packet loss is detected, *dwnd* is set to 0 and *CCN-Compound* goes to *Slow Start* in "Simple1". In contrast, "Smart" version enters *Fast Recovery* which increases the sending of packets resulting in a higher RTT and the decrease of *dwnd*. Therefore, the overall *win* in *CCN-Compound* grows slower with the "Smart" version and this effect is more with the increase of the packet loss rate.

Fig. 4, which shows a comparison of download times of "Simple1" (without *Fast Recovery*) and "Smart" (with *Fast Recovery*) versions when using *CCN-NewReno*, *CCN-Compound* and *CCN-Cubic* under loss rates of 0.1%, 0.2% and 0.5%, confirms the better performance of *CCN-Compound*.

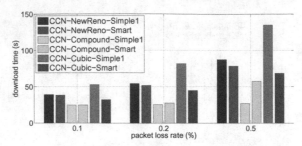

Fig. 4. Download time of *CCN-NewReno*, *CCN-Compound* and *CCN-Cubic* w.r.t. different packet loss rates without *Fast Recovery* ("Simple1") and with ("Smart") *Fast Recovery*

4.2 *Selective Fast Retransmit* Algorithm

The evaluation of *Selective Fast Retransmit* is done using similar versions as in 4.1, but letting "Router 2" in Fig. 2(b) drop multiple *Data* packets continuously at a specified time in order to highlight the effect of *Selective Fast Retransmit*. Here, the comparison is done with "Simple2" and "Smart" versions. In "Simple2", TCP-like *Fast Retransmit* is enabled, while "Smart" is enabled with *Fast Recovery*, *Selective Fast Retransmit* and *Pre-Recovery*. Note that, *Pre-Recovery* is not triggered in this scenario since there are no out-of-order *Data* packets due to the use of a single server in this scenario.

We have compared the recovery time in Fig. 5, which shows the average time that a CCN application stays in *Fast Recovery* when packet losses occur. In case of one packet loss, both "Simple2" and "Smart" shows exactly the same time in *Fast Recovery* for all 3 variants (*CCN-NewReno*, *CCN-Compound* and *CCN-Cubic*). But, recovery time increases drastically with the increase of multiple packet drops for "Simple2", while "Smart" stays almost the same as the single packet drop case.

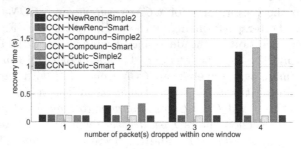

Fig. 5. Recovery time of CCN-NewReno, CCN-Compound and CCN-Cubic w.r.t. number of continuous packet losses

Fig. 6 compares how *cwnd* varies when dropping packets, 1 packet at 305 s, 2 packets at 310 s, 3 packets at 315 s and 4 packets at 320 s. Fig. 6(a) shows that *cwnd* of *Fast Recovery* increases rapidly when the number of packets lost increases continuously, when the *Selective Fast Retransmit* is not used ("Simple2"). In contrast, when *Selective Fast Retransmit* is used ("Smart"), Fig. 6(b) shows that the variations of *cwnd* is not dependant on the number of packet losses. As explained in Section 3.3, this is due to *Selective Fast Retransmit* of CCN continuously sending *Interest* packets of the missing *Data* packets. This is not the case with TCP-like *Fast Retransmit* that waits for in-order data to arrive for the next ACK to be sent.

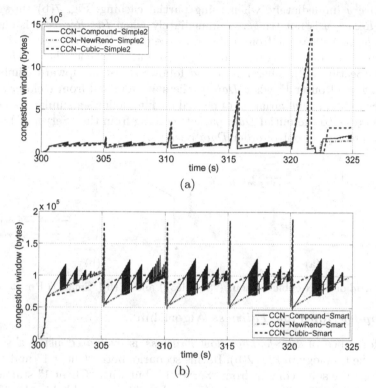

Fig. 6. *cwnd* variations without ("Simple2") and with ("Smart") *Selective Fast Retransmit*

4.3 *Pre-Recovery* Algorithm

The setup shown in Fig. 2(b) is used to evaluate the performance of *Pre-Recovery* by distributing *Data* packets among multiple sources. At the beginning, "Client 1" starts downloading contents while "Router 1" is set to cache segments using LRU caching strategy. "Client 2" is made to start downloading the same content a little later and when "Client 2" starts downloading, "Router 1" has full or part of *Data* packets depending on pre-configured cache sizes. All the results shown here are taken at "Client 2", which gets out-of-order packets due to *Data* packets coming from the "Server 1" as well as from the "Router 1". The results are taken for 3 cases, viz., where all *Data* packets are cached at "Router 1" (full caching), where all *Data* packets are at "Server 1" (no caching) and where the latter part of *Data* packets are cached at "Router 1" (partial caching).

The comparison is done with "Simple3" version, in which *Pre-Recovery* is disabled and "Smart" with *Pre-Recovery* enabled. In this scenario, the effects of packet drops are not emulated.

With TCP-like *Fast Recovery*, even without packet drops, "Simple3" detects a false packet loss through out-of-order *Data* receipts (Fig. 7(a)) and enters *Fast Recovery* immediately, when using partial caching. Fig. 7(b) shows that the *Fast Recovery* is not triggered immediately when *Pre-Recovery* is enabled. When *Data* packets arrive from a closer source (i.e., "Router 1"), *Pre-Recovery* makes sure that *Fast Recovery* is not triggered until it reaches the *Pre-Recovery* threshold (Section 3.2). Therefore, *cwnd* follows the same upward climb as in full caching at "Router 1" when *Data* packets are received from a closer source. At the beginning, *cwnd* variation of partial caching follows a similar trend as in no caching (due to the initial *Data* packets coming from the "Server 1") until it detects the receipt of out-of-order *Data* packets.

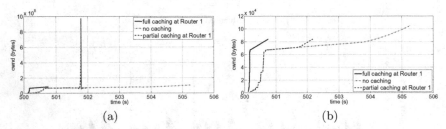

(a)   (b)

Fig. 7. *cwnd* of CCN-cubic without ("Simple3") and with ("Smart") Pre-Recovery

4.4 *Hop-by-Hop Flow Fairness* Algorithm

The performance of *Hop-by-hop Flow Fairness* is evaluated using a scenario based on the topology in Fig. 2(b). In this scenario, both "Client 1" and "Client 2" download the same content from "Server 1", but with "Client 1" starting initially and "Client 2" a little later. LRU based caching is enabled in the "Router 1" and therefore, the download done by "Client 2" initially obtains the content from the cache at "Router 1". The results are compared with and without using the *Hop-by-hop Flow Fairness* algorithm, when using *CCN-NewReno* with different levels of Background Traffic Loads (BTL) in the network. The BTL is created as a percentage of the link capacity.

Table 3 shows the performance comparison of without *Hop-by-hop Flow Fairness* (Case 1) and with *Hop-by-hop Flow Fairness* (Case 2), for the different

Table 3. Hop-by-hop Fairness Performance Comparison

	Client 1				Client 2			
	No BTL		80% BTL		No BTL		80% BTL	
	Case 1	Case 2	Case 1	Case 2	Case 1	Case 2	Case 1	Case 2
Download time, sec	24.19	24.19	230.13	180.5	23.43	23.43	208.44	209.44
Throughput, Kbps	826.8	826.8	86.9	110.8	853.4	853.4	95.9	95.5
Packet losses	0	0	26	0	0	0	0	0

clients under no BTL and with an 80% of BTL. Due to the cached content in "Router 1", the FC-CC application in "Client 2" becomes aggressive as the content can be retrieved faster, initially. During this initial period, since the RTT is smaller, the *cwnd* grows rapidly, thereby becoming aggressive. But, after a while, when the cache is exhausted, "Client 2" also starts fetching the content from the "Server 1". In this way, "Client 1" is disadvantaged. But when *Hop-by-hop Flow Fairness* operates at the "Router 1", the aggressive flow is slowed down by limiting the bandwidth it is able to use. Thereby, both content flows are given a fair share of the bandwidth. This is evident from the better performance (lower download time, better throughput and no packet losses) experienced by "Client 1" for 80% BTL. One other observation made was that the benefits of *Hop-by-hop Flow Fairness* becomes more evident when the amount of BTL increases which is the usually expected when networks are congested (higher BTL).

5   Conclusion

The work presented here discussed about the adoption of FC-CC in CCN based networks. Our contribution focussed on adapting the most widely used TCP flavours of *CCN-NewReno*, *CCN-Cubic* and *CCN-Compound*. We have discussed a number of aspects that need to be considered when adapting TCP due to the architectural differences in CCN compared to TCP/IP, the adaptation of these 3 flavours and the additional algorithms (*Pre-Recovery*, *Selective Fast Retransmit* and *Hop-by-hop Flow Fairness*) identified to address some of the issues relevant to CCN. The *Pre-Recovery* algorithm was identified to avoid the false detection of packet losses in CCN when content arrives from multiple sources. The *Selective Fast Retransmit* algorithm was identified to perform selective resending of *Interest* packets during the loss recovery period. The *Hop-by-hop Flow Fairness* algorithm that considers both *Interest* and *Data* flows was identified to provide fair sharing of bandwidth for competing content flows. The flavour adaptations

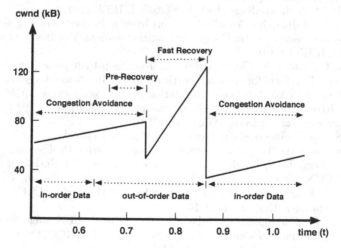

Fig. 8. Operation of the Different FC-CC Algorithms

and the identified algorithms were implemented in an OPNET based simulator and the performance was evaluated. Fig. 8 shows the operation of the different algorithms discussed in our work.

The analysis of the results obtained show that *Fast Recovery* makes *CCN-NewReno* and *CCN-Cubic* more efficient in downloading content under stable loss rates. However, *CCN-Compound* has a larger throughput when losses are only detected from a retransmission timeout. The *Selective Fast Retransmit* algorithm in CCN has a better recovery efficiency than TCP-like *Fast Retransmit*. The *Pre-Recovery* shows the advantages of detecting whether out-of-order *Data* packets are as a result of multiple sources or packet losses. *Hop-by-hop Flow Fairness* enhances the performance of less aggressive flows in terms of goodput and download efficiency by providing a fair share of the use of faces.

We intend to further improve the performance of our work by evaluating these scenarios in large scale network topologies.

References

1. Jacobson, V., Smetters, D.K., Thornton, J.D., Plass, M.F., Briggs, N.H., Braynard, R.L.: Networking named content. In: Proceedings of the 5th International Conference on Emerging Networking Experiments and Technologies, pp. 1–12. ACM (2009)
2. Zhang, L., Estrin, D., Burke, J., Jacobson, V., Thornton, J.D., Smetters, D.K., Zhang, B., Tsudik, G., Massey, D., Papadopoulos, C., et al.: Named data networking (NDN) project, NDN-0001, Xerox Palo Alto Research Center-PARC (2010)
3. Floyd, S.: The NewReno Modification to TCPs Fast Recovery Algorithm, RFC3782 (April 2004)
4. Tan, K., Song, J., Zhang, Q., Sridharan, M.: A Compound TCP Approach for High-speed and Long Distance Networks. In: IEEE Infocom, Barcelona, Spain (April 2006)
5. Ha, S., Rhee, I., Xu, L.: CUBIC: A New TCP-Friendly High-Speed TCP Variant. ACM SIGOPS Operating System Review (2008)
6. Allman, M., Paxson, V., Stevens, W.: TCP Congestion Control, RFC 2581 (April 1999)
7. Oueslati, S., Roberts, J., Sbihi, N.: Flow-aware traffic control for a content-centric network. In: 2012 Proceedings IEEE INFOCOM. IEEE (2012)
8. Rozhnova, N., Fdida, S.: An effective hop-by-hop Interest shaping mechanism for CCN communications. In: Computer Communications Workshops (INFOCOM WKSHPS). IEEE (2012)
9. Carofiglio, G., Gallo, M., Muscariello, L.: Joint hop-by-hop and receiver-driven interest control protocol for content-centric networks. In: Proceedings of the Second Edition of the ICN Workshop on Information-centric Networking. ACM (2012)
10. Palo Alto Research Centre, Draft CCN Protocol Specification, http://www.ccnx.org, (accessed on May 2013)
11. Keshav, S.: An Engineering Approach to Computer Networking: ATM Networks, the Internet, and the Telephone Network. Addison-Wesley Professional (1997)
12. Psaras, I., Clegg, R.G., Landa, R., Chai, W.K., Pavlou, G.: Modelling and Evaluation of CCN-Caching Trees. In: Domingo-Pascual, J., Manzoni, P., Palazzo, S., Pont, A., Scoglio, C. (eds.) NETWORKING 2011, Part I. LNCS, vol. 6640, pp. 78–91. Springer, Heidelberg (2011)
13. Muscariello, L., Carofiglio, G., Gallo, M.: Bandwidth and Storage Sharing Performance in Information Centric Networking. In: ACM SIGCOMM Workshop on Information-centric Networking, pp. 26–31 (2011)

Multipath Transmission
in Content Centric Networking
Using a Probabilistic Ant-Routing Mechanism

Jonas Eymann and Andreas Timm-Giel

Hamburg University of Technology
Institute of Communication Networks
{jonas.eymann,timm-giel}@tuhh.de

Abstract. Content Centric Networking (CCN) is a new networking paradigm that names pieces of content rather than network nodes. It promises more efficient transmissions due to in-network caching and easier realization of mobile and multihomed devices. However, in order to leverage multipath transmission for multihomed devices, routing and forwarding mechanisms are needed that support this functionality. In this paper, we present a probabilistic ant-routing mechanism that enables multipath transmissions for CCN nodes. Using an OMNeT++ based simulation model, we show that our routing mechanism can support transmissions of data streams over multiple links to achieve higher throughput than any single link could provide.

Keywords: Content Centric Networking, CCN, Named Data Networking, NDN, Information Centric Networking, ICN, Routing, Forwarding, Multipath, Ant Colony Optimization.

1 Introduction

The architecture and core protocols of today's Internet, TCP/IP, were developed more than 30 years ago and have proven to be remarkably versatile. The Internet supports applications that were never foreseen and the number of users has exceeded all expectations, for which the exhaustion of IPv4 addresses is a very apparent sign.

However, besides the scarcity of IPv4 addresses, several other fundamental design decisions are no longer in line with today's requirements and prevalent usage of the Internet. Nowadays, users are mostly interested in content or information regardless of which specific server (i.e., which IP address) it is hosted on, yet the network still requires IP addresses to operate. The host-centric architecture with "fixed" IP addresses for hosts is becoming increasingly incongruous for mobile devices that feature more than one network interface (e.g., WiFi and UMTS) and hence have changing network addresses. Seamless mobility, while theoretically solved [1], has never reached a widespread adoption. For instance, switching from WiFi to the mobile phone network on a smartphone still breaks

D. Pesch et al. (Eds.): MONAMI 2013, LNICST 125, pp. 45–56, 2013.

existing TCP connections of running applications. Security was also not part of the original design, therefore numerous additional protocols were developed as an afterthought. Likewise, many services have to make a significant effort to overcome deficiencies in the original TCP/IP architecture. For example, the problems induced by Network Address Translation (NAT) require Skype and other applications to implement NAT traversal mechanisms like STUN [3,4] and due to the lack of in-network caching, services such as YouTube have to rely on Content Distribution Networks [2] to efficiently deliver its services.

Content Centric Networking, or CCN [5], is a new approach that sets out to close this widening gap between architecture and usage of the Internet by naming information chunks rather than addressing nodes.[1] Instead of sending packets to a destination specified by an IP address, CCN nodes send out requests (called Interests) for pieces of content (called Data) specified by a unique, hierarchically structured name. Any node that has matching Data to a traversing Interest can answer immediately because the name unambiguously identifies the Data. If an Interest cannot be answered locally at a node, it will be forwarded to one or more neighboring nodes. The unique name of Data packets enables in-network caching as the content can be stored by any node or router in the network. To prevent unauthorized alteration of content, each Data packet contains a digital signature. Optionally, Data packets can also be encrypted, hence security is a central part of the architecture though this is beyond the scope of this paper (see [6] for further information).

The absence of a fixed destination node address in CCN also facilitates multipath transmissions for multihomed devices with more than one network interface. Unlike IP packets, CCN Interests can be forwarded via several interfaces simultaneously to increase resilience to packet loss. For increased throughput, link bandwidths can be aggregated by forwarding Interests in an interleaving order. However, little research has been done so far on how such multipath forwarding mechanisms for CCN should be designed.

In this work we describe a probabilistic routing and forwarding mechanism for CCN to find multiple paths to sources of content. The mechanism is based on the idea how ant colonies in nature find paths to food sources. Using an OMNeT++ based simulation model of CCN, we demonstrate how such a probabilistic ant-routing mechanism makes it possible to use the paths to transmit constant bit rate data streams over multiple links to increase throughput.

The remainder of this paper is structured as follows: Section 2 discusses related work on probabilistic ant-routing. The basic forwarding mechanism of CCN and existing routing options are explained in Section 3. In Section 4 we present our probabilistic routing and forwarding mechanism for CCN. To test multipath transmission using probabilistic routing and forwarding, two different simulation scenarios are evaluated in Section 5. Finally, Section 6 gives some hints on future work and concludes the paper.

---

[1] Content Centric Networking is also known as Named Data Networking or NDN, see http://www.named-data.net

2   Related Work

The idea of applying the optimizing behavior of ant colonies (Ant Colony Optimization) to telecommunication networks has been studied in several previous works [9,11,12]. It has also been shown that due to their ability to adapt to changing environments, ant-like mechanisms are also suitable for dynamic networks such as MANETs (mobile ad-hoc networks) [13].

A common property in the publications above is the differentiation between "ants" or agent packets that explore the network and find paths, and data packets that transfer user data. As CCN operates by coupled pairs of Interest and Data packets, the existing mechanisms are not directly applicable. However, we can interpret Interests similar to "ants" which simplifies the design, as discussed later.

Ant-based routing and forwarding has also been proposed for CCN. In Services over Content Centric Routing (SoCCeR) the concepts of content centric networking and service centric networking are combined [14]. SoCCeR uses an ant-like approach as an additional routing mechanism for the communication of services, but not as a general routing mechanism for Interests to sources of static content. As all services are assumed to be known, special Interest ants are sent out at regular intervals towards randomly selected services in order to find and update paths. In our approach, we assume unknown destinations, thus use a broadcasting mechanism instead.

A second proposal for ant-routing in CCN is Greedy Ant Colony Forwarding (GACF [15]). GACF uses "Hello ants" created by routers to measure paths to all sources, thus, like SoCCeR, assumes known destinations. Client nodes (consumers) send out "Normal ants" for requesting user data packets. In contrast, our scheme only uses normal CCN Interest and Data packets, which in our view is sufficient and also more closely complies with the architecture of CCN.

Both SoCCeR and GACF showed that Ant Colony Optimization mechanisms are suitable for CCN and can achieve low delays. However, none of the related work on ant-routing investigates the aggregation of links. In this paper, we analyze the multipath behavior and aggregation of multiple links for higher throughput, which to our knowledge was not addressed before.

3   Forwarding and Routing in CCN

Similar to IP packet forwarding, the CCN forwarding process of Interests relies on a structure called Forwarding Information Base (FIB). The FIB contains name prefixes of content collections and one or more associated interfaces through which the content can be reached (Fig. 1). An interface can be either a physical link such as a network interface or a local application, hence the term "faces" to distinguish this generalized concept.

The names of incoming Interests that cannot be answered from the cache[2] are matched against the prefixes in the FIB using longest prefix matching and

---

[2] In Content Centric Networking, the cache is called Content Store.

then forwarded to potential sources of content. Additionally, the node also keeps the information from which interface the Interest arrived in a data structure called Pending Interest Table (PIT). If another Interest arrives for the same Data (i.e., same name), the node adds the arrival interface to the existing PIT entry but does not forward the Interest again. When the Data packet comes back in response to the Interest, the node caches the Data and sends it to all faces for the corresponding PIT entry, which is subsequently deleted. The aggregation of Interests thus saves Data packets from being transmitted more than once over the same link.

Prefix entries in the FIB can be configured manually, which is the method currently used for the prototype implementation of CCN that is developed in the project CCNx[3]. While manual configuration is sufficient for small testbeds with only a few nodes, larger networks will have to use other mechanisms that are also capable of dynamically reacting to changes in the network. It is possible to use existing routing protocols such as Open Shortest Path First (OSPF) and adapt them for CCN, which is the goal of OSPFN [7]. However, in order to

Prefix	Faces
/de/tuhh	2,3
/de/tuhh/comnets	3
/de/uni-bremen	4

Fig. 1. Example of the Forwarding Information Base (FIB)

leverage cached data that is nearby a node but not on the direct path to the original server, routing protocols such as OSPFN cannot adapt quickly enough to capture the locations of highly dynamic cached data which changes at line speed. Previous research suggested that probabilistic routing and forwarding without algorithmically calculated shortest paths might therefore be beneficial for CCN [8].

4 A Probabilistic Ant-Routing Mechanism for CCN

Our probabilistic routing and forwarding scheme is based on the idea of Ant Colony Optimization [9] which is inspired by the way biological ant colonies find paths to sources of food. In nature, each single ant leaves a pheromone trail on the ground. Other ants usually follow trails with strong pheromone traces, thus further increasing the trail. With a some small probability, ants diverge from the trail looking for other paths to the known source or to discover new sources of food. As short paths to sources will generally be used more often (as an ant can cover a short path more often than a long path), there is an implicit optimization towards shorter paths [10]. Over time, pheromones evaporate and thus unused paths slowly fade.

---

[3] http://www.ccnx.org

Applying the idea of Ant Colony Optimization to CCN, we can interpret Interests as ants looking for food, and the corresponding Data packets as the ants carrying food back. The pheromone traces that real ants leave on the ground can be compared to the PIT entries and changes to the FIB that influence how Interests are forwarded. For this reason, we extended the FIB with additional information indicating the quality of a face for each prefix (i.e., the path to a source of content), as shown in Fig. 2. The algorithm of our probabilistic routing

Prefix	Face	q
/de/tuhh	2	0.7
	3	0.3
/de/tuhh/comnets	3	1
/de/uni-bremen	4	1

Fig. 2. Example of an extended Forwarding Information Base (FIB) augmented with information on the quality q of each face for a prefix

and forwarding mechanism consisting of three phases can then be described as follows:

1. In the beginning FIBs are empty, i.e., do not contain any entries. When an Interest arrives and there is not entry for the prefix, the node broadcasts the Interest to all faces except the one that it arrived on.
2. When a Data packet arrives and there is no entry in the FIB for the Data's prefix, a new entry is created and the quality indicator is set to 1 since there is only one face for the prefix. If there is already an entry for the prefix, the quality indicator q_i for the arrival face i is updated to

$$q_i \leftarrow q_i + r(1 - q_i) \qquad (1)$$

where the factor r, $0 < r \leq 1$, influences the reinforcement of the quality value depending on the observed RTT (see below). For all other entries of faces $j \neq i$, the quality indicator is updated by

$$q_j \leftarrow q_j - r q_j \qquad (2)$$

The quality indicator of the arrival face i is therefore increased while the quality indicators of all other faces are decreased. The factor r is calculated based on the round trip time d_{RTT} of the Data that has arrived according to

$$r = r(d_{\mathrm{RTT}}, \alpha) = e^{-\alpha d_{\mathrm{RTT}}} \qquad (3)$$

For very small RTTs r approaches 1, indicating a very good connection and thus resulting in a larger reinforcement in Equation (1) and decrease in Equation (2). The additional parameter α in Equation (3) is used to adjust the influence of an arrived Data packet, i.e., how strongly new RTT values are taken into account to change the quality indicators of the links. A small value of α results in a faster reinforcement of good paths and evaporation of unused paths.

3. When Interests arrive at the node with a matching prefix in the FIB, the quality indicator determines the probability with which each face is used for forwarding. For example, in Fig. 2, for the first entry, face 2 is used with a probability of 0.7 while face 3 is used with a probability of 0.3. However, with a small probability p_b, the Interest is broadcast to all faces as if there was no entry. This way the node can discover new sources of Data and adapt to changes in the network. The normal probabilistic forwarding described above is therefore only applied with the probability $1 - p_b$.

The goal of the developed probabilistic ant-routing mechanism is to achieve high throughput using multipath transmission and at the same time minimize the RTTs of Interest/Data pairs. To test the mechanism, we simulated two different scenarios for different values of α, described in the following section.

5   Simulation Scenarios and Results

We implemented a model of CCN and our probabilistic ant-routing algorithm using the event-based OMNeT++ simulation framework[4]. In order to analyze the mechanism in changing network conditions, we simulated a simple dual path scenario where one path is deactivated during the simulation run and reactivated later. The behavior in a more complex network is simulated using a realistic backbone (NSFNET scenario) under static conditions.

5.1   Dual Path Scenario

The first scenarios is a network with one client that can receive a constant bit rate (CBR) stream from two different servers as shown in Fig. 3 (dual path scenario). To receive the streams, the client sends out an Interest every 20 ms.

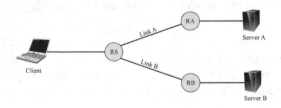

Fig. 3. Dual path scenario with two servers A and B offering the same streams. Link A and B are the bottleneck links with a transmission rate of 250 kbit/s and a delay of 100 ms.

The splitting router RS forwards the Interests either via link A, link B or both links at the same time in case of a broadcast (the broadcast probability is set to $p_b = 0.1$). Link A and B are configured as bottleneck links with 250 kbit/s.

---

[4] http://www.omnetpp.org

Both servers contain the same content and can answer to the Interests with Data packets. In one simulation configuration, the size of the Data packets is 500 B, resulting in a CBR stream of 200 kbit/s, which is less than the bottleneck transmission rate of one link. In the second configuration, Data packets of 1000 B result in a CBR stream of 400 kbit/s. This stream can only be successfully transmitted when both bottleneck links are aggregated and used simultaneously. In order to examine how the ant-routing algorithm adapts to changes in the network, link A is deactivated at $t = 50$ s, i.e., drops all packets. At $t = 150$ s, the link comes up again.

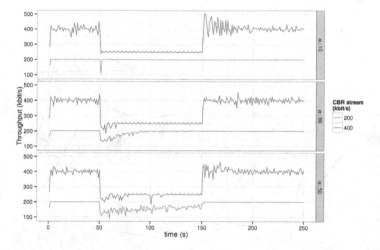

Fig. 4. Received throughput of CBR streams at the client in dual path scenario for α=10, 30 and 50 (single runs). Link A is deactivated between $t = 50$ s and $t = 150$ s.

Fig. 4 shows the achievable throughput for the dual path scenario for three different values of α. As expected, the lower CBR stream with 200 kbit/s can be transmitted, since the Data rate is lower than the bottleneck link speed. The higher CBR stream also achieves its nominal transmission rate, though the throughput fluctuates due to the queueing that occurs at the bottleneck links. The influence of α becomes visible at $t = 50$ s. For larger values of α, the low CBR stream needs much longer to shift to the one remaining link while for smaller α it adapts faster to the change. However, for small values of α, the routing does not stabilize well, as can be seen from the larger fluctuation for the higher CBR stream after the link comes up again at $t = 150$ s.

During the period that link A is deactivated, the high CBR stream can only transmit with the transmission rate of the bottleneck link of 250 kbit/s. Many Data packets are therefore queued and eventually dropped at router RB as the stream of Interests to the server still remains unchanged. After link A is reactivated, the 400 kbit/s stream can again achieve its full transmission rate as the ant-routing algorithm adapts to again using both links simultaneously.

5.2   NSFNET Scenario

The second scenario we simulated is based on the backbone of the National Science Foundation Network (NSFNET) as shown in Fig. 5. The NSFNET backbone consists of 14 routing nodes to which we connected a client and a server. All routing nodes are connected by links with a maximum transmission rate of 1.5 Mbit/s. The propagation delays are indicated by the values next to each link in Fig. 5. Since we are interested in the multipath transmission, the client and server links are faster (10 Gbit/s and a delay of 1 μs) to prevent that they are the bottlenecks. All simulations were repeated 10 times and the broadcast probability p_b was set to 0.1.

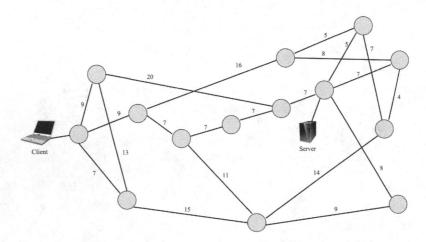

Fig. 5. NSFNET scenario with transmission rate of 1.5 Mbit/s for each link. The numbers indicate propagation delays in milliseconds [9].

Similar to the first scenario, the client sends out a constant stream of Interests. The inter-arrival times of the Interests are 12, 6, 4 or 3 ms. The server has matching Data to the Interests and answers with Data packets of 1.5 kB, resulting in CBR streams of 1, 2, 3 or 4 Mbit/s, respectively. Since any single link only has a data rate of 1.5 Mbit/s, the client can only fully receive the higher CBR streams when more than one link is used. The maximum aggregated link speed of the router to which the client is connected is 4.5 Mbit/s, thus all configured data streams can be transmitted in the ideal case.

Fig. 6 shows the measured throughput at the client for the four different CBR streams and values for α between 0.2 and 100. While the CBR stream with 4 Mbit/s never reaches its full throughput, the three other streams can be transmitted for values of α between 10 and 70.

The surprisingly low throughput of the 1 Mbit/s stream for small values of α can be explained by Fig. 7, which shows the loss rate (ratio of sent Interests to received Data packets) for the different streams. As can be seen in Fig. 7, the loss rate reaches over 10 % for α ≤ 1, thus resulting in the low throughput.

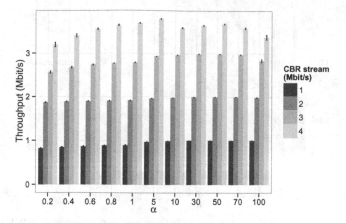

Fig. 6. Measured throughput of CBR streams at the client in NSFNET scenario for different values of α. Error bars indicate 95 % confidence intervals.

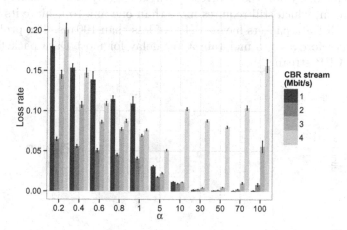

Fig. 7. Average loss rates at client in NSFNET scenario for different values of α. Error bars indicate 95 % confidence intervals.

For $30 \leq \alpha \leq 70$, the loss rates of the three lower CBR streams are very small. The highest CBR stream always experiences loss rates of more than 5 %, explaining the low throughput that is achieved.

Similar to the loss rates, the received delays also decrease for higher values of α (Fig. 8). As mentioned before, the value of α influences the impact the update of the quality indicator of an arrived Data packet. Small values of α therefore result in a highly fluctuating behavior. For $\alpha \approx 50$, we can observe the lowest delays and loss rates.

Fig. 9 shows the Cumulative Distribution Functions of the delay for $\alpha = 50$. As we can see, many packets of the 4 Mbit/s stream suffer from high delays. For the stream of 3 Mbit/s, over 75 % of all packets arrive within 100 ms

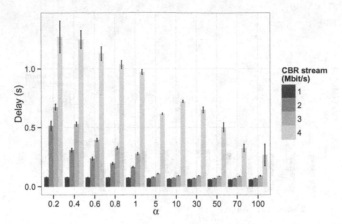

Fig. 8. Average delay of received data packets from server to client in NSFNET scenario for different values of α. Error bars indicate 95 % confidence intervals.

(the minimum delay for the shortest path is slightly above 60 ms). For the 2 Mbit/s stream, which still requires more than one link to achieve its full data rate, nearly all Data packets have a delay of less than 100 ms. The probabilistic routing is therefore able to maintain a low delay for most Data packets for the three lower CBR streams.

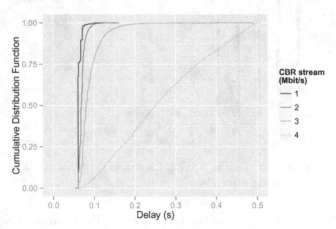

Fig. 9. Cumulative Distribution Functions of delay in NSFNET scenario for $\alpha = 50$ (single run)

6   Conclusion and Future Work

In this paper we presented a probabilistic routing and forwarding mechanism based on the idea of Ant Colony Optimization. Using an OMNeT++ based simulator, we demonstrated that such a mechanism can enable multipath transmission for CCN by using several paths simultaneously to aggregate link bandwidths. This way we can achieve higher transmission rates than any single link could support. Furthermore, the simulations showed that our ant-routing mechanism is capable to adapt to link failures. The time needed for adaptation depends on the parameter α.

Currently, the value for α has to be identified and adjusted manually to achieve good performance for the data transmission. In our future work we plan to investigate how the optimal value for α depends on the network topology and load. Subsequently, we will extend our ant-routing algorithm to dynamically adjust the value of α in order to minimize packet loss and delays and at the same time aim for the highest possible throughput.

References

1. Perkins, C.: IP Mobility Support for IPv4, Revised. RFC 5944 (Proposed Standard) (November 2010)
2. Rafetseder, A., Metzger, F., Stezenbach, D., Tutschku, K.: Exploring youtube's content distribution network through distributed application-layer measurements: a first view. In: Proceedings of the 2011 International Workshop on Modeling, Analysis, and Control of Complex Networks, Cnet 2011, pp. 31–36. ITCP (2011)
3. Rosenberg, J., Weinberger, J., Huitema, C., Mahy, R.: STUN - Simple Traversal of User Datagram Protocol (UDP) Through Network Address Translators (NATs). RFC 3489 (Proposed Standard) (March 2003), Obsoleted by RFC 5389
4. Baset, S.A., Schulzrinne, H.G.: An analysis of the skype peer-to-peer internet telephony protocol. In: Proceedings of 25th IEEE International Conference on Computer Communications, INFOCOM 2006, pp. 1–11 (2006)
5. Jacobson, V., Smetters, D.K., Thornton, J.D., Plass, M.F., Briggs, N.H., Braynard, R.L.: Networking Named Content. In: Proceedings of the 5th International Conference on Emerging Networking Experiments and Technologies, pp. 1–12 (2009)
6. Smetters, D.K., Jacobson, V.: Securing Network Content. Tech report, PARC (October 2009)
7. Wang, L., Hoque, M., Yi, C., Alyyan, A., Zhang, B.: OSPFN: an OSPF based routing protocol for named data networking. NDN Technical Report NDN-0003 (July 2012)
8. Rossini, G., Rossi, D.: Evaluating ccn multi-path interest forwarding strategies. Computer Communications 36(7), 771–778 (2013)
9. Di Caro, G.A.: Ant Colony Optimization and its application to adaptive routing in telecommunication networks. PhD thesis, Faculté des Sciences Appliquées, Université Libre de Bruxelles, Brussels, Belgium (November 2004)
10. Dorigo, M., Birattari, M., Stützle, T.: Ant colony optimization. IEEE Computational Intelligence Magazine 1(4), 28–39 (2006)
11. Di Caro, G.A., Dorigo, M.: AntNet: Distributed stigmergetic control for communications networks. Vivek, a Quarterly in Artificial Intelligence 12(3 & 4), 2–37 (1999), Reprinted from JAIR
12. Costa, A.: Analytic modelling of agent-based network routing algorithms. PhD thesis, University of Adelaide (2002)

13. Di Caro, G.A., Ducatelle, F., Gambardella, L.M.: AntHocNet: an adaptive nature-inspired algorithm for routing in mobile ad hoc networks. European Transactions on Telecommunications 16(5), 443–455 (2005)
14. Shanbhag, S., Schwan, N., Rimac, I., Varvello, M.: SoCCeR: services over content-centric routing. In: Proceedings of the ACM SIGCOMM Workshop on Information-centric Networking, ICN 2011, pp. 62–67. ACM, New York (2011)
15. Li, C., Liu, W., Okamura, J.: A greedy ant colony forwarding algorithm for named data networking. In: Proceedings of the APAN – Network Research Workshop (2012)

Learning Based Proactive Handovers
in Heterogeneous Networks

Seppo Horsmanheimo, Niwas Maskey, Heli Kokkoniemi-Tarkkanen,
Lotta Tuomimäki, and Pekka Savolainen

VTT Technical Research Centre of Finland
Vuorimiehentie 3, Espoo, 02044 VTT, Finland
`firstname.lastname@vtt.fi`

Abstract. Today, the number of versatile real-time mobile applications
is vast, each requiring different data rate, Quality of Service (QoS) and
connection availability requirements. There have been strong demands
for pervasive communication with advances in wireless technologies.
Real-time applications experience significant performance bottlenecks in
heterogeneous networks. A critical time for a real-time application is
when a vertical handover is done between different radio access technologies. It requires a lot of signalling causing unwanted interruptions to
real-time applications. This work presents a utilization of learning algorithms to give time for applications to prepare itself for vertical handovers
in the heterogeneous network environment. A testbed has been implemented, which collects PHY (Physical layer), application level QoS and
users context information from a terminal and combines these Key Performance Indicators (KPI) with network planning information in order
to anticipate vertical handovers by taking into account the preparation
time required by a specific real-time application.

Keywords: Vertical Handover, Heterogeneous Network, Key Performance Indicator, Machine Learning, Quality of Experience.

1 Introduction

Next generation communication systems provide a wide range of services and aim
to provide sufficient QoE (Quality of Experience) to users anywhere and any-
time. This involves using heterogeneous networks to provide services effectively
and efficiently. It is very challenging for mobile operators to balance the load
in networks of multiple radio access technologies, for example LTE, UMTS and
GSM. On the other hand, with the advent of smart mobile terminals supporting
multiple network technologies, mobile applications also have options to select
the most appropriate network to support their own requirements. This leads to
the requirement of transition from one access network to another seamlessly providing better quality options for users. These challenges are dealt with emerging
IEEE 802.21 specification, which supports handovers between IEEE 802 and
non-IEEE 802 (3GPP) access technologies to enable seamless mobility in next

D. Pesch et al. (Eds.): MONAMI 2013, LNICST 125, pp. 57–68, 2013.
© Institute for Computer Sciences, Social Informatics and Telecommunications Engineering 2013

generation heterogeneous wireless network [1]. To facilitate better management of multi-access networks for operators and to assist users in making suitable network selection, automation through cognitive management mechanisms is seen as a potential solution for optimal utilization of multiple access networks. Our motivation was to implement a platform to evaluate different learning based algorithms to be utilized in the vertical handover decision-making. The objective was to fuse real-time monitored KPIs and predicted location and speed dependent KPIs in order to enable foresight decision-making, and thus give mobile applications enough time to prepare themselves for vertical handovers.

Network performance can be estimated based on three orthogonal dimensions: coverage, capacity and QoS [2]. Better user experience requires better QoS and large capacity while network operators are more focused on coverage and capacity. The current trend seems to be moving towards a QoE centric approach, as device intelligence is increasing. However, the operators viewpoint cannot be overlooked as they are providing the network services. Our motivation is to find configurations that satisfy both viewpoints and hence maximize mutual benefits. However, it requires real-time information from both terminal and network sides to find correct configurations. Cross-layer communications and network monitoring play a key role in providing real-time context information.

To investigate the topic, we used the testbed called HET-Q. HET-Q is designed to collect location, real-time PHY/MAC (Medium Access Control) and application level QoS information from a user in all available networks. Intelligent elements observe current network conditions, learn from their earlier decisions, and adapt their operations accordingly. For implementing an intelligent handover mechanism, different machine learning algorithms can be applied, such as Self-Organized Map or a Normal Bayesian Classifier [3] [4]. Both terminal and network sides are designed to have cognitive functionalities. Foresighted selection of the best network requires utilization of the users location and network planning information. Furthermore, along with multi-radio access network aspects, multi-operator aspects with different service classes need to be considered.

In this paper, we will present the architecture of our testbed that supports cognitive handovers. We also present cognitive concepts to assist in making proactive handovers among available networks. The test cases illustrate the ability of the testbed to make use of machine learning algorithms for selecting an appropriate network and to allow time for a mobile application to prepare for a vertical handover.

2   HET-Q Architecture

The architecture of the HET-Q testbed is depicted in Fig. 1. The testbed includes a server side application, HET-Q server and a client side application called HET-Q client. Communication between the applications is done over UDP or TCP/IP connections. The mobile HET-Q client collects MAC/PHY level KPIs, application level QoS KPIs, and location information. Location information is retrieved from a GPS device while outdoors. While indoors, location information is retrieved from an indoor positioning system. The QoS parameters are collected with the measurement tool QoSMeT [5] [6] which is installed on the HET-Q client and server. The QoSMeT server is monitoring a large set of application level QoS KPIs over a point-to-point connection. The PHY/MAC layer information is obtained from wireless modules locked on specific radio access technologies. The PHY/MAC data is retrieved using low level interface queries, such as Hayes command set, also called AT commands. The testbed enables both real-time as well as offline measurements. A commercially available network monitoring tool (Nemo Outdoor) was used to provide offline measurements for validation purposes. The server combines the incoming information with network planning information, and gives the aggregated data to a decision-making algorithm. The algorithm makes a proactive decision beforehand whether the terminal using specific service class (web browsing, video streaming or FTP downloading) should make a vertical handover to another available network or not. The decision is sent as a forced-HO or proposed-HO command to the terminal. In the latter case, the terminal decides whether it obeys the proposal or not. The handovers are executed either using an Intelligent Vertical Handover (IVHO) controller [7] or by directly commanding wireless modules through internal interfaces.

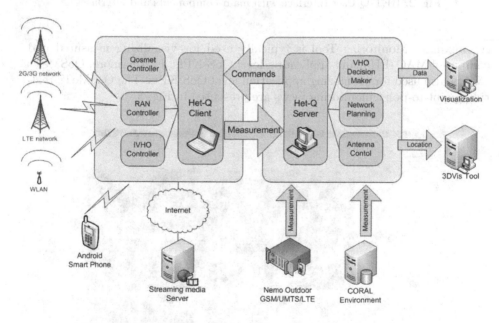

Fig. 1. HET-Q testbed with main components and interfaces

The HET-Q server is run on a server computer. Its GUI is shown in Fig. 2. It shows detailed information about the defined network layouts and a view of a 3D propagation environment including terrain height, clutter and building information. The real time measurement can be controlled by the HET-Q server.

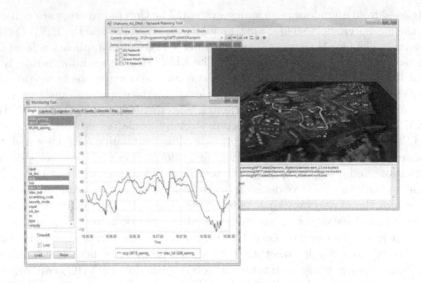

Fig. 2. HET-Q User Interface with main components and interfaces

An auxiliary Monitoring Tool is typically used for visualizing measured and computed MAC/PHY and application level QoS KPIs. Furthermore, QoSMeTs GUI is also used for visualizing application level QoS KPIs. The QoSMeTs real-time point-to-point monitoring views are presented in Fig. 3.

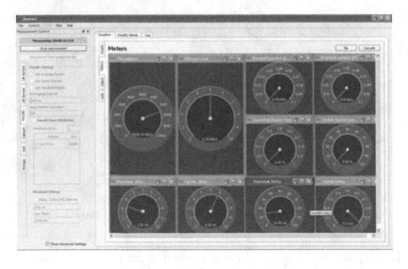

Fig. 3. QoSMeT GUI for monitoring QoS KPIs

3 Utilization of Cognitive Concepts

Cognitive functionality is utilized in the HET-Q testbed in three ways:

- Machine learning algorithms
- Network planning information
- Cognitive radio parameters

3.1 Utilization of Machine Learning Algorithms

Machine learning algorithms were experimented to assist vertical handovers in heterogeneous networks. Experimented algorithms were K-Nearest Neighbors (KNN), Support Vector Machine (SVM), Normal Bayesian Classifier (BAYES), Expectation-Maximization (EM), Multi-Layer Perceptron (MLP), Boosting algorithm (BOOST), Decision Tree (DTREE) and Random Tree (RTREE). We used the OpenCV library implementations of these algorithms [8]. The algorithms were implemented in the HET-Q servers decision-making module. The data flow of the decision-making process is shown in Fig. 4.

Learning algorithms are taught to select the most appropriate radio access technology for a user based on the used service type, measured and predicted KPIs, and location. Training data consists of aggregated information from real-time measurements, network planning data, and users location. Classifying the training samples is done by using prior knowledge of human experts by continuous scrutiny of PHY and MAC parameters. Classifying means that we select the most suitable radio access technology for the application being used. The classified data provides the most suitable network for each measurement sample. Learning algorithms construct their knowledge according to training data. The

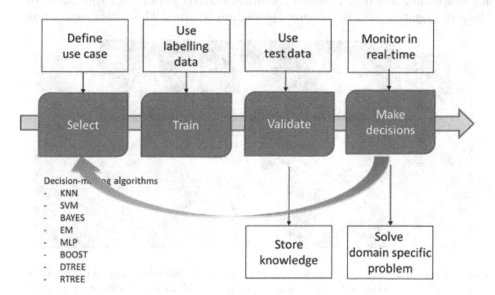

Fig. 4. Data flow of the decision-making process

reliability of the trained algorithm is validated with test data. An algorithm having the highest percentage of correctly classified samples (reliability) is selected for operational use.

3.2 Utilization of Network Planning Information

The HET-Q server uses network planning information in order to give a terminal enough time to prepare for a vertical handover which is critical for real-time streaming applications. Coverage, interference, and data rate prediction results are computed beforehand for the test scenario area using a network scenario and appropriate propagation model. These predictions are fine-tuned and validated with field measurements. Predicted KPIs are calculated at a presumed location of a user using the users current location, heading, and speed. The foresighted decision whether to make a handover relies on the accuracy of network planning information, e.g. coverage, and a users predicted location.

Coverage, interference, and data rate predictions depend on a base stations radio parameters and the modelling precision of the propagation environment. Measurements from dedicated measurement tools e.g. HET-Q client, Nemo Outdoor can be used for fine-tuning prediction models in order to get better equivalence between measured and predicted values.

The availability of digital map information has significantly increased in recent years. Moreover, the 3D virtual modelling and similar tools have matured enough to enable the creation of realistic 3D propagation environments, which include terrain, vegetation, and building information. The used 3D propagation environment models were obtained from National Land Survey of Finland. Unfortunately, most propagation models (called 2.5D models) take neither vegetation nor building shapes into account. Therefore, additional clutter parameters were added to those propagation models to improve prediction accuracy. The clutter parameters

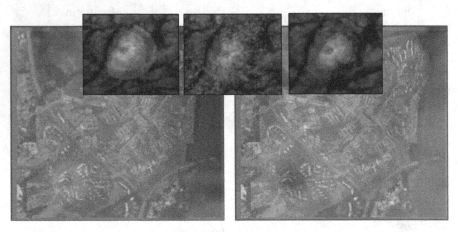

Fig. 5. Predicted coverage of a base station (background) calculated with a propagation model and then optimized (top) with the help of field measurements and location information

are optimized using field measurements. The tuning of a propagation model is illustrated in Fig. 5. The first picture shows a base stations coverage computed with a coverage prediction model, the second one after the clutter parameter tuning, and the last one after a so-called sanity-check. The last step ensures that clutter types attenuation factors are obeying laws of physics e.g. a forest type cannot amplify the signal. During the sanity-check, coverage areas are typically optimized to be a bit pessimistic in order to provide sufficient margins e.g. for fast fading.

3.3   Utilization of Cognitive Radio Parameters

Channel utilization level of WLAN APs is obtained from a CORAL platform which is designed for research purposes to experiment with Cognitive Radio Networking features [9]. The platform reports, which reports the occupancy level of each WLAN channel. The information is used to avoid unnecessary handovers to WLAN if WLAN channels are highly congested. Performance indicators given by CORAL can be considered as cognitive radio parameters. The CORAL platform plays an important role in the HET-Q testbed when a WLAN network is included in the scenario. The monitored PHY/MAC and QoS parameters cannot give adequate indication of what is the load level in the target access point (AP) when a vertical handover is about to occur. Moreover, the end to end QoS measurement tool QoSMeT is limited to measure QoS KPIs only in the active network (network the terminal is currently connected to). If the target AP has a high load, then the terminal is likely to be forced to return to the original network or to re-select another AP. The drawback is that much control signalling is required in the case of a vertical handover, and re-selection will degrade the users experienced QoS. The CORAL framework is used to tackle this problem. The AP is storing information about the channels utilization levels, which can be translated into load percentage. This information can be queried from a CORAL database before making a vertical handover, and thus unnecessary handovers can be prevented. HET-Q server queries data from the CORAL database and uses channel utilization information in decision-making.

4   Experimental Results

An experimental drive test was performed in Otaniemi, Espoo, Finland. The trial included experimentation with real-time vertical handover decision-making. The platform is designed to be real-time so that changes in network performance after a VHO decision can be assessed and the selected decision-making algorithm can be adjusted accordingly. The training of a decision-making algorithm was done with offline measurements, because outliers and other deficiencies can be removed before decision-making. VHO decision-making mechanisms were based on the following factors.

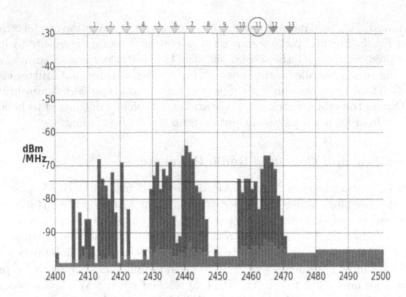

Fig. 6. Interference level for different WLAN channels as shown by CORAL

- *Reference*, Radio Access technology is selected automatically by the connected wireless module
- *Signal Strength*, Vertical handover is based on measured signal strength and coverage prediction results.
- *Proactive*, Vertical handover is done using a machine learning algorithm assisted with network planning and location information. (see chapter III A and B)

The driving route and relevant landmarks are depicted in Fig. 7. The drive test started from Digitalo building, went around it, passed the water tower, and continued down a small hill towards Micronova building. At the lowest location, the car was turned around and driven the same route back to Digitalo. The aim was to test whether WLAN APs in Digitalo as well as the AP installed on top of the water tower connected to CORAL were accessible from a moving car. The route was driven back and forth in order to study whether there are differences in entering and leaving cell boundaries. The turning at the lowest location was selected so that a NLOS condition occurred at the closest base station. In this experiment, we used DNAs (commercial network operator) UMTS and GSM networks, and our own WLAN access point installed at the water tower. The signal strength is indicated with colors. Warm color indicates high received signal level and cold color a low one. In the picture, blue color is indicating areas where surrounding buildings and terrain are shadowing the connection between a base station and the car. From the measurement, we observed that a measured signal strength value depends on the drive direction and serving cell boundaries. The network tends to keep a user connected to a serving base station as long as possible (even if not feasible). Therefore, we also measured signal strengths

Fig. 7. Measurement route with signal strength colours

of neighbouring cells. Similar drive tests were also carried out using another operators network (Sonera) in order to study multi-operator aspects.

When a wireless module was making VHO decisions (reference case), the terminal stayed the throughout whole measurement in the UMTS network even though the used traffic load (QoSMeT control traffic) could have been serviced by the other available networks. This case is shown in Fig. 8 A. In order to study the use of learning algorithms in VHO, we used service type specific constraints to classify the training and testing data. A classifier assigns the most suitable network for each measurement sample. The reference with 100 % reliability is shown in Fig. 8 B. The color indicates the active network - green color is UMTS, blue WLAN, and red GSM. When the measurement car turned around Digitalo, the velocity was so low that connection to Digitalos WLAN APs was possible. In areas where the communication link from car to a GSM base station was shadowed, the terminal switched to UMTS.

The classified training data (see chapter III A.) was used to train all six selected machine learning algorithms. The outcome of training was validated with test data obtained from the drive test and the reliability percentages were computed. The latter one indicates how many correct decisions were made by the trained algorithm. In addition, Self-Organized Map (SOM) classification algorithm was also tested. The achieved reliability percentage was 88 % with the same training and testing data.

In this trial measurement, the best algorithm (SVM) reached 95.6 % reliability. Although this seems good, the algorithm did make tens of wrong decisions. The sequence of wrong decisions was often bursty indicating that the decision-making algorithm was hesitating between two or more alternatives. This hesitation caused unnecessary ping-pong effects. To alleviate this problem, a minimum threshold time was added to the decision-making logic.

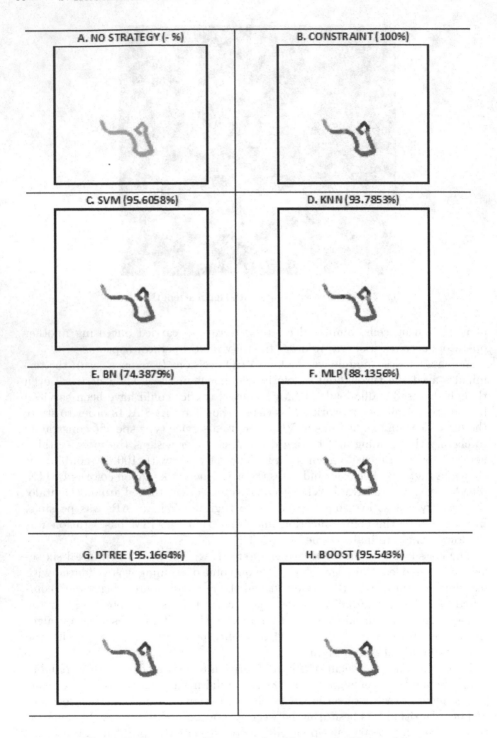

Fig. 8. Performance of learning algorithms in decision making

Based on the trial, we learned that the problem is not purely in the decision-making algorithms. It is more in the data we give them. If the data does not contain clear and systematic indicators to guide the algorithm, then it is possible for the algorithm to make too many incorrect decisions. In the worst cases, the reliability dropped even under 50 %. The measurement data collected from operational networks contain more outliers and deficiencies, which need to be removed before the training. The training in a laboratory environment is easier, because external interference can be isolated and network loads can be controlled in a step-by-step manner. It appeared that in operational networks, more sophisticated learning algorithms, like MLP, have more problems with incorrect training data than the simpler ones. The simple SVM algorithm gave the best results, which indicated that it was more robust and immune to unusual deviations in data.

5   Future Work

In the future, we are planning to test learning algorithms with a mobile terminal running several types of applications. So far, we have focused on a single application (web browsing, video streaming, data downloading with UDP or TCP/IP). The objective is also to integrate adaptive video coding to the HET-Q testbed in order to give video streaming applications opportunity to choose between a vertical handover and an adaptation of video streaming quality. In addition, the aim is to extend the testbeds applicability to support M2M (machine-to-machine) communication for indoor applications. Moreover, we found out that the same learning algorithms used for vertical handovers can also be utilized to automate network coverage tuning with steerable antenna solutions [2] and real-time measurements.

6   Conclusions

This paper describes the implemented testbed and the preliminary results obtained from using learning algorithms for the proactive handover decision-making in heterogeneous networks. The decision-making utilizes real-time PHY/MAC information, application level QoS, network planning information, users movements as well as cognitive radio parameters. The testbed utilizes several learning algorithms.

It was found out that the idea of utilizing learning based decision-making algorithms is plausible for terminal to select the suitable network based on networks load conditions. However, training of learning algorithms turned out to be challenging. Lack of clear patterns as well as outliers and deficiencies in the data tend to decrease the performance of the learning algorithms. Hence, the training of the algorithm is crucial and needs to be done with caution. The results obtained from the field trials confirm that learning algorithms are potential especially for real-time streaming applications in heterogeneous network benefiting from foresighted VHO decisions.

Acknowledgement. This work was performed within the ITSE (Intelligent Telecommunication Systems with Enhanced cognitive processing) project funded by VTT. The work is a follow-up to the prior work carried out in the IST-TALOS [10](Transportable Autonomous patrol for Land bOrder Surveillance system).

References

1. Lampropoulos, G., Salkintzis, A.K., Passas, N.: Media-independent handover for seamless service provision in heterogeneous networks. IEEE Communications Magazine 46(1), 64–71 (2008)
2. Hämäläinen, S., Sanneck, H., Sartori, C.: LTE Self-Organizing Networks (SON): Network Management Automation for Operational Efficiency. John Wiley & Sons (January 6, 2012)
3. Kliazovich, D., Sutinen, T., Kokkoniemi-Tarkkanen, H., Makela, J., Horsmanheimo, S.: Hierarchical Management Architecture for Multi-Access Networks. In: 2011 IEEE Global Telecommunications Conference (GLOBECOM 2011), pp. 1–6 (December 2011)
4. Horsmanheimo, S., Eskelinen, J., Kokkoniemi-Tarkkanen, H.: NES Network Expert System for heterogeneous networks. In: 2010 IEEE 17th International Conference on Telecommunications (ICT), April 4-7, pp. 680–685 (2010)
5. Prokkola, J., Hanski, M., Jurvansuu, M., Immonen, M.: Measuring WCDMA and HSDPA Delay Characteristics with QoSMeT. In: IEEE International Conference on Communications, ICC 2007, June 24-28, pp. 492–498 (2007)
6. VTT Converging Networks Laboratory (CNL) QoSMeT, http://www.cnl.fi/qosmet.html
7. Makela, J., Pentikousis, K.: Trigger Management Mechanisms. In: 2nd International Symposium on Wireless Pervasive Computing, ISWPC 2007, February 5-7 (2007)
8. OpenCV Machine Learning Library (MLL), http://opencv.willowgarage.com/documentation/cpp/ml_machine_learning.html
9. CRC Canada, CORAL - Cognitive radio learning platform, http://www.crc.gc.ca/files/crc/home/wificr/coralbrochureen.pdf
10. TALOS EU FP7 project, http://talos-border.eu/

Enhancing Path Selection in Multihomed Nodes

Bruno Sousa[1], Kostas Pentikousis[2], and Marilia Curado[1]

[1] CISUC, University of Coimbra
Polo II, Pinhal de Marrocos 3030-290, Coimbra, Portugal
{bmsousa,marilia}@dei.uc.pt
[2] Huawei Technologies
Carnotstrasse 4, 10587 Berlin, Germany
k.pentikousis@huawei.com

Abstract. Path selection in multihomed nodes can be enhanced by optimization techniques that consider multiple criteria. With NP-Hard problems, MADM techniques have the flexibility of including any number of benefits or costs criteria and are open regarding the functions that can be employed to normalize data or to determine distances. TOPSIS uses the Euclidean distance (straight line) while DiA employs the Manhattan distance (grid-based) to determine the distance of each path to ideal values. MADM techniques have been employed in distinct areas, as well. Such openness and flexibility may lead to sub-optimal path selection, as their optimality is associated with functions that determine distance as a straight line or as grid path, and not inside an ideal range determined by the type of criteria. In this paper we propose the MeTH distance which considers the type of criteria, whether benefits or costs. In addition, we establish a MADM evaluation methodology based on statistical analysis that enables an objective comparison between MADM mechanisms and respective functions for path selection. With the proposed MADM evaluation methodology, we demonstrate that our MeTH distance is more efficient for the path selection problem than Euclidean and Manhattan distances.

Keywords: MADM, DoE, TOPSIS, path selection, multihoming, evaluation.

1 Introduction

Through the diversity of interfaces, modern device multihoming is characterized by the availability of multiple traffic paths for diverse flows, with different features. However, when considering multiple criteria, optimal path selection becomes a NP-Hard problem [1]. Different approaches exist to solve such kind of problems, namely Linear Programming (LP) or Multiple Attribute Decision Mechanism (MADM). LP techniques are able to provide optimal solutions but with the price of being tied to the problem being optimized [2, 3]. Thus, linear programming cannot be employed, without any adaptation to other problems

D. Pesch et al. (Eds.): MONAMI 2013, LNICST 125, pp. 69–82, 2013.

and scenarios or even to include additional criteria. For instance, overlay multicasting solutions relying on linear programming [4] cannot be applied to path selection optimization.

MADM techniques cope with the limitations of linear programming solutions by supporting optimization without being tied to a particular problem. The Technique for Order Preference by Similarity to Ideal Solution (TOPSIS) [5] a MADM technique, is employed in distinct areas, ranging from social sciences to path selection optimization problems [6,7]. The flexibility of incorporating criteria, the possibility of weighting the diverse attributes and the simplicity of use, make MADM preferable in comparison to LP. MADM formulates a score for each path, which is based on the distance that each path has regarding ideal values. To determine such distance, several functions are applied, such as normalization of data and maximum and minimum procedures, to determine ideal values. While determination of the ideal values is similar between techniques, normalization and distance functions are distinct, as the examples of Euclidean employed by TOPSIS [5], Manhattan used by Distance to Ideal Alternative (DiA) [8], Mahalanobis in Novel Method based on Mahalanobis Distance (NMMD) [9], or distance in a geometric plane [10]. But the effect that such function has on the path selection cannot simply rely on handover performance (e.g., ping-pong effects [9]), as such kind of evaluation does not consider the effects that weights of different criteria have on the score. Other kinds of evaluations only consider specific functions in MADM. For instance, normalization techniques [11] are compared, but such an approach is rather incomplete, as distance or scoring functions MADM are ignored.

The contributions of this paper are twofold: First, we specify a distance function that considers the type of criteria. Second, an evaluation methodology is specified to assess the performance of MADM regarding their rankings according to data from networks with multihomed nodes and respective criteria (i.e. bandwidth, round trip time, jitter, loss). The evaluation methodology, publicly available in [12], relies on statistical analysis from the Design of Experiments (DoE) [13]. With DoE diverse experiments are executed to assess the sensitivity on ranking that techniques have with different criteria weights. With Analysis of Variance (ANOVA), the ranking of MADM techniques is compared regarding the model fitness in terms of completeness, coefficient of determination and variance between experiments or inside experiments. We conducted a comparative evaluation of TOPSIS, DiA and MeTH with our proposed methodology, using data from multihomed nodes collected in testbeds. Achieved results demonstrate that MeTH is the only technique that is able to detect interaction between criteria (i.e. if bandwidth increases, round trip time and jitter may decrease).

The remainder of this paper is organized as follows: Section 2 overviews related work. Section 3 introduces MeTH in a comparative approach to TOPSIS and DiA techniques. The evaluation methodology is introduced in Section 4 and evaluations details are described in Section 5. Results are presented and discussed in Section 6. Finally, Section 7 concludes the paper.

2   Related Work

This section reviews related work regarding path optimization employing MADM techniques. Associated evaluation mechanisms are also included. Other kind of optimization techniques like Linear Programming are outside the scope of this paper.

In the path selection problem, TOPSIS is employed as a mechanism to select the best path to enable flow distribution [7]. Nonetheless, the article only addresses implementations issues, as authors aim to demonstrate that MADM techniques can be employed on Linux hosts. The DiA [8] is a MADM mechanism that aims to cope with the ranking abnormality of TOPSIS. An issue in score occurs when one less performant alternative is removed from selection. The NMMD [9], based on the Mahalanobis distance, enables correlation between criteria to overcome ranking abnormality of TOPSIS. The M-TOPSIS [10] uses a modified distance based on geometric planes with the argument of solving the ranking abnormality of TOPSIS. The evaluation of the previous techniques compares the performance of the respective techniques with TOPSIS in ranking abnormality situations. Nonetheless, we argue that such type of evaluation is sub-representative to enable an efficient comparison of MADM techniques in the path selection problem. Furthermore, in scenarios without failures, multihomed nodes may have all the interfaces available without any instability associated.

As stated, MADM techniques comprise several steps. Normalization, one initial step, is evaluated in TOPSIS by considering different normalization functions [11]. Vector normalization is presented as the one providing better support for different problem sizes. For instance, to choose between 2 or 10 paths. Considering the configuration of multihomed nodes, nowadays the path selection problem may include gigabit and wireless interfaces, not exceeding a few paths. Moreover, the evaluation performed is based on synthetic data.

DoE [13] has been employed to assess TOPSIS efficiency in computer-integrated manufacturing technologies [14,15]. Despite, employing DoE there are no comparisons between different MADM techniques, as TOPSIS is assumed to have a better performance than other related techniques. In the path selection problem we do not have such assumption, instead we employ DoE to determine objectively the most performant MADM technique, regarding its statistical results.

3   MADM for Path Selection

This section introduces MeTH, a MADM technique that enhances path selection by introducing correlation between criteria. The correlation support is based on simple functions, such as average and variance. We follow a comparative approach to introduce MeTH. Namely, we perform a comparison with TOPSIS and DiA, highlighting the main differences between the techniques, as described in the next paragraphs.

Table 1. Distance Functions

Step	TOPSIS^{a,c}	DiA^{a,c}	Meth^{a,b,c}
Distance	$D_i = \sqrt{Id_j - v_{i,j}}$	$D_i = \|Id_j - v_{i,j}\|$	$D_i = \frac{(Id_j - v_{i,j})^2}{\|Id_j - Sd_j\| + 0.001}$
Score	$S_i = \frac{D_i^-}{D_i^- + D_i^*}$	$S_i = \sqrt{(D_i^*)^2 + (D_i^-)^2}$	$S_i = \sqrt{D_i^* + D_i^-}$
Rank	Best=descend(S_i)	Best=ascend(S_i)	Best=ascend(S_i)

^{a} Id_j is the Ideal solution.
^{b} Benefits: $Sd_j = \overline{X_j} + Var(X_j)$; Costs: $Sd_j = \overline{X_j} - Var(X_j)$
^{c} Benefits: D_i^*; Costs: D_i^-

Step 1 - Decision Matrix. Gather the decision matrix with nb-benefits criteria and nc-costs criteria for the m paths (i.e. alternatives in MADM nomenclature).

Step 2 - Normalization. The decision matrix is normalized using the vector normalization, as it is agnostic to the problem size [11]. Normalized scores r_{ij} are obtained by employing the following relation $r_{ij} = \frac{x_{ij}}{\sqrt{\sum x_{ij}^2}}$ for $i = 1, \cdots, m; j = 1, \cdots, n$. x_{ij} correspond to the original values in the decision matrix.

Step 3 - Weighting. The normalized decision matrix is weighted by multiplying the weights w_j of criterion j with the respective normalized score r_{ij}, as follows: $v_{ij} = w_j \cdot r_{ij}$.

Step 4 - Ideal Solutions. Positive-ideal and negative-ideal solutions are determined by A^* and A^- terms, respectively:

$$A^* = \{v_1^*, v_2^*, \cdots, v_{nb}^*\} \tag{1}$$

$$A^- = \{v_1^-, v_2^-, \cdots, v_{nb}^-\} \tag{2}$$

$$\text{Where: } v_j^* = max(v_{i,j}) \; \forall i = 1, \cdots, m \; j = 1, \cdots, nb$$

$$v_j^- = min(v_{i,j}) \; \forall i = 1, \cdots, m \; j = 1, \cdots, nc$$

Step 5 - Distance. This step computes the separation that each path has to the ideal solution. TOPSIS uses the Euclidean distance, DiA employs the Manhattan distance. For path selection, we introduce the MeTH distance that has the advantage of introducing correlation between criteria, through the arithmetic average and variance functions, as summarized in Table 1. It has been demonstrated that correlation avoids ranking abnormalities of TOPSIS and DiA [9]. MeTH also considers the type of criteria type in the formulation of distance.

Step 6 - Score. Scoring is obtained by combining the separation from positive and negative ideal solutions, D_i^* and D_i^-, respectively. Each technique has different forms of combining distances, as depicted in Table. 1.

Step 7 - Ranking. Ranking relies on ordering score vectors Si. Since scoring is different between techniques, ordering is performed in descending for TOPSIS and in ascending order for DiA and MeTH.

Table 2. Decision matrix for 3 criteria with 2^k factorial design

Id	x_1	x_2	x_3	Effect
1	-	-	-	(1)
2	+	-	-	x_1
3	-	+	-	x_2
4	+	+	-	x_1x_2
5	-	-	+	x_3
6	+	-	+	x_1x_3
7	-	+	+	x_2x_3
8	+	+	+	$x_1x_2x_3$

$$Y = \beta_0 + \beta_1 x_1 + \beta_2 x_2 + \beta_3 x_3 +$$
$$\beta_4 x_1 x_2 + \beta_5 x_1 x_3 +$$
$$\beta_6 x_2 x_3 + \beta_7 x_1 x_2 x_3 + \epsilon \qquad (3)$$

As demonstrated, MADM share functions in some steps. Functions performing the same goal (e.g., distance determination) but with different formulations, justify the performance difference between these techniques. The following section presents a methodology to assess such difference in performance.

4   An Evaluation Methodology for MADM Techniques

This section specifies an evaluation methodology for MADM techniques, which can be used in the context of multihoming nodes for path selection. The aim is to compare MADM techniques more efficiently and without relying on sub-representative evaluation metrics, such as handover ratios, in the path selection problem.

The DoE or experimental design [13] allows to plan experiments, in such a way that facilitates analyses and conclusions. DoE has different techniques to promote analyses, specially the 2^k factorial design that allows to assess the effect of several variables over a response. In the path selection problem, the criteria may include benefits, such as security, coverage, bandwidth and costs like round tip time, jitter and packet loss. The 2^k factorial design specifies full factory experiments for the k main effects, $\left(\frac{k}{2}\right)$ two-factor interactions, $\left(\frac{k}{3}\right)$ three-factor interactions, and so on, in a total of $2^k - 1$ effects. By applying full factorial a decision matrix is obtained for the k effects, considering two levels: (-) representing the minimum values and (+) representing maximum values. Table 2 exemplifies the decision matrix for 3 factors (x_1, x_2, x_3), considering a 2^k factorial design. The n^k factorial design considers n levels of the criteria. In the path selection problem with 3 paths, the n levels can correspond to the maximum values of the diverse criteria, $max_{p1}(x1)$, $max_{p2}(x1)$, $max_{p3}(x1)$ and so on.

With the results of several experiments, Y (score), the response variable, can be estimated through a regression model, as depicted in Eq. 3, where x_1, x_2 and, x_3 represent effects/criteria, β_0 is the intercept coefficient, β_1, β_2 are effect coefficients and σ is the error estimate. Experiments include the same data for the diverse criteria but with different weight sets.

ANOVA applies regression to formulate a linear model in the form of the Eq. 3 and has associated statistical values that determine the efficiency of the model. The goodness of fit can be assessed by the coefficient of determination R^2, which corresponds to the total variance in response variable (Y) by effects/criteria. Higher values of R^2, close to one, indicate that the model explains almost 100% of the variation in Y due to the effects/criteria and their possible interactions. The F-statistic is also important to assess the variation between groups and within groups. Such groups represent the different experiments. For instance, higher values of F-statistic indicate that mean variation between experiments is greater than variation within experiments. If variation is between experiments, it highlights that the score varies due to the different configured weights.

The proposed methodology to compare MADM techniques includes several steps, as detailed bellow:

Step 1 - Gather data of the different paths for each criteria. Such step can be performed in a controlled way or relying on data collected by others, outside control. In this step n decision matrices $dM_n[m, k]$ are obtained, with m measurements for the n paths with k criteria.

Step 2 - Determine the levels of each criteria for the diverse paths. Levels correspond to the minimum, min_j, and maximum, max_j, for path i in the n overall paths. *LevelMin* corresponds to the minimum level (-) while *LevelMax* corresponds to the maximum level (+), and are determined according to Eq. 4 and Eq. 5, respectively.

$$LevelMin_j = min(dM_1[, j], dM_2[, j], \cdots, dM_n[, j]) \; with \; j = 1, \cdots, k \quad (4)$$
$$LevelMax_j = max(dM_1[, j], dM_2[, j], \cdots, dM_n[, j]) \; with \; j = 1, \cdots, k \quad (5)$$

This step determines the logic of employing 2^k or n^k factorial design. If there are no zeros in both levels, 2^k factorial design can be followed, otherwise n^k factorial design must be employed. Data with zeros can represent issues in ANOVA, such as outliers. With a 2^k factorial design levels correspond to the vectors $LevelMin_j$ and $LevelMax_j$. In a n^k factorial design, levels for criteria j are based on the maximum (+) values for the n paths, assuming maximum values are different from zero.

$$lMax_j = \left[max(dM_1[, j]), \cdots, max(dM_n[, j]) \right] \; with \; j = 1, \cdots, k \quad (6)$$

Step 3 - Specify weights sets for the different z experiments. Each j criterion in the k criteria has associated a weight. $dW_{sets}[z, k]$, the matrix with weight sets is determined for the z experiments. Weights define how important a criterion is over another, tailoring the final ranking determined by MADM techniques.

Step 4 - Determine factorial design matrix $dF[a, k]$, with a relying on the factorial design, $a = 2^k$ or $a = n^k$. For instance, Table 2 depicts the combinations of three criteria under 2^k factorial design, resulting in $a = 8$, $dF[8, 3]$.

Step 5 - Run MADM technique for the full set of factors specified in the $dF[a, k]$ matrix with the respective weight sets in the $dW_{sets}[z, k]$ matrix. Experiments lead to scores, which are combined with the full set of factors to form the input matrix $dI[a, k + z]$ as illustrated in Matrix 7, where $level_{a,k}$ holds the minimum or maximum values.

$$
dI[a, k+z] = \begin{array}{c} \\ 1 \\ 2 \\ \vdots \\ a \end{array} \begin{bmatrix} level_{1,1} & \cdots & level_{1,k} & Score_{1,k+1} & Score_{1,k+2} & \cdots & Score_{1,k+z} \\ level_{2,1} & \cdots & level_{2,k} & Score_{2,k+1} & Score_{2,k+2} & \cdots & Score_{2,k+z} \\ \vdots & \vdots & \vdots & \vdots & \vdots & \vdots & \ddots \\ level_{a,1} & \cdots & level_{a,k} & Score_{a,k+1} & Score_{a,k+2} & \cdots & Score_{a,k+z} \end{bmatrix}
$$
$$
\begin{array}{ccccccc} k_1 & \cdots & k_k & z1 & z2 & \cdots & z_z \end{array}
$$
(7)

Step 6 - Perform ANOVA where the response variable is $Y = Score$ determined by MADM techniques depending on the diverse covariates (k criteria). The initial linear model must include all the covariates and their possible interactions, as exemplified in Table 2 and Eq. 3 for 3 covariates (x_1, x_2, x_3). Interactions are important as the values of one criterion might be related with the values of other criteria. For instance, the score, besides being based on bandwidth, round trip time and jitter can be based on a relation between these parameters. We stress on interactions between criteria, as they can be typical in path selection problems. For instance, higher bandwidths have associated lower RTT, as well as lower jitter values.

Step 7 - Reformulate linear model by including only the effects that are significant, those with $p\text{-value} < 0.05$. Run ANOVA with the reformulated model and validate if assumptions for ANOVA models are fulfilled. Namely the model must comply with normality, homogeneity and independence assumptions [13]. Normality assumes that under the same conditions, the observations are normally distributed for each value of X (recall Eq. 3). Homogeneity assumes that the variance for all X values is the same. Independence means that Y values of one observation (X_i) should not influence the Y values for other observations. In DoE, with the factorial design, the independence assumption is assured. The normality assumption can be checked via histograms, where bars must follow the trend of the normal curve. Homogeneity can be checked by plotting the residuals versus the fitted models. If the model complies with normality and homogeneity assumptions, statistical analysis of the regression model must be performed as detailed in the next step.

Step 8 - Analyse the model regarding its completeness, if all the criteria is included, as well as interactions. The analysis must also rely on coefficient of determination, R^2 that assesses how the model explains the variance of Y (score) and F-statistic that complements R^2 in the sense that it measures if variance is inside experiments or between experiments. F-statistic assesses how a MADM technique deals with weights. Higher values of R^2 (close to one) and higher values of F-statistic are preferred. In addition, the significance of the effects and interactions must be considered. Significant effects indicate strong contribution to the score.

Next section presents examples of the TOPSIS, DiA and MeTH evaluation using the evaluation methodology herein proposed and publicly available in [12].

5   Evaluation

The proposed methodology has been applied in two distinct scenarios: *Dropbox* and *Heterogenous* scenarios, which are describe bellow. These scenarios use the same criteria for benefits and costs. Benefits include security (Sec), coverage (Cov) in meters, and bandwidth (BW) in Mb/s. Costs include round trip time (RTT) in milliseconds, Jitter in milliseconds and packet loss (Loss) criteria common in the path selection problems [2].

5.1   Dropbox Scenario

The Dropbox scenario considers a cloud environment where Dropbox services [16] were evaluated. The evaluation of this scenario uses data collected from TCP applications in a university campus, accessing Dropbox facilities. The collected traces contain application network performance values, such as RTT, jitter, retransmissions and duplicates. The evaluation considers a multihomed node with four distinct paths for a Dropbox service. In addition, the collection of data was beyond our control, since data acquisition was performed by Drago et al. [16]. The wireless environment is configured as follows: one path is set according to the IEEE 802.11n and the remaining are configured according to the IEEE 802.11g standard. Moreover, the different paths are configured with different security values, to simulate open networks and networks with security mechanisms. The values used in the evaluation are included in the paper to allow the reproduction of results.

Table 3. Levels of each criteria for the different paths in Dropbox scenario. Levels are represented in the form of min;max.

Paths	Benefits Criteria			Costs Criteria		
	(Sec)	(Cov)	(BW)	(Jitter)	(RTT)	(Loss)
P1	1; 7	0; 250	0; 300	0.20; 575.31	62.48; 171.79	0; 0.40
P2	1; 7	0; 100	0; 54	1.5; 999.1531	46.32; 166.27	0; 0.11
P3	1; 3	0; 100	0; 54	0.20; 10105.49	75.35; 5141.21	0; 0
P4	1; 5	0; 100	0; 54	0; 1126.61	0; 259.78	0; 0.18

5.2   Heterogeneous Scenario

The Heterogenous scenario comprises a multihomed node with three available paths, provided through a wired link (IEEE 802.3ab) and two wireless links, namely IEEE 802.11n and IEEE 802.16e. This scenario was under our control and includes data acquired during several weeks. To collect criteria values, the OWAMP protocol [17] was used, since it allows to gather values according to standardized recommendations from IETF. Owping [18] and bwctl [19] tools were employed, as these implement OWAMP protocol and enable an accurate data acquisition of RTT, jitter, loss and bandwidth, respectively. The clock of machines was synchronized using Network Time Protocol (NTP), to meet the requirements of OWAMP protocol.

Table 4. Levels of each criteria for the different paths in Heterogenous scenario. Levels are represented in the form of min;max.

Paths	Benefits Criteria			Costs Criteria		
	(Sec)	(Cov)	(BW)	(Jitter)	(RTT)	(Loss)
P1	1; 7	0; 54000	0.8821144; 16.81217	0.0; 312.0	0.0; 202.7	0; 0.67
P2	1; 7	0; 250	32.27258; 56.85376	0.1; 6.4	1.1; 21.6	0; 0
P3	1; 7	0; 100	89.99288; 91.26333	0.0; 3.5	0.2; 21.2	0; 0

5.3 Methodology

The different experiments, in light of DoE, were based on ranking determination with different criteria weights. Weights, for both scenarios, were organized in sets to include a full representation of the possible and most representative combinations $dW_{sets}[z, k]$. Table 5 depicts the different combinations of benefits and costs weights, for the $z = 16$ experiments.

Table 5. Configured weights. Weigths sets have been configured regarding the possible and most representative combinations.

Set	W_{Sec}	W_{Cov}	W_{BW}	W_{Jitter}	W_{RTT}	W_{Loss}
1	0.33	0.33	0.33	0.33	0.33	0.33
2	0.33	0.33	0.33	0.6	0.2	0.2
3	0.33	0.33	0.33	0.2	0.6	0.2
4	0.33	0.33	0.33	0.2	0.2	0.6
5	0.6	0.2	0.2	0.33	0.33	0.33
6	0.6	0.2	0.2	0.6	0.2	0.2
7	0.6	0.2	0.2	0.2	0.6	0.2
8	0.6	0.2	0.2	0.2	0.2	0.6
9	0.2	0.6	0.2	0.33	0.33	0.33
10	0.2	0.6	0.2	0.6	0.2	0.2
11	0.2	0.6	0.2	0.2	0.6	0.2
12	0.2	0.6	0.2	0.2	0.2	0.6
13	0.2	0.2	0.6	0.33	0.33	0.33
14	0.2	0.2	0.6	0.6	0.2	0.2
15	0.2	0.2	0.6	0.2	0.6	0.2
16	0.2	0.2	0.6	0.2	0.2	0.6

The n^k factorial design was chosen, as many parameters had values of zeros in both scenarios. The factorial design matrices rely on maximum values for each criteria of the distinct paths, depicted in Table 3 and Table 4 for Dropbox and Heterogenous scenarios, respectively. Indeed the matrices for these scenarios were $dF_{Drop}[4^6, 6]$ and $dF_{Het}[3^6, 6]$. The input matrix $dI[a, k + z]$ for ANOVA considers the defined experiments (Table 5) and factorial design matrices. In this evaluation, $dI_{Drop}[4^6, 6 + 16]$ and $dI_{Het}[3^6, 6 + 16]$ matrices were set for Dropbox and Heterogenous scenarios, respectively.

6 Results and Discussion

This section presents and discusses the results achieved with the evaluation performed. All the evaluation has been performed using R-project [20], and models are compared using model completeness, effects significance, R^2 and F-statistics metrics. The beta terms of the ANOVA regression model (recall Eq. 3) are not specified in the models obtained to simplify comparison between MADM techniques.

6.1 Dropbox Scenario

$$Y_{lmTOP} = BW + RTT + Jitter + Loss + Cov \tag{8}$$

The model obtained by TOPSIS (lmTOP) using the methodology presented in this paper includes all the criteria, and is specified according to Eq. 8. DiA also results in the same model. This model, lmTOP, does not include any interactions, and defines score as a function of bandwidth, RTT, jitter, loss and coverage (e.g., all criteria). The model is not fully complete, as interactions are not detected.

$$Y_{lmMeth} = BW + RTT + Jitter + Loss + Cov + BW{:}Cov + BW{:}RTT{:}Cov+$$
$$BW{:}Jitter{:}Cov + BW{:}Loss{:}Cov + BW{:}RTT{:}Jitter{:}Cov+$$
$$BW{:}RTT{:}Loss{:}Cov + BW{:}Jitter{:}Loss{:}Cov \tag{9}$$

MeTH, our proposed MADM technique, outputs a different model (lmMeTH) and besides including all the criteria, it also includes interactions between them, as per Eq. 9. lmMeTH demonstrates that criteria has relations, and can be considered as a complete model, in comparison to lmTOP, since criteria and respective interactions are included.

Table 6. Results of Dropbox

method	model	signif	interactions	R^2	F-statistic
TOPSIS	lmTOP	yes	no	0.5274	14624.2727
DiA	lmTOP	yes	no	0.4452	10518.2098
MeTH	lmTOP	yes	no	0.7240	34376.5185
TOPSIS	lmMeth	no	yes	0.5274	6093.3300
DiA	lmMeth	no	yes	0.4452	4382.2384
MeTH	lmMeth	yes	yes	0.7413	15649.5765

Table 6 summarizes the statistical values obtained in the dropbox scenario. With lmTOP model, the TOPSIS technique can explain $\approx 53\%$ of variation of data, since $R^2 = 0.5274$. DiA is only able to explain $\approx 45\%$ of the variance, nonetheless, MeTH is able to explain $\approx 72\%$ of the score variance. Recall that values close to 1 are fully explained by the model. The F-statistic also reports higher values in MeTH, namely, $F_5 = 34376.5185, p < 0.005$, which means that the variation of score is higher between experiments than in experiments. Thus, MeTH considers more properly the weights sets configured on the diverse experiments, when compared to TOPSIS or DiA approaches. F-statistic for TOPSIS follows MeTH model, namely, $F_5 = 14624.2727, p < 0.005$. MeTH within the lmTOP model is the technique with more satisfactory statistical values, followed by TOPSIS. The main issue with this model is that is lacks interactions, that is, it does not consider the relations between criteria (e.g., if one criterion increases the other criterion will increase as well, or vice-versa). In this context the lmMeth model is more complete and is obtained with MetH, mainly due to the distance function (recall Table 1) that correlates data of the distinct paths. In the lmMeTH model, MeTH presents, again, the best performance regarding statistical values, since R^2 is higher and F-statistic is also higher $F_{12} = 15649.5765, p < 0.005$, in comparison to TOPSIS and DiA results. In addition, when comparing both models, (the main difference relies on the interactions), lmMeTH model with MeTH technique is able to explain $\approx 74\%$ of score variance, against the $\approx 72\%$ of lmTOP. F-statistic in the lmMeTH model is not higher in comparison to lmTOP model, but the 14 terms in Eq 9 against 5 in Eq. 8 justify such fact. It is also relevant to point out for the lmMeTH model that with TOPSIS and DiA not all the effects are significant, which means that these techniques are not able to find relations between criteria.

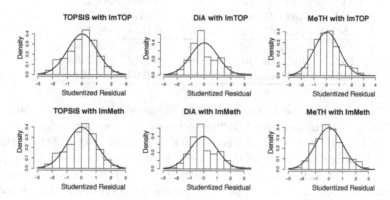

Fig. 1. Normality for analysed MADM in Dropbox scenario

According to the Step 7 of the evaluation methodology, assumptions for ANOVA need to be checked, in order to guarantee that the results have higher confidence. Fig. 1 depicts a graphical test to assess normality of lmTOP and lmMeTH models within the different MADM techniques evaluated, relying on histograms and normal curve. At a first glance, DiA is the only technique violating normality in lmTOP and lmMeTH models, which may indicate that the distance or scoring functions (recall Table 1) perform transformations that break such assumption. MeTH and TOPSIS are able to present normality in the scoring for both models. In these techniques bars follow the trend of the normal curve (pictured in blue), that is, there is a pattern of ascending and descending "stairs", without any exception.

The results in this scenario demonstrate that the distance and associated score functions lead to different results, mainly in terms of supporting interactions and statistical importance.

6.2 Heterogenous Scenario

The model obtained by TOPSIS (lmTOP) using the methodology presented in this paper for heterogenous scenario includes all the criteria, and is similar to Dropbox scenario. The DiA technique has the same model. Despite having fewer data (3^6 rows when compared to 4^6 in Dropbox scenario), MeTH is also able to provide interactions, as per Eq. 10. In particular, the lmMeTH model in the heterogenous scenario is more complete with 14 effects, in comparison to the Dropbox model, which has only 12 effects, compare Eq. 10 and Eq. 9.

$$Y_{lmMeTH} = BW + RTT + Jitter + Loss + Cov + \text{BW:Jitter} + \text{BW:Loss} +$$
$$\text{BW:Cov} + \text{BW:RTT:Cov} + \text{BW:Jitter:Cov} + \text{BW:Loss:Cov} +$$
$$\text{BW:RTT:Jitter:Cov} + \text{BW:RTT:Loss:Cov} + \text{BW:Jitter:Loss:Cov} \qquad (10)$$

Table 7. Results of Heterogenous

method	model	signif	interactions	R^2	F-statistic
TOPSIS	lmTOP	yes	no	0.5352	2684.5152
DiA	lmTOP	yes	no	0.4313	1768.3257
MeTH	lmTOP	yes	no	0.7514	7046.4885
TOPSIS	lmMeth	no	yes	0.5352	958.0181
DiA	lmMeth	no	yes	0.4313	631.0595
MeTH	lmMeth	yes	yes	0.7963	3253.4246

Table 7 summarizes the statistical values obtained in the heterogenous scenario. With lmTOP model, the TOPSIS technique can explain $\approx 53\%$ of variation of data, since $R^2 = 0.5352$. DiA is only able to explain $\approx 43\%$ of the variance. MeTH is able to explain $\approx 75\%$ of the score variance. The F-statistic also reports higher values in MeTH, namely, $F_5 = 7046.4885, p < 0.005$, what means that the variation of score is higher between experiments than inside the respective experiment. TOPSIS follows the MeTH performance in terms of F-statistic. This indicates that DiA is the technique that less impacts scoring regarding weights configurations. Considering weights as applications preferences (i.e., one might prefer more security other prefers higher bandwidths), DiA may not provide a scoring adapted to the requirements of distinct applications. Regarding the lmMeTH model, MeTH technique is able to explain $\approx 80\%$ of score variation. Thus, contrasts with TOPSIS and DiA techniques that do not increment values of R^2 in the lmMeTH.

Fig. 2 depicts a graphical test to assess normality of lmTOP and lmMeTH models within the different techniques, relying on histograms and normal curve. With the lmTOP model, normality is supported only by MeTH technique, as bars follow the trend of the normal curve (pictured in blue). DiA and TOPSIS present some exceptions to the normality assumption.

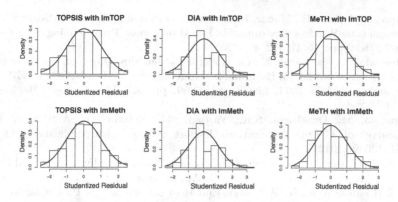

Fig. 2. Normality for analysed MADM in heterogenous scenario

The values in the heterogenous scenario regarding R^2 are higher for MeTH and TOPSIS techniques in comparison to the Dropbox scenario. The reason for such performance increase relies on the complexity of the scenario, with 3 paths against 4 paths. This fact indicates that TOPSIS and MeTH adapt more efficiently to the problem size in comparison to DiA. In fact, MeTH is able to explain $\approx 80\%$ of the values of score with all the criteria and respective interactions.

7 Conclusion

This paper specified MeTH as a MADM technique best suited for path selection problems, as it does not assume distance to be a straight line or grid-based, but, instead a composite function between benefits and costs criteria. In MeTH distance is considered for ideal values and relevant ranges. The evaluation methodology relying on statistical analysis, specified in this paper, has the advantage of being easily reproducible. Results based on data from controlled and uncontrolled path selection scenarios and with different number of paths, demonstrate that MeTH is able to perform optimal path selection more efficiently regarding the configured weights and multihoming nodes configurations.

Acknowledgment. The first author acknowledges the support of the PhD grant SFRH/BD/61256/2009 from Ministério da Ciência, Tecnologia e Ensino Superior, FCT, Portugal. This work is supported by CoFIMOM project PTDC/EIA-EIA/116173/2009 and TRONE project CMU- PT/RNQ/0015/2009.

References

1. Hou, R., Lui, K., Leung, K., Baker, F.: Approximation Algorithm for QoS Routing With Multiple Additive Constraints. In: ICC 2009, pp. 1–5. IEEE (2009)
2. Li, X., Mehani, O., Agüero, R., Boreli, R., Zaki, Y., Toseef, U.: Evaluating User-Centric Multihomed Flow Management for Mobile Devices in Simulated Heterogeneous Networks. In: Timm-Giel, A., Strassner, J., Agüero, R., Sargento, S., Pentikousis, K. (eds.) MONAMI 2012. LNICST, vol. 58, pp. 84–98. Springer, Heidelberg (2013)

3. Choque, J., Agüero, R., Muñoz, L.: Optimum Selection of Access Networks Within Heterogeneous Wireless Environments Based on Linear Programming Techniques. Mob. Netw. Appl. 16(4), 412–423 (2011)
4. Kucharzak, M., Walkowiak, K.: On modelling of fair throughput allocation in overlay multicast networks. In: Balandin, S., Koucheryavy, Y., Hu, H. (eds.) NEW2AN 2011 and ruSMART 2011. LNCS, vol. 6869, pp. 529–540. Springer, Heidelberg (2011)
5. Behzadian, M., Otaghsara, S.K., Yazdani, M., Ignatius, J.: A State-of The-Art Survey of TOPSIS Applications. Expert Systems with Applications 39(17), 13051–13069 (2012)
6. Sun, C.-C.: A Performance Evaluation Model by Integrating Fuzzy AHP and Fuzzy TOPSIS Methods. Expert Systems with Applications 37(12), 7745–7754 (2010)
7. Nacef, B., Montavont, N.: A Generic End-Host Mechanism for Path Selection and Flow Distribution. In: Proc. PIMRC 2008. IEEE (September 2008)
8. Tran, P.N., Boukhatem, N.: The Distance to The Ideal Alternative (DiA) Algorithm for Interface Selection in Heterogeneous Wireless Networks. In: Proc. Mobi-Wac 2008 (October 2008)
9. Lahby, M., Cherkaoui, L., Adib, A.: New Optimized Network Selection Decision in Heterogeneous Wireless Networks. International Journal of Computer Applications 54(16) (September 2012)
10. Ren, L., Zhang, Y., Wang, Y., Sun, Z.: Comparative Analysis of a Novel M-TOPSIS Method and TOPSIS. Applied Mathematics Research eXpress 2007, 1–10 (2010)
11. Chakraborty, S., Yeh, C.-H.: A Simulation Comparison of Normalization Procedures for TOPSIS. In: CIE 2009, pp. 1815–1820. IEEE (2009)
12. Sousa, B.: Evaluating MADM techniques, http://mcoa.dei.uc.pt/doe/ (last Visit: May 12, 2013)
13. Montgomery, D.C.: Design and Analysis of Experiments. John Wiley & Sons (2008)
14. İç, Y.T.: An Experimental Design Approach Using TOPSIS Method for The Selection of Computer-Integrated Manufacturing Technologies. Robot. Comput.-Integr. Manuf. 28(2), 245–256 (2012)
15. Sandanayake, Y., Oduoza, C., Proverbs, D.: A systematic modelling and simulation approach for jit performance optimisation. Robotics and Computer-Integrated Manufacturing 24(6), 735–743 (2008)
16. Drago, I., Mellia, M., Munafò, M.M., Sperotto, A., Sadre, R., Pras, A.: Inside dropbox: Understanding personal cloud storage services. In: Proceedings of the 12th ACM Internet Measurement Conference, IMC 2012 (2012)
17. Shalunov, S., Teitelbaum, B., Karp, A., Boote, J., Zekauskas, M.: A One-way Active Measurement Protocol (OWAMP). IETF Request for Comments: 4656 (September 2006)
18. Boote, J., Karp, A.: Internet 2 One-Way Ping (OWAMP) (2013), http://www.internet2.edu/performance/owamp/index.html (last visit: May 12, 2013)
19. Boote, J., Brown, A.: Internet 2 Bandwidth Test Controller (BWCTL) (2013), http://www.internet2.edu/performance/bwctl/index.html (last visit: May 12, 2013)
20. R Core Team, R: A Language and Environment for Statistical Computing. R Foundation for Statistical Computing, Vienna, Austria (2012), ISBN 3-900051-07-0

Correlation-Based Cell Degradation Detection for Operational Fault Detection in Cellular Wireless Base-Stations

Muhammad Zeeshan Asghar[1], Richard Fehlmann[2], and Tapani Ristaniemi[3]

[1] Magister Solutions Ltd, Hannikaisenkatu 41, Jyväskylä, Finland
[2] Nokia Siemens Network Research, Linnoitustie 6, Espoo, Finland
[3] Department of Mathematical Information Technology,
University of Jyvaskyla, Jyvaskyla, Finland
muhammad.asghar@magister.fi, richard.fehlmann@nsn.com,
tapani.ristaniemi@jyu.fi

Abstract. The management and troubleshooting of faults in mobile radio networks are challenging as the complexity of radio networks is increasing. A proactive approach to system failures is needed to reduce the number of outages and to reduce the duration of outages in the operational network in order to meet operator's requirements on network availability, robustness, coverage, capacity and service quality. Automation is needed to protect the operational expenses of t he network. Through a good performance of the network element and a low failure probability the network can operate more efficiently reducing the necessity for equipment investments. We present a new method that utilizes the correlation between two cells as a means to detect degradations in cells. Reducing false alarms is also an important objective of fault management systems as false alarms result in distractions that eventually lead to additional cost. Our algorithm is on the one hand capable to identify degraded cells and on the other hand able to reduce the possibility of false alarms.

Keywords: Mobile Networks, Fault Managements, Degradation Detection, Correlation, Operational Expenditures (OPEX), Capital Expenditures (CAPEX), Long Term Evolution (LTE), Self-Organizing Networks(SON).

1   Introduction

The huge amount of network elements in the mobile communication networks and consequently handling of huge amount of measurements recorded at each base station is a great challenge. The tasks of operation and maintenance of mobile cellular networks are not only vulnerable to errors as wireless network is complex to handle but also requires a huge amount of human resource to monitor and execute these tasks. A lot of effort is being put on this area of operations and maintenance of mobile communication systems that aims at simplifying the management of cellular network on the one hand and improving the efficiency by introducing automation, on the other hand. The fundamental requirement to tackle this challenge is to automate the

D. Pesch et al. (Eds.): MONAMI 2013, LNICST 125, pp. 83–93, 2013.

operations and maintenance functionalities. This triggered the concept of self-healing networks. Self-healing is an important domain of Self-Organizing Networks (SON). Other major domains of SON enabled networks are self-configuration and self-optimization.

Self-healing enabled cellular networks are generally defined as the wireless cellular networks where the tasks of troubleshooting including detection, diagnosis, corrective actions are largely automated but the operator will have final control over the decisions. The self-healing use cases defined by 3GPP [1] are given as: Self-Recovery of NE Software, Self-Healing of Board Faults, Cell Outage Detection, Cell Outage Recovery, Cell Outage Compensation and Return from Cell Outage Compensation. Although 3GPP use cases are focused on "cell outage", we adopt a more general concept of "cell degradation" which refers to the case where the actual performance of the cell in handling traffic is significantly lower as it is supposed to be. Degradations may not be measured directly as they do not necessarily trigger alarms. Degradations can be classified in terms of their severity i.e. from worse performance to complete outage. Usually a faulty cell starts degradation in prior to go in outage state. It is not enough to just detect the faults in a timely manner, but it is equally important to detect the degradations of the performance of cells (sectors) before real failures occur so that counter measures can be taken in time.

Recently two books are published on "Self-organizing networks" [2][3]. The class of 'Operational Fault Detection' OFD algorithms are introduced by Cheung [4]. The OFD algorithm analyze performance indicators detect fault signatures without the need for operators to manually set thresholds. The profile of the system is built by either looking at its earlier behavior or comparing it to similar systems. The correlation-based algorithm uses the correlations of cells (sectors) within a geographical neighborhood. It is assumed that there exists an appreciable level of correlation between neighboring cells. The same OFD approach is followed by a statistical hypothesis test framework for determining faults [5]. A method to detect coverage and dominance problems and identify interferers in WCDMA networks is introduced in [6]. Signaling messages exchanged through the radio interface are used to calculate certain metrics for every cell during normal network operations reflecting real traffic distributions and geographical user locations. Competitive neural algorithms are used for fault detection and diagnosis in 3G cellular networks in [7]. Another cell outage detection algorithm based on the neighbor cell list reporting of mobile terminals is introduced by Mueller in [8] . A framework is presented in [9] using Minimization of Drive Tests (MDT) databases, for detecting sleeping base stations, network outage and dominance areas in a cognitive and self-organizing way. Diffusion maps for reduction of high dimensionality and nearest neighbor classification methods were used. An experimental system for comprehensive testing of SON use cases is presented in [10]. A self-healing framework for 3GPP LTE networks is presented in [11] where detection and compensation of cell outages are evaluated in a realistic environment.

This paper is organized as follows: Section 2 describes the proposed algorithm for degradation detection. Section 3 discusses the procedure to choose the well-correlated cell pairs /comparing cells. Section 4 shows the investigations with the data recorded at a real 3G network. In this paper we do not give precise values of the performance metrics rather we address the vague terminologies in a better and clear way using empirical results.

2   The Proposed Algorithm

In our approach we exploited the idea that there are many cells in the network coverage area having similar behavior irrespective of their geographical locations. The terms "faultless situation", "load" and "appreciable level of correlation" will be used in the following sections, therefore, we give definitions of these terms here as follows.

The term "faultless situations" means the cells are functioning normally, i.e. they handle the traffic as they are supposed to and have no interior problems. Such cells are also called healthy cells. Although there might always be minor problems in the cell, for the sake of simplicity we may ignore them as long as they do not have significant impact on the performance of the cell.

"Load" can be represented by several key performance indicators. Some of the load related key performance indicators (KPIs) include traffic demand by users and others not. For example the KPI "throughput" is highly dependent on user traffic demands while "number of active users" is not. As the first one includes a higher degree of randomness, it is less usable in monitoring the correlation level of the load of the cell and so the number of active users in a cell is better suited to be used as a load level KPI to monitor the correlation levels.

"Appreciable level of correlation between two cells" refers to the fact that the relationship between the two cells is strong enough in faultless situations such that a diminishing of this correlation could be well noticed. We consider a correlation level as appreciable if for two cells whose correlation stay above that level in normal conditions a degradation of one of the cells is clearly visible as the correlation values start to drop then. It requires an effort to determine that level in a real network. However, network operators can identify a good value for appreciable correlation levels based on their field experience. Based on our empirical results we identified the value 0.5 as a good value to be used as appreciable level of correlation between two cells but this might be different in other networks. Two cells having an appreciable level of correlation, we call "well correlated cells". At this point we note that such cells need not to be adjacent cells.

Let us consider a KPI or a function of KPIs expressing the load handled at a cell, e.g. the number of active users allocated to the cell or the transferred downlink load. In regular time steps these values are recorded, let us denote the values for the target cell by $x_1, x_2, ..., x_n$ and for a comparing cell by $y_1, y_2, ..., y_n$. The correlation coefficient r (X,Y) is given below where the vectors X and Y consist of the components $x_1, x_2, ..., x_n$, $y_1, y_2, ..., y_n$, respectively. Here, the sum is taken over the sliding window size n:

$$r(X,Y) = \frac{\sum_{i=1}^{n}(x_i - \overline{x})(y_i - \overline{y})}{\sqrt{\sum_{i=1}^{n}(x_i - \overline{x})^2}\sqrt{\sum_{i=1}^{n}(y_i - \overline{y})^2}} \tag{1}$$

The above mentioned formula is used to calculate the correlation values of each pair of cells. In a first step we have to choose cells where these correlation values consistently stay above some reasonable value, e.g. 0.5 as we proposed above. These chosen cells are fixed and referred to as the comparing cells. The appreciable level of correlation can be defined differently by the operator as stated above. The correlation threshold does not need to be the same for all networks.

We assume now that for each target cell a set of comparing cells has been determined. The correlation coefficients with each chosen comparing cell are now monitored. If a target cell's correlation coefficient with all its chosen comparing cells drops below the predefined reasonable bound there is a good reason to assume that a performance degradation of the target cell has started and a suspicion is raised therefore. At least if there is more than one comparing cell showing this behavior this is a good reason for an alarm. If there is only one such cell some additional cell performance monitoring is needed in order to determine if a cell is degrading and if yes which one. Such additional performance monitoring includes tracking KPIs of the cells and checking if they pass certain thresholds that operators have set in the traditional way. In any case it can be concluded that two or three comparing cells suffice to make a decision if an alarm shall be raised because if the target cell is degrading then it will be visible in all the correlation levels with comparing cells except for very unlikely exceptional situations. So if two or three comparing cells show decrease in correlation below that appreciable level it can be concluded that the target cell is degrading. On the other hand if the target cell is healthy the degradation levels with two or three comparing cell stay above that appreciable level and it can be concluded that the target cell is healthy without checking further comparing cells.

The question of precisely how many comparing cells should be required to detect the degradation should be answered by the operator. The question is how many comparing cells are needed in order for the operator to decide if a target cell needs some recovery measures.

We used a flexible critical time duration that has to be computed every time we utilize a fixed critical duration in connection with the sliding window. In a state of suspicion the target cell is locked. The monitoring follows more steps to see if this drop below the appreciable level is temporary only. The algorithm now waits for more steps. If during a few following steps the correlation of the target cell with its comparing cell(s) does not rise above the predefined level then an alarm will be triggered. Based on empirical results we have seen that the correlation between the comparing cell pair becomes stable as we increase the window length. Using this idea, we define the condition that must be met before triggering an alarm.

3   Investigations with Real Network Data

We had the opportunity to get access to a real 3G network and observe its performance data over a period of time. The observed network consists of thousands of cells and is located in a European city. The granularity of the performance data is one hour, thus each sample corresponds to a one hour measurement. In what follows we present a couple of typical correlation values statistics. They have been collected over a period of two weeks. In regular steps KPI values were measured and correlation coefficients calculated. The window size was 64 steps. The KPI represented the number of active users in the cell.

Cell pairs having high correlations (>0.8)

Fig. 1. Cell pairs having high correlations (>0.8)

The empirical results in Figure 1 show that the assumption of having high correlation with the geographical neighbors is not always correct. In the available data, out of all the cell pairs showing high correlation only 4% are neighbors whereas about 96% are cell pairs that are not geographical neighbors. Thus it proves that there are many more cells with high correlation than just the ones in the geographical neighborhood. For detection we can take all the available cells into account where the similarities in the performance with the target cell are reasonably high. It is up to the operator to decide how long to observe this similarity among the cells.

Neighboring cell paris correlation

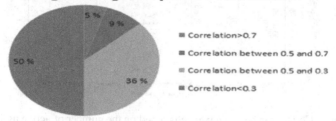

Fig. 2. Correlation of neighboring cell pairs

Figure 2 presents the statistics of the correlation values of all neighboring cell pairs. As can be seen, in spite of showing high resemble in the behavior over time the cells being geographical nearby show often low correlation. In this performance data collected from this real operational network, only 5 percentage of the cell pairs that are geographically nearby show high correlation and 14% show for our purposes still a good correlation level (above 0.5). So, one out of seven cells has an appreciable level of correlation. On the other hand 86 percentage of the cell pairs that are geographically neighbors, exhibit low correlation. This data shows that it is not reliable only to base the decision on the cell pairs that are neighbors to each other. However, two or three comparing cells for a target cell are enough for the algorithm as will be explained in section 5. Therefore, it can be expected that enough good correlated cells can be found among the closest 20 cells. There could be networks where relying on the geographical neighborhood gives good results. But this is not true always.

3.1   Degradation Types

As degradations are rare events and did not occur in our observed real data, we have introduced artificial errors in the real data. In order to produce degradation we have reduced the number of active users in the data as they would have been in case of a healthy cell. There are two types of degradation that we have introduced for the evaluation of the proposed methodology.

- Slow degradation
- Fast degradation

We introduced the slow degradation in the data collected from operational network by decreasing the number of active users in samples over time. Each step corresponds to a one hour measurement and thus the number of active users was decreased in every hour. Fast degradation indicates severe malfunction caused by the failing hardware component or software entity of the base station. We introduced fast degradation in the data collected from operational network by decreasing the number of active users to zero instantly.

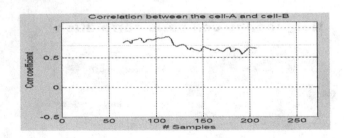

Fig. 3. Correlation between two cells based on the number of active users

Figure 3 presents a typical correlation value track represented by blue color. The green line shows the mean of the correlation curve and red line gives the threshold or the critical level of correlation. As can be seen the correlation curve starts at 65 (because the window size is 64) and show some variation of the correlation coefficient over time. In this example, however, these values stay consistently above

0.5 and are therefore useful for monitoring a possible degradation. The correlation value between cell-A and cell-B remains higher than the critical level in healthy conditions. The curve then ends at step 205 where monitoring had ended.

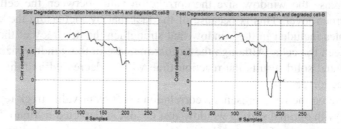

Fig. 4. a)Degradation type I: Cell-B degraded b) Degradation type II: Cell-B degraded

Figure 4 depicts the same coefficient as Figure 3 but with an artificially introduced slow degradation of the target cell (curve on the left) and a fast degradation (curve on the right) that starts at step 168. The slow degradation continues stepwise and as can be seen the curve falls down slowly. Such a type of degradation is easily spotted, however with a latency that depends on the window size.

In the fast degradation the number of active users in the cell is reduced to 0 all at once. As can be seen such a type of degradation is spotted fast and easily.

3.2   Window Size Analysis

There is a trade-off between the reaction time and accuracy of detection. For high reaction time less number of samples will be utilized whereas for accuracy it is better to have more samples to get the statistical confidence. An optimal number is required that satisfies both requirements. For instance, in our analysis, we proposed at least a two days period for an accurate detection on one hand and a quicker response to the network changes on the other hand. However, it is not easy to find a global optimum number that is valid for all cells in the network. For this reason, we emphasized the need of different observation time for each cell pair.

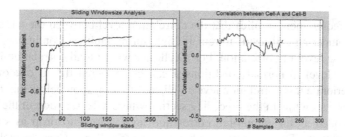

Fig. 5. a)Minimum Correlation Vs Window Size b) Correlation based on the window size 44

In the curve on the left in Figure 5, the optimal window size is depicted for an arbitrarily selected well correlated cell pair. In this example it turns out that 44 is the optimal window size meaning large enough for giving an accurate correlation value and as small as possible guaranteeing the smallest possible reaction time. As we further increase the window size the correlation value between the cell pairs stays above a certain level. This is because of the fact that by increasing the window size more samples included in the window that strengthen the accuracy of the correlation value between the cells. Although the further increase in the window size yields high correlation and solid results the reaction time will be decreased and this results in a slower detection process.

The curve on the right presents a correlation coefficient value track represented by blue color, with optimal sliding window size i.e. 44, as depicted in figure 5. The green line shows the mean of the correlation curve and red line gives the threshold or the critical level of correlation. As can be seen the correlation curve starts at 45 (because the window size is 44) and show some variation of the correlation coefficient over time, however, these values stay consistently above 0.5 and are therefore useful for monitoring a possible degradation.

4   Choice for Comparing Cells

In real networks user behavior varies strongly depending on the time of day, the geographic location and other factors. Although it might be that cells located near to each other would experience similar environmental conditions this is not always true as shown in the preceding section. It is also possible that some cells perform similar to other cells independent of their geographic location. This might be caused due to a similar kind of user behavior depending mainly on the time of the day. It is vital to choose the right cells as comparing cells. This is done in an initial cell pair selection process. In this section we describe this initial process.

In deciding how to choose comparing cells to a given target cell we follow two principles or requirements:

1. A degradation of the performance of a cell shall be detected
2. False alarms shall be avoided as good as possible

The first requirement implies that the correlation level between the target cell and its chosen comparing cell needs to remain high during faultless conditions, i.e. above the appreciable level of correlation. For a cell pair whose load correlation level stays above such a level in normal conditions it can be expected that if one of the cells starts to deteriorate this correlation levels will start to drop soon below that reasonable level. We have seen this in the preceding section where a degradation of the cell could easily be spotted as the monitored correlation level started to drop as soon as the degradation sets in. This suggests to observe all the cell pairs and to pick the ones whose correlation levels stay high.

However, this is very costly as the number of pairs grows like the square of the number of cells in question. It is therefore advisable to start with each target cell and a smaller group of cells to be monitored as potential comparing cells.

We have seen that the cell degradation implies a drop in the correlation level. But the converse is not true. If the target cell experiences a drop of the load correlation level with a comparing cell chosen as explained above then this is only one indication that the target cell is degrading. But there could be other reasons as well that the correlation level is dropping.

This information has to be combined with further information before the cell performance degradation can be declared. This can be done by looking at the correlation level with other chosen comparing cells or by taking traditional cell performance monitoring indicators into account. Only if several indicators have shown that the target cell is giving signs of deterioration it can be logically concluded that the target cell is degrading and an alarm should be raised.

We illustrate this by an example. Given a target cell let us assume we have two cells (green in figure 6) that can be paired with the target cell (purple) as both have correlation levels to the target cell above the critical level. Let us further assume that one of the cells is near the target cell and the other far away. The question is if there is an advantage by choosing one or the other.

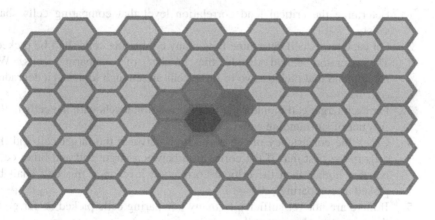

Fig. 6. Example, near and far away cells with good correlation in green

Let us now assume such a scenario as explained above where a peak in user density affects a group of cells (sky blue in the figure) around the target cell, including the comparing cell nearby. As the correlation level with the cell nearby is still preserved a false alarm could be avoided if this cell is chosen as comparing cell as no suspicion is raised by it. However, the correlation level with the cell far away is decreasing as the cell far away does not experience the load changes by the local peak and so a suspicion is raised also there. Hence, if the comparing cell had been chosen far away, then both sides raise a suspicion and we have a false alarm. In this case it is an advantage to choose the comparing cell nearby.

So, we can say, if we have to pick a comparing cell out of two possibilities, one nearby and the other far away, then there is no reason to choose the one far away.

In order to follow the second principle we consider situations where traditional monitoring methods can lead to false alarms, i.e. situations where a suspicion for a fault is raised but the target cell is not degrading. For instance, KPIs like load levels, number of unsuccessful call attempts, channel quality, etc. are monitored and traditionally suspicions are raised if they cross certain thresholds. Such situations can occur by unusual and hence unexpected user behavior. If for instance a peak in user density affects a group of cells it can be that the traditional performance indicators of some of the cells interpret this as being a cell performance degradation. However, the load correlation level might still be preserved as the unexpected peak in user density affects the whole group of cells. In that case the performance indicators raise a suspicion while the correlation level monitoring does not. Hence a combined logic would still not raise an alarm if the combined logic requires a suspicion from both sides. A false alarm would be avoided.

So, while the second principle suggests to choose comparing cells nearby and the first principle to choose them with correlation levels above a certain critical correlation level, we summarize the steps to choose comparing cells for the target cells:

1. Determine the critical load correlation level that comparing cells shall satisfy
2. For each target cell determine how many comparing cells shall be picked. The operator should decide the number of comparing cells. We recommend that picking two or three cells are enough to detect a degraded cell.
3. For each target cell monitor the load correlation levels with the cells in the first tier of surrounding cells
4. Check the consistency of the correlation between the target cell and the cells in the first tier. If the correlation between target cell and other cells remains higher than the critical correlation level then this cell shall be picked as comparing cell.
5. If there are not yet sufficiently many comparing cells picked so far go to the next tier and continue there, etc.

Steps 3 to 5 in our procedure therefore aim at choosing possible candidates near the target cell. If we find candidates we can stop, otherwise we enlarge the neighborhood to look for further cells. In this way comparing cells can be picked such that the two principles for the choice are followed as good as possible.

5   Conclusion and Future Work

In this paper we proposed a new method of cell degradation detection using the correlation between cells. In particular, the use of correlation between cell pairs is studied in detail and we used performance data collected from a real operational network in a European city for evaluation of the method. Our analysis suggests that the correlation coefficient between cell pairs can be utilized as a means for the detection of degradations in cells. The future work includes observing data in a real network together with the operators knowledge if problems in cells have occurred or not and to test the algorithm in this way.

References

[1] 3GPP TS 32.521, Self-Optimization OAM; Concepts and Requirements. Release 9, (June 2009)

[2] Hämäläinen, S., Sanneck, H., Sartori, S.: LTE Self-Organising Networks (SON): Network Management Automation for Operational Efficiency (January 2012)

[3] Ramiro, J., Hamied, K.: Self-Organizing Networks (SON): Self-Planning. Self-Optimization and Self-Healing for GSM, UMTS and LTE (January 2012)

[4] Cheung, B., Kumar, G.N., Rao, S.: Statistical Algorithms in Fault Detection and Prediction: Toward a Healthier Network. Bell Labs Technical Journal 9(4), 171–185 (2005)

[5] Rao, S.: Operational Fault Detection in Cellular Wireless Base-Stations. IEEE Transactions on Network and Service Management 3(2) (2006)

[6] Zanier, P., Guerzoni, R., Soldani: Detection of Interference, Dominance and Coverage Problems in WCDMA Networks. In: PIMRC (2006)

[7] Barreto, G.A., Mota, J.C.M., Souza, L.G.M., Frota, R.A., Aguayo, L., Yamamoto, J.S., Macedo, P.E.O.: Competitive Neural Networks for Fault Detection and Diagnosis in 3G Cellular Systems. In: Telecommunication and Networking –ICT (2004)

[8] Mueller, C.M., Kaschub, M., Blankenhorn, C., Wanke, S.: A Cell Outage detection Algorithm Using Neighbor Cell List Reports. In: IWSOS Proceedings of the 3rd International Workshop on Self-Organiznig Systems (2008)

[9] Turkka, J., Chernogorov, F., Brigatti, K., Ristaniemi, T., Lempiäinen, J.: An Approach for Network Outage Detection from Drive-Testing Databases. Journal of Computer Networks and Communications Article ID 163184, 13 pages (2012), doi:10.1155/2012/163184

[10] Asghar, M.Z., Hämäläinen, S., Meinke, N.: Experimental System for Self-Optimization of LTE Networks. In: 15th ACM International Conference on Modeling, Analysis and Simulation of Wireless and Mobile Systems (2012)

[11] Asghar, M.Z., Hämäläinen, S., Ristaniemi, T.: Self-Healing Framework for LTE Networks. In: 17th IEEE International Workshop on Computer-Aided Modeling Analysis and Design of Communication Links and Networks (2012)

Cloudifying Mobile Network Management: Performance Tests of Event Distribution and Rule Processing

Sumit Dawar[1,2], Sven van der Meer[1], John Keeney[1],
Enda Fallon[2], and Tom Bennet[2]

[1] Ericsson Network Management Labs,
Ericsson Software Campus, Athlone, Co. Westmeath, Ireland
{sumit.dawar,sven.van.der.meer,john.keeney}@ericsson.com
[2] Athlone Institute of Technology, AIT, Athlone, Co. Westmeath, Ireland

Abstract. With the ever increasing number of devices, nodes and the events they create, scalability and performance become important aspects for Operation Support Systems (OSS). One solution is to distribute the work load, i.e. 'cloudify' the formerly centralized monitoring and decision functions. This requires remodeling Complex Event Processing (monitoring) and Policies (decision making) towards a distributed yet coordinated system. This paper describes an extended architecture, implementation and performance tests for a policy-based event processing system. The main advantage of our approach is that we use policies for event pattern matching (an advanced form of Complex Event Processing) and for the selection of corrective actions (called Distributed Governance). Policies are (a) distributed (over multiple components) and (b) coordinated (using centralized authoring). The resulting system can deal with large numbers of incoming events, as is required in a telecommunication environment. Peak load will be well above 1 million events per second, combining different data sources of a mobile network. This paper presents the motivation for such a system, along with a comprehensive presentation of its design, implementation and evaluation.

Keywords: Complex Event Processing, Rule System, Distributed Processing, Performance.

1 Introduction

Mobile networks are growing, cell sizes are decreasing and the number of connected devices is exploding. These conditions result in an ever increasing number of events from the network. The situation becomes critical and requires scalable solutions for event processing and the selection of corrective actions, i.e. for alarm events. Our work combines rule systems to encode event processing knowledge and messaging to provide for a distributed system. Other earlier work used centralized rules over a distributed system [5-8], which drastically limits the scalability. We use distributed rules that are coordinated by centralized authoring to address this limitation. In this paper, we describe the general architecture, the reference implementation we have

D. Pesch et al. (Eds.): MONAMI 2013, LNICST 125, pp. 94–107, 2013.

developed and performance tests with regard to end-to-end message processing. The work is integrated into a wider research project in the Ericsson Network Management labs that deals with extreme volumes of mobile network events.

This paper is organized as follows: section 2 introduces core concepts, technologies and products from messaging systems and rule systems. Section 3 briefly discusses the architecture and main design decisions of our system. The sections 4 and 5 then detail the implementation and provide a discussion of test results, mainly looking into the performance for the end-to-end event processing. Section 6 discusses related work from academia and industry. Finally, a conclusion summaries this paper and discusses future work items of our project.

2   Conceptual Background, Products and Tools

Combining concepts from messaging systems with concepts from rule systems requires an understanding of two disjoint domains. In general, messaging system provides the main communication links between the components of a distributed system. A rule system provides the intelligence to manage and process events and event patterns to trigger appropriate actions. In this section we look into the fundamental idea of both to introduce relevant terms and concepts.

2.1   Messaging System

A distributed system has multiple components that may be built independently, with potentially different languages and platforms, dispersed at different locations. There are a number of approaches including: distributed data stores, streamed data, query-response models, or asynchronous messaging. Using a message-based approach distributed components share and process data in a responsive asynchronous way and it is this approach we focus on in this work. Our works use Advanced Message Queuing Protocol (AMQP) messaging due to external project requirements, namely RabbitMQ, an open source AMQP implementation.

AMQP is "an open standard for passing business messages between applications" [1]. Data (the messages) is sent in a stream of octets, thus it is often called a 'wire protocol'. Version 1.0 of the AMQP standard defines three main components: the networking protocol, a message representation and the semantics of broker services. All of these components address core features such as queuing, routing, reliability and security. Message encoding is separated into links, sessions, channels and connections, with links being the highest level and connections the lowest level of abstraction. A link connects network nodes, also known as distributed nodes in AMQP.

RabbitMQ [2] is an open source implementation of the AMQP standard. It facilitates 'producers' to send messages to 'brokers', which in turn deliver them to 'consumers'. Messages can also be routed, buffered and made persistent, depending on runtime configuration.

AMQP is designed to be programmable, allowing application to configure 'entities' and 'routing schemas'. The three important entities in RabbitMQ realizing the programmability are 'exchange', 'queue' and 'binding'. An exchange receives events from a producer and realizes different routing schemes. A queue is bound to an exchange and handles consumer-specific message reception. A binding defines the rules for message transfer between an exchange and a queue. See [3] for details.

2.2   Rule System

Rule systems provide the means to define and process rules. In our work, we are focusing on Production Rule Systems (PRS) due to external project requirements. The computational model of PRS implements the notion of a set of rules, where each rule has a sensory precondition ("left-hand-side", LHS, or "WHEN" clause) and a consequential action ("right-hand-side", RHS, or "THEN" clause). Rules are also referred to as productions and they are the primary form of knowledge representation. The rule engine also maintains knowledge-base of facts. When the facts stored satisfy the precondition of a rule, the rule "fires", thus invoking the action part of the rule. Often, the action part of the rule can change the fact knowledge-base, potentially triggering more rules.

Drools Expert is an open source implementation of a PRS. In Drools Expert, Rules and facts of a PRS constitute a knowledge base. Rules are present in the production memory and the facts are kept in a database called working memory, which maintains current system knowledge. There is an Inference Engine based on Charles Forgy's Rete Algorithm, which efficiently matches the facts from working memory to conditions of the rules in the production memory.

Also, a conflict resolution is required when there are multiple rules on the agenda. As firing a rule may have side effects on working memory, the rule engine needs to know in what order the rules should fire (for instance, firing 'ruleA' may cause 'ruleB' to be removed from the agenda). The default conflict resolution strategies employed by Drools Expert are: Salience and LIFO (last in, first out). [4]

3   Architecture and Design

We receive events from streams (using other Ericsson software), process them and forward them via queues. Each component employs a rule engine to process events. A typical process is to receive an event or a number of events (pattern) and create/send composite events. The events we process are actual mobile network events, such as performance events (counters) or alarm events. However, for simplification we refer to events as characters, e.g. 'A', 'B' and 'C'. Figure 1 shows how an incoming event stream (ABABCA…) is directed to a dedicated queue (CEP) and processed.

Events are received, one by one, by the Complex Event Processing (CEP) component. It takes simple events ('A', 'B') and generates complex events ('@A', '@AA'). These complex events represent patterns, i.e. sequences of events that are of special interest. The rules in the CEP component specify which patterns need to be matched and which corresponding complex event needs to be generated. Finally, complex events are sent to the next queue.

The Distributed Governance (DG) component receives complex events and selects appropriate actions to respond to them. The rules in the DG component define which complex events are being processed and what actions are associated with them. The number of associated actions can be zero or more, with zero action indicating an un-decidable situation, while more than one indicates multiple possible actions. DG then sends the actions to a new queue, which can feed into multiple applications of a broader management process, e.g. as part of Network Operation Center (NOC).

Combining messaging (AMQP) and rule systems (PRS) allows for a design of a flexible and scalable system. Using queues for communication not only facilitates the CEP and DG components to be distributed, but also for multiple redundant or load-balanced instances of each component to be run in parallel at runtime. If one CEP instance reaches its performance limits a new CEP instance can be executed, connected to the CEP queue and some patterns of the original CEP instance allocated to the new CEP instance. Figure 1 shows a scenario with three CEP instances and two DG instances.

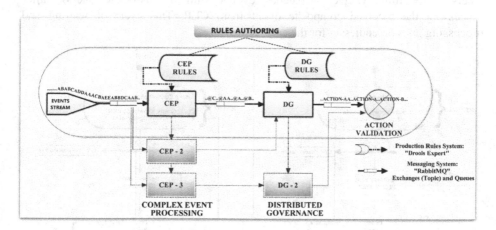

Fig. 1. Architecture and deployment scenario

One characteristic of the described system design requires special attention: the processing of patterns and the selection of actions is (a) distributed over two components (CEP and DG in the architecture) and can also be (b) distributed over multiple instances (CEP and DG instances in design and runtime). An effective and efficient coordination is required to guarantee that all patterns are processed and that the resulting complex events find related rules for action selection. Figure 1 shows a process for 'Rule Authoring' which is responsible for the coordination. The details of this process are out of scope for this paper, which focuses on the implementation and testing of the message processing.

4   Implementation

This section details the implemented system. We have built four components (which we call nodes), developed in Java 7. Two nodes realize the core of the event processing and two are used to automate tests. The two core nodes are CEP and DG (Figure 2). The other two supporting nodes are the input and output consoles (Figure 3). CEP and DG are built in a very similar way: they read events (messages) from a topic, invoke a rule engine to process events and then publish the results of the rule evaluation on another topic in form of complex events (CEP) or actions (DG).

4.1   Core Nodes

Both nodes, CEP and DG, start with an initialization of their respective topics and knowledge base (rules, for rule processing). CEP waits to get events from the input console, processes it (applies rules) and sends it out on another topic where DG receives it. Similarly, DG dispatches events with the associated action after processing the received composite event from CEP. This cycle of waiting and processing goes on endlessly for the core nodes.

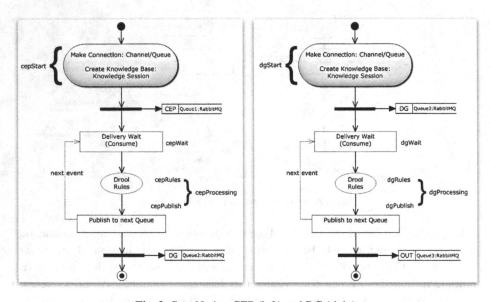

Fig. 2. Core Nodes, CEP (left) and DG (right)

4.2   Complex Event Processing (CEP) Node

Figure 2 (left) shows the CEP node with its three main parts: start, wait and processing. Start creates the knowledge base and two topics CEP and DG. When an event is received on CEP topic, a corresponding fact is inserted into the knowledge base and all rules are 'fired' (processed). Rules evaluate to match patterns as the knowledge base holds the information (facts) of previously received events. To keep the knowledge base light and efficient these facts are retracted when they are of no use to match patterns. In our system we have kept up to four facts in knowledge base to match the pattern, we call it the window of events. This window size can be changed per event pattern required to be matched. After rules evaluation complex events are generated and published to the DG topic.

4.3   Distributed Governance (DG) Node

Figure 2 (right) shows the DG node with its three main parts: start, wait and processing. Similar to the CEP node, DG creates its knowledge base and two topics called DG and OUT. The topic DG is the same as that created by the CEP node for its output, thus the two nodes a bound via that topic. When a complex event is received, a corresponding fact is inserted into the knowledge base and all appropriate triggered rules are then fired. Rules evaluate in DG to associate identified patterns to actions, which are then published to OUT topic.

Table 1. Single and Multi-event Pattern (examples)

Single event Pattern			Multi-event Pattern		
Incoming Event	Composite Event	Associative Action	Incoming Events	Composite Event	Associative Action
A	@A	Action-A	A-A	@AA	Action- AA
B	@B	Action-B	A-B†	@AB	Action- AB
C	@C	Action-C	A-A-B	@AAB	Action- AAB
D	@D	Action-D	A-A-B-B	@AABB	Action- AABB
E	@E	Action-E			

†A-B implies that 'B' occurs after 'A'

Table 1 shows an example of events (single and multi) and corresponding complex events with associative action. This pattern matching can be extended to generate new complex events, by simply writing the new CEP rules and corresponding rules in the DG for associative action.

4.4   Supporting Nodes

For testing, we have added an input and an output console, which will later be replaced by real systems for event processing and action respond. For the current system the input node provides the functionality of reading a file containing events, and then splitting the string to publish events on the CEP topic one by one. The output node receives the actions on the OUT topic and prints them out.

Figure 3 shows the two supporting nodes and their main phases (input console on the left and output console on the right). The input console starts and publishes as described above. When all events read from a file are published, it terminates. The output console starts once and waits indefinitely (until the process is terminated). Start creates the topic OUT and wait waits for actions from the DG node to print them to the console as they arrive.

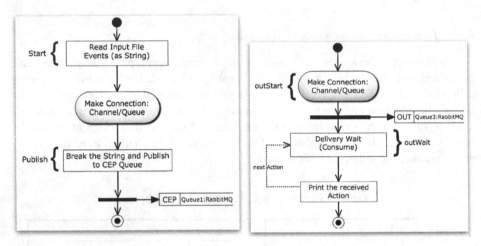

Fig. 3. Input (left) and Output (right) Console support Nodes

5   Testing and Evaluation ("Strings" as Alarm Events)

The tests we have performed are modeled to provide a good understanding about the performance of the overall system. Special attention focuses on the impact the message processing and the rule processing have on the overall system performance. The goal is to understand the technology impact on an end-to-end event processing. Tests have been run for 10 up to 1,000,000 events in a single stream with 10 test runs per input stream size. The numbers of rules and the actual rules have not been changed between test runs, so the results show the processing of a fixed set of 10 rules for CEP and 9 rules for DG. Further test runs will be needed to understand the impact of increasing rule sets on the performance. All tests have been run on a Intel i5 (dual core) Windows 7 laptop.

Each component of the system has fixed measurement points. They are shown in the figures in the implementation section. Initialization phases (called start) are not part of the measurement. The following list shows all measurement points of each component:

- Core nodes (Figure 2): Start, Wait, Rules, Publish (for CEP and DG)
- Supporting Nodes (Figure 3: Publish (Input node) and Wait (Output node)

Figure 4 shows the overall processing time, i.e. the time it takes to process all events from input console to output console. The time for up to 1,000 events is negligibly small. From 10,000 events onwards the time rises in proportion with the increasing number of event in the input stream.

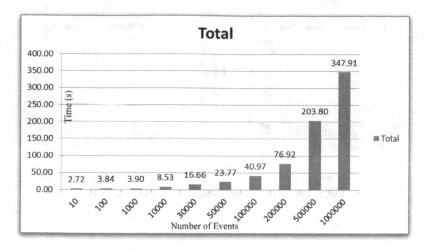

Fig. 4. Averaged Maximum Time for system (with String events)

5.1   Time Consumption on Core Nodes

The different times within CEP and DG namely Start, Wait, Rules, Publish, Processing and Total are measured and plotted on the graphs shown in Figure 5. The initialization phase of the nodes (Start) has been included here to show that it has no impact on the overall system performance (note: the number of rules and topics did not change).

An important metric evaluated is the time consumed during rule evaluation and the wait a node does before fetching the next event from the queue. These times, Wait and Rules, shown in Figure 6 and discussed in the following section, depict the performance of Drools Expert.

Another Important metric is the time each node takes to publish events to the topic. There are three nodes doing this task on their corresponding topics; the input console, CEP and DG. The publish time of these nodes measures the efficiency of RabbitMQ.

5.2   Discussion

Drools Expert rules are used on the nodes CEP and DG. DG's Wait is directly proportional to the time the CEP node takes for rule evaluation. The output console also waits with DG for CEP rules evaluation and then waits for the DG rules evaluation. Hence it has the longest wait time. Figure 6 compares wait time with the rules evaluation time with increasing number of events.

CEP rules are complex and identify patterns that take more time compared to DG rules which are used to select actions associated to patterns.

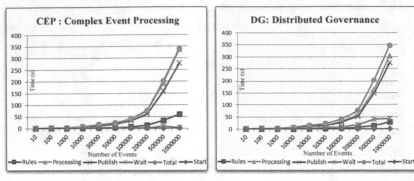

Fig. 5. Different time consumptions in CEP and DG

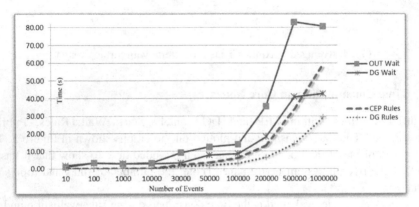

Fig. 6. 'DG and OUT node Wait' vs 'CEP and DG Rules'

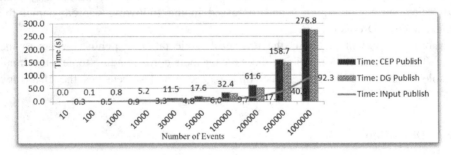

Fig. 7. Publish time for Input, CEP and DG nodes

There are three locations where events are published: CEP, DG and the input console. Figure 7 shows the time it takes to publish. The time taken by the input console to publish all the events is very small (virtually negligible) for up to 30,000 events finishing even before CEP starts processing events.

Above 30,000 events, as the number of events increases it affects the CEP processing time and generates a cascading effect for the overall system performance. Thus, separating the input console from CEP (and subsequently DG) is important for any event stream above 30,000 events.

6   Testing and Evaluation ("Maps" as Alarm Events)

Extending our distributed system to work with Maps (*LinkedHashMap<String, Object>*). Maps are closer to the real world mobile network alarms and by hence replacing Strings with Maps (alarms); we will be able to find out the real world performance of our distributed system. The main information that a Map event contains are the alarm ID, the language, its type, timestamps and payload. With Maps we have a flexibility to add some critical information during processing that could help in final decision for action in response to the alarm.

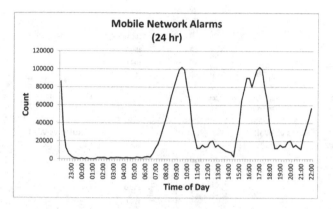

Fig. 8. Number of Mobile Network Alarms during a day

Figure 8 shows a possible event pattern of a mobile network for 24 hour period. During the event storms (at the peaks in figure above), we require a system that could work seamlessly and provides for an efficient alarm management system.

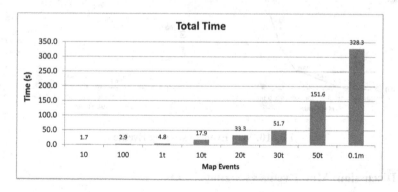

Fig. 9. Averaged Maximum Time for System (with Map events)

We need our system to perform at a speed of thousands of events per second. So that with multiple nodes we could make it more efficient for congestion free peak hours. For such performance the response time of a system should not be more than 5-6 minutes for an event storm. We have kept our experiments bound to a limit of 5 minutes of total system run. We went up to 1 million events with Strings but with Maps we are able to go up to 100k events within our time bound.

Figure 9 shows the mean processing time for Map events, for 100k events it exceeds 5 minutes which is considered under our test environment but not acceptable in real world mobile networks scenario.

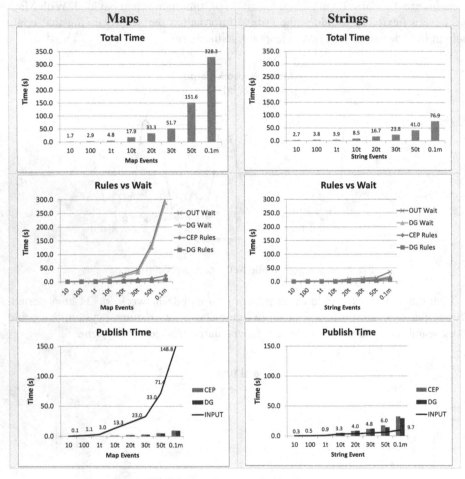

Fig. 10. Map Events vs String Events

6.1   Discussion: Map Events vs String Events

The comparison of Maps as events to the Strings as events is shown in Figure 10. The important difference we noted by the comparison is that input takes a very long time to publish as the number of events increase. This increases the wait time of cascaded system (CEP-DG-OUT) and hence the total processing time. For Maps messaging system has to hold and process more than 10 times of data per event compared to Strings and hence becomes slow.

We observe that RabbitMQ is not the best for messaging system when the load becomes high during events storm and hence we get a backlog processing at that time; which is not be acceptable for real world mobile networks. We have considered a couple of alternatives for messaging system which are under testing to be made compatible and function in parallel with our rule processing system.

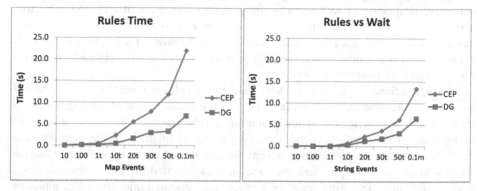

Fig. 11. Rules Processing time: Maps and Strings

Rules for CEP and DG are re-written to work with Maps but rules processing. For CEP which holds the knowledge of 4 concurrent events for pattern matching, it takes longer now with heavier data of maps. But for DG it is almost equal as the rules are simple and no pattern matching is done.

This time consumption is not critical as it is still under 25 seconds for 100k events. With highly complex pattern matching, which is a part of our future work, we can safely assume that rule system would take longer time without going critical.

We conclude that with maps we have gathered a better analytics for the performance of our distributed system in real environment.

7   Related Work

In the Policy-Based Information Sharing in Publish/Subscribe Middleware [5] author describes a control of sensitive information system in health care environment. The criticality of information sharing and data access is controlled by rules, precisely hook rules (Postgres SQL). Information that travels on the messaging system is tailored for a particular subscriber, on need-to-know basis. We have found that this paper has similar architecture as of our system with a slightly different implementation. Our system analyzes the patterns inside the incoming messages and modifies the forwarded message to correspond to the identified pattern, whereas it analyses the incoming messages and modifies it for particular subscriber according to information relevant to that subscriber.

A rule-based middleware for business process execution [6] implements rules over messaging middleware to provide a simple and efficient way of describing executable business processes. The complex conditional workflows and enterprise integration patterns are implemented in terms of rules. The Prova rule language and the Rule Markup Language (RuleML) are used to implement rules over an Enterprise Service Bus (ESB).

Policy-driven middleware for self-adaptation of web services compositions [7] focuses on specifying and enforcing monitoring-policies to help in fault detection and corrective adaptation of web services compositions. Since monitoring and corrective action selection is combined in a single policy, this work does not scale well when the number of faults increases drastically. It also does not allow for smart filtering of fault events, which is essential to address high-priority events immediately and add lower-priority events to maintenance reports.

Message oriented middleware with integrated rules engine [8] is a patented invention addressing deficiencies in respect to the management of message oriented middleware. It describes the integration of a rule engine with message-oriented middleware. Their method includes creating a shared memory in the memory of a computer and adding or deleting tokens in the shared memory corresponding to objects such as messages and message queues, created in and removed from, respectively, in a messaging component of message oriented middleware, or topics or subscriptions or log file space for messages queues in the messaging component. The method additionally includes applying rules in a rules engine to the tokens in the shared memory.

Our work differs from the above in that we use distributed and coordinated policies (between two components for event processing and governance), while policy instances in each component are atomic, i.e. do not effect each other. This results in a system that is hugely scalable, since only a combination of event processing policy and governance policy depend on each other.

8   Summary and Future Work

This paper describes the second phase of our work on building a rule-based event processing distributed system, which combines a messaging system with a rules system. We start by describing the underlying technologies, tools and products being used. Messaging using AMQP is implemented by RabbitMQ and our rule system uses Drools-Expert.

The architecture we have created consists of several interconnected components with communication links, realizing a distributed system. In our architecture we introduce 2 rule governing nodes; Complex Event Processing (CEP) and Distributed Governance (DG). We have streams of events entering the system which are being processed by CEP to generate complex events, essentially identifying patterns within the events. These complex events are then fed into DG for analysis and decisive action. The communication links between these components is provided by the messaging system. There are topic exchanges (channels and queues) between components which provide forwarding with selective filtering capability.

In our previous paper, we focused on the evaluation of performance of the products RabbitMQ and Drools by running several tests with events ranging from 10 to 1 million. In effect we are measuring the performance of rules and publishing of complex events. The wait state, introduced due to dependency of a node on processing time of previous node, is also considered.

In this paper we extended our work for evaluating the performance and take to closer to the real world alarm events. We introduced Maps as events with several parameters stored inside one event. Then we critically analyzed the performance of the system and compared the results with our previous work with Strings as events.

Part of the future work planned is to deploy multiple CEP and DG nodes/engines on multiple machines that can work simultaneously to distribute the load at required times. We also have planned to increase the complexity of the governing rules in CEP and DG to test the highly complex patterns matching. A higher performance is the main objective of our work, currently we have all our nodes tested under constrained environment, working on a single machine (Intel i5, dual core) with Windows 7. Running our nodes across distributed servers in a cloud-based deployment should see the approach scale to a level appropriate for a high throughput, telecommunication grade management process.

References

1. AMQP Architecture,
   http://www.amqp.org/architecture (last visited: February 22, 2013)
2. RabbitMQ Tutorial,
   http://www.rabbitmq.com/tutorials/tutorial-one-java.html
   (last visited: February 22, 2013)
3. RabbitMQ AMQP Concepts,
   http://www.rabbitmq.com/tutorials/amqp-concepts.html
   (last visited: February 22, 2013)
4. JBoss.org, http://docs.jboss.org/drools/release/5.5.0.Final/
   drools-expert-docs/pdf/drools-expert-docs.pdf
   (last visited: February 1, 2013)
5. Singh, J., Vargas, L., Bacon, J., Moody, K.: Policy-Based Information Sharing in Publish/Subscribe Middleware. In: IEEE Workshop on Policies for Distributed Systems and Networks, POLICY 2008, Computer Lab., Univ. of Cambridge, Cambridge, June 2-4, pp. 137–144 (2008)
6. Paschke, A., Kozlenkov, A.: A rule-based middleware for business process execution. In: Multi-konferenz Wirtschaftsinformatik, MKWI (2008)
7. Erradi, A., Maheshwari, P., Tosic, V.: Policy-Driven Middleware for Self-adaptation of Web Services Compositions. In: van Steen, M., Henning, M. (eds.) Middleware 2006. LNCS, vol. 4290, pp. 62–80. Springer, Heidelberg (2006)
8. Winn, G.M., Young, N.G.S.: Message oriented middleware with integrated rules engine International Business Machines Corporation: US Patents US20130007184 (2012), http://www.google.com/patents/US20130007184

A Distributed Control Plane for the Internet of Things Based on a Distributed Hash Table

Jaime Jiménez Bolonio[1], Manuel Urueña[2], and Gonzalo Camarillo[1]

[1] Ericsson Research, NomadicLab, Finland
{jaime.j.jimenez,gonzalo.camarillo}@ericsson.com
[2] University Carlos III of Madrid, Spain
muruenya@it.uc3m.es

Abstract. As any other communication system, the Internet of Things (IoT) requires a functional control plane. However developing such control plane in a centralized way presents a number of challenges given the multiple stakeholders, the huge number of devices distributed worldwide, their limited connectivity, and specially that most IoT devices are battery-powered and thus must be sleeping most of the time. This paper explores the possibility of employing a distributed control plane for the IoT that leverages the intrinsic scalability and flexibility of peer-to-peer Distributed Hash Tables (DHTs). In particular, it proposes using a so-called "command mailbox" resource to remotely control sleeping sensors and actuators in an asynchronous way, while also solving important issues such as device bootstrapping and security.

Keywords: Internet of Things (IoT), Peer-to-Peer (P2P), Distributed Hash Table (DHT), REsource Location And Discovery (RELOAD).

1 Introduction

The future vision of Internet of Things (IoT) is being realized by the interconnection of a wealth of heterogeneous devices [1]. Due to their ubiquity, such devices are likely to be connected to various types of networks, from NAT-based home networks to cellular or low-range wireless sensor networks. Many of them will have limited resources (i.e. computation, memory, etc.), power limitations being the most notable constrain (e.g. battery powered). Thus, it will be likely that such devices will be sleeping most of the time in order to save energy.

IoT has been defined in various ways, for our purposes we will use the definition given by [2]: *"The pervasive presence around us of a variety of things or objects which, through unique addressing schemes, are able to interact with each other and cooperate with their neighbors to reach common goals"*

Such cooperation is achieved by collaboration between **sensors** that gather data from their surroundings and **actuators** that interact with the physical world. A control entity, the **master**, is the one issuing the commands to the actuators and who configures both sensors and actuators. These masters are just logical entities that may be IoT devices (e.g. a light sensor that controls a shades' actuator), a simple user

D. Pesch et al. (Eds.): MONAMI 2013, LNICST 125, pp. 108–121, 2013.
© Institute for Computer Sciences, Social Informatics and Telecommunications Engineering 2013

application (e.g. a home automation web page), or a complex management software orchestrating many sensors and actuators (e.g. a smart city). Moreover an IoT device may be controlled by several masters simultaneously, which may be unknown at the time the device was deployed.

When analyzing the IoT traffic we consider two main types of communication: commands (i.e., sent by a master to a sensor or actuator) and data (e.g., measurements sent periodically by a sensor). Since each type of traffic has quite different communication patterns, we refer to those types of traffic using the *control-plane* and *data-plane* terms, respectively.

This paper is focused on the challenges of building a **control-plane** for the IoT, mainly the limited communication patterns of these devices, given that most IoT devices will be behind firewalls/NATs and, more importantly, that they will be sleeping most of the time in order to save battery, and thus cannot be contacted directly by their masters. A simple solution to this problem may be employing centralized servers that act as gateways between IoT devices and their masters (which may be other IoT devices themselves). However any centralized solution has a limited scalability and may complicate the multi-tenant requirements for the IoT.

Therefore this paper proposes a fully decentralized solution based on a Distributed Hash Table (DHT) that is employed as a rendezvous mechanism between IoT devices and their masters. In particular we specify how such solution may be implemented using RELOAD/Chord, although, in order to do so in an efficient and secure way, we propose a number of enhancements to the current RELOAD specification.

2   Related Work

Some works in the literature propose to connect wireless sensors with the network by using some kind of local gateway, such as a mobile device [3][4]. Some of these data-plane solutions try to decentralize those gateways, for instance by means of a distributed overlay as in [4]. Sensors then connect to peers that are equipped with both cellular and local Wireless Sensor Network (WSN) radio interfaces. The distributed gateway overlay provides functions for resource discovery, network management, storage and a rendezvous mechanism, featuring also the usual characteristics of P2P systems, such as scalability and NAT traversal.

Albeit limited, P2P systems can be implemented by constrained devices [8][9] and fit with the IoT requirements previously stated. Therefore the new enhancements we propose in this paper will be also suitable for the deployment of a fully distributed IoT scenario that does not require such local gateways, but devices will autonomously connect to the P2P IoT.

3   Background and Problem Statement

We take REsource Location And Discovery (RELOAD) [5] as the reference P2P protocol since it provides a standard, generic, self-organizing overlay network service. On top the RELOAD overlay layer different application protocols can be plugged in, such as the Session Initiation Protocol (SIP), Extensible Messaging and Presence

Protocol (XMPP) or even the Constrained Application Protocol (CoAP) [7], a lightweight client-server protocol for sensors [6] that will probably be employed in the data-plane of the IoT.

RELOAD proposes Chord [10] as its default Distributed Hash Table (DHT) algorithm to organize the overlay. It also has an integrated Network Address Translator (NAT) traversal mechanism, the Interactive Connectivity Establishment (ICE) [11]. In a distributed and heterogeneous IoT scenario, this mechanism comes very handy for interconnecting the autonomous devices, which will use whatever communication technology is available. The DHT allows for storing information in the overlay, where resources are identified by their *resource-ID*, which is usually obtained by hashing some resource's information, i.e. name, data, URI, owner ID, etc. As with other DHTs, RELOAD identifies devices by their *node-ID*, usually calculated with the same hash algorithm as the resource-ID. RELOAD supports two types of nodes: *peers* and *clients*. Peers are nodes that run the DHT algorithm, route messages, and store data on behalf of other nodes. Clients are nodes that do not run the DHT algorithm, and neither provide message routing nor storage services. Instead, they use other peers as proxies to the DHT.

Therefore, given the connectivity and resource constraints of most IoT devices, it is reasonable that they connect as RELOAD clients to a DHT composed by stable peers. However, there are some limitations in the way clients operates in the current specification, related to enabling sleeping devices and adapting current access control policies to the open and multi-stakeholder nature of IoT.

3.1   Enabling Sleeping IoT Devices in RELOAD

Although there has been a lot of research on network scalability, including P2P networks, the sleepy behavior of network devices has been considered only recently [1]. The main reason being that it changes one of the main assumptions about Internet hosts, that is, that they can be contacted at any time. Both P2P protocols, like RELOAD, and sensor protocols, like COAP, assume that nodes, either peers/clients or COAP servers/gateways, are always able to receive messages. However, this would require IoT devices to be fully awake all the time, or at least its wireless interface, which will severely limit the lifetime of any battery-power device.

Still, many do not consider this an issue, since it is assumed that wireless sensor devices just awake periodically to send one or few COAP messages with the last sensor measurement to a gateway or central server, and immediately go to sleep again [13]. Although in the data plane this client-only behavior of sensors is possible in most scenarios, this is no longer the case for the control and management planes. Although they have been overlooked by the research literature, they are essential for the correct operation of all kind of networks, including the Internet of Things. For example in order to configure a sensor with the COAP URI where to send its measurements to, the time between those measurements, or a threshold to filter unimportant events. Other example of management plane operation may be obtaining the statistics about transmitted/received packets in order to troubleshoot a problem.

To save space and cost, many IoT devices will not have a dedicated control/management interface (e.g. an USB port), but will rely on the same network interface employed for the data plane, which should be sleeping most of the time. Therefore, *it is not possible to send control or management commands to sleeping sensors or actuators*, unless some additional synchronization or rendezvous mechanism is in place. Our proposal is that low power devices can use a Distributed Hash Table (DHT) as a rendezvous mechanism to receive commands from their masters, since they may be behind a firewall or NAT and be sleeping most of the time. To do so, a sensor device creates a resource in the DHT, called *Command Mailbox*, and polls it periodically to check if it has new commands from its (potentially unknown) masters, while always-on actuators may receive these commands immediately by becoming DHT peers. Masters only need to know the node-ID of the device (either a sensor or actuator), in order to send commands to it through the DHT.

3.2   Security Considerations for the IoT Control-Plane

Although current sensor-based applications are vertically integrated, and thus a single vendor provides the whole stack, which is usually specifically designed for a given application and client, we envision the future IoT as an open and multi-stakeholder network, where interoperable devices can be provided by multiple vendors, and new applications can be deployed dynamically over the existing infrastructure. However, such open environment poses clear security challenges. In our particular case, although the commands from the master are encrypted and signed using a Message Authentication Code (MAC), the main security problem is how to allow an arbitrary number of masters (e.g. the users of a given IoT application) to write in the Command Mailbox resource of an already deployed device without using a dedicated server or directory [14].

Currently RELOAD has two control policies that can be employed to protect this kind of resource sharing: *node-based* and *list-based*, although they have some drawbacks:

- *Node-based* (USER-NODE-MATCH in RELOAD) [5] policy allows **any node of the DHT** to write one entry in any Dictionary resource applying it. However, in order to protect their own memory, peers responsible for the storage of the Dictionary resource will certainly limit its size. This could easily lead to a Denial of Service (DoS) attack, because an attacker with multiple valid certificates would be able to store a high volume of data to overflow such limit, preventing legitimate masters from storing their information. This happens because the peer storing the resource does not know which nodes are the valid masters of a device.

- *List-based* (USER-CHAIN-ACL in RELOAD) [15] policy is not vulnerable to this attack, because only the nodes **explicitly allowed** by the owner of the resource are able to write data. However, this requires the device to know the list of legitimate masters beforehand. Moreover, a device cannot be shared by an arbitrary number of users, because that would be too great a burden for the peer managing such list, as well as all associated certificates - thus the dedicated server approaches such in [14]. In the IoT context, it implies that our sensor device should have to know beforehand the user-IDs or node-IDs of all possible masters before being deployed. This obviously complicates the management and deployment of IoT devices, especially in the cases of embedded ones that do not have a dedicated control interface. Therefore, a simpler mechanism to enable initially unknown masters to write commands in the resource of a deployed embedded device would be useful.

4   Proposed Solutions

As we have seen in the previous section, controlling sleeping IoT devices is problematic because those devices are asleep most of the time. In addition, current DHTs do not implement access control policies suitable for the large amount of devices that will be part of the IoT future scenario and their multi-stakeholder management. In this section we tackle those problems and present solutions to them.

4.1   A Command Mailbox for DHTs

Taking Chord's implementation in RELOAD [5] as a model, devices that want to use this method should be pre-configured at least with the following information:

- The node-ID of the device, which must be globally unique.
- A valid certificate from the Enrollment Server of the DHT.
- The DNS name of the overlay, or the IP addresses of Bootstrap Servers.
- An optional, randomly generated, *secret key*. The master can later change this key, but if the device is reset, it goes back to this initial secret key.

In order to issue commands to the device, its masters must know the device's node-ID and its current secret key. This information may be shared in several ways, for instance it can just be printed in the manual or in the device itself. In any case, the master should change the secret-key as soon as possible (i.e. the very first control command). Notice that it is not necessary neither that the master knows whether the device is a sensor or an actuator, nor the device has to know whom its master or masters are beforehand, which greatly simplifies the bootstrapping and the dynamic ownership of IoT devices.

The proposed command mailbox resource is to be used by sensors, actuators and masters. The initial operation procedure after being reset (see Figure 1) is the same for devices plugged to the grid (e.g. actuators), thus awake and connected all the time, and for battery-powered, or otherwise intermittent-connected, devices (e.g. sensors).

After booting, an IoT device contacts the Bootstrap Server to obtain the overlay configuration and to identify its Admitting Peer, i.e. the one responsible for the node-ID of the joining node. Then, in the case of an always-on actuator, since it has enough resources to be a full peer, it joins the DHT as a RELOAD peer through its Admitting Peer. A sensor, on the other hand, attaches to its Admitting Peer as a RELOAD client, and thus has no routing or storage responsibilities.

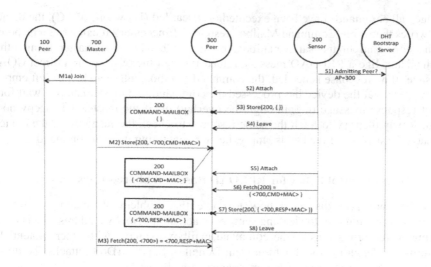

Fig. 1. Issuing a command to a sleepy client device (e.g. a battery-powered sensor)

Then the booting device creates in the DHT a Dictionary resource with the new *COMMAND-MAILBOX* kind-ID and the proposed *CLIENT-ID-MATCH* policy that enables it to store it with the same key as its own node-ID. Note that this behavior is not contemplated in current RELOAD specification because, to limit resource consumption and provide more availability, data can only be stored when the resource-ID are either a hash of the owner's user-ID or node-ID. In the case of an actuator peer, since it is the responsible for its own command mailbox resource, it is not necessary to create a real resource (e.g. reserve memory or replicate it), but just to process the DHT messages targeting it. In the case of a sensor device, the command mailbox is created in its Admitting Peer by performing a DHT store operation with the same key as the sensor's node-ID.

At this point, once the Command Mailbox resource has been created, a sensor device may leave the Admitting Peer and go to sleep for some pre-defined amount of time between command checks (e.g. 10 minutes). Conversely, an actuator remains connected as a peer in order to receive messages from its masters, requesting a store operation in its Command Mailbox resource. Then, when the sensor awakes, it attaches again as a client to its Admitting Peer and fetches its mailbox looking for any new command. Both types of devices can verify the MAC code of the incoming command, and optionally decrypt it, to guarantee that it comes from a valid master that knows its current secret key.

Therefore, when a master has to issue commands to any of the IoT devices it controls, it only has to be connected to the same DHT (either as a peer or as a client). Then it can issue control messages just by storing the encrypted and signed command into the Command Mailbox resource with the same resource-ID as the target device's node-ID. Thus, if the target device is an actuator, the command will be received directly by the actuator peer and act accordingly. Sensors on the other hand will only receive such command after checking the Command Mailbox at its Admitting Peer.

Once all commands have been executed or discarded (i.e. wrong MAC), the device overwrites the whole Command Mailbox resource. If necessary it can write a response to the command in the same mailbox, or sent it back to the master using other mechanisms, like a RELOAD message routed through the overlay, or a direct COAP message. If no response is needed, the command-mailbox entry can be just left empty.

To check that the device has processed the command, the master can just wait for a direct response message (e.g. through the overlay) or, if the master is a sleepy node itself, it may then try to fetch the same resource to check the response of the device, or that at least verify if the key is empty, i.e. not containing its own command.

4.2   Access Control Policy for RELOAD Based on Shared Keys

Previously we have discussed how to solve the problem of sending control or management commands to sleeping sensors or actuators. Now we address the issue of sharing write permissions of the command mailbox resource with other (potentially unknown) nodes in the overlay to prevent Denial of Service (DoS) attacks. To do so, we propose the use of a shared-key mechanism (see Figure 2).

In our IoT deployment scenario every embedded device can be deployed without a pre-configured list of masters, but rather just with a randomly generated secret key. Any master would only need to know the device's identifier and its initial secret key, which can be printed in the manual or in the device itself. Therefore a device can be easily controlled by an arbitrary number of masters without managing an explicit access control list.

A device that wants to create a Command Mailbox resource and share its write permissions with its (unknown) masters by means of the proposed shared-key mechanism should follow two steps:

1. Establishing a Write Key: The device sends a `Store Request` message with the same ID as the Command Mailbox resource being protected and a value identifying it as a Write Key (in RELOAD this can be done by editing part of the `StoreKindData` with an additional `key_sign_type = WRITE_KEY` attribute). The message should also define the Message Authentication Code (MAC) algorithm to be employed by other nodes, and include the **shared key** associated to that resource, and that may be derived (e.g. by hashing) from the device's secret key. The Write Key is encrypted with the public key of the peer storing the resource, so it can be securely forwarded through the overlay. Only the owner node can change the secret key or the MAC algorithm at any time by sending a new `Store Request` message with a different `write_key` field.

2. Storing in the Resource: After establishing the Write Key of the Command Mailbox, any node that knows such key is also able to store information in the shared resource. Those messages need to include a `write_sign` signature field containing the MAC value of the whole message structure including the resource-ID, by using the current Write Key. The MAC algorithm must be the one specified in the `mac_algorithm` field of the `Store Request` operation by the owner device. When considering RELOAD, other operations (i.e. Fetch, Stat, etc.) are not affected since the `write_key_sign` field only appears in Store messages.

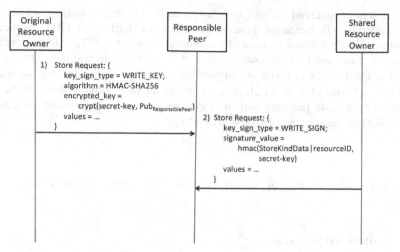

Fig. 2. RELOAD resource being shared between two owners

When the responsible peer needs to **replicate** the shared resource in one or more replicas, it should also include the whole `write_key` field in the `Store Request` message sent to the replica, and optionally encrypting the write key with the replica's public key. Usually the certificates of the replicas should be in the responsible peer's cache, but if not, the key can be obtained by sending a RELOAD ping message to the replica's node-ID.

5   Scalability Analysis

This section analyzes the scalability of the proposed DHT-based IoT control plane by comparing it with using centralized servers, as well as analyzing the effect of the proposed enhancements to RELOAD. To do so, let us define N as the total number of nodes in the Internet of Things (IoT):

$$N = N_S + N_A$$

Where N_S and N_A are, respectively, the total number of sensors and actuators in the IoT. We will assume that actuators are mains-powered and have a permanent connection (although they may be behind NATs/firewalls), so they can behave as DHT peers. On the other hand, sensors are sleeping most of the time so they only wake up periodically to check their command mailboxes. Due to this intermitted connection sensors are not full peers, but connect as RELOAD clients to their Admitting Peers.

To model the IoT control traffic, we will also define Ox as the average rate, measured in messages per time unit, of control operations issued to a given node of type x. Thus, O_s and O_a are the average rate of control operations issued to a sensor and an actuator, respectively (e.g. $O_a = 1$ means that each actuator receives on average one control operation per time unit). P_s and P_a are defined as the rate sensors and actuators poll their associated Command Mailbox (e.g. $P_s = 1$ means that each sensor polls its command mailbox once per time unit).

Now we can define M_X as the total number of control messages exchanged (either sent or received) per time unit by all nodes of type X. Then M_C is the total number of messages sent or received per unit time by all servers in the centralized scenario, and M'_{DHT} specifies all messages generated within the RELOAD DHT. Notice that forwarding a control message, either by a central server or a RELOAD peer, involves one reception and one transmission, and thus it is accounted as two messages.

Finally, the metric employed to compare the scalability of the different scenarios is L_x, the average load of a node of type x, measured as the average number of messages exchanged by a node per time unit. It is computed as the total number of messages (M_X) divided by the number of type X nodes (N_X):

$$L_x = \frac{M_X}{N_X}$$

Next we provide an analytic model for this load metric in the three evaluated scenarios.

5.1   Centralized Scenario

In this scenario, the control plane of the IoT is provided by a set of N_c centralized servers. We will assume a perfect load balancing strategy so all servers handle exactly the same number of messages. Then, actuators have a permanent connection with one of these servers, which acts as a proxy of control commands, sending back and forth the operation requests from masters and the replies from actuators. Therefore, the total number messages exchanged by all IoT actuators is just two times (i.e. request + reply) the average control operation rate of a single actuator (O_a) multiplied by the total number of actuators (N_A):

$$M_A = 2O_aN_A$$

Sensors, on the other hand, do not have such permanent connection and thus cannot receive control commands from their masters directly. Instead these masters' operations are stored in a Command Mailbox at the central servers while the master waits for a response. Sensors poll its mailbox periodically (at P_s rate), and when it contains a new operation request, it is executed and the response is sent back to the user through the central server. Therefore the total number of messages exchanged by the sensors is the sum of the polling ones plus the two request/response messages exchange with the master:

$$M_S = 2P_sN_S + 2O_sN_S = 2N_S(P_s + O_s)$$

Then, the total number of messages exchanged by all masters is:

$$M_M = 2O_aN_A + 2O_sN_S$$

Therefore, since the central servers forward all messages exchanged among masters, sensors and actuators, the total number of messages handled by all servers (M'_C) and the average load per server (L_c) are:

$$M_C = 4O_aN_A + 2N_S(P_s + 2O_s)$$

$$L_c = \frac{M_C}{N_C}$$

5.2   Standard DHT without the Proposed RELOAD Enhancements

To avoid the extra cost and single point of failure of centralized servers, in the following scenarios the control plane is provided by a global DHT comprised by all IoT actuators that are powerful enough to act as RELOAD peers. Sensors act as RELOAD clients and are connected to the DHT through their Admitting Peers. Masters that want to issue control commands are also connected as RELOAD clients in order to write the desired operation in the Command Mailbox of the target IoT node and then, as in the previous case, wait for a direct response forwarded through the DHT. Both operations are acknowledged to provide a reliable service.

However in the second scenario we will first not consider the proposed RELOAD enhancements. Therefore the Command Mailbox resource of a sensor or an actuator is stored by some (random) peer in the DHT obtained by hashing its node-ID, and both sensors and actuators have to periodically poll it in order to check if there is any new operation request. In that case, they execute it and send the reply back through the DHT to the master (which has provided its node-ID in the command request) that finally acknowledges back to the device. Therefore the number of messages exchanged by all masters, sensors and actuators among them, as well as with the peers storing their respective Command Mailboxes are:

$$M'_S = 2P_S N_S + 2O_S N_S = 2N_S(P_S + O_S)$$

$$M'_A = 2P_a N_A + 2O_a N_A = 2N_A(P_a + O_a)$$

$$M'_M = 4O_S N_S + 4O_a N_A$$

However each of these messages, exchanged either with the peer storing the command mailbox or with the master, must be forwarded through the DHT. For a Chord ring with N_{DHT} peers, the average number of hops is $H = log_2 N_{DHT}$ [10] and, since each hop requires receiving and sending each forwarded message, the total number of forwarded messages doubles. Moreover there is certain overhead in order to maintain the DHT structure. In case of RELOAD/Chord an update message must be sent to all neighbor peers every 10 minutes ($U_{Neighs} = 6$ msg/hr), while a search for best fingers is performed each hour ($U_{Fingers} = 1$ msg/hr). Given that each peer must have 16 fingers and 22 neighbors (i.e. 3 predecessors + 3 successors + 16 fingers) [5], the total number of overhead messages per time unit to maintain the DHT is:

$$M_{DHT} = 22U_{Neighs}N_{DHT} + 4H16U_{Fingers}N_{DHT} = N_{DHT}(22U_{Neighs} + 64HU_{Fingers})$$

Then, the total number of messages (exchanged among masters, sensors and actuators) sent and received by all DHT peers (M'_{DHT}), and the average peer load (L'_{DHT}) are:

$$M'_{DHT} = 2H(2P_S N_S + 2P_a N_A + 4O_S N_S + 4O_a N_A) + M_{DHT}$$

$$L'_{DHT} = \frac{M'_{DHT}}{N_{DHT}}$$

5.3   Enhanced RELOAD DHT

In the third scenario, the IoT control plane is also provided by a global DHT, but now it employs the proposed RELOAD enhancements. This way, the Command Mailboxes of sensors and actuators are not stored in remote peers, but in the sensor's Admitting Peer or at the actuator itself. This greatly reduces polling overhead because allows actuators to receive commands immediately, and polling messages from sensors are not forwarded several hops away through the DHT, but just target the local Admitting Peer. Therefore the total number of messages exchanged among masters, sensors and actuators in this distributed scenario are:

$$M''_A = 4O_a N_A$$

$$M''_S = 2N_S(P_s + O_s)$$

$$M''_M = 4O_s N_S + 4O_a N_A$$

Now only the messages among masters and actuators, sensors or their Admitting Peers have to be forwarded in the DHT (still with H hops on average), while sensors' polling messages reach the Admitting Peer directly, leading to the following total number of messages (also considering the M_{DHT} overhead) in the DHT and the average load per peer:

$$M''_{DHT} = 2H(4O_s N_S + 4O_a N_A) + 2P_s N_S + M_{DHT}$$

$$L''_{DHT} = \frac{M''_{DHT}}{N_{DHT}}$$

6   Evaluation

In order to evaluate the scalability of the three analyzed scenarios, we should compare them with similar parameters. Therefore let us assume that the control operation rate for sensors is just one operation per node and day ($O_s = 1$ op. per node and day = 1/24 op. per node and hour) while actuators receive one operation per hour ($O_A = 1$ op. per node and hour). The Command Mailbox polling rate is also the same for sensors and actuators, but faster to reduce the response time ($P_s = P_a = 1$ poll per node every minute = 60 polls per node and hour). To do not favor any device type, let us assume that half of the IoT devices are sensors and the other half actuators ($N_s = N_a = N/2$). Moreover, all actuators form the IoT control-plane DHT ($N_{DHT} = N_a$).

Figure 3 shows the scalability of the three proposed scenarios. Each curve represents the average load per node measured in messages per hour of each solution. That is, L_c, L'_{DHT} and L''_{DHT} that were defined in the previous section. Since the average load depends on the number of nodes, the centralized solution has four curves for different number of servers, ranging from one to 10,000. Notice that both axes are in log scale.

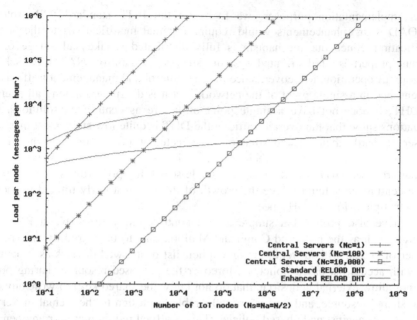

Fig. 3. Load per node in the three evaluated scenarios (L_c, L'_{DHT}, L''_{DHT})

It can be clearly seen that the centralized solution requires deploying a high number of servers in order to maintain the same average load as the DHT-based solutions, which is low enough (2,351 msg/hr = 0.65 msg/sec with one billion - 10^9 - IoT nodes) to be supported even by constrained devices. Moreover, the proposed enhancements for RELOAD reduce one order of magnitude the total number of messages in the DHT by avoiding polling remote Command Mailbox resources, which constitute a high share of the total traffic.

However, due to the overhead to maintain the DHT, a distributed IoT control plane does not make sense for small IoT deployments that may simply rely on few centralized servers. On the other hand, a DHT composed by IoT actuators does not require deploying and maintaining additional infrastructure, and continuously upgrades as the IoT grows, given that the new actuators will help providing the IoT control plane.

7 Conclusion

This paper provides the foundation of a fully distributed control plane for the Internet of Things (IoT). It provides an asynchronous mechanism to send control plane commands (e.g. CoAP, SNMP or custom ones) to intermittently connected devices. Moreover this solution enables the IoT to be managed by different stakeholders, which do not need to deploy its own infrastructure but may rely on the existing IoT devices themselves.

For implementation purposes, we focus on the IETF standard P2P protocol: RELOAD. Our enhancements would require minimal modifications to the current specification. Since our mechanism is fully distributed it takes advantage of the inherent properties of distributed systems such as scalability, NAT traversal and autonomous operation. Moreover, since the IoT control and management traffic is not concentrated in a single point of the network, but it is distributed among all peers of the DHT, it does not have a single point of failure as centralized solutions. Our estimations show that the overall traffic in the DHT is quite low since most messages are sent towards their final destinations (i.e. actuator peers), or through a direct connection (e.g. sensors polling their Admitting Peers). Moreover, our analysis shows that the proposed DHT solution has remarkable scalability properties when compared with a centralized solution, since the growth of the IoT as a fairly limited impact on the control-plane load of DHT peers.

We have also provided a simple access control policy to enable a RELOAD resource, such as the proposed Command Mailbox one, to be shared by an arbitrary number of nodes, without requiring an explicit list of allowed devices as it happens now with access list-based policies. Moreover the proposed resource sharing policy does not allow external nodes (i.e. that do not know the shared key) to write any data in the shared resource, and thus is not vulnerable by design to the Denial of Service (DoS) attacks against node-based policies. This is a final requirement for an open, but secure, distributed management of IoT devices.

Acknowledgments. The authors would like to thank Heikki Mahkonen and Petri Jokela for their help with this work and for reviewing the final document.

References

[1] Mazhelis, O., Luoma, E., Warma, H.: Defining an Internet-of-Things Ecosystem. In: Andreev, S., Balandin, S., Koucheryavy, Y. (eds.) NEW2AN/ruSMART 2012. LNCS, vol. 7469, pp. 1–14. Springer, Heidelberg (2012)

[2] Atzori, L., Iera, A., Morabito, G.: The Internet of things: A survey. Computer Networks 54(15), 2787–2805 (2010)

[3] Hu, F., Rajatheva, N., Latva-aho, M., You, X.: Sensor Integration to LTE/LTE-A Network through MC-CDMA and Relaying. VTC Spring, 1–5 (2012)

[4] Mäenpää, J., Bolonio, J.J., Loreto, S.: Using RELOAD and CoAP for wide area sensor and actuator networking. EURASIP Journal on Wireless Communications and Networking 2012(1), 121 (2012)

[5] Jennings, C., Baset, S., Schulzrinne, H., Lowekamp, B., Rescorla, E.: REsource LOcation And Discovery (RELOAD) Base Protocol. In: 2013 IETF Internet-Draft, Intended status: Standards Track

[6] Shelby, Z., Hartke, K., Bormann, C.: Constrained Application Protocol (CoAP). In: 2013 IETF. Internet-Draft, Intended Status: Standards Track (2013)

[7] Jimenez, J., Lopez-Vega, J.M., Maenpaa, J., Camarillo, G.: A Constrained Application Protocol (CoAP) Usage for REsource LOcation And Discovery (RELOAD). In: 2013 IETF. Internet-Draft, Intended Status: Standards Track (2013)

[8] Mäenpää, J., Bolonio, J.J.: Performance of REsource LOcation and Discovery (RELOAD) on Mobile Phones. In: 2010 IEEE Wireless Communications and Networking Conference (WCNC). IEEE (2010)

[9] Tozlu, S., Senel, M.: Battery lifetime performance of Wi-Fi enabled sensors. In: 2012 IEEE Consumer Communications and Networking Conference (CCNC). IEEE (2012)

[10] Stoica, I., Morris, R., Liben-Nowell, D., Karger, D.R., Kaashoek, M.F., Dabek, F., Balakrishnan, H.: Chord: a scalable peer-to-peer lookup protocol for internet applications 11, 17–32 (2003)

[11] Rosenberg, J.: Interactive Connectivity Establishment (ICE): A Protocol for Network Address Translator (NAT) Traversal for Offer/Answer Protocols. RFC 5245 IETF (2010)

[12] Chawathe, Y., Ratnasamy, S., Breslau, L., Lanham, N., Shenker, S.: Making gnutella-like p2p systems scalable. In: Proceedings of the 2003 Conference on Applications, Technologies, Architectures, and Protocols for Computer Communications, pp. 407–418. ACM (2003)

[13] Vial, M.: CoRE Mirror Server. Draft-vial-core-mirror-proxy-01, IETF Internet-Draft, Intended Status: Standards Track (2013)

[14] Sturm, C., Dittrich, K.R., Ziegler, P.: An access control mechanism for P2P collaborations. In: Proceedings of the 2008 International Workshop on Data Management in Peer-to-Peer Systems. ACM (2008)

[15] Knauf, A., Schmidt, T.C., Hege, G., Waehlisch, M.: A Usage for Shared Resources in RELOAD (ShaRe). Draft-ietf-p2psip-share-01, 2013 IETF Internet-Draft, Intended status: Standards Track (2013)

Route-Over Forwarding Techniques
in a 6LoWPAN

Andreas Weigel[1], Martin Ringwelski[1], Volker Turau[1], and Andreas Timm-Giel[2]

[1] Institute of Telematics
[2] Institute of Communication Networks
Hamburg University of Technology, Hamburg, Germany
{andreas.weigel,martin.ringwelski,turau,timm-giel}@tuhh.de

Abstract. 6LoWPAN plays a major role within the protocol stack for
the future Internet of Things. Its fragmentation mechanism enables transport of IPv6 datagrams with the required minimum MTU of 1280 bytes
over 802.15.4-based wireless sensor networks. With the envisioned goal of
a fully standardized WSN protocol stack currently necessitating a route-
over approach, i.e. routing at the IP-layer, there are two main choices for
any 6LoWPAN implementation with regard to datagram fragmentation:
Hop-by-hop assembly or a cross-layered direct mode, which forwards individual 6LoWPAN fragments before the whole datagram has arrived. In
addition to these two straightforward approaches, we propose enhancements based on adaptive rate-restriction for the direct forwarding and
a retry control for both modes to reduce the number of losses of larger
datagrams. Our evaluation of the basic and enhanced forwarding modes
within simulations and a hardware testbed indicate that the proposed enhancements can considerably improve packet reception rate and latency
within 6LoWPAN networks.

Keywords: 6LoWPAN, fragmentation, 802.15.4, CometOS, forwarding, route-over, wireless sensor networks.

1 Introduction

Wireless sensor networks (WSNs) have a broad field of possible applications,
starting from smart homes via monitoring of industrial plants, agricultural fields
and personal health through to smart metering. WSNs are typically characterized by nodes with only constrained resources in terms of memory, computation
power and available energy and by wireless links which often exhibit lossy and
transient behavior. Until recently, these networks usually employed proprietary
protocols and therefore off-the-shelf solutions were either not available or not
interoperable.

The vision of the "Internet of Things" aims at providing each and every sensor with its own IPv6 address to make it accessible via proven and established
standard protocols. This idea has given rise to the development of a standardized
protocol, Transmission of IPv6 Packets over IEEE 802.15.4 Networks (RFC 4944

D. Pesch et al. (Eds.): MONAMI 2013, LNICST 125, pp. 122–135, 2013.

[1]; 6LoWPAN), which enables the use of IPv6 with the link layer protocol IEEE 802.15.4 [2]. The routing protocol for low power and lossy networks (RPL [3]) and its recent acceptance as a proposed standard as well as the constrained application protocol (CoAP [4]) complement the development towards a completely standardized IPv6 protocol stack for wireless sensor networks.

The 802.15.4 standard offers physical- and MAC-layers for low power wireless personal area networks (LoWPAN). While the MAC-frame size of those networks is only 127 bytes, IPv6 depends on a maximum transmission unit (MTU) of at least 1280 bytes.

6LoWPAN offers an intermediate layer between the IP- and the data link layer to overcome this issue. It defines compression algorithms for IPv6 headers and a fragmentation mechanism for larger IPv6 datagrams to be transportable within 802.15.4 MAC frames. Concerning the routing within a multi-hop wireless network, 6LoWPAN specifies two possibilities: mesh-under and route-over. With mesh-under, routing decisions are made at the adaption layer by some not specified routing protocol; the entire 6LoWPAN network appears to the IP layer as a single hop network. Following an approach with completely standardized protocols, we are only concerned with route-over, where routing decisions are made by a routing protocol at the IP layer, e.g. RPL.

Applying strict separation of layers with route-over, a node then needs to buffer incoming fragments in order to reassemble the complete datagram. If the arriving packet is in transit to another node, it has to be reassembled, handed to the IP layer for routing decisions and again has to be fragmented and sent to the next node. During the whole process, buffer space has to be reserved for the whole datagram. Considering the resource limitation of WSN hardware, where a buffer is likely to be not much larger than the MTU, this may necessitate dropping additional incoming datagrams for which no buffer space is left.

This is a known issue and the informational implementation guidelines [5] recommend the use of a virtual fragmentation buffer, which immediately forwards fragments which are just in transit to the next hop and only stores information necessary to identify and dispatch the following fragments. While such a direct forwarding scheme may overcome the buffering issue and even decrease the latency on longer paths by enabling pipelining of fragments, it is also likely to cause more collisions on the channel due to the hidden terminal problem.

Considering that lost fragments will inevitably lead to lost datagrams, the forwarding strategy has a tremendous impact on the performance within a 6LoWPAN-based wireless sensor network. Therefore, we evaluated the basic schemes and additionally propose rate-restriction mechanisms to prevent performance degradation using the direct mode and a retry-control mechanism to prevent the loss of nearly completely transmitted datagrams. These different modes are described in more detail in Section 3. An overview about past research in concerning 6LoWPAN fragmentation strategies is given in Section 2. Sections 4 and 5 provide information about the used simulation and testbed scenarios and the results of the experiments, respectively. Section 6 concludes this work.

2   Related Work

Different forwarding techniques for 6LoWPAN for IPv6 datagrams without and with fragmentation were evaluated by Ludovici et al. [6]. They analyzed end-to-end delay and loss-rate of a single sender for two route-over[1] and two mesh-under schemes within a line topology of up to five TelosB nodes, yielding a maximum network diameter of 4. One main result of their studies was the dramatically higher reliability of the route-over scheme compared to mesh-under and enhanced route-over, up to a datagram size at which maximum buffer capacity is approached and datagrams have to be dropped due to the lack of buffer space. On the other hand, end-to-end delay has been observed to be better for the three non-reassembling schemes.

A similar approach was adopted by Bhunia et al. [7]. Within a similar setup, they analyzed the end-to-end delay and loss rate for a single sender node within a small testbed with a line topology. Their observations are in line with those of [6].

In a draft of the IETF working group "Routing over low power and Lossy networks"[2], Thubert and Hui [8] describe an extension to RFC4944 which adds negative acknowledgements and fragment recovery mechanisms to 6LoWPAN. By means of recovery from individual fragment losses, the loss (and potentially congestion-causing upper layer retransmission) of whole datagrams is meant to be prevented. While certainly worth investigating, this can be seen as an orthogonal approach to the mechanisms proposed by us and will not be further evaluated here.

Wang et al. [9] proposed a method for mesh-under routing in 6LoWPANs, which reassembles packets at some intermediate nodes. Evaluating route-over, mesh-under and their chained mesh-under routing (C-MUR) in a testbed consisting of 6 nodes arranged in a line topology, they observed that C-MUR achieves a latency between mesh-under and route-over and a better packet reception rate than both for an increasing number of fragments.

An important issue when applying direct forwarding within a 6LoWPAN is the possible self-interference of fragments of the same datagram along a multihop path. Gnawali et al. acknowledged this problem of collisions with formerly forwarded frames, though within the slightly different context of their routing protocol for WSNs (CTP: Collection Tree Protocol [10]). To minimize the possibility for such self-interference, a restriction is introduced to the rate with which frames are forwarded by CTP. This technique is adopted by our rate-restricted modes which are introduced in Section 3.

---

[1] Route-over: the "classic" re-assembling mode; enhanced route-over: a virtual reassembling mode, which actually directly forwards individual fragments and thereby corresponds to our "Direct Mode"

[2] http://tools.ietf.org/wg/roll/

3 Forwarding Techniques

In the following, we call the approach of treating fragments of IPv6 datagrams corresponding to a strictly layered network stack **Assembly Mode**: Each datagram is completely reassembled at each intermediate IPv6 hop. In contrast, we use the term **Direct Mode** for the mechanism which works according to the implementation guidelines for 6LoWPAN [5]. Fragments of datagrams which are not destined to the receiving node are directly forwarded by determining the next hop from the IPv6 routing table. At arrival of the first fragment, a node creates an entry in a so-called virtual reassembly buffer, which is used to identify the following fragments and keep track of the status of in-transit datagrams.

3.1 Enhanced Direct Modes

When a node forwards an arrived fragment immediately to the next node it will compete for the channel with the previous node trying to send the next fragment. While this problem is solved by the CSMA/CA of the MAC Protocol, adding another hop will in many cases cause a hidden terminal problem and drastically increase the probability for collisions at the intermediate node. CTP (see Section 2) uses a rate restriction to decrease the impact of the hidden terminal problem in high traffic scenarios, i.e. in case nodes have several frames stored in their send queue: Every node, after having forwarded a frame, will delay the transmission of consecutive frames.

We adopted this strategy in two different ways: First, we defined and implemented a mode which is identical to the rate restriction proposed by the collection tree protocol. We observed a mean transmission time for a 96 bytes 6LoWPAN fragment of $t_{tx} = 6\,\mathrm{ms}$, including backoffs and transmission time. Under the assumption that a routing protocol will choose shortest paths, the channel will be free again after waiting for the duration of two transmissions following the initial one[3]. Therefore, after each transmission, we randomly schedule a delay t_d, with

$$1.5 \cdot t_{tx} \leq t_d \leq 2.5 \cdot t_{tx} \tag{1}$$

We call this mode **Direct Mode with Rate Restriction (Direct-RR)**.

This strategy, however, also has some obvious issues. First, the average transmission time can be different for different nodes, depending on their position within the network and the current traffic situation. Second, the transmission time strongly depends on the configuration of the 802.15.4 link layer, e.g., changing the minimum backoff exponent will dramatically increase the average duration of a transmission. To mitigate the impact of these issues, we propose an adaptation of the used transmission delays to the actual transmission time. We call this mode **Direct Mode with Adaptive Rate Restriction (Direct-ARR)**. Instead of setting a fixed rate restriction, the 6LoWPAN layer continuously measures the actual transmission time and calculates an exponentially

---

[3] Consider $A \to B \to C$ – when C has finished, the danger of a collision at B is greatly reduced.

weighted moving average (EWMA) to estimate the average transmission time: $t_{tx} = \alpha t_{tx} + (1-\alpha)t_{tx,curr}$. The actual delay is again determined by Equation (1). Note that, as the number of link layer retries also influences the transmission time, Direct-ARR mode essentially implements a local congestion avoidance.

3.2   Retry Control

Transmitting larger datagrams with several frames will increase the risk of one fragment getting lost on the way. One lost fragment results in the loss of the complete datagram. When such a loss occurs, all transmissions of fragments before have been in vain and worthlessly produced network traffic. For this reason and with IPv6 following a best-effort delivery, link layer retries are desperately needed to prevent unacceptably high end-to-end loss rates. Therefore we set the number of link layer retries to 7 in our experiments and simulations.

Additionally, we propose a retry control mode to decrease the probability of unnecessary transmitted frames in the network. If a large part of a datagram has already been transmitted successfully to the next hop, we put more effort on transmitting the following parts. We call this method **Progress-Based Retry Control (PRC)**. The number of retries is calculated as follows, where s is the size of the fragmented datagram and s_{trans} the already transmitted size:

$$N_{Retries} = 7 + 8 \times \frac{s_{trans}}{s} \tag{2}$$

This results in a number of 7 to 15 MAC retries, with 15 being the maximum number of retries provided by the hardware-supported automatic acknowledgement mechanism of the transceiver used within our testbed.

4   Methodology

We integrated all forwarding techniques into our 6LoWPAN implementation for CometOS[4] [11]. CometOS enables the reuse of its C++ module implementations for simulations within the OMNeT++ framework and for the testbed deployment. To avoid influence of any routing mechanism to the measurement result, we applied a static routing scheme during all experiments. CometOS' physical channel model is based on the MiXiM framework[5]. For our simulation runs, we used a channel model resembling a LogNormal Shadowing with a given fixed average signal strength and a variance. Different from a standard propagation model, we configured each link individually by means of a configuration file.

4.1   Scenarios

For simulations we considered four different network topologies as shown in Figure 1. The chain-like network (Fig. 1a) was chosen because we expect that the

---

[4] http://www.ti5.tuhh.de/research/projects/cometos/
[5] http://mixim.sourceforge.net/index.html

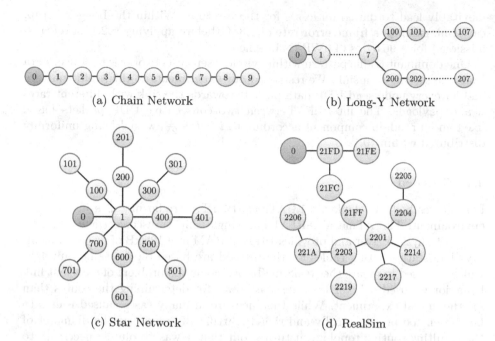

(a) Chain Network

(b) Long-Y Network

(c) Star Network

(d) RealSim

Fig. 1. Simulated networks. Edges represent static routes, the dark gray node is the sink.

benefits of pipelining fragments are most clearly visible in this setup. In contrast, the "Star" network (Fig. 1c) exhibits paths with a maximum of three hops and therefore does not yield any potential for pipelining and clearly favors the assembly modes in this regard. On the other hand, it contains enough nodes routing their traffic over the central node to reveal potential bottlenecks concerning the available buffer space. The Y network (Fig. 1b) again provides tremendous potential for pipelining while at the same time it contains a potential bottleneck.

The RealSim network (1d) was modeled after a real world network and thereby represents a more typical WSN topology. It was created by collecting link data (received signal strength indicator (RSSI) mean and variance, packet reception rate (PRR)) from the testbed itself and installing the corresponding links into our physical channel model. Static routes for this scenario were created by executing the Dijkstra algorithm on the collected link data, where the weight of the edges was set as the product of the ETX values for incoming and outgoing links. Although this approach does not capture the transient properties of links within a real world deployment, where links may exhibit dramatic changes of the experienced PRR, or the possible interference from other networks (IEEE 802.11), it enables the comparison of results from the testbed with those from a equivalent simulated network topology.

Within the Chain and Star networks, the links were set to artificially achieve a PRR of virtually 100% at the link layer, frame collisions on the other hand inevitably lead to datagram losses for those setups. Within the Long-Y setup, each link exhibits a frame error rate of 8.3 % (before applying 802.15.4 retransmissions) for a 96 bytes 6LoWPAN fragment.

One dominant traffic pattern within wireless sensor networks is to collect data from the sensors to a sink. We restricted our experiments to this traffic pattern and let every node send UDP data packets towards the sink with different rates λ and payloads. The interval i between two consecutive UDP packets has a fixed and a random component according to $i = I + \frac{1}{2\lambda}$, with I being uniformly distributed within $\left[0, \frac{1}{\lambda}\right]$.

4.2   Testbed

For the testbed, we deployed 13 ATmega128RFA1 radio modules in an office environment. The ATmega128RFA1 is a single chip transceiver/mcu using an 802.15.4 physical layer and provides 16 kB of RAM and 128 kB of program memory. The static routing tables for the testbed are based on the same link data which are used to create the RealSim. To overcome the problem of transient link behavior we used a lower transmission power for determining the routes than for the actual experiment. While this measure in many cases caused routes to be chosen too pessimistically and thereby artificially increased the diameter of the resulting routing topology, it turned out that it was absolutely necessary to guarantee that the network was connected most of the time.

To be able to determine the latencies of UDP packets within the testbed we introduced a time synchronization mechanism which makes use of timestamps within the transceiver driver. In order to keep the traffic overhead introduced by this mechanism low, we reduced the rate at which new synchronization beacons are sent to an average of once every 75 s.

The 6LoWPAN layer of our implementation has an assembly buffer of 2000 bytes, which is also used for buffering enqueued fragments. In the assembly mode it is possible to reassemble up to 10 datagrams (given that their combined size fits into the buffer). In the direct modes, only 4 datagrams can be reassembled; instead a tiny fragment buffer can forward up to 15 datagrams. With this configuration both modes use exactly the same amount of RAM yielding a basis for a fair comparison.

5   Evaluation

In this section we compare the different forwarding techniques in terms of packet reception rate (PRR) and latency. Our RealSim network is used to verify the comparability of the simulation results with the testbed network. In the simulations we used five runs with each node sending 2 000 UDP packets each run. In the testbed we send 48 000 bytes in UDP packets of 100, 400 and 1200 bytes payload. This results in 40 packets of 1200 bytes to 480 packets of 100 bytes per

Table 1. Configuration of the underlying 802.15.4-based MAC layer

macMinBE	macMaxBE	macMaxCSMABackoffs	macMaxFrameRetries
3	8	5	7

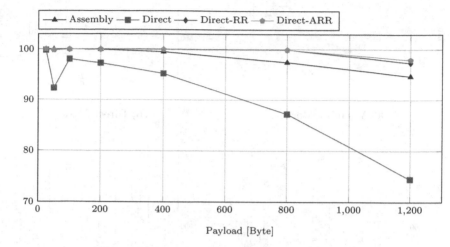

Fig. 2. PRR of the Chain Network 37.5 B/s

run in the testbed. Nine runs were executed per configuration. During all experiments and simulations, the 802.15.4 MAC was set to use the configuration shown in table 1.

For depicting the latencies, we use boxplots, depicting the minimum and maximum measurements by its whiskers, the 10th and 90th percentile by the box and the median by the line in the middle.

5.1   Chain Network

In the Chain Network, the Direct-RR Mode achieves a better PRR and latency than the Assembly Mode (Figure 2) while the Direct mode suffers from heavy packet losses due to collisions caused by self-interference. Up to packet sizes of 800 bytes, Direct-ARR has a PRR of almost 100%, which drops to 96.9% at 1200 bytes packet size. As expected, the Direct modes exhibited significantly better latency for large fragmented datagrams (shown for 1200 bytes in Figure 3), although for a small percentage of datagrams the maximum values exceed those of the assembly mode. For nodes farther away from the sink, the advantage of pipelining datagrams by reusing the channel becomes obvious.

As the PRR is near optimum for the Chain Network, PRC has limited impact on the results and is omitted here. Only the Direct Mode without any Rate Restriction can profit from PRC with an increased PRR by 3%, but is 17% worse than the Assembly Mode.

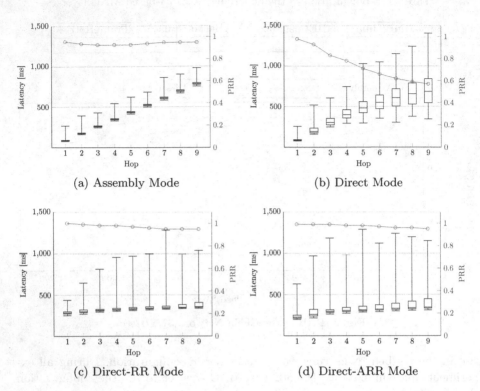

(a) Assembly Mode

(b) Direct Mode

(c) Direct-RR Mode

(d) Direct-ARR Mode

Fig. 3. Per hop latency and PRR in the Chain Network with 37.5 B/s and 1200 bytes payload

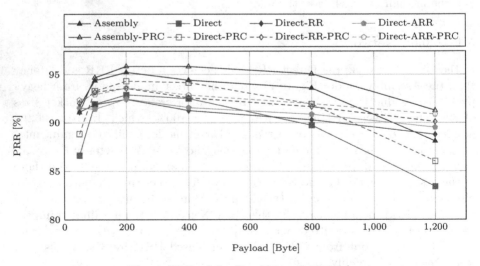

Fig. 4. PRR of the Star Network 37.5 B/s

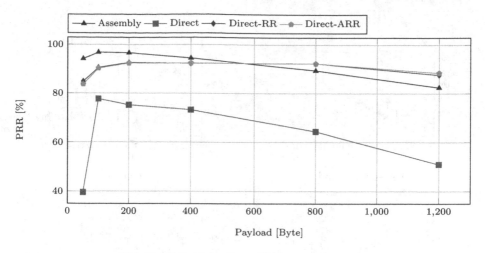

Fig. 5. PRR of the Long-Y Network 37.5 B/s

5.2 Star Network

Within the Star Network, no forwarding mode achieves a PRR of 100% (Figure 4). Multiple opportunities for hidden-terminal-caused collisions exist in every branch and at the centering node, whereas the possibilities for self-interference (and pipelining) on the short way are rare. For these reasons, assembly and direct modes perform similarly in terms of PRR and latency (which we omitted). The comparatively steep drop in PRR of the assembly mode at 1200 bytes is due an increased number of drops caused by lack of buffer space at the central node. For the Star Network, the usage of retry control increases the PRR by 2% to 4%.

5.3 Long-Y Network

In the Long-Y Network, the Direct-RR and Direct-ARR Mode show almost no difference and perform comparably to the Assembly Mode regarding the PRR (Figure 5). For payloads over 800 bytes these modes exhibit an even better PRR than the Assembly Mode. With PRR getting down to 60% and only up to less than 90%, the classical Direct Mode performs impractically even with the PRC enhancement.

In terms of average latency (see Fig. 6), the rate-restricted direct modes outperform the Assembly Mode significantly: For 1200 bytes and at a distance of 15 hops, the median of the direct modes (RR: 395 ms, ARR: 392 ms) is less than a third of that of the Assembly Mode (1311 ms).

All of the PRR results show that the PRR with 100 bytes is higher than with 50 bytes payload. This can be explained by the fact that 50 and 100 bytes payload both result in a datagram with two fragments (with the corresponding control overhead), but the datagrams of 100 bytes payload are sent at only half the rate.

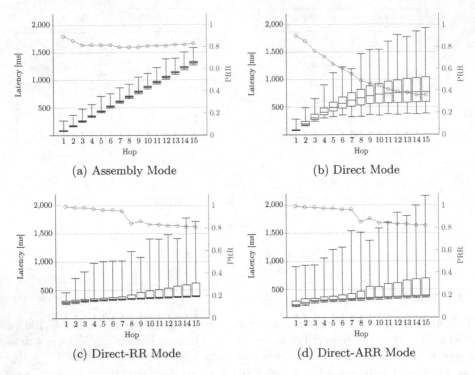

Fig. 6. Per hop latency and PRR in the Long-Y Network with 37.5 B/s and 1200 bytes payload

5.4 RealSim and Testbed

Figures 7a and 7b show the PRR of the RealSim and Testbed Network with a byte rate of 37.5 B/s. Note that payloads of 50, 200 and 800 Bytes have not been used in the testbed, but only within the simulation. Naturally, some differences can be observed between simulation and experiments in the real network. The overall PRR for all modes are lower and the confidence intervals of averages from the testbed are more widespread. We explain these differences with the nature of a real world environment. During the experiments, there were people moving in the office building, which also contains various WiFi hotspots causing additional interference. The mechanism for time synchronization additionally puts a small load on the real network. Nevertheless, the results show similar tendencies and confirm the simulation results as an accurate-enough estimation of the real world.

As a first result we can see that the Direct Mode has the worst PRR of all modes. Direct-ARR outperforms Direct and Direct-RR, but has still a worse PRR than the Assembly Mode. This trend can be observed in the testbed even stronger than in the RealSim.

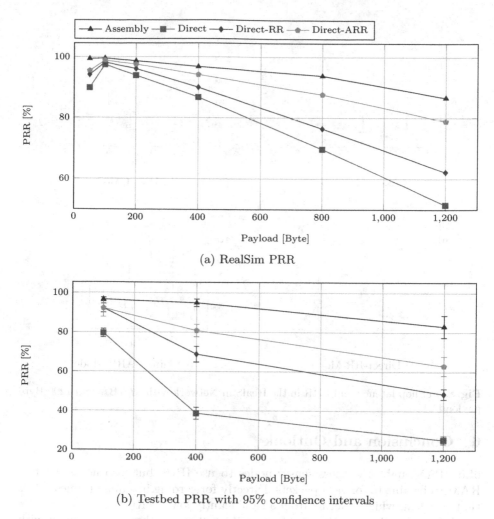

(a) RealSim PRR

(b) Testbed PRR with 95% confidence intervals

Fig. 7. Comparing the packet reception rates of the RealSim and the Testbed Network with a byte rate of 37.5 B/s. Note the different scaling of the y-axes.

Figures 8a, 8b, 8c and 8d show the latency results for the RealSim Network with the Assembly, Direct, Direct-RR and Direct-ARR Mode. We can see that the Direct Mode has no significant difference in latency, but the PRR drops dramatically for further hops. The rate restriction of the Direct-ARR mode achieves similar latencies, while achieving a higher PRR, though the latency is more widespread. It has to be noted that the static routes chosen for RealSim and testbed did not reflect the actual transmission range of the nodes (see 4.2), and the "real" network diameter most of the time was rather 4 instead of 7. Therefore, the direct modes could not benefit from pipelining and exhibit latencies not better than the Assembly Mode.

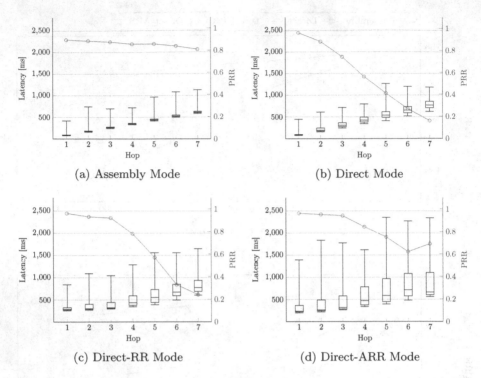

(a) Assembly Mode

(b) Direct Mode

(c) Direct-RR Mode

(d) Direct-ARR Mode

Fig. 8. Per hop latency and PRR in the RealSim Network with 37.5 B/s and 1200 Byte payload

6   Conclusion and Outlook

6LoWPAN enables wireless sensor nodes to use IPv6, but also needs a lot of RAM to be able to forward packets. Directly forwarding incoming frames solves that problem, while suffering from a significantly lower PRR.

We introduced three advanced forwarding techniques that are compliant with the 6LoWPAN standard. These can increase the PRR of the direct mode to almost the same level as the Assembly Mode. In scenarios with many hops tailored for pipelining these direct modes with a rate restriction exhibited a significantly lower latency than the Assembly Mode while at the same time having a better or similar PPR. On the other hand, the assembly mode beats all direct modes in the testbed configuration.

Of the two enhanced direct modes, Direct-ARR yielded the better results regarding PRR and latency within all simulations and the testbed. The PRR of all modes could be slightly increased by the introduced retry control, although the impact is not as large as hoped.

In the future work the selective retry control will have to prove itself against a flat increase of retries. While the latter may even further increase the PRR in many situations, we want to explore the behavior in high traffic situations, where it may also cause additional congestion.

To further increase the performance of 6LoWPAN implementations, we plan to implement a fragment recovery mechanism (see Section 2) and combine it with the (adaptive) rate restriction and/or retry control.

So far, we used only a single and rather aggressive configuration of the 802.15.4 MAC for our experiments. We are going to explore the influence of different parameter sets in the future.

References

1. Montenegro, G., Kushalnagar, N., Hui, J., Culler, D.: Transmission of IPv6 Packets over IEEE 802.15.4 Networks. RFC 4944 (Proposed Standard) (September 2007)
2. IEEE Standard for Local and Metropolitan Area Networks— Part 15.4: Low-Rate Wireless Personal Area Networks (2011)
3. Winter, T., Thubert, P., Brandt, A., Hui, J., Kelsey, R., Levis, P., Pister, K., Struik, R., Vasseur, J., Alexander, R.: RPL: IPv6 Routing Protocol for Low-Power and Lossy Networks. RFC 6550 (Proposed Standard) (March 2012)
4. Shelby, Z., Hartke, K., Bormann, C.: Constrained Application Protocol (CoAP) (May 2013), http://tools.ietf.org/pdf/draft-ietf-core-coap-17.pdf (accessed: June 11 2013)
5. Bormann, C.: 6LoWPAN Roadmap and Implementation Guide (draft) (April 2013), http://tools.ietf.org/pdf/draft-bormann-6lowpan-roadmap-04.pdf (accessed: May 30, 2013)
6. Ludovici, A., Calveras, A., Casademont, J.: Forwarding Techniques for IP Fragmented Packets in a Real 6LoWPAN Network. Sensors (Basel) 11(1), 992–1008 (2011)
7. Bhunia, S.S., Sikder, D.K., Roy, S., Mukherjee, N.: A comparative study on routing schemes of IP based wireless sensor network. In: 2012 Ninth International Conference on Wireless and Optical Communications Networks (WOCN), pp. 1–5 (September 2012)
8. Thubert, P., Hui, J.: LLN Fragment Forwarding and Recovery (draft) (February 2013),http://tools.ietf.org/html/draft-thubert-roll-forwarding-frags-01 (accessed: June 11, 2013)
9. Zhu, Y.-H., Chen, G., Chi, K., Li, Y.: The Chained Mesh-Under Routing (C-MUR) for Improving IPv6 Packet Arrival Rate over Wireless Sensor Networks. In: Wang, R., Xiao, F. (eds.) CWSN 2012. CCIS, vol. 334, pp. 734–743. Springer, Heidelberg (2013)
10. Gnawali, O., Fonseca, R., Jamieson, K., Moss, D., Levis, P.: Collection tree protocol. In: Proceedings of the 7th ACM Conference on Embedded Networked Sensor Systems, SenSys 2009, pp. 1–14. ACM, New York (2009)
11. Unterschütz, S., Weigel, A., Turau, V.: Cross-Platform Protocol Development Based on OMNeT++. In: Proceedings of the 5th International Workshop on OMNeT++ (OMNeT++ 2012) (March 2012)

An Adaptive Algorithm to Optimize the Dynamics of IEEE 802.15.4 Networks

Javier Hurtado-López and Eduardo Casilari

University of Malaga,
ETSI Telecomunicacion, Campus de Teatinos, 29071
{jhurtado,ecasilari}@uma.com

Abstract. IEEE 802.15.4 standard is becoming one of the most popular technologies for the deployment of low rate Wireless Personal Area Networks with strong power constraints. In order to reduce the energy consumption, beacon-enabled networks with long network inactive periods can be employed. However, the duration of these inactivity periods, as some other configuration parameters, are conventionally set to default values and remain fixed during the whole network operation. This implies that if they are misconfigured the network will not adapt to changes in the conditions of the environment, particularly to the most determining one, i.e. the traffic load. This paper proposes a simple procedure for the dynamic adaptation of several key parameters of IEEE 802.15.4 networks. Under this procedure, the 802.15.4 parameters are modified as a function of the existing traffic conditions.

Keywords: IEEE 802.15.4, Wireless Sensor Networks, optimization, CSMA/CA.

1   Introduction

IEEE 802.15.4 standard [1] defines the Physical layer (PHY) and the Medium Access Control layer (MAC) for the communication of low-power Wireless Sensor Networks (WSN). Specifications such as ZigBee [2] or 6LoWPAN [3] are built on IEEE 802.15.4 standard to complete the protocol stack for Low-Rate Wireless Personal Area Networks (LR-WPAN). This stack is designed to satisfy the market needs for energy efficient, low cost (bellow one dollar) and low rate wireless embedded devices. IEEE 802.15.4 compliant transceivers operate in the Industrial Scientific and Medical (ISM) radio bands with a maximum transfer rate of 250 kbps at 2.4 GHz (with 16 available channels), which can be decreased to 40 kbps or even down to 20 kbps at the 915/868 MHz bands (channels 0 to 10). The standard also contemplates the possibility of providing real time services through Guaranteed Time Slots (GTS).

There are two different modes for the MAC sublayer to operate: (1) the beaconless mode, also denominated point to point, in which unslotted CSMA/CA is used between nodes to communicate, and (2) the beacon-enabled mode, which utilizes slotted CSMA/CA. In this last case communications are synchronized through the transmission of beacons, i.e. a special type of frame that is periodically emitted by specific nodes (coordinators). In order to keep synchronized, nodes must associate to

D. Pesch et al. (Eds.): MONAMI 2013, LNICST 125, pp. 136–148, 2013.

a coordinator and stay active to receive the Beacon. Under this beacon mode, transmissions are only allowed within a special period, the Contention Access Period (CAP), which begins immediately after the Beacon emission and whose duration is defined by the coordinator. After the CAP, GTS (Guaranteed Time Slots) may take place. During the remaining time until the next Beacon, the nodes enter into a low consumption state (or sleeping mode) reducing their duty cycle and consequently saving battery power. Although the beaconless operation mode is less complex and does not present any scalability problem (as far as it allows nodes to transmit at any moment), it may force the nodes to be listening to the radio channel continuously. This leads to a useless waste of energy while GTS are not possible. On the other hand, the beacon-enabled mode is more complex to configure and implement as it may demand a strict synchronization of the nodes.

The main challenge and also the main attractiveness of IEEE 802.15.4 is its potentiality to set up self-organizing networks capable of adapting to diverse topologies, node connectivity and traffic conditions. In fact, most advantages of employing IEEE 802.15.4 strongly depend on the configuration of the Medium Access Control (MAC) sublayer.

This paper proposes several enhancements for the dynamics of the IEEE 802.15.4 MAC layer. The proposal includes different algorithms to adapt and optimize the activity periods and the time of transmission of the nodes in an IEEE 802.15.4 compliant star network according to the traffic load. The analysis of the performed simulations shows that a wrong election of the beacon-enabled mode parameters may severely affect the global network behavior.

This paper is organized as follows: Section 2 briefly describes the configuration and operation of beacon-enabled IEEE 802.15.4 network. The section also reviews some existing proposals to adapt the configuration to the traffic load. Section 3 presents the algorithms proposed to optimize the network performance while Section 4 compares them by means of simulations. The final Section 5 summarizes the main conclusions and suggests some possible research lines.

2   Configuration of 802.15.4 Networks

The IEEE 802.15.4 standard defines two types of devices: Full-Function Devices (FFD) and Reduced-Function Devices (RFD). The last ones are only enabled to communicate with its coordinator. Typical leaf nodes, such as sensors, will be RFDs. FFDs may play any role in the network, i.e. coordinator (PAN coordinator or intermediate router in multihop networks) or leaf node. A coordinator manages and centralizes the communications of a star topology formed by a set of associated nodes. When operating in a beacon-enabled mode a coordinator announces itself and the corresponding network identifier by broadcasting beacons periodically. The nodes associated with a coordinator must synchronize to this frame. The time between two consecutive beacons is called the Beacon Interval (*BI*) and its structure is called Superframe (see Figure 1). The Superframe can be divided into two periods: an active part and an inactive one. All the communications between a coordinator and its 'children' must take place during the active portion of the Superframe, also known as Superframe Duration (*SD*). All nodes, including the coordinator may go into a power saving mode or sleeping state during the inactive period to extend their batteries lifetime.

The whole structure of the Superframe is governed by the values of two MAC numerical parameters: the *macBeaconOrder* (*BO*) and the *macSuperframeOrder* (*SO*). *BO* and *SO* define the values of *BI* and *SD* as it follows:

$$BI = a \cdot 2^{BO} \text{ for } 0 \leq BO \leq 14 \tag{1}$$

$$SD = a \cdot 2^{SO} \text{ with } 0 \leq SO \leq BO \leq 14 \tag{2}$$

where *a* is the Base Superframe duration (15.36, 24 or 48 ms depending on the employed bit rate: 250, 40 or 20 kbps respectively). The values of *BO* and *SO* are limited to the [0, 14] interval. In addition the value of the *SO* must remain equal or lower than *BO*. The ratio *SO/BO* is called the duty-cycle. The lower the duty-cycle the larger the inactive period. If *SO=BO* (i.e. duty-cycle is 1) no inactive period would exist and the Superframe Duration would coincide with the whole Beacon Interval.

The active period of the superframe is divided into sixteen slots. The first one (slot 0) is reserved for the beacon. This frame must be received by all the associated devices so that they must be awake for this first slot. Up to seven Guaranteed Time Slots may be assigned to some nodes at the end of the *SD* in order to provide QoS (Quality of Service). This is called the Contention Free Period (CFP). The Contention Access Period (CAP) extends between slot zero and the CFP. Within the CAP, devices contend for the channel and communications are regulated by slotted CSMA/CA.

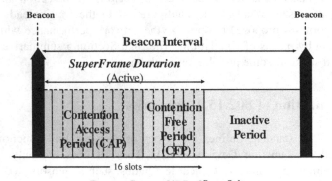

Beacon Interval (*BI*)=2$^{\text{Beacon Order}}$
Superframe Duration (*SD*)=2^{SuperFrameOrder}

Fig. 1. 802.15.4. Superframe

2.1   CSMA/CA

Slotted CSMA/CA channel access algorithm shall be normally used in IEEE 802.15.4 beacon-enabled networks to transmit data or commands within the CAP. Figure 2 illustrates the Slotted CSMA/CA algorithm flow chart.

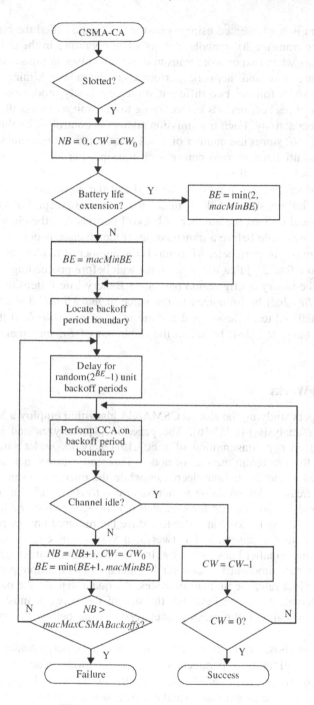

Fig. 2. Stotted CSMA/CA algorithm [1]

The algorithm is implemented using its own unit of time called the backoff period (time required to transmit 20 symbols: 320 μs when operating in the 2.4 GHz band). A collision occurs when two or more transmissions take place at the same time. If this happens data are lost and network performance degrades. Aiming at avoiding collisions CSMA/CA follows two different strategies: firstly, nodes must wait for a random number of backoff periods before trying to transmit and secondly the channel is sensed to detect activity. Each transmission attempt is controlled by three variables: *NB*, *CW* and *BE*. *NB* stores the number of times that the current transmission has been attempted. It is initialized to zero before each transmission and incremented in one unit if the channel is sensed to be busy. If *NB* rises above the threshold defined by *macMaxCSMABackoffs*, transmission is aborted and the algorithm terminates with a channel access failure status. *CW* is initialized to two (except for the 950 MHz Japanese band) and defines the number of backoff periods that the channel has to be consecutively sensed idle before a transmission. If the channel is detected to be busy, CW is reset to zero. The parameter *BE* controls the number of random backoff periods (in the range from 0 to 2^{BE}) that the nodes must wait before proceeding to the channel assessment. If the binary configuration parameter Battery Life Extension (BLE) is set to false (zero) *BE* shall be initialized to the value of *macMinBE*. Otherwise, if true, *BE* shall be initialized to the lesser of 2 and the value of *macMinBE*. If the channel is assessed to be busy, *BE* shall be set to the minimum of *BE* incremented by 1 and *macMaxBE*.

2.2   Related Works

Most of the papers studying the slotted CSMA/CA algorithm employ a Markov chain model for their analysis [4] [5] [6]. The paper in [4] analyzes and simulates the throughput and energy consumption of a 802.15.4 network under saturated traffic conditions and for a different number of nodes. This study shows that, as the number of nodes increases, the throughput decreases while the energy consumption per one slot payload increases. An extension to non-saturated traffic conditions can be found in [5]. Their analysis probes that for saturated networks, it is preferable to choose a large exponential delay backoff in order to reduce the required energy per useful bit. On the other hand, for unsaturated networks, a very small energy saving can be achieved by setting smaller backoff values. In [6] the authors characterize (also using the theory of discrete time Markov chains) the interaction of multiple parameters such as the packet arrival rate, the number of nodes, the queue length, the packet size and the Beacon Interval. They conclude that the size of the network must be kept very small in order to maintain the mean packet service time below the duration of the superframe.

As it refers to those works that study the MAC layer performance for different values of its configuration parameters (e.g. *macMinBE, macMaxFrameRetries, macMaxCSMABackoffs*), those in [7], [8], and [9] should be highlighted. In [7] and [8], the authors evaluate by simulation and experimentation the reliability of the MAC layer. They conclude that, when using the default values proposed by the standard, as the number of network nodes increases, the rate of delivery or delivery ratio, rapidly decreases. This performance decline is shown to be significant even for only five network nodes. In [9] a cross-layer solution to the various problems encountered is proposed.

Aiming at maximizing the throughput for a beaconed star topology the article in [10] focuses on the impact of the Backoff Exponent (*BE*). According to their ns-2 simulations the authors state that reducing the minimum default value of BE from three to one and adjusting it individually for every node (basing on the data to be transmitted) can result in an increase in the transfer rate of up to 45%. On the other hand, in the slotted version of CSMA/CA, if it is not possible to transmit in the a certain CAP, the packets are stored by the nodes so that their transmission is deferred until the beginning of the next CAP. This causes transmission attempts to be concentrated at the beginning of the CAP, which results in an increment in the packet collision probability. This is known as the access congestion problem. The more the network is saturated the more this problem will arise. The origin of the access congestion problem according to [11] is that, to reduce the consumption of the network, the initial value of BE is too small. This provokes that many nodes will calculate the same random delay value and consequently they will try to transmit simultaneously, which will induce packet collisions. The authors propose an algorithm that adapts the value of BE to the particular circumstances of the network to alleviate the problem. Authors suggest that the same algorithm may be applied to check the network load and to adapt the superframe duration appropriately to fit the requirements of the network under the current traffic load. However, the proposal is left for further research.

The main way to adapt a beaconed 802.15.4 network to the traffic conditions is to modify the duty-cycle, i.e. the ratio between the Superframe Order and the Beacon Order. A traffic adaptive Superframe Order is proposed in [12]. In this work if the queue occupation of a node exceeds a certain threshold it issues a special packet to the coordinator. Once that it is received, the coordinator sets a 100% duty cycle in the next superframe. When the coordinator does not receive any of these packets during several superframes it diminishes the value of the Superframe Order. The weakness of this approach is that it requires that the node can communicate with the coordinator. Thus if the node's queue is full because of the device's difficulties to transmit, the coordinator will not receive the packet and no adaption will be performed to the SO. A possible solution can be found in [13] where a special broadcast tone is emitted by a node after the CAP if it is unable to transmit or have not received the acknowledgement packets. The coordinator extends the CAP when it receives this tone. However this idea is not fully compatible with the standard as it requires the coordinator to be active after the CAP. Moreover it cannot be easily extendable to clustered networks. A different approach can be found in [14] and [15] where the coordinator is in charge of estimating the need of adaption by tracing the frequency of the communications of its children. In these papers the same duty-cycle adaptation to traffic can be achieved by modifying the Beacon Order parameter instead of the Superframe Order. The main conclusion of these studies is that certain trade-offs between the desired power saving and the delay have to be found. Energy can be saved if delay is sacrificed.

Our study is focused in relatively large networks (101 nodes) under heavy traffic conditions.

3   Proposed Algorithms

In the following subsection we present two strategies that are intended to reduce the impact of a bad election of the Superframe Order (SO) and the initial random CSMA/CA backoff wait time on the performance of a 802.15.4 star network.

3.1   Superframe Order Adaptation Algorithm

As it can be observed in expressions (1) and (2), for beacon-enabled networks, both *BO* and *SO* are key parameters. It is important to notice that they are defined as constant parameters. Thus, once they are configured, their value will never change regardless of the circumstances of the network (in particular, the traffic load). It may occur that real traffic network conditions or traffic patterns differ from those assumed during the design and the deployment of the network leading to a performance degradation which will be caused by a misconfiguration of these parameters.

The time between two consecutive Beacons i.e. the Beacon Interval, only depends on the *BO* parameter, therefore it seems reasonable that, in a star network, the whole average latency strongly depends on the *BO* selection. This is why the *BO* value is typically dictated by the application level and the actual requirements of the corresponding WSN. For this reason, in this paper we do not consider the adaptation of the *BO*. Thus, regarding the SuperFrame Structure only the *SO* parameter can be modified in order to try to accommodate the network configuration to the traffic.

Selecting a wrong Superframe Order value can have serious implications for the performance of the network even if the traffic is always the same. If the value configured for the *SO* is low and the traffic is high, the network will most probably not be able to process all the packets properly since contention access periods will be too small. On the other hand, suppose the extreme case of a network in which the SuperFrame Order is set to a high value and there is no traffic; this configuration would unnecessarily force the coordinator to be active during long periods, increasing the consumption and reducing the battery lifetime. This fact is aggravated in the case of cluster multihop networks where more nodes acting as intermediate routers exist.

A different scenario could be that of a network where traffic conditions vary. For example, consider a WSN in which several types of sensors coexist. Suppose that most of the time there is little or no traffic, in this case it seems appropriate to fix the value of the *SO* to its minimum, i.e. zero. However it may happen that some of the sensors, according to their nature, periodically turn on and transmit data causing local traffic peaks. In this scenario it would be adequate to dynamically adapt the value of *SO*, increasing it when those sensors activate and returning to the minimum once the traffic is processed. So, the main goal of our adaptive scheme consists in trying to detect the local variations that may occur in the traffic and then decide whether the *SO* should be changed or not.

In our solution, as a first strategy, we propose that the network coordinator performs a count of the number of frames received from each of its children at every interval between beacons and computes the relative increase or decrease of the traffic load. Then there are three possibilities. Firstly, if an important traffic growth is detected the coordinator will assume that the traffic has considerably increased so that the duty cycle of the nodes (*SO/BO* ratio) should be augmented. In that case, the value of *SO* is incremented in 1 unit in order to enlarge the Superframe Duration and to make more time available for data transmissions. Secondly, if a significant reduction is computed, traffic is considered to have decreased and *SO* should be decremented (if possible). If not relevant changes in the traffic load are detected, the Superframe Order is left unchanged.

The modification of the Superframe Order in a Start Network is extremely easy to propagate to the whole network as it only involves the transmission of the new value of the *SO* in the next Beacon (every Beacon contains a reserved field to inform about the value of the *SO*) and every node must listen to the coordinator's Beacons. So this algorithm is fully compatible with the standard and does not introduce any protocol overload in the sense that it requires no additional information. In our implementation we have included two different control parameters so that two thresholds (U_1, U_2) can be set to determine if a change in the relative traffic received from a node is significant or not. The first one (U_1) determines when the *SO* must be increased while the second one (U_2) governs the reductions of the superframe order.

Mathematically the adaptation of *SO* can be described as:

$$\begin{rcases} [x[n+1]-x[n]] > U_1 \\ and \\ SO[n+1] < BO \end{rcases} \Rightarrow SO[n+2] = SO[n+1]+1 \tag{3}$$

$$\begin{rcases} [x[n+1]-x[n]] < -U_2 \\ and \\ SO[n+1] > 0 \end{rcases} \Rightarrow SO[n+2] = SO[n+1]-1 \tag{4}$$

where *x[n]* and *SO[n]* respectively represents the traffic (number of packets) received by the coordinator and the value of the Superframe Order during the *n-th* beacon interval, while and U_1 and U_2 are the aforementioned decision thresholds.

3.2   Backoff Exponent Adaptation Algorithm

This is the second adaptation strategy presented in this paper. As seen in the section 2.1 the Backoff Exponent (*BE*) parameter is another fundamental parameter in the CSMA/CA algorithm. Depending on its value a node determines the random delay time before every transmission to minimize the probability of collision. By default, 802.15.4 standard establishes an initial value of three for *BE*, which can be incremented up to five if the radio channel is sensed to be busy twice. Even if *BE* is 5, just a maximum of thirty-one different backoff waiting periods are possible, while a CAP enables up to 786,432 backoff periods. So it is not unusual that some nodes will calculate the same random delay value and try to transmit simultaneously causing a collision. This may become a major problem for those configurations of star networks in which the CAP is not large enough to process all the traffic load or if there is a high traffic density within the active Superframe, which may be caused by a misconfiguration of the *SO* parameter. Another related problem is the access congestion which was previously described.

As a solution to alleviate these problems we propose an algorithm that adapts the value of *BE* to the particular circumstances of the network. The idea behind the algorithm is to calculate the random delay time that precedes every transmission following a uniform distribution along a configurable percentage of the overall duration of the Contention Access Period. By increasing the random wait before the packet emission, the algorithm aspires to reduce the Access Congestion Problem with a better distribution of the traffic within the CAP. This is obviously achieved at the cost of increasing the packet delay.

4   Simulation and Results

In order to evaluate the performance of the precedent algorithms, we have implemented and simulated them in the OMNeT++ 4.2.2 Inetmanet IEEE 802.15.4 UndertTest environment [16], [17]. The selected scenario consists of a star network topology formed by a hundred leaf nodes and a coordinator. Neither the network creation phase nor Guaranteed Time Slots are considered. There is no possible hidden node effect because every node is in the range of interference of the rest. In our study there only exists uplink traffic, i.e. from the nodes to the coordinator, except for the Beacons. This could be a realistic scenario of a wireless sensor network in which the sensors (leaf nodes) consist of simple RFD end devices while the coordinator could be a more complex FFD node acting as a sink of the information sent by the sensors.

The network is programmed to operate at the channel 11 (2.4 GHz band) at 250 kbps. As the performance metrics we define:

-Queue Drops: percentage of packets discarded by nodes' queue. A node queue drops a packet when it is full. The selected queue length is 10 packets.

-Transmission losses, which reflect the percentage of packet transmissions that have reached the maximum number of allowed retries so that the packet is dropped by the node.

-Average delay: for every packet received by the coordinator we compute the difference between its generation and arrival times. Thus the average delay in seconds is defined as the average of all these differences.

-Collisions: The overall number of collisions that take place in the network.

-Energy per bit: global cost (miliJoules) involving the transmission of a single bit, defined as:

$$\text{Energy/bit} \left(\frac{\text{mJ}}{\text{bit}} \right) = \frac{\text{Network Consumed Energy (W·s)}}{(\text{Total Received } Bytes) \text{x } 8} \text{ x } 1000 \tag{5}$$

For all the simulations the Beacon Order is set to 5 and the packet size is 10 bytes while the inter arrival time of the packets follow an exponential distribution with a mean value of 1 s. For most typical applications of WSN, this configuration of the network (100 leaf nodes and one packet per second and node) can be considered an example of heavy traffic load conditions as long as an average of 100 packets will be sent to the coordinator every second. Most of these packets will contend for the same radio resource during the CAP. Thus many collisions, delays and packets drops are expected to occur.

The employed energy model storages the time a device stays in each of the four possible states idle, reception, sleep and transmission in seconds. Table 1 presents the current consumption in mA for a typical 802.15.4 device [18].

The device energy consumption (mW·s) for each state can be easily computed as the product of Vcc (V), the current consumption (mA) and the time the node expends in that state (s).

Table 2 tabulates the reference results obtained after the simulation of the network when no adaptive policy is applied.

Table 1. Consumption of a device depending on the status of the radio transceiver for a supply voltage (V_{CC}) of 3.3 V [18]

Status	Consumption (mA)
Idle	0.42
Reception	19.70
Sleep	0.02
Transmission (0 dBm)	17.40

Table 2. Reference results

SO	Queue Drops (%)	Transmission Loss (%)	Average Delay (s)	No. of Collisions	Energy/bit (mJ/bit)
0	89.28	66.29	16.256	6,408,421	0.759
1	83.28	33.20	1.561	11,008,155	0.309
2	71.96	24.67	0.407	15,749,402	0.194
3	47.19	34.36	0.224	15,760,231	0.118
4	0.00	18.31	0.089	2,467,858	0.021

Note that the traffic generated by nodes is the same for every simulation, so if we observe the evolution for the queue drops as the *SO* value increments we can see a logical decrease. We should take into account that a unit increase in the value of the *SO* means duplicating the duration of the CAP so that the probability of successfully transmitting a packet and releasing a queue position significantly increases. When *SO* is bigger than three, the coordinator's Superframe Duration is long enough to accommodate all the traffic transmitted by the nodes so that there are no queue drops. On the other hand, for lower *SO* values the CAP is too short, the nodes have to store the packets and the queue begins to reach its full capacity at some instants (dropping some packets). A misconfiguration of the Superframe Order to zero will cause serious saturation problems, with loss rates higher than 80%. The same evolution with the *SO* is followed by the Average Delay. A *BO* of 5 corresponds to a Beacon Interval of approximately half a second (0.49152 s). As it can be noticed from Table 1, the average delay for *SO* values over two is below a Beacon Interval, which is a desired property. If *SO* equals to 0 the average delay exceeds more than one order of magnitude the duration of a Beacon Interval, which will most probably be not tolerable.

The relationship between collisions and the Superframe Order is not so simple. In fact, if we compare with the case with *SO*=0, we can observe that collisions initially increase when a higher *SO* is utilized. The reason for this trend is that if *SO* is zero, the CAP is too short even to try to transmit most packets, which are directly dropped without provoking any collision. In this sense, just for the longest CAP (*SO*=4), the collisions tend to decrease.

Table 3 reflects the main results obtained after the simulation of the first policy. The values for U_1 and U_2 were heuristically set to 20 and 70, respectively.

Table 3. Results with Superframe Order Adaptation

Queue Drops (%)	Transmission Losses (%)	Average Delay (s)	Global Collisions	Energy/bit (mJ/bit)
72.08	15.34	0.274	13,981,844	0.153

The results show that the Superframe Order adaptation algorithm presents a good behavior. The average delay remains under the Beacon Interval while the transmission fail rate is lower than any of the reference values. However this policy does not reduce the number of collisions, mainly caused by the heavy traffic conditions existing during the initial phase of the CAPs. This problem can be mitigated by ignoring the initial default value of *BE*. Table 3 shows the results of the reference experiments when the Backoff Exponent Policy is utilized. In this case, before any transmission, a random waiting time between 0 and a percentage of the remaining CAP is selected. As it is shown in Table 4, under this policy both collisions and transmission losses are mitigated while more traffic is transmitted for any value of *SO* (see Table 5).

Table 4. Results with the Backoff Exponent adaptation Policy

SO	Queue Drops (%)	Transmission Loss (%)	Average Delay (s)	Global Collisions	Energy/bit (mJ/bit)
0	87.44	63.24	39.089	5,319,702	0.474
1	78.33	40.69	27.762	9,299,981	0.251
2	60.28	26.58	19.208	11,926,301	0.155
3	21.59	16.81	9.479	9,007,508	0.116
4	0.00	1.05	0.436	803,265	0.022

Table 5. Improvement of the transmitted traffic under Backoff Exponent adaptation Policy

SO	Increment of transmitted Bytes (%)
0	1.00
1	1.63
2	8.10
3	30.56
4	17.27

Furthermore, the energy per bit is kept within very reasonable values improving the reference ones in practically all cases. The main disadvantage of this technique is the delay, which is substantially increased. This was expected since the technique postpones the transmission of the packets increasing the random average waiting time. The percentage of the CAP employed by the algorithm to calculate the random waiting time prior to each transmission is 100% in this paper.

Finally Table 6 collects the results obtained if both policies are simultaneously applied.

Table 6. Results of the combined policy

Queue Drops (%)	Transmission Fails (%)	Average Delay (s)	Global Collisions	Energy/bit (mJ/bit)
0.00	1.48	0.436	797,991	0.022

The combination of both techniques yield reasonable values for the queue losses, transmission fails and the energy per bit while the average delay is still smaller than a beacon interval. Furthermore the number of collisions has noticeably decreased and it improves all previous results. Also, the increase in the number of transferred bytes is of 172.11%.

If none of the presented techniques is applied the best record for the transmission losses (18.31%) is reached for a value of SO=4. A slightly better result is obtained with the Superframe Order Adaptation policy with 15.75%. However, after combining the two techniques the obtained value plummets down to 1.48%.

5   Conclusions and Future Work

This paper has investigated the dynamic optimization of two key IEEE 802.15.4 MAC sublayer parameters, the Superframe Order, and the Backoff Exponent. The Standard defines the Superframe Order parameter but does not mention how to determine it. Furthermore, SO is defined as a constant. We have shown that SO value has a deep impact on the network performance so we propose its dynamic adaptation to the network conditions, particularly to the traffic load. In this regard it has been proposed, implemented and simulated a technique which adapts the size of the Contention Access Period to the actual traffic load by reconfiguring the SO. We have also studied the collisions and access congestion problem and presented a policy to avoid them. One of the most promising features of IEEE 802.15.4 networks is its capability for self-configuring. This is why we consider that adaptive policies can be of great interest for the optimization of 802.15.4 networking applications. Finally, we have presented the most significant results obtained by the simulation of the proposed techniques when they are applied both separately and jointly being particularly. Results show that the combination of both techniques leads to a better network performance. Future work should extend these studies to the cluster-tree topologies where problems as the Access Congestion will become even more important. Additionally, we propose the study of other policies for network reconfiguration where the adaptability to traffic should be managed in the end (leaf) nodes.

Acknowledgments. This work was partially supported with public funds by the Spanish National Project No.TEC2009-13763-C02-01.

References

1. IEEE-WG802.15, 802.15.4-2011 - IEEE Standard for Local and metropolitan area networks–Part 15.4: Low-Rate Wireless Personal Area Networks (LR-WPANs), IEEE standard for Information Technology (2011)
2. ZigBee-Alliance, ZigBee specification (2013), http://www.zigbee.org/
3. Kushalnagar, N., et al.: IPv6 over Low-Power Wireless Personal Area Networks (6LoWPANs): Overview, Assumptions, Problem Statement, and Goals, RFC. 4919, Internet Engineering Task Force (IETF) (August 2007)
4. Park, T.R., et al.: Throughput and energy consumption analysis of IEEE 802.15.4 slotted CSMA/CA, Electronics Letters (September 2005)
5. Pollin, S., et al.: Performance Analysis of Slotted Carrier Sense IEEE 802.15.4 Medium Access Layer. IEEE Trans. on Wireless Communication 7(9), 3359–3371 (2008)
6. Mišic, J., et al.: The impact of MAC parameters on the performance of 802.15.4 PAN. Ad Hoc Netw. 3(5), 509–528 (2005)
7. Anastasi, G., et al.: The MAC unreliability problem in IEEE 802.15.4 wireless sensor networks. In: Proceedings of the 12th ACM International Conference on Modeling, Analysis and Simulation of Wireless and Mobile Systems, pp. 196–203. ACM, Spain (2009)
8. Anastasi, G., et al.: A Comprehensive Analysis of the MAC Unreliability Problem in IEEE 802.15.4 Wireless Sensor Networks. IEEE Trans. Industrial Informatics 7(1), 52–65 (2011), doi:10.1109/TII.2010.2085440
9. Di Francesco, M., et al.: Reliability and Energy-Efficiency in IEEE 802.15.4/ZigBee Sensor Networks:An Adaptive and Cross-Layer Approach. IEEE J. Sel. Areas Commun. 29(8), 1508–1524 (2011)
10. Ko, J.G., et al.: Performance Evaluation of IEEE 802.15.4 MAC with Different Backoff Ranges in Wireless Sensor Networks. In: Proceedings of the 10th IEEE International Conference on Communication systems (ICSS), Singapore, pp. 1–5 (October 2006)
11. Rao, V.P., Marandin, D.: Adaptive backoff exponent algorithm for zigbee (IEEE 802.15.4). In: Koucheryavy, Y., Harju, J., Iversen, V.B. (eds.) NEW2AN 2006. LNCS, vol. 4003, pp. 501–516. Springer, Heidelberg (2006)
12. Kwon, Y., Chae, Y.: Traffic Adaptive IEEE 802.15.4 MAC for Wireless Sensor Networks. In: Sha, E., Han, S.-K., Xu, C.-Z., Kim, M.-H., Yang, L.T., Xiao, B. (eds.) EUC 2006. LNCS, vol. 4096, pp. 864–873. Springer, Heidelberg (2006)
13. Lee, J., et al.: ECAP: A Bursty Traffic Adaptation Algorithm for IEEE 802.15.4 Beacon-Enabled Networks. In: Proceedings of the IEEE 65th Vehicular Technology Conference (VTC2007-Spring), Ireland, pp. 203–207 (April 2007)
14. Neugebauer, M., et al.: A new beacon order adaptation algorithm for IEEE 802.15.4 networks. In: Proceedings of the Second European Workshop on Wireless Sensor Networks, pp. 302–311 (2005)
15. Neugebauer, M., et al.: Duty cycle adaptation with respect to traffic. In: Proceedings of the 10th IEEE Conference on Emerging Technologies and Factory Automation (ETFA 2005), Italy, pp. 425–432 (September 2005)
16. OMNeT++, http://www.omnetpp.org
17. InetManet FrameWork, https://github.com/aarizaq/inetmanet-2.0
18. Texas Instruments homepage, http://www.ti.com/product/cc2420

A Novel Machine-to-Machine Traffic Multiplexing in LTE-A System Using Wireless In-Band Relaying

Safdar Nawaz Khan Marwat[1], Yasir Zaki[2], Jay Chen[2], Andreas Timm-Giel[3], and Carmelita Göerg[1]

[1] Communication Networks (ComNets), University of Bremen,
Otto-Hahn-Allee NW1, 28359 Bremen, Germany
{safdar,cg}@comnets.uni-bremen.de
[2] Computer Science Department, New York University Abu Dhabi (NYUAD),
Abu Dhabi, United Arab Emirates (UAE)
{yasir.zaki,jay.chen}@nyu.edu
[3] Communication Networks, Hamburg University of Technology,
Schwarzenbergstrasse 95E, 21073 Hamburg, Germany
timm-giel@tuhh.de

Abstract. In Long Term Evolution Advanced (LTE-A) several new features have been added to deal with the ever-increasing demands for higher data rates and spectral efficiency. One of the key features that the Third Generation Partnership Project (3GPP) has introduced is the Relay Node (RN), a low power low cost device used to increase the spectral efficiency, especially at the cell edge. In this paper, we propose to use RNs to address a challenging new problem emerging on the horizon: the expected tsunami of Machine-to-Machine (M2M) traffic in cellular and mobile networks (in LTE, and LTE-A). By taking advantage of RN's low cost, low power, and small size we outline the challenges of and one possible design for using RNs to integrate M2M traffic in LTE-A. To the best of our knowledge, this is a novel idea that has not yet been proposed and may give RNs more longevity and therefore greater value.

Keywords: LTE/LTE-A, Machine-to-Machine (M2M), wireless in-band Relay.

1 Introduction

The cost of using cellular services has fallen dramatically over recent years and cellular broadband connectivity has become globally available. In addition, the ever-decreasing costs and sizes of the devices with integrated sensors, network interfaces, and enhanced power capabilities have led manufacturers to offer a variety of hardware leading to new applications, and services. The term M2M communication denotes these devices, known as machines, which have the capacity to communicate and are expected to vastly outnumber conventional devices [1].

Long Term Evolution (LTE) and LTE-Advanced (LTE-A) are currently considered to be the best candidates to incorporate future technologies such as M2M. M2M applications are expected to have narrowband requirements with infrequent data transmission, but the development of these standards was primarily for broadband data

D. Pesch et al. (Eds.): MONAMI 2013, LNICST 125, pp. 149–158, 2013.

services. With narrowband M2M applications, these existing standards may not achieve spectrum and cost efficiency. Therefore, the integration of M2M communication having low data rates, small packet sizes, and higher number of devices may cause a substantial reduction to the overall performance of future network systems, as shown in [2].

The main goal of this paper is to highlight the challenges of providing M2M services in future mobile networks with an emphasis on LTE-A. In addition, we propose a practical solution for the integration of M2M traffic in the LTE standard. The use of mobile network resources by swarms M2M devices for applications such as remote monitoring can have a significant impact on the performance of regular data traffic such as voice, video and file transfer. This paper illustrates the key M2M issues and challenges for LTE-A radio resource management and proposes a novel solution which leverages RNs to cope with these problems.

2   Machine-to-Machine (M2M)

M2M communication is a rapidly developing research field. The M2M core concept is the interconnection of different devices without human intervention. Due to tremendous growth in this area, the diversity and number of M2M devices as well as the mobile data traffic is expected to grow significantly in the near future [3]. It is also anticipated that the "Internet of Things" will augment the existing Internet with a variety of connected devices [4]. Subsequently, several application domains could benefit from these concepts. Example application areas could be: remote supervision in logistical processes, smart metering and monitoring, intelligent transport system, e-healthcare, etc. Recent advances in research have shown a great interest in remote monitoring of homes, vehicles and places with M2M devices [5,6,7], for example, energy monitoring, traffic surveillance, and environmental monitoring.

Contemporary M2M communications are based on available wireless communication technologies like Global System for Mobile Communications/General Packet Radio Service (GSM/GPRS). At the moment, these standards fulfill the requirements of the existing M2M applications adequately because these technologies offer low-cost deployment of M2M devices with convenient deployment and roaming facilities. However, the expected exponential growth of the M2M traffic and the different new trends and many application scenarios mean that legacy mobile systems like GSM/GPRS will soon be insufficient. It is also worth mentioning that, in contrast to typical end-to-end communications, M2M devices transfer their data without direct human intervention; thus, traffic generated differs from human generated traffic.

3   Relaying in Long Term Evolution Advanced (LTE-A)

The 3GPP has been exploring new ways to increase overall data-rates and to reduce latency. One of the biggest challenges that current mobile communication systems, like LTE, face is low throughput for cell-edge users. The 3GPP has begun studying different techniques to address this problem including: the usage of different low power heterogeneous nodes with the normal micro and macro base stations. These nodes can be femto cells, pico cells, or relay nodes. In this paper, we focus on low cost low power Relay Nodes (RNs). A relay is a device used to extend the cell coverage area [8]. Relaying refers to the communication of the terminal with the network using a node that is wirelessly connected to a donor cell over the LTE air interface [9]. The RN would appear as an ordinary cell to the terminal. The RN is a low-power base station, wirelessly connected to the Donor eNodeB (DeNodeB). RNs also have the capability to improve coverage by simply placing them at locations with poor channel conditions or coverage holes where they perform radio scheduling independently [10]. The protocol stack of a relay is shown in Fig. 1. The 3GPP specifications support both in-band and out-band operations of the relays. The in-band operation means that the link between the DeNodeB and the RN (Un interface) as well as the link between the RN and the terminal (Uu interface) uses the same LTE carrier frequency. In out-band operations; both links have different carrier frequencies. In-band operations can be achieved by time multiplexing the two different links, that is the Un and Uu interfaces. Out-band operations, generally, may not be feasible because they require separate frequency carriers that are scarce resources in the first place. In addition, using isolated antennas for both links to achieve out-band operations would increase the implementation cost and complexity.

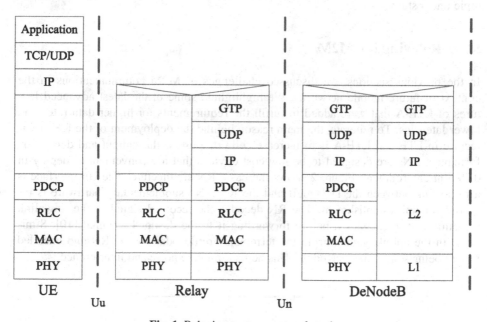

Fig. 1. Relaying system protocol stack

4   State-of-the-Art (SoA)

In the literature on RNs most research efforts are directed towards the implementation aspects and improving system performance. In [11], the performance evaluation of relaying system is achieved using actual deployment environments and propagation models of an urban location in central London instead of employing traditional metrics of artificial environments and models. In [12], the uplink performance of LTE-A with RN deployment is investigated and a resource allocation scheme is proposed to meet the relay requirements. In [13], the authors have performed field trial measurements for indoor relaying with full frequency reuse using a test-bed. The study is extended to outdoor relaying in [14]. Several other works are based on performance evaluation of relaying in LTE-A. Authors of [15] suggest improvements in relaying protocols and frame structure to improve system performance. In [16], the authors propose a user multiplexing scheme for relaying with the aim of reducing multiplexing overhead. The influence of site planning on the performance of relay networks is studied in [17] The system performance enhancement of LTE-A and intercell interference mitigation is shown to be achieved by applying the power control scheme both at the DeNodeBs and the RNs. Out-band relaying operations performance optimization is investigated in [18]. In [19], the reduction in relaying latency is discussed by extending the available relaying schemes. The issue of QoS-aware scheduling for relays with in-band operations is discussed in [20]. The M2M communication over amplify-and-forward relays, also known as repeaters, is discussed in [21]. From our literature review, the facilitation of M2M communication by employing RNs is not a topic under study.

5   Relaying for M2M

In the previous sections, we discussed challenges of M2M communications in the context of future mobile networks. We highlighted some of the latest advanced features of LTE-A that were added to fulfill the requirements for higher data rates and lower latencies. To reiterate, the main reason behind the deployment of the RN architecture in LTE and LTE-A is to increase cell edge users' throughput and delay performance. RNs are designed to be low cost devices that are convenient to deploy in different environment. Figure 2 shows the basic RN architecture. The Un interface is a radio link between the DeNodeB and the RNs. No supplementary hardware is required for link establishment. The RN decodes the received signal in the downlink direction and re-encodes it before forwarding it to the destined terminal [10]. Similarly, in the uplink, signals from the terminals are decoded by the RN and encoded before being sent to the DeNodeB. This helps minimize noise and interference.

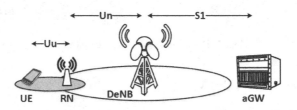

Fig. 2. Relay Node Architecture

The nature of M2M traffic is usually very low data rates; a machine sends a very small number of bits every couple of minutes or hours. Looking at the LTE physical resources and their structure, the 3GPP standardize that the smallest resource unit that the base station can allocate/schedule to a certain LTE users is a Physical Resource Block (PRB). A PRB consists of the aggregation of 12 OFDM sub-carriers, and is capable for transmitting, in favorable channel conditions, several hundred bytes of data. The mobile communication spectrum is a scarce resource of great value and operators pay huge amounts of investment capital to obtain the licenses to operate in a certain spectrum. If an entire PRB is allocated to a single machine a severe degradation in the overall spectrum utilization/efficiency will result. A design change will likely be necessary so that LTE/LTE-A networks are able to incorporate the M2M traffic without affecting the Quality of Service (QoS) of its normal user traffic.

5.1   Possible M2M in LTE-A Integration Solutions

As discussed earlier, the main problem of serving the M2M traffic in LTE network is the inefficiency of the transmission, since each M2M node is going to utilize a full PRB only to send a few bits. There are a number of possible solutions that can be used to increase the efficiency of the M2M transmission:

- Each M2M node can delay the transmission and aggregate a number of its data together before sending it over the LTE network. This can increase the efficiency of the transmission, however the M2M devices normally sends data every couple of minutes or hours and delaying the transmission in order to aggregate several data together will have an impact on the service the M2M node is providing. So this solution may not always be practical.
- The LTE network can schedule M2M devices with less than one PRB, e.g., 1 sub-carrier instead of 12. This means that the 3GPP standard has to be modified in order to reflect this change. In addition, reducing the transmission to a single sub-carrier will also mean that more gap intervals have to be inserted to avoid inter symbol interference that will lead to a reduction of the spectrum. This is not a very practical solution and is also not feasible.
- Several M2M traffic, coming from different nodes, is aggregated and multiplexed together for the transmission over a single PRB. This can be a feasible solution that can solve the aforementioned problems. However, a number of technical challenges must be addressed first before this solution can be implemented in practice. For example, where to aggregate the different M2M traffic? What kind of identification can be used to differentiate between the different multiplexed traffic? The algorithm proposed by this paper falls within this solution category.

5.2   Efficient Relay Node PDCP Algorithm for M2M Traffic Multiplexing

In this paper, we focus on the layer-3 type RNs, where these nodes are used as an Aggregator/Multiplexer entity for the different M2M devices. The wireless in-band RN architecture is probably the most reasonable and cost effective method to be used in conjunction with the M2M traffic. These RNs are low cost devices that can multiplex the different M2M traffic without the use of any additional backhaul. Since these RNs uses the same wireless spectrum that the operator already owns as the backhaul link to the DeNodeB.

In order to incorporate the M2M traffic efficiently in the LTE network, we propose the following functionalities to be implemented in the in-band layer-3 RNs:

- An M2M QoS-aware Relay Node Scheduler (RNS): the RNS is responsible for scheduling the air interface resources over the RN Uu interface. The RNS schedules the transmissions of the different M2M traffic. In order to have efficient M2M transmission, the RNS has to be aware of the different M2M QoS characteristics and correlate this with the varying wireless backhaul of the Un interface between the RN and the DeNodeB.
- An efficient PDCP algorithm in the RN has to be implemented. This algorithm will operates hand-in-hand with the RNS, and will multiplex different uplink data sent by the M2M nodes together to be sent over the Un interface.

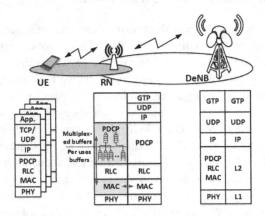

Fig. 3. Proposed RN M2M multiplexing solution

This means that instead of requesting uplink resources from the DeNodeB for individual terminals, the resource request is made by the RN for a group of multiplexed users. This is possible when IP (Internet Protocol) packets of different M2M terminals are multiplexed intelligently into one single large PDCP packet. The DeNodeB would see this as a single radio resource request making it possible to allocate one PRB to several M2M devices and enhance spectral efficiency many folds. Figure 3 shows a high level overview of the proposed scheme.

5.3   Proposal Challenges

The proposed solution can be viewed as aggregating and multiplexing the traffic of several M2M nodes into one packet, similar to what is done currently for several bearers of one user. This RN scheme for M2M communication can be implemented to work only in narrowband so that it fits the requirements of M2M applications and the interference with the signals of DeNodeB is minimized.

Given that the idea is novel, it is not free of challenges and issues. In this subsection a number of research challenges and issues are discussed. One of the main challenges that have to be addressed is the RN Scheduler (RNS) algorithm. As can be seen from the protocol architecture of the RN, it has two MAC layers; one is responsible for the Uu interface towards the RN UEs and one for the Un interface towards the DeNodeB. The RNS is located in the Uu MAC layer; it schedules the access of the M2M devices to the Uu interface. This scheduling is correlated to whatever scheduling grants the DeNodeB is given to the RN, since the RN will ask for uplink transmission by the Un MAC layer. The challenge presents itself in the way the RNS should be designed, i.e., the RNS has to schedule the M2M devices based on their QoS correlating this to the grant given by the DeNodeB for the backhaul transmission. In addition, the multiplexing scheme done at the PDCP layer of the RN is another issue. As stated earlier, several M2M traffic coming from different M2M devices are going to be multiplexed into a single PDCP bearer that will be seen by the DeNodeB by the Un interface. The question still remains, how many multiplexed bearers need to configured? Which M2M traffic should be multiplexed together and in which frequency this should be done?

Since the use of wireless in-band RN seems to be the most feasible option for economical reasons, an additional challenge has to be addressed. Wireless in-band relaying, as it was explained earlier, require a separation between the two different links (Uu and Un), because the RN cannot send and receive at the same time due to self-interference. As a result, the RN has to utilize a Time Division Duplex (TDD) scheme to separate the transmissions of the different interfaces in time. This would imply, that an additional delay is introduced due to the use of the TDD scheme. The RNS has to be designed in such a way that it can balance between the different time slots of the Uu and Un air interfaces. The ratio of split between the two interfaces is far from trivial, and proper investigations and research is required to address the most optimum splitting strategy. Such splitting strategies can either be static or even dynamic depending on the different traffic loads on each wireless interface.

Another very interesting challenge that need to be addressed come from the situation when the RN is also serving regular LTE-A users. The issue here would be that the RNS has to differentiate between the M2M devices and the regular users, and how the RNS can still guarantee the QoS of the regular LTE/LTE-A users since the communication is done over a two hop transmission. Similarly, if the M2M devices are in the range of the DeNodeB but not in the range of the RN, how the DeNodeB should deal with these devices. These challenges are tricky but not impossible to tackle.

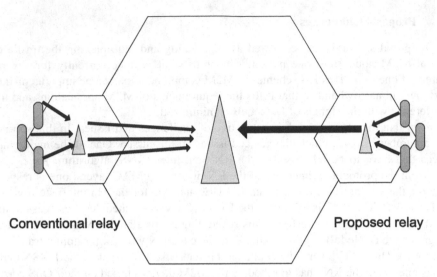

Fig. 4. Relaying schemes

6   Conclusion and Outlook

In this paper we provided an overview of the recently introduced features of the LTE-A system. We focused on Relaying, which is a prominent new feature of LTE-A. The primary aim of relaying is to extend cell coverage and enhance cell edge user performance. We propose to exploit this functionality to facilitate the integration of M2M communication by designing an intelligent RN MAC scheduler and PDCP multiplexing scheme. This proposal would handle the M2M narrowband requirements and boost the spectral efficiency.

In our future work, we plan to implementing an innovative and QoS aware RNS as well as a PDCP multiplexing architecture into our LTE simulation model. The design and implementation of the RN with this special multiplexing capability would help in evaluating the system performance and the impact of the proposed scheme. Finally, we plan to perform several performance evaluations and demonstrate how the proposed solution would help to easily integrate the M2M traffic within the LTE/LTE-A network without any degradation or penalties to the regular network performance.

Acknowledgments. Many thanks to the University of Engineering and Technology, Peshawar, Pakistan and the International Graduate School for Dynamics in Logistics, University of Bremen, Germany for their financial support of this research work.

References

[1] Lawton, G.: Machine-to-Machine Technology Gears up for Growth. Computer 37(9), 12–15 (2004)
[2] Pötsch, T., Marwat, S.N.K., Zaki, Y., Goerg, C.: Influence of Future M2M Communication on the LTE system. In: Wireless and Mobile Networking Conference, Dubai, United Arab Emirates, April 23-25 (2013)

[3] Cisco Systems Inc., Cisco Visual Networking Index: Global Mobile Data Traffic Forecast Update, 2011-2016. Digital Publication (February 2012)

[4] Coetzee, L., Eksteen, J.: The Internet of Things - promise for the future? An introduction. In: IST-Africa Conference Proceedings, Pretoria, South Africa, May 11-13, pp. 1–9 (2011)

[5] Shin, S.H., et al.: Intelligent M2M network using healthcare sensors. In: 14th Asia-Pacific Network Operations and Management Symposium, September 25-27, pp. 1–4 (2012)

[6] Chang, Y.-C., Chi, T.-Y., Wang, W.-C., Kuo, S.-Y.: Dynamic software update model for remote entity management of machine-to-machine service capability. IET Communications 7(1), 32–39 (2013)

[7] Yunoki, S., Takada, M., Liu, C.: Experimental results of remote energy monitoring system via cellular network in China. In: Proceedings of SICE Annual Conference, Tokyo, Japan, August 20-23, pp. 948–954 (2012)

[8] Cox, C.: An Introduction to LTE: LTE, LTE-Advanced, SAE and 4G Mobile Communications, 2nd edn. John Wiley & Sons (2012)

[9] Dahlman, E., Parkvall, S., Sköld, J.: 4G LTE/LTE-Advanced for Mobile Broadband. Academic Press (2011)

[10] Holma, H., Toskala, A.: LTE for UMTS: Evolution to LTE-Advanced, 2nd edn. John Wiley & Sons (2011)

[11] Irmer, R., Diehm, F.: On coverage and capacity of relaying in LTE-advanced in example deployments. In: IEEE 19th International Symposium on Personal, Indoor and Mobile Radio Communications, Cannes, France, September 15-18, pp. 1–5 (2008)

[12] Rasheed, A.A., Redana, S., Raaf, B., Hamalainen, J.: Uplink resource partitioning in relay enhanced LTE-Advanced networks. In: IEEE 20th International Symposium on Personal, Indoor and Mobile Radio Communications, Tokyo, Japan, September 13-16, pp. 1502–1506 (2009)

[13] Venkatkumar, V., Wirth, T., Haustein, T., Schulz, E.: Relaying in Long Term Evolution: Indoor full frequency reuse. In: European Wireless Conference, Aalborg, Denmark, May 17-20, pp. 298–302 (2009)

[14] Wirth, T., Venkatkumar, V., Haustein, T., Schulz, E., Halfmann, R.: LTE-Advanced Relaying for Outdoor Range Extension. In: IEEE 70th Vehicular Technology Conference, Anchorage, AK, USA, September 20-23, pp. 1–4 (2009)

[15] Huang, Q., Ni, M.-J., Tang, L., Chai, R., Chen, Q.-B.: Relay protocol improvement and frame structure design base on overhearing mechanism and physical network coding. In: IEEE Youth Conference on Information Computing and Telecommunications, Beijing, China, November 28-30, pp. 319–322 (2010)

[16] Teyeb, O., Frederiksen, F., Phan, V.V., Raaf, B., Redana, S.: User Multiplexing in Relay Enhanced LTE-Advanced Networks. In: IEEE 71st Vehicular Technology Conference, Taipei, Taiwan, May 16-19, pp. 1–5 (2010)

[17] Bulakci, O., Redana, S., Raaf, B., Hamalainen, J.: Performance Enhancement in LTE-Advanced Relay Networks via Relay Site Planning. In: IEEE 71st Vehicular Technology Conference, Taipei, Taiwan, May 16-19, pp. 1–5 (2010)

[18] Krishnan, N., Yates, R.D., Mandayam, N.B., Panchal, J.S.: Bandwidth Sharing for Relaying in Cellular Systems. IEEE Transactions on Wireless Communications 11(1), 117–129 (2012)

[19] Bradford, G.J., Laneman, J.N.: Low latency relaying schemes for next-generation cellular networks. In: IEEE International Conference on Communications, Ottawa, ON, Canada, June 10-15, pp. 4294–4299 (2012)

[20] de Moraes, T.M., Bauch, G., Seidel, E.: QoS-aware Scheduling for In-Band Relays in LTE-Advanced. In: 9th International ITG Conference on Systems, Communication and Coding, Munich, Germany, January 21-24, pp. 1–6 (2013)

[21] Elkheir, G.A., Lioumpas, A.S., Alexiou, A.: Energy efficient AF relaying under error performance constraints with application to M2M networks. In: IEEE 22nd International Symposium on Personal Indoor and Mobile Radio Communications, Toronto, ON, Canada, September 1-14, pp. 56–60 (2011)

Service and Communication Management in Cooperative Vehicular Networks

Olivia Brickley and Dirk Pesch

NIMBUS Centre for Embedded Systems Research,
Cork Institute of Technology, Cork, Ireland
{olivia.brickley,dirk.pesch}@cit.ie

Abstract. With the increasing demand for traffic safety and efficiency and constant search for innovative solutions within the automotive market coupled with supporting initiatives from regulatory domains, the potential of Intelligent Transportation Systems (ITS) is immense. Basic vehicle and roadside infrastructure collaboration allows an increase in efficiency and safety and acts as the foundation for an extensive application set to achieve the ITS goals of cleaner, safer and more efficient travel. There are some important considerations however. Taking into account the wide array of communication technologies and plethora of proposed applications, this paper aims to address one of the major and largely unexplored challenges facing the ITS research community in relation to service and communication management (SCM), whereby the underlying communications capability is sufficiently exploited to assure satisfactory operation of deployed ITS applications. A complete SCM solution is proposed under an "Always Satisfactorily Connected" (ASC) objective; two probing techniques are examined to assess the performance of the candidate communication networks and simple policy and Grey Relational Analysis (GRA) based selection policies are considered. In addition, a standard indicative measure to analyse the effectiveness of the SCM scheme is introduced. The performance of the proposed SCM schemes is evaluated using CALMNet, a comprehensive network-centric simulation environment for CALM-based cooperative vehicular systems. Results highlight the effect of different techniques on system performance and user satisfaction.

Keywords: Cooperative Vehicular systems, ITS, CALM, VANET, Network Selection, Heterogeneous Networks.

1   Introduction

The concept of Intelligent Transportation Systems (ITS) presents new R&D challenges in the transportation and ICT sectors and is currently receiving considerable interest from the research community. The primary objective of ITS is the creation of advanced road traffic systems for improved traffic safety, efficiency, and travelling comfort. Basic vehicle and roadside infrastructure collaboration allow for an increase in efficiency and safety and acts as the foundation for

D. Pesch et al. (Eds.): MONAMI 2013, LNICST 125, pp. 159–171, 2013.

an extensive application set to achieve ITS goals. Allowing cooperation among ITS entities to the degree envisioned requires a persistent, stable and reliable underlying communications service.

The ITS community are working towards a full-scale system solution for the provision of value-added services, all of which are fundamentally based on the vehicle-to-vehicle (V2V), vehicle-to-roadside (V2R) and vehicle-to-infrastructure (V2I) information exchange paradigm. Bodies including the Institute of Electrical and Electronic Engineers (IEEE), International Standards Organisation (ISO) and Car-to-Car Communications Consortium (C2CCC), among others, propose communications solutions to facilitate the envisaged ITS operational capabilities where a diverse spectrum of applications are supported [1,2,3]. The ISO propose CALM (Continuous Air-interface for Long to Medium range), a complete high speed ITS communication solution using a heterogeneous mix of new and existing complementary media, enabling V2V, V2R and V2I communication modes providing terrestrial, regional and short range connectivity alternatives [3].

In parallel with the ISO and IEEE standardisation efforts, organisations such as the European Telecommunications Standards Institute (ETSI) and the C2CCC, as well as a large number of funded research projects and commercial content providers have identified many beneficial application and service concepts [4,5,6,7,8]. Considering the heterogeneous mix of communication technologies and plethora of proposed applications, it is possible that at any one time there are multiple mobile network service options available. Selection of an inappropriate network interface or dissemination strategy for data transmission can result in unsatisfactory performance in terms of user or service requirements and constraints, having potentially fatal consequences in the vehicular environment. Identification of the most appropriate transmission strategy therefore becomes a fundamentally important element of any ITS communication solution and directly impacts the perceived system performance. The ultimate challenge is to properly specify the communication requirements of projected ITS applications and derive the corresponding dissemination strategy based on these, taking into account the user preferences and current environmental context.

The remainder of this paper is structured as follows. The next section reviews research efforts in the area of access network selection in heterogeneous network environments. In Section 3, the complete SCM solution is proposed under an "Always Satisfactorily Connected" (ASC) objective; two probing techniques are examined to assess the performance of the candidate communication networks and multiple selection policies are considered. Section 4 introduces CALMnet, the comprehensive simulation environment used for evaluation of various selection approaches in the cooperative vehicular environment. Both quantitative and qualitative analysis of results is carried out in Section 5. In addition, standard indicative measures to analyse the effectiveness of the SCM scheme are introduced. Conclusions are drawn in Section 6.

2 Candidate Network Selection in Heterogeneous Networks

The issue of heterogeneous network management has been studied comprehensively in recent years, with most emphasis on the integration of cellular technologies and WLAN with cellular networks. While the vehicular network solution combines both ad-hoc and infrastructure based communication modes and integration on a larger scale than that previously proposed, the subject of communications management in terms of selection of the best alternative given multiple candidate networks remains.

Network selection involves the implementation of some decision-making policy within the multi-access environment. Design of a complete network selection solution involves four key considerations:

- *Selection Objectives*
  Definition of the "best" network is a core task and drives the solution design process. Therefore, the objectives of the selection system must be clearly defined; will the preferred solution be that which maximises profits, minimises monetary cost or power consumption, optimises QoS, or a combination of these, for example. Typically, the overall objective is multi-dimensional and specific to the system operating environment. Resolution of the overall system objectives will identify the criteria integral to the decision making process. [10,11,12]
- *Parameter Significance*
  Network selection is often a trade off between multiple factors in order to achieve the cited objectives. Therefore, it is necessary to identify the relative significance of the decision criteria; each should be assigned a weighting value proportional to the magnitude it endows on the decision. Parameter weighting can be fixed or dynamically adjusted in relation to the situational context, can be set by user or application, and in some cases utilises fuzzy logic or analytic hierarchy process (AHP) techniques. [10,13,14,15]
- *Condition Monitoring*
  The network selection policy generally relies on a number of static and dynamically changing metrics. A good solution should ensure that information regarding current conditions is suitably accurate. This requires an information gathering process where all parameter values can be quantified and is fundamentally dependent on the selection deployment strategy. The use of network-assisted selection solutions for example, is one approach for data monitoring, while machine learning and user rating propagation (i.e. gossiping) techniques have also been proposed. [11,17,18]
- *Candidate Ranking*
  Once the relevant information has been gathered, all candidates are ranked in relation to their ability to meet the identified selection objectives. This is achieved through simple fixed policies or more complex techniques employing fuzzy logic theory, cost and utility functions, game theory, or other multi-attribute decision making (MADM) techniques including GRA, TOPSIS, and ELECTRE. [10,11,15,16]

These considerations should be used as the template for complete system design in a heterogeneous network setting. The following section describes the proposed SCM approach.

3   Service and Communication Management for Cooperative Vehicular Systems

In the literature, few studies propose a complete network selection solution; most concentrate their efforts on the ranking of candidates for a given objective/parameter set. This paper proposes the SCM framework; a complete solution for cooperative vehicular environments which is directly applicable to the ISO CALM stack. Here, two communication interfaces (CI) are assumed. UMTS provides a wide area cellular connection facilitating V2I communication while 802.11p WAVE is employed for V2V and V2R connectivity.

3.1   Selection Objectives

The principal objective of any system for the ITS scenario will be in ensuring adequate service provision; this prompts a move away from the traditional "Always Best Connected" (ABC) paradigm, so dominant throughout the literature, towards the concept of "Always Satisfactorily Connected" (ASC). In this case, the "best" is defined as that candidate which most closely satisfies user preference and the operational requirements of the requesting services rather than that which maximises these.

Application data in vehicular networks has spatiotemporal properties; all information has a finite lifetime and is typically only relevant to specific geographic areas. Should the intended destination receive stale or spatially non-relevant information, then ITS service requirements may be compromised. Reliability also has elevated importance in the ITS scenario; the loss of information can have considerable consequences. It is obvious then that the application requirements will centre on data lifetime and reliability requirements. Data lifetime defines the time after which the data becomes stale and is of no relevance to the receiver any longer; reliability describes the loss tolerance for each deployed service.

User preference in the form of cost will also have a significant impact on selection of a suitable carrier network and will often dictate the selection decision. This cost can be expressed in monetary or data usage terms. Here, users specify their willingness to pay (WTP) in relation to the offered ITS services and the selection strategy must strive to satisfy this.

3.2   Parameter Significance

Given the large scope for development in the ITS domain and the diverse set of applications that will be deployed, it is necessary to classify the service sets in relation to their operational requirements. This enables the SCM to identify the parameter significance for a given set of services. In this study, three classes are defined; these are generic categories within which individual applications can be specified.

- Safety Services
  This category encompasses a variety of applications necessary for improved safety and traffic management. Such services include collision, hazard and emergency vehicle approach warnings, as well as information regarding dynamic speed limits, lane usage and traffic light state notification etc. Applications in this service category have very strict spatiotemporal properties; data has a short lifetime and is relevant only at a local level. In this category, information is generally transmitted via broadcast communication.
- Subscriber Services
  This includes a number of commercial and informational services to which a traveller can subscribe. Drivers may wish to receive information regarding the traffic state on their chosen route to a particular destination, for example. Commercial advertising and vehicle platooning are also envisaged as subscriber based services where travellers express interest in receiving certain update information. This category comprises of an information push based model where notification data is delivered to subscribed users; temporal and reliability constraints are more relaxed than those defined for the safety service.
- Personalised Services
  This category encompasses applications which cater for individual traveller requirements. Transaction based services such as parking space reservation and temporary bus lane usage, as well as route planning applications and commercial vehicle agent systems fall into the category of personalised services. This class of services has strict requirements relating to reliability while data has longer lifetimes.

3.3   Condition Monitoring

Candidate ranking is fundamentally dependent on the quality of the context information regarding current network conditions. Therefore, the quantification of parameters which reflect this is a cornerstone in any network selection strategy. Here, two approaches to candidate condition monitoring are considered:

- Constant Probing takes into consideration the general performance of each candidate network over time. This is based on the CVIS-CALM implemented approach whereby the vehicle Mobile IP Home Agent (HA) is periodically polled using ICMP Echo Request messages. Network latency, jitter, throughput and loss information is recorded and weighted sliding window analysis calculates updated performance indicators for these.
- Dynamic Probing reports on the performance of the direct communication path between source and destination endpoints. This approach also uses ICMP Echo Request messages to determine the latency, jitter, throughput and loss performance of each candidate network. This polling is aperiodic; probing is initiated with every new service request and the intended destination for the calling service is polled.

3.4   Candidate Ranking

Once the relevant information has been gathered, all candidates must be ranked in relation to their ability to meet the identified selection objectives. In this study, a GRA based approach is proposed. This has been shown to be the best MADM technique for network selection since reference solutions can be customised for a varying mix of attributes and optimisation objectives [19].

Grey Relational Analysis (GRA) is a well-known MADM technique, used across many disciplines, which measures the strength of the relationship between data sequences. Here, the set of criteria $\{k_1, k_2...k_n\}$ for each of the alternatives $\{x_1, x_2...x_m\}$, are represented by the decision matrix, D

$$D = \begin{vmatrix} x_0(k_1) & x_0(k_2) & \cdots & x_0(k_n) \\ x_1(k_1) & x_1(k_2) & \cdots & x_1(k_n) \\ \vdots & \vdots & \vdots & \vdots \\ x_m(k_1) & x_m(k_2) & \cdots & x_m(k_n) \end{vmatrix} \tag{1}$$

A reference solution, x_0, is also defined, to which all candidates are compared. D is normalised, becoming D', typically following a larger-the-better, smaller-the-better or nominal-is-best normalisation policy. The Grey Relational Grade (GRG), η, used to describe the similarity between each candidate network x_i, and x_0, is then computed using the following:

$$\eta = \frac{1}{n} \sum_{i=1}^{n} \frac{\Delta_{min} + \Delta_{max}}{\Delta_i + \Delta_{max}} \tag{2}$$

where
n   = number of decision criteria
Δ_i $= |x_0(k) - x_i(k)|$
$\Delta_{max} = \max(\Delta_i)$
$\Delta_{min} = \min(\Delta_i)$

The GRG identifies the distance to the reference solution and therefore the alternative achieving the highest GRG score is deemed the most suitable candidate.

Determining a suitable data dissemination alternative for the GRA-based SCM is a three stage process involving the following tasks:

1. Definition of reference solution, x_0
   This represents the ideal solution with which all candidates x_i are compared. In an effort to ensure the ASC objective, here x_0 is taken to be the operating requirements of the requesting applications. Therefore, x_0 is defined dynamically with every communication request from upper layer ITS applications. This provides a flexible SCM solution which can cater for a diverse mix of newly deployed and existing ITS services and also ensures the ASC objective.

2. Criteria Normalisation

This involves expressing and evaluating the observed network conditions in a form where they can be easily compared. In this study, the criteria are normalised with respect to the reference solution, x_0. Normalisation therefore, is a measure of the degree of fulfilment of the ITS service requirements by the network characteristics and is calculated using a set of utility functions. Since the objective of the proposed SCM solution is ASC, the nature of these utility functions is dependent on the service category and the requirement under consideration. The normalised value, δ, is then used to calculate the GRG score. The utility functions are designed so that only exact matches for x_0 are awarded the highest δ of 1. For candidates which cannot meet or exceed x_0, δ is negatively assessed with varying degree; those unable to meet the requirements experience sharper decay than those which can exceed them and is based on the distance between the reported performance and x_0. For this reason the utilities are modelled using exponential behaviour.

- Safety

   Safety services are of the highest priority in the ITS environment; these applications broadcast information at frequency f_{safety} and have strict temporal requirements. Network delay and loss statistics reported by the network monitoring process are normalised for safety services using the utility functions in (3) and (4) respectively. Safety services have a hard upper limit on the lifetime of data ($x_0(d)$); therefore, any network delay value satisfying this requirement is normalised to 1. Network delay values exceeding $x_0(d)$ achieve a zero utility. Safety services also require 100% reliability; this means that all neighbouring vehicles should receive the data at least once within its lifetime. In equation 4, the smaller the $x_i(l)$, the greater the normalised value, $\delta_{safety}(l)$. For increasing $x_i(l)$, $\delta_{safety}(l)$ decays exponentially, the rate of which is dictated by the frequency, f_{safety}, at which the data is broadcast, and the decay constant, τ_{safety}.

$$\delta_{safety}(d) = \begin{cases} 1 & x_i(d) <= x_0(d) \\ 0 & \text{otherwise} \end{cases} \tag{3}$$

$$\delta_{safety}(l) = e^{-\frac{x_i(l)}{f_{safety} * \tau_{safety}}} \tag{4}$$

- Subscriber

   Subscriber services have longer data lifetimes and are somewhat tolerant of fluctuations in reliability. Following the ASC objective, equations 5 and 6 are designed to ensure that the highest normalised value is the one which most closely matches x_0. For network delay, the maximum normalised value, ($\delta_{sub}(d)$) of 1 is achieved as the delay value approaches $x_0(d)$ at a rate defined by the distance from $x_0(d)$ and $\tau_{sub}^{in(d)}$. For values exceeding the maximum data lifetime, $x_0(d)$, $\delta_{sub}(d)$ exponentially decreases at a rate of $\tau_{sub}^{dc(d)}$. Candidates whose reported losses are within the limits defined in $x_0(l)$ achieve the maximum normalised value, $\delta_{sub}(l)$.

Losses that exceed this threshold cause an exponential decrease in $\delta_{sub}(l)$ according to the distance from $x_0(l)$ and constant $\tau_{sub}^{dc(l)}$.

$$\delta_{sub}(d) = \begin{cases} e^{-\frac{(x_0(d)-x_i(d))*\tau_{sub}^{in(d)}}{x_i(d)}} & x_i(d) <= x_0(d) \\ e^{-(x_i(d)-x_0(d))*\tau_{sub}^{dc(d)}} & \text{otherwise} \end{cases} \quad (5)$$

$$\delta_{sub}(l) = \begin{cases} 1 & x_i(l) <= x_0(l) \\ e^{-(x_i(l)-x_0(l))*\tau_{sub}^{in(l)}} & \text{otherwise} \end{cases} \quad (6)$$

- *Personalised*
  The personalised service category is sensitive to network reliability and data lifetimes are bounded. Network delay values falling in the range $[0,x_0(d)]$ achieve a utility score, $\delta_{pers}(d)$, approaching 1 as dictated by the constant $\tau_{pers}^{in(d)}$ and the distance from $x_0(d)$. In cases where these bounds are exceeded, $\delta_{pers}(d)$ experiences an exponential decay at a rate of $\tau_{pers}^{dc(d)}$, dictated by the distance from $x_0(d)$. Data losses are not tolerated in this service class; therefore, $\delta_{pers}(l)$ exponentially decreases according to $\tau_{pers}^{dc(l)}$ for any $x_0(l) <1$.

$$\delta_{pers}(d) = \begin{cases} e^{-\frac{(x_0(d)-x_i(d))*\tau_{pers}^{in(d)}}{x_i(d)}} & x_i(d) <= x_0(d) \\ e^{-(x_i(d)-x_0(d))*\tau_{pers}^{dc(d)}} & \text{otherwise} \end{cases} \quad (7)$$

$$\delta_{pers}(l) = e^{-(x_i(l)-x_0(l))*\tau_{pers}^{dc(l)}} \quad (8)$$

The performance of the candidate networks in relation to the cost parameter, C_n, is normalised according to equation 9. Since the WAVE network has no associated cost to the user this (and any other free alternative) will always achieve the maximum score of 1. For candidate networks that exceed the maximum desired cost, $x_0(c)$, defined by the user for each category of service, the utility value exponentially decreases at a rate associated with the users willingness to pay (WTP) value.

$$C_n = \begin{cases} 1 & x_i(c) <= x_0(c) \\ e^{(x_0(c)-x_i(c))*(1-wtp)*SF} & \text{otherwise} \end{cases} \quad (9)$$

3. GRG calculation
   Once the normalised decision matrix D' has been computed, equation(2) is used to calculate the GRG for each alternative. Candidates are ranked in order and the x_i achieving the highest GRG is deemed the most suitable communication medium for ITS data dissemination.

Analysis of the GRA-based SCM is carried out through simulation, the details of which are outlined in the following section.

4   CALMnet Simulation Environment

Simulations are carried out using CALMnet, a comprehensive network-centric simulation environment, built on top of the OPNET simulation tool, for CALM-based cooperative vehicular systems [20]. UMTS has ubiquitous coverage within this environment and 10 RSUs are placed 1km apart along this roadway, acting as gateways to the network backbone.

The proposed GRA-based candidate ranking scheme is compared with two other approaches.

- Random Selection: the carrier network for the ITS application traffic is randomly selected. Safety services use broadcast communications and can be carried over any WAVE channel and UMTS. However, since the WAVE control channel (CCH) is for non-IP traffic, this is not considered as a candidate for Subscriber and Personalised services.
- Simple Matching based Selection: here, the selection requirements are simply matched with the candidate network abilities. The CCH is designed specifically to meet the need of safety applications; therefore a policy is adopted whereby safety traffic is always carried on this channel. For all other data traffic, the selection is based on simple candidate scoring. Here, all input parameters are equally weighted in importance to the overall decision and candidate scores are incremented to reflect a match with service requirements and user preferences. The candidate with the highest score is deemed the best solution.

Mobility

The open source Simulation of Urban MObility (SUMO) v0.11 package was used as the road traffic simulator to generate realistic microscopic vehicular mobility patterns. Vehicles move in each lane on the highway with varying speeds that are restricted to a maximum speed of 120km/h. The vehicle density for the simulated scenario is illustrated in Figure 1. The high density of vehicles seen at approximately 3000m is caused by the presence of a toll plaza. Here the maximum speed is capped at 50kmph resulting in a build up of vehicles in this location and thus ensuring that both free flow and congested road traffic conditions are observed.

Application Modelling

Six distinct applications are defined, the details of which are presented in Table 1. These specify their data lifetime and reliability requirements, which are used as inputs to the ranking procedure.

User preference in relation to the WTP is modelled based on data plans currently offered by mobile operators. Three categories of user are defined:

- All you can eat (AYCE)
  Users in this category have no limit on their data usage. Therefore, they are not concerned with the cost of using any ITS services; their WTP = 1 for all services.

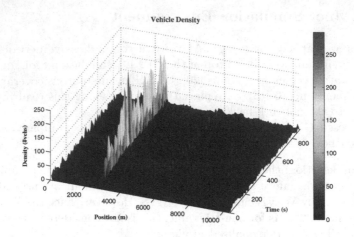

Fig. 1. Vehicle Density for simulated highway mobility scenario

Table 1. Application specifications

Service Class	Application	Communication Mode	Frequency	Data Lifetime	Reliabilty
Safety	Hazard warning	V2V Broadcast	10Hz	100ms	1.0
	Flexible lane change	V2V Broadcast	1Hz	500ms	1.0
Subscriber	Platoon	V2V	exp(45)s	15s	0.98
	TUS	V2I	exp(180)s	30s	0.95
Personalised	CVAS	V2V	-	15	1.0
	Buslane reservation	V2I	-	10	1.0

– 2GB limit
  Users on this plan have a moderate data usage plan and can afford to run
  ITS services. In this category the WTP ranges between [0, 0.7] for subscriber
  services and [0, 0.8] for personalised services.
– 200MB limit
  These users have limited data usage and will have a low WTP; between [0,
  0.4] for subscriber services and [0, 0.5] for personalised services.

5   SCM Performance Analysis

Assessing the performance of the proposed SCM framework in the cooperative
vehicular environment requires examination of the random, simple matching and

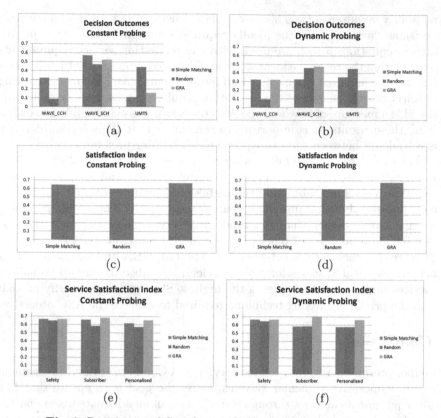

Fig. 2. Decisions and Satisfaction Index for all selection schemes

GRA based ranking algorithms as well as the two proposed monitoring methods. Two main factors are considered:

– Selection Decisions
   This gives an insight into the operation of the ranking procedure, demonstrating the choices made under the varying working conditions experienced. Figures 2(a) and 2(b) illustrate the selection decisions for each of the selection methods using both constant and dynamic probing. Here, it is evident how the network condition monitoring technique has an effect on the candidate ranking procedure with the proportions of CI selection differing for both probing schemes. As expected, the Simple Policy and GRA schemes have identical values for the WAVE CCH since all safety services are transported over this CI. Simple policy matching the WAVE SCH 57% and 33% and UMTS 10% and 35% for all decisions using constant and dynamic probing respectively. GRA has a breakdown of 52%/16% for the SCH and 47%/20% for UMTS in the constant/dynamic probing scenarios.

– Satisfaction Index (SI)
   The SI is defined as the degree to which the chosen communications network satisfies the WTP user preference and the service data lifetime and

reliability requirements. This is calculated using GRA to determine each decisions' distance from the ideally required solution. To assess the performance, equations 3 to 9 are used, with the requesting service requirements representing the reference ideal solution. The maximum grade of 1 will therefore only be achieved when exactly all requirements have been met. Referring to selections which exceed the requesting requirements will not score highly; the SI is a measure of how well the ASC objective was achieved. When examining these results, it is important to remember that the selection decision is a trade off between service requirements and user preference.

The overall SI values for each scheme is presented in Figures 2(c) and 2(d). Here, GRA-based ranking outperforms the random and simple matching selection techniques, obtaining the highest index values of 0.67 and 0.68 in constant and dynamic probing scenarios respectively. The simple matching scheme scores higher than the random selection, achieving an SI of 0.64 and 0.6. The final set of plots in 2(e) and 2(f) illustrate the breakdown of SI scores for each service category. As expected, GRA and simple matching achieve identical SI scores for safety services. For subscriber and personalised services however, GRA achieves the highest SI scores, again verifying that it is the principal ranking technique required to achieve the ASC objective.

6 Conclusions

This paper presented a framework for Service and Communication Management (SCM) in cooperative vehicular systems. Here, the goal is to ensure that ITS service requirements are met through the selection of an adequate dissemination medium from the underlying heterogeneous communication network. Specifying an objective of "Always Satisfactorily Connected" (ASC), random, simple matching and GRA-based selections are examined for both constant and dynamic probing techniques. Results show that GRA-based selection better services user and application requirements in the CALM-based cooperative vehicular environment. Constant probing proved to be the best condition monitoring technique for simple matching based selection, while the highest satisfaction index was achieved for GRA-based selection using dynamic probing.

Future work will study the affect of RSU density on the decision process; the urban scenario will also be examined. Also, the comparison of an "Always Best Connected" objective with the proposed ASC will be carried out. Additional communications technologies will also be considered.

References

1. 802.11p-2010 - IEEE Standard for Information technology– Local and metropolitan area networks– Specific requirements– Part 11: Wireless LAN Medium Access Control (MAC) and Physical Layer (PHY) Specifications Amendment 6: Wireless Access in Vehicular Environments
2. Car-to-Car Communication Consortium, Car-to-Car Communications Manifesto, Overview of the C2C-CC System (August 2007), http://www.car-to-car.org/

3. Continuous Air-interface for Long to Medium range (CALM)
4. Telematics Update, White Paper: The Connected Car Business Model: Will a standardised approach propel further adoption, or inhibit brand differentiation? (April 2013)
5. Electromagnetic compatibility and Radio spectrum Matters (ERM); Intelligent Transport Systems(ITS); Part 1: Technical characteristics for pan-European harmonized communication equipment operating in the 5 GHz frequency range and intended for critical road-safety applications
6. CoOperative Vehicle Infrastructure Systems (CVIS), http://www.cvisproject.org
7. Electromagnetic compatibility and Radio spectrum Matters (ERM); Intelligent Transport Systems (ITS); Part 2: Technical characteristics for pan-European harmonized communications equipment operating in the 5 GHz frequency range and intended for road safety and traffic management, and for non-safety applications related ITS applications
8. Cooperative Systems for Intelligent Road Safety (COOPERS), http://www.coopers-ip.eu
9. Huang, L., Chew, K.A., Tafazolli, R.: Network Selection for One-to-Many Services in 3G-Broadcasting cooperative networks. In: IEEE Vehicular Technology Conference VTC Spring (May 2005)
10. Dhar, S., Ray, A., Nath Bera, R.: A Context Aware Vertical Handover Algorithm for Vehicular Communication. International Journal of Electronics, Computer and Communications Technologies 2(1) (October 2011)
11. Mitra, S.: Optimal Network Selection Algorithm for Heterogeneous Wireless Networks. In: 5th International Conference on Industrial and Information Systems ICIIS (August 2010)
12. Sibanda, C., Bagula, A.: Network Selection for Mobile Nodes in Heterogeneous Wireless Networks using Knapsack Problem Dynamic Algorithms. In: 20th Telecommunications Forum TELFOR (November 2012)
13. Wang, L., Binet, D.: TRUST: A Trigger Based Automatic Subjective Weighting Method for Network Selection. In: Advanced International Conference on Telecommunications AICT (May 2009)
14. Cui, H., Zhu, L., Yang, S., Li, J.: A Novel Network Selection Algorithm of Service-Based Dynamic Weight Setting. In: 4th International Symposium in Wireless Pervasive Computing ISWPC (2009)
15. Chai, R., Tang, L., Xiao, M., Chen, Q.: Adaptive network selection algorithm based on user application profile. In: 5th International ICST Conference on Communications and Networking in China (CHINACOM) (August 2010)
16. Bouland Mussabbir, Q., Yao, W., Niu, Z., Fu, X.: Optimized FMIPv6 using IEEE 802.21 MIH Services in Vehicular Networks. IEEE Transactions on Vehicular Technology, Special Issue on Vehicular Communications Networks (November 2007)
17. Lungaro, P.: Word-of-Mouth in Radio Access Markets. In: IEEE 63rd Vehicular Technology Conference VTC Spring (May 2006)
18. Bari, F., Leung, V.: Network Selection with Imprecise Information in Heterogeneous All-IP Wireless Systems. In: Wireless Internet Conference (WiCon) (October 2007)
19. Bari, F., Leung, V.: Use of Non-monotonic Utility in Multi-attribute Network Selection. In: Wireless Telecommunications Symposium (April 2007)
20. Brickley, O., Koubek, M., Rea, S., Pesch, D.: A Network Centric Simulation Environment for CALM-based Cooperative Vehicular Systems. In: SIMUTOOLS (March 2010)

Investigation of Different Approaches for QoE-Oriented Scheduling in OFDMA Networks*

Florian Wamser, Sebastian Deschner, Thomas Zinner, and Phuoc Tran-Gia

University of Würzburg, Am Hubland, Germany
{wamser,deschner,zinner,trangia}@informatik.uni-wuerzburg.de

Abstract. QoE- and application-aware scheduling is a new paradigm for mobile communication networks. It aims at making better use of network resources with respect to the perceived quality of the users. To achieve this, it specifies an interaction between application and networking layers. Previous work has shown that such a resource management is possible by the weighting of applications and the definition of key quality indicators. However, quantification of the benefits and the impact on the application itself is hardly studied, since it requires precise modeling of both the data transmission in the mobile network as well as the application itself. In this paper the influence of different cross-layer scheduling heuristics on the application is examined for the air interface of LTE mobile networks. For this, not only the physical data transmission but also the application behavior is simulated in detail for Skype, YouTube, web browsing, and downloads. For each application quality indicators are defined that provide information on the current performance of the application. The investigated scheduling approaches take into account detailed application information of different levels like the application type, the current status of the application, or the ability of an application to adapt to the network situation.

1 Introduction

Nowadays, high data rates in mobile networks are possible. They allow high quality streaming or similar services that were usually reserved only for fixed network users. The requirements for these applications are diverse and typically vary over time due to video encoding, download patterns, or user behavior. Today's networks support them based on Quality of Service (QoS) parameters. However, compliance with the QoS policies on the network level does not necessarily guarantee a good quality of applications. From the user's perspective, a good application quality is defined by parameters related to the application such as video quality, waiting times or responsiveness of the application. A major challenge for network operators is therefore the consideration of these requirements within the network to meet the user expectations.

* This work has been funded by the German Research Foundation under grant TR 257/28-2 (FunkOFDMA).

D. Pesch et al. (Eds.): MONAMI 2013, LNICST 125, pp. 172–187, 2013.
© Institute for Computer Sciences, Social Informatics and Telecommunications Engineering 2013

Quality of Experience (QoE) and application-aware scheduling is a new paradigm for mobile communication networks based on the interaction between application and network layer. It enhances traditional scheduling approaches that rely on objective measures such as packet loss rate, channel quality, transfer delay or delay variation, by additionally taking application information into account. This requires an identification of the key influence parameters on the application quality as well as means to monitor these parameters. Depending on the type of application, these parameters may be measured at the end-device or in the network using techniques like deep packet inspection. Today's packet schedulers in cellular networks are based on hard QoS parameters, i.e., they either can provide the requested QoS or not. This differs for QoE-based schedulers which may provide several thresholds for a certain, as well as, for a varying application quality. Accordingly, this flexibility can be used to exploit the temporal variability of the transmission channel to better support applications or compensate local load peaks by using fewer resources.

Previous work has shown that QoE scheduling for applications is possible through the utilization of certain information and the definition of key quality indicators. Kahn et al. [1] define cross-layer scheduling with a so-called utility function. The aim is to maximize the utility in order to optimize the QoE. In [2], QoE influence factors are determined and measured for web traffic. According to them, a QoE-oriented scheduling is defined. Wamser et al. [3] utilize the buffered YouTube playtime for QoE-aware scheduling in OFDMA networks. All solutions consider QoE or application information. Nevertheless, quantification of the benefits and the impact on the application itself are hardly studied, since it requires precise modeling of both the data transmission in the mobile network as well as the application itself.

In this paper, a simulative investigation is performed on how application information of varying degrees of detail may provide a more effective packet scheduling in the air interface of LTE mobile networks. All simulation runs are performed within an LTE system level simulator which involves a detailed application-layer model of YouTube, Skype, and TCP, as well as the LTE protocol stack and wireless channel models. The scheduling approaches that are proposed and investigated are of increasing complexity. First, fixed service flows for applications are arranged with respect to the recognized application type. Then, approaches are proposed that require more information about the application such as application status. Finally, a direct signaling of QoE-related application parameters is assumed. Issues such as scalability are not addressed in this paper. Furthermore, only one single cell is simulated.

The remainder of the paper is structured as follows. In Section 2 the technical background for scheduling is summarized as well as an overview of various scheduling approaches is given. Section 3 describes the investigated scheduling algorithms. In Section 4 the application models are introduced that are used for the evaluation of the schedulers. After that follows the description of the simulation in Section 5. In Section 6 a scheduling taking into account the adaptation behavior of Skype is presented. Finally, a comprehensive statistical evaluation of different scheduling approaches is done in Section 7. At the end, conclusions are drawn in Section 8.

2   Background and Related Work

Unlike random access-based networks, the transmission of data packets in mobile networks is controlled by the base station. It performs a scheduling of the pending packets that determines when data is transmitted to a user and when a user is allowed to send data to the base station. The basic idea of the scheduling is to dynamically assign resources for the transmission according to their required data rate and QoS conditions.

Previous approaches often aim at maximizing the potential total throughput in a cell while providing some degree of fairness. This includes common scheduling approaches that take advantage of time-varying channel conditions such as proportional fair scheduling or variants of opportunistic scheduling. Current approaches, however, consider more and more the application or the user as well as his demands on the network.

For example, there is utility-based scheduling. The idea of utility-based scheduling [1,4,5] is based on the fact that different QoS parameters have a different effect on the QoE of an application. Thus, the QoS parameters are weighted and a utility function is defined based on them. The aim is to maximize the utility in order to optimize the QoE. Furthermore, there are cross-layer approaches that consider directly the QoE that the end user experiences. In [6,7], the continuously monitored QoE of voice connections is considered for scheduling and admission control decisions for IEEE 802.16 networks. In [3], the buffered playtime of YouTube video streaming is utilized for a dynamic prioritization of YouTube traffic to increase the QoE. In [2], a mapping for web traffic is presented to allow for a direct consideration of web browsing within the scheduling.

In contrast to specific scheduling approaches, there is also a 3GPP working group to study general mechanisms and approaches to avoid user plane congestion in LTE networks [8]. One use-case of this working group is the specification of congestion-based policy rules for the radio access network for crowded cells.

3   Description of the Studied Scheduling Algorithms

The objective of the paper is to investigate and simulate different scheduling concepts or heuristics and have a look at the benefits and the impact on the applications.

For comparison, we first specify a simple proportional fair scheduler as a reference scheduler. Afterwards, we start with arranging fixed service flows for Skype. This is based on the concept of QoS provisioning for applications in mobile networks where QoS profiles are assigned to LTE bearers or IEEE 802.16 service flows. The idea however is that the classes are selected in such a way that the throughput is restricted for application that are able to adapt to low network resources such as Skype. Hence, there are resources that are available for other applications. Then, we move on to signaling approaches that provide direct feedback on the requirements of the applications to the scheduler.

3.1 Proportional Fair Scheduling

The proportional fair scheduler addresses both fairness and throughput in the network. This is achieved by assigning each user i at transmission frame f a priority M which is based on the present achievable transmission rate r and the previously achieved overall throughput R.

$$M_i^R(f) = \frac{r_i^\alpha}{R_i^\beta}. \tag{1}$$

It should be noted that the available total bandwidth B depends on the scheduling since different assignments lead to different user throughputs due to the adaptive modulation and coding of the users.

3.2 Fixed Service Class for Skype

Service classes define QoS parameters such as maximum throughput and minimum latency for all users of the class. The service class schedulers used in this work are specifically designed for Skype video calls to take advantage of the adaptation capabilities of Skype. The idea is to restrict a Skype user to a specified bandwidth in order to gain resources for other users. The constraint is selected in such a way that only a small QoE degradation occurs since Skype adapts to the given conditions. More precisely, the goal is to avoid that Skype changes the resolution but adjusts the frame rate and image quality.

Application-Based Service Class. The application based service class is a service class with a guaranteed bandwidth for all Skype users in the cell. This requires the base station to know whether the packets belong to Skype or not. All packets belonging to Skype users are assigned to this class. It is the simplest approach to set a restriction for Skype. Within the class a proportional fair scheduling is done. The scheduling is depicted in Algorithm 1.

Flow-Based Service Class. Flow-based service classes guarantee QoS parameters for single flows instead of application groups. In this case, we guarantee 30 % of the maximum transmission rate of Skype to each Skype user since this is slightly higher than the throughput at which Skype changes the resolution of the video encoding according to our model.

On Demand Flow-Based Service Class. The on demand flow-based service class is similar to the previous one but instead of throttling the throughput of the Skype users all the time, this is only done if there is another application that requires bandwidth. Hence, Skype is able to get more throughput if the situation allows it. In this paper, the limitation in throughput is only triggered by the YouTube users. If there is a YouTube flow in its initial best effort phase, or with a low buffer level (less than 3 s), the service class is activated and all Skype users get the guaranteed but limited throughput as long as enough resources are available.

Algorithm 1. Application-based Service Class Scheduling

1: $bandwidth\_skype\_class = 0$
2:
3: **while** $bandwidth\_skype\_class < max.$ $bandwidth$ for the $class$ **do**
4:    $packet\ list \leftarrow ProportionalFair(skype\ packets)$
5:    $bandwidth\_skype\_class + = packet.size$
6: **end while**
7:
8: **while** $bandwidth\ available$ **do**
9:    $packet\ list \leftarrow ProportionalFair(\neg skype\ packets)$
10: **end while**

3.3   QoE Scheduling Using Application Parameters

The QoE scheduler is similar to the proportional fairness scheduler, but instead of using a priority proportional to the possible throughput, a throughput inversely proportional to the current estimated QoE is used. Hence, if the application is currently in a very good condition, it is assigned a very low priority. However, if the application is in a poor condition, it gets a higher priority. While this scheduler achieves good results since every application only is assigned as much bandwidth as it really needs, it makes signaling between the end-users and the base station necessary. In our case, we assume that a logical feedback channel exists between the client application and the scheduling entity in the base station [3]. The application condition is mapped onto a mean opinion score (MOS) scale by the metrics presented in Table 1. The MOS value is the arithmetic mean of individual subjective ratings of test users for the quality of a service. It ranges from 1 (poor) to 5 (excellent). According to the QoE model in [9], stalling (interruption in the video playback) is by far the main influence factor of YouTube QoE. Therefore, the current buffer level of the YouTube player is reported to the base station. For web browsing, the loading time of a web page is monitored and for downloads the current throughput is measured, c.f. [10]. In the following, we call this scheduler QoE feedback scheduler.

Table 1. QoE metric for the different applications

QoE	file download	web browsing	YouTube	Skype		
	throughput	page loading	buffer	frame rate	image quality I	resolution
[MOS]	[Mbps]	time [s]	level [s]	F [fps]		
1	< 0.25	> 5	< 2	-	-	160x120
2	0.25 - 0.5	3 - 5	2 - 4	-	-	320x240
3	0.5 - 1	2 - 3	4 - 8	$3 + \frac{F}{35fps} + (2I - 1)$		640x480
4	1 - 2	1.5 - 2	8 - 16			
5	> 2	< 1.5	> 16			

4   Modeling of the Investigated Applications

For application-aware scheduling, it is important to model the application accurately. This section describes the modeling of the four investigated applications for the evaluation, namely file download, web browsing, YouTube, and Skype.

4.1   File Download

The file download is the most simple application in the simulation. It represents the download of a big data file. Therefore, a best effort transmission over TCP is simulated. The HTTP protocol is not simulated. The size of the downloaded data can be specified by the user. Hence, the download only depends on the simulated physical link and the behavior of the TCP congestion avoidance algorithm.

4.2   Web Browsing

Web browsing of a user is modeled as follows. A web session consists of the download of a web page followed by an exponentially distributed reading time of a mean of 3 s. The web page itself consists of a main object and several embedded objects. Embedded objects are images, JavaScript code or CSS style sheet instructions. The number of embedded objects, the size of these objects and the size of the main object follow random variables whose distributions are listed in Table 2. TCP is used as transport protocol. The web server takes care about the TCP connection handling. The keep-alive timeout for HTTP/1.1 connections is set to 5s based on the values of the default configuration of the Apache web server. Furthermore, no speed or connection limit is set.

Table 2. Web session simulation parameters [3]

reading time	neg. exponential: $\mathrm{Exp}(3s)$
volume main object	log-normal: $\ln \mathcal{N}(10 \text{ kbytes}, 25 \text{ kbytes})$ $\in [100 \text{ bytes}, 2 \text{ Mbytes}]$
number of embedded objects	truncated Pareto(scale, shape, max): $Pr(1.1, 2, 55)$
volume embedded object	log-normal: $\ln \mathcal{N}(8 \text{ kbytes}, 126 \text{ kbytes})$ $\in [50 \text{ bytes}, 2 \text{ Mbytes}]$

4.3   YouTube

The YouTube Flash Player and a YouTube download server is simulated for YouTube users. The player processes HTTP data to display the YouTube video. In particular, it calculates the current buffered video playtime in seconds. The player may stall if the playtime buffer is empty. The play-out delay after stalling is set to 3 s buffered playtime which is the current value of the YouTube video player. The YouTube download server behavior follows [11] with refinements according to own measurements. The download speed is controlled by the server in two phases. The size S_{ip} of the initial best effort phase depends on the mean data rate x of the Adobe Flash video. It corresponds to a buffered playtime of 40 s, hence it is calculated as

$$S_{ip} = 40s \cdot x. \tag{2}$$

The periodic phase sends data in blocks of 64 kB with a fixed inter-arrival time. The inter-arrival time ΔT_{arr} depends on the target transmission rate which is 125 % of the mean data rate x of the Flash video, but has a maximum of 2.096 s. Therefore it is calculated as

$$\Delta T_{arr} = min(2.096s, \frac{64kbytes}{1.25x}). \tag{3}$$

4.4   Skype-Like Video Conferencing

The objective is to model a Skype-like application that dynamically adjusts the video parameters depending on the network quality. For this purpose, measurements of Skype from February 2012 serve as a basis for modeling. This section is separated into two different parts, describing the server model for the sending behavior on the one hand, and the self-adapting client behavior on the other hand.

Sending Behavior. We consider only video calls. A call can be started and finished. Hence, it cannot be degraded to a voice call or instant messaging. Additionally, no connection process and buddy list updates take place in background. Only the downlink direction is taken into account. Due to this, the application in the simulation only performs unidirectional transmitting of data directly from a so-called Skype server to a client with UDP transport protocol. Consequently, server and client must be started two times for a realistic video call, as in both directions usually video is transmitted. It is assumed that Skype can adjust three parameters in order to adapt to the current network performance. According to our measurements, the frame rate p_{mfr}, the resolution p_{res}, and the image quality p_{qua} can be adjusted during video calls. The maximum frame rate is set to 35 fps. The image quality is modeled by a factor between 0 and 1. An image quality of 1 corresponds to the best quality. Values below 1 indicate that some kind of lossy compression is used. There are three resolutions available. They are '640x480', '320x240', and '160x120' which result in a data rate ratio of 100 %, 25 %, and 6.25 %. The Skype server periodically sends data blocks to the client. The block inter-arrival time can be described by

$$\Delta T_{ar} = 1/p_{mfr}. \tag{4}$$

Next to p_{res} and p_{qua}, the blocksize additionally depends on a total data rate. It is set to $p_{tdr} = 1.2\,Mbps$. The maximum frame rate is set to $p_{mfr} = 35$. Consequently, the blocksize for our Skype-like application is described by

$$B_{size} = p_{tdr} \cdot p_{qua} \cdot p_{res}/p_{mfr}. \tag{5}$$

Self-adapting Behavior. In order to instantly react to poor network conditions, the application in our model measures packet delay. A high packet delay is assumed to be caused by high network load. Therefore, the client signals the server that it should enter a "poor network" routine in order to decrease the quality of the video call. This is exactly done if the measured mean packet delay during the last second exceeds the threshold of 75 ms. In the next step, the application resets the parameters for the frame rate and the image quality. Afterwards, periodic requests of the current packet delay serve to estimate the current performance of the connection. In case the packet delay stays below the threshold of 75 ms, the frame rate is increased in our model up to 17 fps. In case the packet delay exceeds the threshold, the image quality is decreased in steps of 0.1 to a minimum of 0.5. Afterwards, the resolution is decreased, while the image quality is set to 1. The algorithm stops if either the minimum resolution and image quality or the targeted frame rate is reached.

In addition, the application in our model also performs a second routine in order to increase the video quality, if possible. This routine runs periodically every 10 s during the complete Skype video call. It is only activated if the previous described routine is not active. If the packet delay is lower than a threshold of 35 ms, the algorithm starts to increase the video encoding until the packet delay exceeds the threshold. The encoding is increased every 500 ms. Our model first tries to increase the resolution, afterwards the image quality is increased and finally the frame rate is increased. If the packet delay exceeds the threshold during this procedure, the encoding is set back to the last working encoding and the routine stops.

5 Description of the Simulation

One mobile cell is simulated with a time-discrete event-based simulator for LTE mobile networks. The physical data transmission is performed on the basis of precalculated link-level curves for packet error and goodput from separate simulations with the LTE Downlink Link Level Simulator of the Technical University of Vienna[1]. The simulator implements a complete signal processing chain for the traffic channel. PHY and MAC functions are implemented according to LTE release 8 [12] as specified in [13,14]. A carrier frequency of 2.5 GHz, a bandwidth of 5 MHz, and a cell diameter of 250 m have been chosen. The signaling and control channels are simulated as error-free. Based on this physical simulation a complete system model is implemented with TCP transport protocol and application layer. TCP Cubic with congestion control, error detection and flow control is simulated for each user to obtain realistic scenarios even in overload situations. The propagation model for the data transmission consists of path loss, shadow fading, and multipath fading. Path loss is calculated according to the Winner II urban macro-cell model [15]. Furthermore, the shadow fading decorrelation distance is set to 50 m. The users move around randomly within the cell with a speed of 1 m/s. For this purpose, 200 SNR channel traces has been precalculated

---

[1] http://www.nt.tuwien.ac.at/ltesimulator

since on the fly computation is very time consuming. One SNR channel trace is assigned to each user with a random time offset. The users are able to watch YouTube videos, conduct Skype video calls, download files, or surf the Internet. On the packet level, a queue based scheduling at the base station is done.

Only the downlink is considered in this work, since it is assumed that this constitutes the bottleneck of the access network. The transmission is controlled by a packet scheduler. Each user has a packet buffer which is limited in size. The packet scheduler chooses the packets from the user queues according to the scheduling algorithm and passes them to the resource allocator. The resource allocation then selects the appropriate modulation and encoding based on the link-level curves depending on the users channel and places it in the frame.

6 Scheduling Taking into Account the Adaptation Behavior of Skype

As an example for semi-static scheduling, we demonstrate in the following how the adaptive capabilities of Skype can be exploited to gain bandwidth for other users. In overload situations an application like Skype, which adaptively adjusts to different network situations, is restricted to a reasonable extent to obtain resources for other applications. Such a redistribution of resources does not necessarily mean that the network resources are shared fairly. A reasonable allocation must be achieved depending on the application type (video, browsing, gaming, e.g.) because a high definition video obviously needs more bandwidth than a user surfing the Internet. The overall goal is a consistent and equal QoE on application level for all users.

The simulated scenario includes 7 Skype and 7 YouTube users and is simulated for 80 s. One Skype user and two YouTube users are shown exemplarily in the figures. The explanation of the scheduling behavior is based on these users. The channel conditions of the Skype user and the two YouTube users during the simulation are depicted in Figure 1. The YouTube users have good channel conditions at the beginning and up to a simulation time of 50 s. During this time period they achieve the maximum possible bandwidth.

Figure 2 shows the resulting behavior of the applications. In this case the proportional fair scheduler is used. Figure 2(a) depicts the throughput of the YouTube users, their corresponding buffer levels during the simulation and the mean data rates of the videos. YouTube user A with a mean data rate of about 1.2 Mbps maintains full video playback buffers during the complete simulation. In contrast, the video playback of YouTube user B is interrupted for 5 times during the simulation since his throughput is below the mean data rate of his video. Figure 2(b) shows the throughput of the Skype user and resulting video quality during the simulation. The resolution is not shown here since it stays at the maximum during the whole simulation. However, the frame rate and the image quality is changed often after the YouTube users have started their transmission. This can be explained by the insufficient channel quality of the user and the congestion in the cell. As soon as the channel conditions for the Skype user are better, the video encoding returns to its maximum.

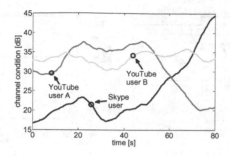

Fig. 1. Channel of users during the simulation

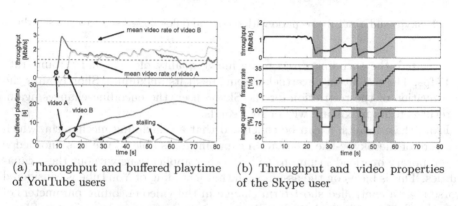

(a) Throughput and buffered playtime of YouTube users

(b) Throughput and video properties of the Skype user

Fig. 2. Skype and YouTube scenario with proportional fair scheduler

After 50 s the channel quality of YouTube user A drops significantly which results in about half of the available bandwidth for this user. The channel for the Skype user is of low quality from 0 s to 50 s, but improves quickly after 50 s.

Figure 3 shows the simulation of the same scenario with the on demand flow-based service class described in Section 3.2. Figure 3(a) depicts the situation for the YouTube users. The restriction for Skype users is activated immediately after the YouTube users start the transmission. The throughput of both YouTube users is significantly higher now, compared to the scenario with the proportional fair scheduler. Between 20 s and 30 s the throughput of user B drops below the mean data rate of his video. Yet this does not lead to stalling (interruptions in the video playback) since YouTube user A enters his periodic phase after 30 s and so the throughput of YouTube user B exceeds the mean data rate of his video again. Both YouTube users experience no stalling during the whole simulation. Their QoE is not degraded. After 50 s the service class is deactivated since both YouTube users completed their initial phases and their buffer levels are higher than three seconds.

Figure 3(b) shows the video encoding of the Skype user for the scheduling with the on demand flow-based service class scheduler. As soon as the service class

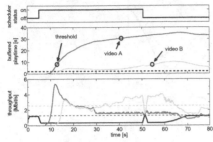
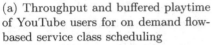
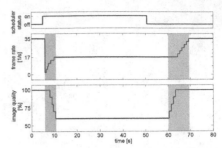

(a) Throughput and buffered playtime of YouTube users for on demand flow-based service class scheduling

(b) Video properties of the Skype user for on demand flow-based service class scheduling

Fig. 3. Skype and YouTube scenario with on demand flow-based service class scheduler

is activated, the encoding drops to an image quality of 60 % and a frame rate of 17 fps. The resolution nevertheless remains at its maximum. Shortly after the deactivation of the restriction for the Skype user, the encoding changes again. It returns to its maximum within 10 seconds.

From these results, it can be concluded that a scheduling mechanism, which is aware of the Skype-like adaptation capabilities, is able to use this knowledge in temporary overload situations to help other applications without these capabilities. This is based on the assumption that a stalling of YouTube is considered worse than a controlled short-term change in the video encoding parameters of Skype [16]. However, the benefit is dependent on a large number of active Skype users in the cell because each Skype-user only provides a small resource gain. For network operators, this means that this solution is only useful if enough Skype users are on the network.

7   Investigation and Comparison of Scheduling Approaches and Their Effect on Applications

In the following, the performance of the schedulers described in Section 3 is statistically evaluated with the aim to compare the benefit and the impact of the different approaches on the applications. The following paragraph describes three different scenarios that have been chosen for the evaluation. 100 runs are conducted per scheduler and scenario. Afterwards the impact of the schedulers is described for each application separately. The evaluation is based on carefully chosen application quality indicators which provide a high QoE correlation: For YouTube the buffered playtime is used, since stalling is the main factor for a QoE degradation [9]. For web browsing the download time of the content is chosen while for file downloads the amount of downloaded data is considered as key quality indicator, c.f. [10]. For Skype the image quality and the steadiness of the video encoding are used.

Scenario Description. Scenario I, II, and III represent different situations in a cell. In the first scenario the cell is frequented only moderately, in the second scenario highly. In the third scenario the system is overloaded. The Skype users, download users, and web browsing users start directly at the beginning of the simulation. The starting time of the YouTube users is calculated from a uniform distribution between second 5 and second 20. For each user one out of 10 videos is randomly chosen. The system is simulated for 100 s. Scenario I simulates 19 users. There are 7 Skype users, two download users, four web browsing users, and 6 YouTube users. Scenario II consists of 25 users. There are 8 Skype users, three download users, 6 web browsing users, and 8 YouTube users. Scenario III simulates 34 users. There are 10 Skype users, four download users, 10 web browsing users and 10 YouTube users.

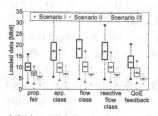 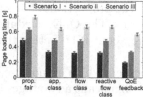 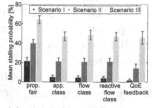

(a) Average loaded data of the file download users   (b) Average loading time of the web browsing users   (c) Average stalling probability of the YouTube users

Fig. 4. Evaluation of the amount of downloaded data, the page load time of web browsing users, and the stalling probability of YouTube

File Download. Figure 4(a) shows the amount of downloaded data of the file download users for the five different schedulers during all three scenarios. The red line indicates the median of the loaded data, the red circle indicates the average loaded data. The box shows the 40 % quantile of the results. The complete range is indicated by the dotted line and the triangles. The results differ but a tendency can be observed. With a higher number of users in the system the amount of data that the users are able to load decreases. Accordingly, the 40 % quantiles and the entire range of the results become smaller indicating less variance. The three service class schedulers provide comparable results. On average, users are able to load about 17 Mbit in Scenario I, 10 Mbit in Scenario II, and 7 Mbit in Scenario III. Both, the proportional fair scheduler and the scheduler with QoE feedback offer less quality to the file download users. The scheduler with QoE feedback however performs slightly better in Scenario I and II (12 and 8 Mbit) than the proportional fair scheduler (10 and 7 Mbit). For the overloaded Scenario III, the proportional fair scheduler shows similar results as the QoE feedback scheduler.

While the scheduling with service classes performs by far the best regarding the file download users, it should be noted that a lower download throughput might be beneficial for the other users. File downloads are flexible applications and a certain delay or a low download throughput can be tolerated. From a QoE perspective, assigning a lot of bandwidth is not necessary or even a waste of resources. Therefore, a more moderate behavior like the one of the QoE feedback scheduler is desirable to gain resources for other applications as explained in the next section.

Web Browsing. Figure 4(b) shows the average page loading time of the web browsing users between second 30 and 80 of the simulation for the five different schedulers during all three scenarios. Only the transfer time within the mobile network is considered. Delays by the web server or the transmission over the Internet are not included here. The 95 % confidence intervals are indicated by the red lines on top of the bars. The results of all schedulers show the same tendencies. If the number of active users inside the system increases, the page loading time increases, too. However, the respective loading times of the scenarios differ with different schedulers. While there is no significant difference between the three service class schedulers, the proportional fair scheduler shows significantly worse performance by about 0.1 s. The QoE scheduler provides loading times of 0.2 s, 0.3 s and 0.6 s which are about 0.1 s better than the times of the service class schedulers.

Even the service class schedulers which do not use detailed information about the web browsing users, show significant advantages in the average page loading times over the proportional fair scheduler. This benefit is gained by the restriction of the Skype users. The QoE scheduler performs also better. It demonstrates that basic knowledge about the application conditions can improve the scheduling process.

YouTube. Figure 4(c) shows the average stalling probability for YouTube users. Stalling is defined as at least one interruption between second 30 and 80 of the simulation. While the stalling probability increases with a larger number of users in the system, the use of the different application-aware schedulers has no significant impact on the results. All application-aware schedulers result in similar stalling probabilities for all three scenarios. These are about 4 % in Scenario I, 21 % in Scenario II, and 47 % in Scenario III. Especially in the overload Scenario III, stalling can not be completely prevented. The proportional fair scheduler achieves the worst results in all three scenarios with stalling probabilities of 21 %, 40 %, and 64 %.

Skype. Figure 5(a) shows the average time period of a steady video quality relative to the usage time of Skype. The video encoding is considered steady if it does not change within 2 seconds. The results for the different schedulers vary. The video encoding is the most stable with the service class schedulers since they guarantee a certain data rate which is necessary for Skype users. The scheduler with QoE feedback achieves the worst results regarding the relative time period of steady video quality with about 62 % in all three scenarios. The proportional fair scheduler shows different results for the three scenarios. The relative time period of steady video quality is very high (about 86 % in

Scenario I), but much lower for Scenario II (72 %) and Scenario III (65 %). The application-based service class performs comparably in the first two scenarios with a relative steady time of about 80 % but decreases in Scenario III to about 70 % due to the overload. The two flow-based service class schedulers achieve by far the best results.

For this it is concluded that for some applications a smaller but more steady throughput is more efficient than a slightly higher but fluctuating one. The video encoding of Skype is very unstable for schedulers like the QoE feedback scheduler or the proportional fair scheduler. The reason for this is the constantly changing bandwidth assignments with these schedulers.

The downgrade algorithm which is essentially responsible for the adaptation to new network conditions always results in a frame rate of 17 fps if there is congestion in the network. The main changing feature is the image quality. Therefore, the crucial question is how often the video encoding is not at its maximum while Skype is in an adaptive mode. Figure 5(b) shows the average time period of Skype's video coding not being at maximum. During all three scenarios and with all five schedulers the results are similar. Skype is in an adaptive mode during 90 % of the time period for all schedulers, but for the proportional fair scheduler. The proportional fair scheduler tries to provide bandwidth fairness with respect to the throughput. Since Skype requires little bandwidth compared to applications like YouTube or file downloads, this is sufficient and it is much more often in a non-adapted state with the maximum video quality. The more users are in the system, the higher is the probability to be in an adapted state. In Scenario I the probability is 18 %, in Scenario II 55 % and in Scenario III it is 93 %.

For some applications certain compromises have to be made. The proportional fair scheduler is the only one able to provide a high and steady bandwidth so that the maximum video encoding can be used with Skype. However, as Figure 5(a) shows, this is achieved at the expense of a constant quality and to the disadvantage of other applications. Even the scheduler with QoE feedback which

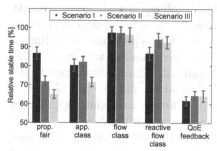

(a) Average time period of steady video quality relative to the usage time of Skype

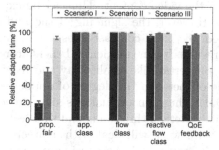

(b) Average time period of Skype's video coding not being at maximum

Fig. 5. Skype video properties

is the most unstable regarding the video quality does not achieve significantly higher probabilities for the maximum encoding. This is due to the load in the network of the other applications which are too greedy to allow this scheduler to assign high bandwidths for flexible applications such as Skype.

Generally considered, the evaluation of the application-aware schedulers in comparison to the proportional fair scheduler demonstrated that application awareness improves the overall situation of the applications in the network. However, there are different results for different applications. For example, the YouTube application has achieved useful results with a scheduler with QoE feedback because the latter can tolerate dynamic changes in the bandwidth due to the video buffer. The Skype application in contrast does not require such a scheduling. For Skype video the QoE scheduling results in a very unstable situation due to the automatic adaptation. In contrast, Skype can benefit from a static service class with guaranteed QoS properties like small delay and fixed throughput.

8   Conclusion

In this paper, we investigated the impact of using application information for scheduling decisions on the downlink within cellular networks on the user perceived quality. In particular, we investigated different scheduling approaches together with varying degrees of available application information like application type, application status or application intelligence, and highlighted their impact on key QoE indicators for web browsing, file downloading, progressive video streaming and Skype video conferencing.

Our results reveal a strong improvement of the overall QoE in case of application-aware scheduling for the investigated use-cases. We further showed that each of the considered applications can benefit from an application-aware scheduling. However, different applications may prefer different types of scheduling. Furthermore, for some applications a large signaling overhead is required. For YouTube a very flexible scheduling can be carried out due to the buffering of the video content. This can be exploited to obtain a multi-user diversity gain. However, the signaling of the buffer level to the scheduling entity is required. Skype in contrast does not require a dynamic scheduling according to our results. It can sufficiently benefit from a static service class with guaranteed QoS properties like small delay and fixed throughput. The results quantify the trade-off between the degree of application information and the gain in terms of QoE. Thus, our evaluations allow to compare different candidate approaches with theoretical thresholds and to select the most appropriate ones.

Future work will deal with a precise evaluation of the signaling overhead, i.e., the costs, and the consideration of other applications for the concept of QoE-oriented and application aware scheduling. In addition combined scheduling approaches will be investigated to allow a scenario-independent optimization of the overall QoE.

References

1. Khan, S., Duhovnikov, S., Steinbach, E., Kellerer, W.: MOS-Based Multiuser Multiapplication Cross-Layer Optimization for Mobile Multimedia Communication. Advances in Multimedia 2007 (2007)
2. Ameigeiras, P., Ramos-Munoz, J.J., Navarro-Ortiz, J., Mogensen, P., Lopez-Soler, J.M.: QoE oriented cross-layer design of a resource allocation algorithm in beyond 3G systems. Computer Communications 33(5), 571–582 (2010)
3. Wamser, F., Staehle, D., Prokopec, J., Maeder, A., Tran-Gia, P.: Utilizing Buffered YouTube Playtime for QoE-oriented Scheduling in OFDMA Networks. In: International Teletraffic Congress (ITC), Krakw, Poland (September 2012)
4. Thakolsri, S., Khan, S., Steinbach, E., Kellerer, W.: QoE-Driven Cross-Layer Optimization for High Speed Downlink Packet Access. Journal of Communications 4(9), 669–680 (2009)
5. Song, G., Li, Y.G.: Utility-Based Resource Allocation and Scheduling in OFDM-Based Wireless Broadband Networks. IEEE Communications Magazine 43(12), 127–143 (2005)
6. Bohnert, T.M., Staehle, D., Kuo, G.-S., Koucheryavy, Y., Monteiro, E.: Speech Quality Aware Admission Control for fixed IEEE 802.16 Wireless MAN. In: IEEE ICC, Beijing, China (May 2008)
7. Bohnert, T.M., Staehle, D., Monteiro, E.: Speech Quality Aware Resource Control for Fixed and Mobile WiMAX. In: Marcos Katz, F.F. (ed.) WiMAX Evolution, p. 227. John Wiley and Sons (January 2009)
8. 3rd Generation Partnership Project., 3GPP TR 22.805 V12.1.0; Feasibility study on user plane congestion management (Release 12), v12.1.0 (December 2012)
9. Hoßfeld, T., Schatz, R., Seufert, M., Hirth, M., Zinner, T., Tran-Gia, P.: Quantification of YouTube QoE via Crowdsourcing. In: IEEE International Workshop on Multimedia Quality of Experience - Modeling, Evaluation, and Directions (MQoE 2011), Dana Point, CA, USA (December 2011)
10. Egger, S., Hoßfeld, T., Schatz, R., Fiedler, M.: Waiting Times in Quality of Experience for Web Based Services. In: QoMEX 2012, Yarra Valley, Australia (July 2012)
11. Alcock, S., Nelson, R.: Application flow control in youtube video streams. ACM SIGCOMM Computer Communication Review 41(2), 24–30 (2011)
12. 3GPP Technical Specification Group RAN, E-UTRA; LTE physical layer – general description, 3GPP, Tech. Rep. TS 36.201 Version 8.3.0 (March 2009)
13. 3GPP Technical Specification Group RAN, E-UTRA; physical channels and modulation, 3GPP, Tech. Rep. TS 36.211 Version 8.7.0 (May 2009)
14. 3GPP Technical Specification Group RAN E-UTRA; multiplexing and channel coding, 3GPP, Tech. Rep. TS 36.212 (March 2009)
15. Winner II consortium, Channel Models Part II: Radio Channel Measurements and Analysis Results, Deliverable 1.1.2," IST-4-027756 WINNER II, Tech. Rep. (September 2007)
16. Zinner, T., Hoßfeld, T., Minash, T.N., Fiedler, M.: Controlled vs. Uncontrolled Degradations of QoE The Provisioning-Delivery Hysteresis in Case of Video. In: New Dimensions in the Assessment and Support of Quality of Experience (QoE) for Multimedia Applications (June 2010)

Model-Free Adaptive Rate Selection
in Cognitive Radio Links*

Álvaro Gonzalo-Ayuso and Jesús Pérez

University of Cantabria,
Department of Communication Engineering,
Santander-39140, Spain
{alvaro,jperez}@gtas.dicom.unican.es

Abstract. In this work we address the rate adaptation problem of a
cognitive radio (CR) link in time-variant fading channels. Every time
the primary users (PU) liberate the channel, the secondary user (SU)
selects a transmission rate (from a finite number of available rates) and
begins the transmission of fixed sized packets until a licensed user reclaims the channel back. After each transmission episode the number of
successfully transmitted packets is used by the SU to update its optimal
rate selection ahead of the next episode. The problem is formulated as
an n-armed bandit problem and it is solved by means of a Monte Carlo
control algorithm.

Keywords: Cognitive radio (CR), rate control, n-armed bandit
problem, reinforcement learning (RL).

1 Introduction

In this work we focus on opportunistic spectrum access (OSA) in hierarchical
cognitive radio (CR) networks where the secondary users (SU's) only use the licensed spectrum when primary users (PU) are not transmitting (in the following
we use "primary user" or PU to refer to the aggregate of primary users). Every
time the PU liberates the channel, the SU begins transmitting until, without
prior notice, the PU reclaims the channel again at any given time.

We consider noncooperative spectrum sharing where each SU makes its own
decision on the spectrum access strategy, based on its error free channel sensing
and the number of data packets successfully transmitted over time. In this work
we focus on a single SU link and we do not take into consideration the compe-
tition between the different SU's. Nonetheless, the proposed scheme would still
work in an scenario with multiple SU's competing to access the channel.

In this work we assume that the SU's support automatic repeat request (ARQ)
protocol, so when a frame is decoded with error, its data is retransmitted in a further frame. Rate adaptation of SU links in CR has been widely addressed in the

* This work was supported by the Spanish Government, Ministerio de Ciencia e Inno-
vación (MICINN), under projects COSIMA (TEC2010-19545-C04-03) and COMON-
SENS (CSD2008-00010, CONSOLIDER-INGENIO 2010).

D. Pesch et al. (Eds.): MONAMI 2013, LNICST 125, pp. 188–201, 2013.

technical literature, [1], [2], [3]. However, none of the above works consider frames retransmission. In [4] frames retransmission was taken into account, but assuming a time independent channel occupancy model. In [5] the authors present a similar problem, however they do not consider time variables scenarios or time dependent occupancy models. In [6] and [7] we considered frames retransmission and we made use of the acknowledgments (ACK's) for rate control, however, in these cases we assumed perfect knowledge of the channel fading and occupancy statistical models. To the best of our knowledge, optimal rate adaptation while considering retransmissions of failed frames, time-dependent channel occupancy and fading models have not been addressed so far in the context of OSA.

In this work we aim to go one step further, we introduce a rate adaptation algorithm in which we do not require any additional information about the channel state and occupancy. The ACK's sent back by the SU receiver are the only information exchanged with the SU transmitter. We propose an energy efficient scheme with a reduce computational cost and hardware complexity with relaxed requirements in terms of delay and transmission rate. This is the main novelty of this work.

We formulate the adaptive rate selection as an n-armed bandit problem [8] where the actions are the different available transmission rates, and the rewards are based on the number of successfully transmitted packets over time and its duration. We propose a Monte-Carlo based algorithm [8] capable of tracking changes in the received signal to noise ratio (SNR), the channel occupancy process and others variables over time to select the optimal rate.

The remaining of this paper is organized as follows; system model is presented in section 2. In section 3 we formulate the problem and we introduce the solving algorithm. In section 4 we present numerical results to evaluate the tracking capacity, the robustness, the speed of convergence and the performance of the algorithm under different scenarios. Finally, section 5 presents the conclusions of this work.

2   System Model

We consider an SU that periodically senses the channel ideally (with zero probability of miss detection and false alarm). Once it detects that the channel is idle, it begins the transmission of a sequence of fixed size data packets until the PU reclaims the channel. Each one of these packets is encoded into a single frame. The SU has the capability of adapting its transmission rate, i.e. the duration of each frame.

The aim of the SU is to maximize its own throughput during the sojourn time of the PU. To achieve this goal, the SU selects a transmission rate from a set $\mathcal{A}$ of $K = |\mathcal{A}|$ different types of available frames, each one with duration T_a and frame error rate (FER) denoted by $p(a, SNR)$, where $a \in \mathcal{A}$ and SNR is the signal to noise ratio at the receiver during the frame transmission. We assume a block fading channel model, namely, the SNR does not change during the transmission of a frame, but it can change from frame to frame.

We consider a conventional and ideal ARQ mechanism to detect frame transmission errors. When the receiver receives a frame, it sends back an ACK packet to the transmitter through an instantaneous error-free feedback channel to inform whether the frame has been correctly decoded or not. Whenever a frame is decoded with error, the corresponding packet must be retransmitted in a further frame.

The SU transmitter does not have access to any information regarding the channel state, the receiver SNR or the PU channel occupancy patterns. The information related to the channel state available to the SU transmitter is:

1. The ACK's sent back by the receiver.
2. The availability of the channel by means of perfect sensing.

We assume that the transmit power constrains on the SU avoid significant interference on the normal operation of the PU. Consistently, whenever the PU occupies the channel, the SU frames are lost.

Primary User Channel Access Model

Figure 1 depicts the channel occupation process by the PU. The channel state changes alternatively between idle and busy periods over time. The duration of the idle/busy periods is given by two random variables denoted by d_i and d_b respectively. Let $F_i(d_i)$ and $F_b(d_b)$ be the corresponding cumulative distribution functions (CDF) that model the occupancy process.

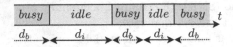

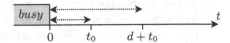

Fig. 1. Channel occupancy process   Fig. 2. Idle period

Regarding figure 2, let $\beta(d|t_0)$ denote the conditional probability that the channel remains idle at time $t_0 + d$ given that it was idle at time t_0. Using Bayes' theorem:

$$\beta(d|t_0) = \begin{cases} \dfrac{1 - F_i(t_0 + d)}{1 - F_i(t_0)}, & t_0 > 0 \\ 1 - F_i(d), & t_0 = 0 \end{cases} \tag{1}$$

Generally, $\beta(d|t_0)$ depends on t_0.

Sensing and Transmission Strategy

Figure 3 illustrates the adopted sensing strategy. The SU periodically senses the channel every T_i seconds and every sensing instance takes T_s seconds. Once it detects that the channel is idle, it begins its own transmission. After transmitting each frame, the SU senses the channel again. As long as the presence of the PU is not detected the SU continues transmitting. Whenever the channel is sensed as busy the SU stops transmitting.

Notice that, when the channel is idle, the time interval between two consecutive sensings depends on the frame duration and it may differ from the interval when the channel is busy. If the PU reclaims the channel during the transmission of a frame, the SU transmitter has no way to detect the collision during the transmission of the current frame. This last frame is usually lost. Figure 3 illustrate this situation, transmission of frame 3 is completed even thought the channel is busy during the last half of the transmission and the frame is therefore lost.

In the following, we will refer to time windows in which the SU transmits, as episodes and we will use T_{eps} to denote their duration. Notice that the actual time interval in which the channel is idle, will in general differ from the observed episode.

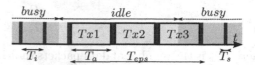

Fig. 3. Sensing and transmission strategy

3   Problem Formulation

We formulate this rate adaptation problem as a n-armed bandit problem [8] with ε-greedy policy, where the set of actions, $\mathcal{A}$, is formed by the set of available rates.

The SU maintains and updates an action-value function, $Q(a)$, which can be understood as an estimated measure of performance for each action (rate). In particular the entries of $Q(a)$ are an estimation of the expected throughput when transmitting each type frame during an episode. After a rate is selected at the beginning of the episode, it will be maintained throughout the entire episode. This approach guarantees that the transmission rate only needs to be changed once per episode (at most). In [6] we showed that for non fading channels, this is optimal or close to optimal. However, it is easy to see that under fading channels and, unless the coherence time of the channel is higher than the average episode duration, this scheme is not optimal, or close to optimal, anymore [7].

Two possibilities arise, exploration and exploitation. Usually, we are interested in exploitation, selecting the action that we expect to yield the best performance, namely the one with the highest Q. However, it is also important to try, or explore, the other actions occasionally in order to keep their estimated values updated. This is of critical importance in a dynamic environment since the expected performance of each action will vary over time. To handle the trade-off between exploration and exploitation we propose to use an ε-greedy policy [8]. With probability $1 - \varepsilon$ the SU selects exploitation, the action with highest current value, $a^* = \arg\max_a Q(a)$, is selected. With probability ε the SU explores and the action is randomly picked from $\mathcal{A}$. An ε-greedy policy is usually expressed as

$$\pi(a) = \begin{cases} 1 - \varepsilon + \varepsilon/K, & a = a^* \\ \varepsilon/K, & a \neq a^*, \end{cases} \tag{2}$$

for $a \in \mathcal{A}$ and where $\pi(a)$ is the probability of selecting action a. The greedier a policy is, the higher the probability of choosing the optimal action.

After each episode concludes, a reward is granted to the decision maker in order to update its value-function. These rewards are a measure of *how good* performed the selected action (rate). In particular, they are an estimation of the throughput during the episode

$$r = \frac{P_{Tx}}{T_{eps}}, \tag{3}$$

where P_{Tx} is the number of data packets that have been successfully transmitted during the episode (number of received ACK's).

Given the reward, the value of the selected action, a, is updated with the following Monte-Carlo [8] rule:

$$Q(a) = Q(a) + \mu(a)\left[r - Q(a)\right], \tag{4}$$

where $0 < \mu(a) \le 1$ is the so called adaptation step. Notice that when $\mu(a) = 1$, the updated value of $Q(a)$ is simply the reward r, the algorithm has no memory of the past episodes.

Large adaptation steps provide a faster convergence in the action-value estimations at the price of smaller precision. On the other hand, smaller values provide slower convergence but can achieve higher precision. Noisy or inaccurate action-value estimations can lead to a noisy ε-greedy policy. If the noise level is high, it can affect the optimal rate selection causing the ε-greedy policy to be unstable continually changing its choice of a^* even in stationary environments. On the other hand, actions that are not currently optimal, are selected less frequently, meaning that their values are most likely outdated. For these actions it makes sense to use a large adaptation step to be sure that a few, or even a single adaptation step, is enough to get a reasonable update of the value.

We propose to use two different step sizes. Optimal action-value estimation is refined with a smaller adaptation step, μ_{opt}, while the other values are kept updated only with less precise estimations by using a larger step size μ_{exp}. Therefore we define $\mu(a)$ as

$$\mu(a) = \begin{cases} \mu_{opt}, & a = a^* \\ \mu_{exp}, & a \ne a^*, \end{cases} \tag{5}$$

with $\mu_{opt} \le \mu_{exp}$. Table 1 illustrates the complete adaptive rate selection algorithm.

4   Numerical Results

In this section we first present the general simulation framework and then, the specific simulations to evaluate the performance of the rate selection algorithm under different realistic scenarios.

Table 1. Adaptive Rate Selection Algorithm

```
Q ← Initialize arbitrarily
π ← Initialize ε-greedy policy from Q
Repeat forever
        ChannelState ← Channel Sensing Output
        If ChannelState = busy
             wait Tᵢ
        Else
             Select rate a using policy π
             P_Tx = 0,  T_eps = 0
             Repeat until ChannelState = busy
                  Transmit a type a frame
                  If an ACK is received → P_Tx = P_Tx + 1
                  T_eps = T_eps + T_a
                  ChannelState ← Channel Sensing Output
                  T_eps = T_eps + T_s
             End
             r = P_Tx/T_eps
```

$$Q(a) = Q(a) + [r - Q(a)] \cdot \begin{cases} \mu_{opt}, & a = a^* \\ \mu_{exp}, & a \neq a^* \end{cases}$$

```
             π ← ε-greedy policy from Q
        End
End
```

4.1 Simulation Framework

Frame Types. Throughout section 4 we assume that there are four different rates available to the SU transmitter, all carrying a payload of 1024 bits. Table 2 shows the frame duration, T_a, for each rate. We also associate each rate with one of the FER curves shown in figure 4. The FER curves of many practical system can be approximated by the exponential function, for this reason we choose to work with the following generic exponential expression to resemble realistic systems

$$FER(a) = A \cdot e^{-B \cdot [SNR + C(a)]},$$

where $A = 10^3$ and $B = 0.6$ are constants, SNR is given in dBs and $C(a)$ represents a SNR shift in dBs and it is also given in table 2 for each rate. All frames encode a single packet of 1024 bits.

In the following we will use *operational SNR range* to refer to the range of SNR values in which a particular rate is optimal. For example, operational SNR range of rate 2 is approximately between 7 and 12 dBs.

Sensing Strategy. We assume that the sensing period $T_i = 0.1$ ms, and negligible sensing time, $T_s = 0$ ms.

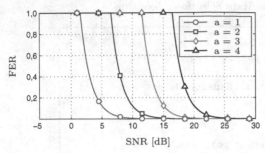

Fig. 4. Frame Error Rate for the four types of frames available

Table 2. Parameters for the four types of frames

rate	T_a [ms]	$C(a)$ [dBs]
1	1.6	10
2	0.8	5
3	0.4	0
4	0.2	-5

PU Channel Access Model. Without loss of generality, and only for simulation purposes, in the following we model d_i and d_b as generalized exponential (GE) random variables with CDF

$$GE_x(x) = \left[1 - e^{-\lambda(x-\mu)}\right]^\alpha, \quad x \geq \mu \tag{6}$$

where $x \geq \mu > 0$, $\lambda > 0$ and $\alpha > 0$. Notice that for $\alpha = 1$ and $\mu = 0$ the GE distribution becomes the exponential distribution with parameter λ

$$\beta(d|t_0) = \frac{1 - \left(1 - e^{-\lambda(t_0+d)}\right)}{1 - \left(1 - e^{-\lambda(t_0)}\right)} = e^{-\lambda d}, \tag{7}$$

which does not depend on t_0. This memoryless exponential model has been extensively used in the literature, however, in many practical cases it is not a realistic one [9].

Specifically, throughout the simulations section we make use of the four different GE distributions described in table 3.

We propose three different distributions, GE_{i1}, GE_{i2} and GE_{i3}, for d_i. In these cases, given $\mu = 0$, d_i can take any value greater than zero. Parameter λ is chosen so that the three distributions share the same mean value. Since $\alpha = 1$,

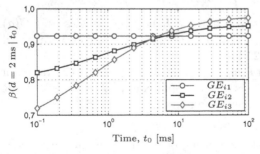

Fig. 5. $\beta\,(d = 1.6\text{ ms}|t_0)$ for the GE_i distributions described in table 3

Table 3. Parameters of the selected CDFs, μ and the mean value in ms

	λ	μ	α	Mean
GE_b	200	2	1	7
GE_{i1}	50	0	1	20
GE_{i2}	30.69	0	0.5	20
GE_{i3}	14.41	0	0.2	20

both GE_{i1} and GE_b are memoryless distributions. Figure 5 illustrates $\beta(d|t_0)$ for $d = 1.6$ ms (the duration of the longest frame), as a function of t_0, for the three GE_i distributions.

The distribution of d_b has an important influence on the performance of the adaptation scheme. In time varying environments, the probability that the learned value-function resembles the real channel state decreases with the duration of the busy intervals.

Channel Fading. We consider both, simple additive white Gaussian noise channels (AWGN) and fading channels. For the fading channels we use a Rayleigh block fading model so the channel gain remains constant at least during the transmission of the longest frame. For our experiments we consider three values for the Doppler frequency for these fading channels: $f_D = \{0.1, 0.5, 1\}$ Hz.

The AWGN channel has a constant unitary channel gain (0 dB), in turn we assume an average channel gain of 0 dB for the fading channels. In all cases the average received SNR is assumed to be 15 dB.

Adaptive Algorithm. Unless otherwise indicated, we also assume that:

- The exploration adaptation step is always $\mu_{exp} = 1$.
- The exploration parameter is fixed as $\varepsilon = 0.1$.
- The action-value function, Q, is initialized to zero.

Performance Metrics and Upper Bonds. As a measure of performance, we use the averaged throughput per episode,

$$Th_{eps} = \mathrm{E}\,[r] \cdot payload,$$

assuming that the four types of frames carry the same payload of 1024 bits. Unless it is otherwise indicated, all the numerical results have been obtained averaging ten thousand independent simulations.

Upper bounds are computed as the throughput achieved by selecting the optimal rate on each episode but taking the exploration parameter into account. The optimal actions are selected *a priori* based on the channel occupancy statistical models, the variable FER of each type of frame and its duration. The upper bound on AWGN channels and fading channels might not be the same, even if the average SNR is the same, simply because the channel gain is not a random variable but a constant in the AWGN channels. In fading channels the upper bound is expected to be above the throughput yield by any of the stationary policies (selecting the same type of frame on every episode). In turn, for the AWGN channel the upper bound will match the throughput achieved by one of the stationary policies.

4.2   Adaptation Step and Tracking Capability

In this section we aim to show how the choice of the adaptation step can affect the tracking capability of the algorithm and hence its performance. We consider a fading channel, with $f_D = 0.1$ Hz, a channel occupancy model described by GE_{i2} and GE_b, three adaptation steps, $\mu_{opt} = \{0.1, 0.5, 1\}$, and we average ten thousand independent runs of the algorithm. Figure 6 show the throughput and the corresponding averaged policy. We can see how there is little difference between $\mu_{opt} = 0.1$ and 0.5, however, for $\mu_{opt} = 1$ the throughput sinks. In the latter case the algorithm relays solely on the last reward obtain with each rate, therefore, and on the face of incomplete information, the algorithm tends to select the safest rate, the one which can work with a lower SNR. Our experiments show than in general a fading channel will lead to a less greedy policy simply because different rates become optimal at different times. The fact that the adaptation step depends on the selected rate is what gives the algorithm its robustness against the selection of μ_{opt}, in general the performance of the algorithm is not strongly dependent on μ_{opt} as long as we choose a small value.

A key feature of our algorithm is its tracking capability at a reduced computational cost and complexity. To illustrate how the algorithm is capable of tracking the changes in the SNR, we generate an independent sampled sequence of the channel fading process with $f_D = 0.5$ Hz, then we run ten thousand independent simulations over the same fading sequence and, considering a channel occupancy process with the memoryless distributions GE_{i1} and GE_b.

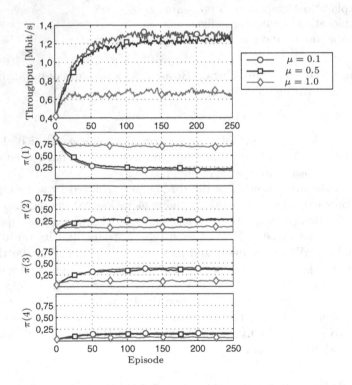

Fig. 6. Throughput per episode (top) and its corresponding policy (bottom) for several values of μ. Fading channel with $f_D = 0.1$ Hz and occupancy model given by GE_{i2} and GE_b.

Figure 7 illustrates the SNR evolution, the achieved throughput and the corresponding policy and action value function. We can see how the throughput varies overtime following the changes in the SNR. By looking at the policy figure we can see how rates 2 and 3 share most of the probability throughout the whole simulation, this is because the SNR remains approximately within the operational SNR ranges of rates 2 and 3. A closer look to the action value figure reveals that rate 3 is optimal most of the time, however when the SNR falls below approximately 10 dB rate 2 becomes optimal. On the other hand rates 1 and 4 are deactivated most of the time because the SNR is above and below their operational SNR ranges respectively. We can see how only rate 4 gains some value and probability of selection precisely when the SNR is maximum.

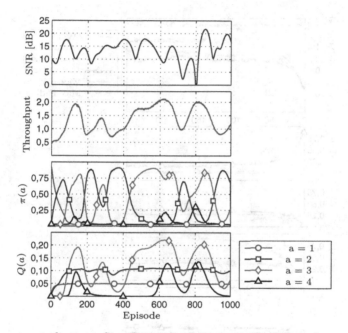

Fig. 7. From top to bottom, Signal to noise ratio evolution, Throughput per episode in Mbit/s, policy and Q value

4.3   Performance over Fading Channels

In this subsection we measure the performance degradation due to the limited tracking capability and we show that the algorithm is still capable of exploiting the transmission opportunities. To do so we consider distributions GE_{i1} and GE_b for the channel occupancy model and we run the simulations for the AWGN channel and for three different values of Doppler frequency, $f_D = \{0.1, 0.5, 1\}$ Hz.

Figure 8 depicts the throughput evolution along with the corresponding achievable rates and the averaged policy. As we increase f_D, the SNR variation within an episode increases reducing the probability that the selected rate remains optimal. Even more important is the fact that, as we increase f_D the correlation between two consecutive episodes decreases, for this reason it is harder for the algorithm to forecast which rate is optimal for the next episode. The gap between the achievable throughput when transmitting over the AWGN channel and when transmitting over a fading channel is due to the random nature of the channel gain in the latter case.

As for the averaged policy evolution we notice that for the AWGN we obtain a greedy policy after convergence. For the other three cases, the policy is roughly the same and it is less greedy because the probability is spread more evenly among the rates. In this particular case $\pi(2)$ and $\pi(3)$ stand out meaning that the SNR oscillates within the SNR operational range of rates 2 and 3 most of the time.

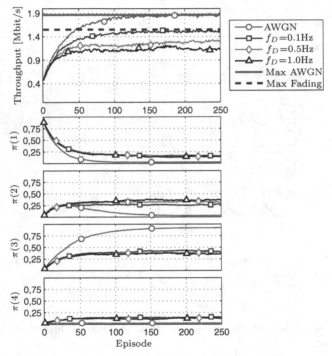

Fig. 8. Throughput per episode and achievable rate (top) and the corresponding policy (bottom) for several values of f_D

4.4   Channel Occupancy Model

Next, we explore the effect of different degrees of memory on the channel occupancy model. To do so, we repeat the same simulation but this time only for the AWGN channel and for the three distributions GE_{i1}, GE_{i2} and GE_{i3}. Figure 9 depicts the throughput evolution along with the corresponding achievable rates and the averaged policy. In this case the achievable rate is strongly influenced by the occupancy model, however, the algorithm is still capable of converging towards the upper bounds.

As the memory effect is more noticeable, episodes much shorter and much longer than the average are more likely to occur. Hence, suboptimal rates might gain value and be selected more often eventually leading to a less greedy policy and a degraded performance. We can see how for the distribution with the largest memory (GE_{i3}), the gap between the achieved rate and the upper bond is larger than for the other distributions. Correspondingly, by looking at the policy evolution we can also see how $\pi(3)$ decreases and $\pi(2)$ increases resulting in a less greedy policy. Notice that this effect is different from the one observed for the fading channels, there is no possibility of tracking here, only the fact that as the episode duration is more variable, some rates may randomly gain value introducing noise in the $Q(a)$ estimation and therefore interfering with the rate selection.

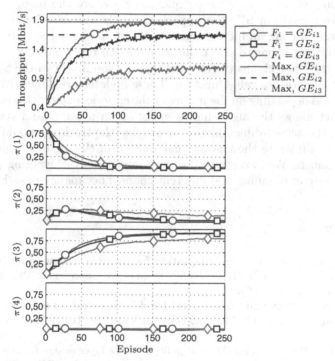

Fig. 9. Throughput per episode and achievable rates (top) and the corresponding policy (bottom) for the three distributions in table 3

4.5   Exploration Parameter, ε

Theory suggests that as we increase the value of ε we explore more and therefore we exploit less, in other words, it takes less time to learn the ε-policy but it learns a less greedy policy which might lead to a lower achievable throughput. This is exactly what we found when we run simulations on static environments, with no fading channels or other variables varying over time. However, when the environment varies over time, for example due to a fading channel, a larger ε does not necessarily lead to a lower throughput. Experiments reveled that in this cases it is critical to explore sufficiently often in order to maintain an estimation of Q that resembles the true value of each rate over time. On the other hand, exploring too often means that we spend less time exploiting what we learned. The optimal ε depends on how fast the environment changes, slow changes require less exploration and fast changes require higher values of ε.

5 Conclusions

In this work we have presented a novel adaptive rate selection scheme for cognitive radio links. We introduce a model free adaptive rate selection with a reduce computational cost and hardware complexity; these are the main novelties of this work. We consider a SU that opportunistically accesses the channel with the goal of transmitting an infinite number of data packets. Every time the SU begins transmitting it has to select the transmission rate following an ε-greedy policy. After the PU reclaims the channel the decision maker in the SU receives a reward and updates its value function. These updates are done with different adaptation steps depending on the nature of the episode, exploration or exploitation. This trick allows the algorithm to maintain an updated and yet accurate estimation of the action-value function improving the tracking capability.

Experiments illustrate the tracking capabilities of the algorithm under variable SNR channels. We also study the performance and converging properties for different degrees of fading and different channel occupancy models.

References

1. Chai, C.C.: On power and rate adaptation for cognitive radios in an interference channel. In: Proc. 71th IEEE Vehicular Technology Conference, PIMRC, Taipei, Taiwan, vol. 2, pp. 1–5 (May 2010)
2. Gao, L., Cui, S.: Power and rate control for delay-constrained cognitive radios via dynamic programming. IEEE Transactions on Vehicular Technology 58, 4819–4827 (2009)
3. Wang, H.H.J., Zhu, J., Li, S.: Optimal policy of cross-layer design for channel access and transmission rate adaptation in cognitive radio networks. EURASIP Journal on Advances in Signal Processing, vol. 2010 (2010)
4. Pérez, J., Khodaian, M.: Optimal rate and delay performance in non-cooperative opportunistic spectrum access. In: 9th International Symposium on Wireless Communication Systems (ISWCS 2012), Paris, France (August 2012)
5. Jouini, W., Ernst, D., Moy, C., Palicot, J.: Upper confidence bound based decision making strategies and dynamic spectrum access. In: 2010 IEEE International Conference on Communications (ICC), pp. 1–5 (2010)
6. Gonzalo-Ayuso, A., Pérez, J.: Dynamic rate adaptation in cognitive radio considering time-dependent channel access models. In: 8th International Conference on Cognitive Radio Oriented Wireless Networks, CROWNCOM (2013)

7. Gonzalo-Ayuso, Á., Pérez, J.: Rate adaptation in cognitive radio links with time-varying channels. In: 21st European Signal Processing Conference 2013, EUSIPCO 2013 (2013)
8. Sutton, R.S., Barto, A.G.: Reinforcement Learning: An Introduction. M.I.T. Press (1998)
9. López-Benítez, M.: Spectrum usage models for the analysis, design and simulation of cognitive radio networks. Ph.D. dissertation, Universitat Politècnica de Catalunya (UPC), Barcelona (May 2011)

Enhancing Quality of Experience (QoE) Assessment Models for Web Traffic

Amanpreet Singh[1], Ahmed Mahmoud[1], Andreas Koensgen[1], Xi Li[1],
Carmelita Göerg[1], Mehmet Kus[2], Muhsin Kayralci[2], and Jasmin Grigutsch[2]

[1] University of Bremen
Otto-Hahn-Allee 1, 28359 Bremen Germany
{aps,ahmed,ajk,xili,cg}@comnets.uni-bremen.de
[2] OTARIS Interactive Services GmbH
Fahrenheitstr. 7, 28359 Bremen
Germany
{kus,kayralci,grigutsch}@otaris.de

Abstract. Web applications are becoming the key services in today's networks (both fixed networks and mobile networks). Consideration of web service quality has become essential to provide the end users with satisfying Quality of Experience (QoE). In order to evaluate and manage the web quality, methods for QoE assessment are desired to estimate the service quality perceived by the end users. In this paper, we study a number of existing objective quality assessment models for assessing the QoE of web applications, and compare their performance with simulations to find out their individual advantages and limitations to use in practice. Simulation results show that the proposed QoE model can be applied for evaluating the quality of different web sources in the Long Term Evolution (LTE) networks, considering the lossy property of mobile networks. A fitting model is presented to describe the correlation between network Quality of Service and User QoE obtained in subjective lab test. To overcome the shortcomings of the existing models, this paper also proposes an enhanced QoE model which considers the effects of parameters such as page download size and content, browser cache setting as well as the packet losses and connection throughput in quality assessment e.g., page response time. To study other user related aspects in the evaluation of QoE, subjective tests in real systems and environments are planned as the next step.

Keywords: Web, Quality of Experience, Quality of Service, Modeling.

1 Introduction

Web applications have always been the key service with the onset of the Internet in both fixed and mobile networks. To provide a high-quality web service for the users, evaluating and managing the quality properly is extremely important. The normal Quality of Service (QoS) measurements that reflect the technical parameters of a service, however, do not reflect the user's perception of the obtained performance. Therefore, in the recent years attention has widely been paid on the concept of Quality of experience (QoE).

D. Pesch et al. (Eds.): MONAMI 2013, LNICST 125, pp. 202–215, 2013.

QoE is defined by ITU as "the overall acceptability of an application or service, as perceived subjectively by the end-user" [1]. QoE is typically represented using the Mean Opinion Score (MOS) [2], which is an empirical quality scale which ranges from 5 (excellent) to 1 (bad), indicating the quality from the user's perspective of the received service. To measure the perceived service quality, QoE assessment methodologies are indispensable, which are important for service quality management as well as for network planning, monitoring and optimization. The QoE assessment methods can be based on subjective tests or objective QoE models. Subjective evaluation of quality is usually carried out by a test panel of real users. Objective evaluation of quality is performed by applying objective QoE assessment models on behalf of a real user, trying to imitate or predict user perceptions by mapping network level QoS parameters into user level QoE. This provides the operators and service providers with a metric of the user satisfaction with the service.

Web traffic contributes a major part to the overall Internet traffic. According to real time monitoring using Akamai platform that handles about 20% of the world's total web traffic, there are 13,639,235 hits per second, 50,794,152 global page views per minute [3].

The key parameter that governs the user web QoE is the page response time i.e., the time it takes for the web page to download completely after the web link was clicked [4]. In other words, the total response time is defined as the time between issuing a web request to the system until the end result is visible to the user. The response time can be affected by the sum of time it takes to transfer the request to the remote server, the time the remote server needs for satisfying the request and the time it takes to transfer the response to the end user [5].

There are three main limits for the subjective response time as mentioned in (Nielsen 1993) [6]:

- 0.1s is the limit when a user feels that the system responds instantaneously.
- 1.0s is the limit until which a user perceives the page to be uninterrupted.
- 10s are the limit to keep the user's attention focused on the web page.

According to a study by Akamai in 2006 [7]:

- 75% of people would not return to websites that take longer than 4 seconds to load.
- Most of the Internet users rank page-loading time as a priority.

Another study [8] suggests that most users are willing to wait only about 2 seconds for simple information retrieval tasks on the web. A similar conclusion was released by Akamai in September 2009 [9]:

- 40% will leave off the web page if it takes more than 3 seconds to load.
- 47% expect 2 second or less to load a web page.

Even fractions of seconds of response time can have significant effects as Google found that by moving from a 10-result search web page which loaded in 0.4 seconds to a 30 result page loading in 0.9 seconds decreased the ad revenues by 20% [10].

The remainder of this paper is structured as follows. A number of selected objective QoE models for web applications are described in section 2. Section 3 discusses the important aspects that should be considered for precise modeling of the web QoE. The subjective tests that were conducted in a lab environment, their results and corresponding fitting models are presented in section 4. Section 5 describes the simulation scenario that is used to compare the different objective QoE models against the proposed fitting models. Finally, section 6 gives the conclusion and also an outlook.

2   Existing Web QoE Objective Models

Since, the page response time is what a user experiences while opening a web page, it is normally assumed to be the parameter that one should map to the web QoE values. Therefore, most of the web QoE models described in the literature which are mainly based on the page response time [11] [12] are explained in sections 2.1 and 2.2. The page response time is dependent on the design of the respective web page and also on the quality of the connection. One of the simplest forms used to identify the quality of a connection is the data rate that the user gets while opening the web page. Therefore in [13], a QoE mapping model is given based on the different user data rates. All these models are based on their respective subjective test results and we also follow the same norm to propose our new model in section 4.2 and 5.

2.1   Fitting Functional Models

In [11], subjective test results were used to map the impact of the web page response time (T) to web QoE (MOS) by different curve fitting function models such as based on the linear, logarithmic or exponential functions (refer Table 1). To measure the closeness of the fitting functions with that of the subjective QoE results, the coefficient of correlation was calculated for each fitting function. The exponential function as well as the logarithmic functions fit the subjective results best. The logarithmic function also has a high correlation as supported by ITU-T Rec. G.1030 [14].

Table 1. Web QoE functional fitting models [11]

Relation	QoE Model	Coefficient of correlation
Logarithmic	$MOS = -1.426 \cdot \ln(T) + 4.469$	0.994
Linear	$MOS = -0.318 \cdot T + 4.158$	0.983
Exponential	$MOS = 4.836 \cdot \exp(-0.15 \cdot T)$	0.995

The QoE values for the different models are depicted in Fig.1 for varying page response times. For the subjective tests to which the different models were mapped, the QoE values were considered in the normal range of 1 (unacceptable) to 5 (excellent) with an additional level of 0 which identified when the users simply disconnected the session. Therefore in Fig.1, the models map the page response time to the web QoE values ranging between 0 and 5.

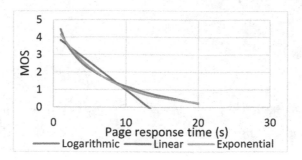

Fig. 1. Mean opinion score (MOS) curve fitting functional models based on page response time

2.2   Fitting Models Based on the Lorentzian Function

Like most of the Quality of Experience models, in [12] an experimental survey of the subjective quality as perceived by the end user was used to develop a mapping function based on the Lorentzian function [13] between the web page response time, T (measured in seconds)) and the user's quality experience (MOS). This model will be referred as the PRT non-linear model in this paper; it is defined as given in Eq. (1).

$$MOS = 5 - \frac{578}{1 + \left(11.77 + \frac{22.61}{T}\right)^2} \tag{1}$$

One of the important factors that influences the page response time is the user data rate for the web connection. The authors in [15] formulated a mapping function between the web QoE and the user data rate, r (measured in kbps) with which the web page was downloaded. This model will be referred as UDR non-linear model in this paper; it is defined as specified in Eq. (2).

$$MOS = 5 - \frac{578}{1 + \left(\frac{r + 541.1}{45.98}\right)^2} \tag{2}$$

The QoE values for these two models based on the Lorentzian function are depicted in Fig. 2. According to these results, a 10s limit exists for a user to fall into the category of being completely dissatisfied i.e., a mean opinion score of less than 2. A similar QoE value is obtained for a user data rate of around 100kbps. The user data rate can also be seen as the goodput of the web connection.

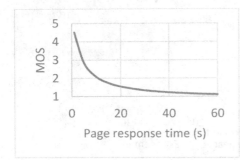 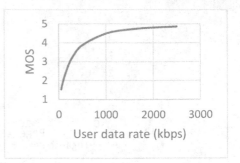

Fig. 2. Mean opinion score (MOS) curve fitting Lorentzian models w.r.t. a) Page response time (PRT non-linear model) and b) User data rate (UDR non-linear model)

3   Important Aspects for Web Browsing Experience

When a user visits a webpage, the browser first performs a DNS lookup to obtain the IP address of the web server. It then establishes a TCP connection with the server before it starts to download the main webpage. The main page may embed many web objects, including CSS, Java scripts, and images, which sometimes are hosted by servers in multiple domains. In that case, the browser has to perform more DNS lookups, establish multiple connections to different servers, and download objects in parallel. This process continues recursively until all the objects are downloaded. Thus the page response time depends on factors such as DNS lookup time, TCP setup and transfer (including the slow start phase and other congestion control aspects), and the client browser itself (the browser's response time and rendering speed of the displayed page). In addition, contents of most of the popular web pages are dynamic i.e., the structure and embedded objects, e.g. advertisements, may change over time.

Some of the important aspects to evaluate web browsing performance (or page response time) are listed here:

- **Total page size:** the page response time is monotonically increasing with the downloaded page size. A web page usually contains several embedded objects and all these add to the total page size.

- **DNS lookup time:** the web page's embedded objects may be hosted under different domains leading to a significant delay caused due to the DNS lookup process. Fig. 3 shows a snapshot of a web page (www.radiobremen.de) download, where the DNS lookup time is depicted for two embedded objects that are hosted at two different domains [16]. Fig.3 also shows other types of delays such as the connection setup delay, the time to first byte and finally the download time.

- **Browser concurrency:** Browsers support concurrent TCP connections within the same domain to improve download efficiency. If no network bottleneck exists, a higher concurrency means better utilization of bandwidth and shorter page response time. The maximum number of concurrent TCP connections within a domain varies for different browsers [17].

- **Cache strategy:** To speed up the web page response, browsers and web page designers allow for caching the web page content for a certain time. Thus if the same page is re-visited then the page can be reloaded from the cache or if only certain parts of the page are updated in the interactive browsing session then only the incremental information (embedded objects) are retrieved from the server.

- **Effective page size:** Due to the cache effect, during an interactive browsing session, a user may click on several embedded links and observe a favorable performance as in most cases the whole page is not required to be retrieved from the web server. The amount of downloaded data is referred to as effective page size. This reduces the load on the network as well as makes the response time shorter and hence should be considered whenever browser cache is used instead of the total page size.

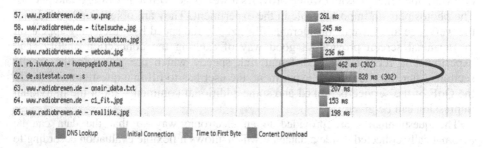

Fig. 3. Waterfall view shows DNS lookup, initial connection and object download time for different domains

4   Subjective Test for Web QoE

The concept of Quality of Experience (QoE) [1] is an approach to measure the network performance from the user's point of view, which means that degradations or disruptions of the service are being considered. The challenge of QoE measurements is that the perception of the user is a subjective phenomenon which varies between different users. Hence, in order to design a model to map QoS to QoE, tests with multiple users have to be performed. This section discusses QoE measurement experiments which were performed in the scope of the investigations discussed in this paper.

4.1   Experimental Setup

The hardware setup is shown in Fig. 4. Six probands can be tested at a time; each of them is provided a netbook (Lenovo S10-2) with a screen size of approx. 26 cm (10 inches) and a screen resolution of 1024×600 pixels. The netbooks are connected via an Ethernet switch to each other as well as to the Internet. The switch is manageable which allows configuring the uplink and downlink speed separately for each port. The switch is also connected to the Internet by a router which is required for the web browsing test. A controlling computer inside the network allows the automatic configuration of the switch and the start of required software on the netbooks.

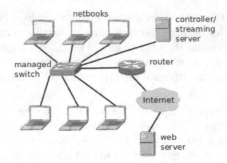

Fig. 4. Experimental setup for the Web QoE subjective tests

For web browsing, the netbooks connect to a preconfigured server on the Internet (www.radiobremen.de/vier) which provides a web page with a mix of text and photos. The photos play an important role in the experiment. They are objects embedded into the web page and have a considerable file size, so the speed by which they appear on the terminal screen provides a good way of ranking the connection quality. The experiment is repeated with different link speeds which are given in the results section. After the end of each experiment, the user has to fill in a questionnaire where the QoE of the service is ranked and some additional comments about the individual impression can be given.

The questionnaires are provided in an electronic way so that the data can be automatically collected inside a database which allows a flexible evaluation according to certain criteria. E.g., for the determination of the QoE/QoS relationship, it is important to consider whether a user is an "expert" with sound knowledge about networking devices or an inexperienced user who might use the Internet only occasionally.

During the preparation phase of the experiment, link speeds suitable to run experiments with the different services were determined by friendly-user tests (FUT). Five speeds have been selected individually for each service, where the number of five is chosen according to the Mean Opinion Score model as described in section 1. For one of the five speeds, the experiment is run twice, once after an experiment with a higher speed and once after a lower speed. The aim is the identification of memory effects, i.e. it is considered that the user has a different perception when coming from an experience worse than the current one or when coming from a better one. During the FUT, the tendency that different users sometimes have different opinions about the same technical service quality already could be observed, which highlights the need to perform the experiment with a large number of users to find the Mean Opinion Score (MOS) for each speed.

4.2   Subjective Test Results

In the subjective tests, 35 users took part which with equal gender distribution (18 male, 17 female). Most of the test users were either university students (21) or employees (10) with sufficient knowledge about the Internet and related terminology to web related applications. Fig. 5 depicts the average number of hours spent per day by the test users for different applications on the Internet. It is clear that web surfing and e-mail are two most often used applications.

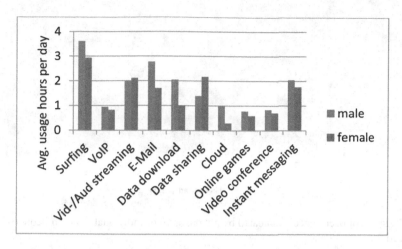

Fig. 5. Average number of hours spent per day on the Internet for different activities

Fig. 6 depicts the QoE results obtained for different link speeds. The test for a link speed of 512kbps was done twice, once after the best speed of 2Mbps and then again after the worst speed of 256 kbps. Both the set of results are not too much apart though the one that follows the speed of 2 Mbps gives a slightly better MOS value.

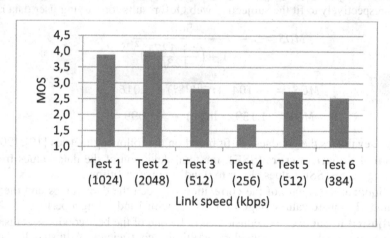

Fig. 6. Web QoE values for the different link speeds in the order of performed tests

Fig. 7 indicates the frequency of the different Individual Opinion Score (IOS) values that the test users gave for different link speeds. As expected, different users rate the quality differently but the trend shows a shift towards higher MOS values for larger link speeds.

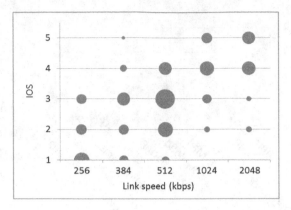

Fig. 7. Number of occurrences (indicated by bubble area) of Individual Opinion Score (IOS) vs. link speed

4.3   Fitting Model for Web QoE

The MATLAB curve fitting toolbox provides graphical tools and functions for fitting curves and surfaces [18]. Regression analysis can be conducted using a library of linear and nonlinear models or by providing custom equations like we did here with the Lorentzian, power and logarithmic (Log_our) functions depicted in Eq. (3), (4) and (5), respectively to fit the subjective web QoE results for varying user data rates.

$$MOS = 5 - \frac{500}{1 + \left(\frac{r + 1271}{123.2}\right)^2} \tag{3}$$

$$MOS = -104 \cdot (r^{-0.6168}) + 5.016 \tag{4}$$

$$MOS = 1.1592 \cdot \ln(r) - 4.6099 \tag{5}$$

Table 2 evaluates the goodness of fit based on the following metrics [19], [20]:

- **Sum of Squares Errors (SSE):** the total deviation of the data values from the fitting values. SSE values closer to 0 indicate better fitting results.
- **R-Square:** the square of the correlation between the data values and the fitting values. R-square values range from 0 to 1, with 1 indicating a perfect fit.
- **Adjusted R-Square:** it is considered to be one of the best goodness statistics for the fitting quality as it considers additional coefficients. Adjusted R-square is particularly useful in the feature selection stage of model building. Unlike R-square, the adjusted R-square increases only if the new term improves the model more than would be expected by chance.
- **Root Mean Squared Error (RMSE):** this statistic is also used to measure the difference between the fitting and the data values with a better fit having RMSE value closer to 0.

From Table 2, it can be seen that the power fitting model gives the best results, and a comparison between the subjective web QoE results and the fitting model results is depicted in Fig. 8.

Table 2. Web QoE fitting models goodness of fit statistics

Fitting method	SSE	R-Square	Adjusted R-square	RMSE
Power	0.05992	0.9845	0.9689	0.1731
Log_our	0.1971	0.9489	0.9319	0.2563
Lorentzian	0.1708	0.9557	0.941	0.2386

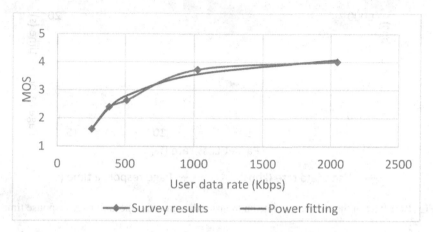

Fig. 8. Power fitting model for the obtained web QoE subjective test results

5   Simulation Scenario and Results

This section discusses the results obtained by the simulation of an LTE Scenario in the OPNET simulator. To realize controlled packet losses and link delay, an impairment object is added on the link between the eNB1 and router R2, as depicted in Fig. 9.

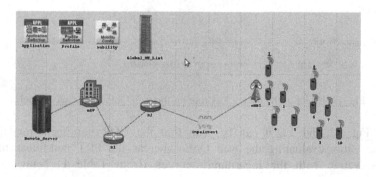

Fig. 9. Simulation scenario for a LTE network in OPNET simulator

Fig. 10 depicts the variation of the user data rate and the corresponding page response time for different packet loss rate configurations in the LTE scenario described in Fig. 9. The web QoE results for different fitting models with respect to varying packet loss rates and link delays are shown in Fig. 11 and 12, respectively. The logarithmic curve is the fitting model taken from Table 1, while the PRT non-linear and UDR non-linear models are described by equation (1) and (2), respectively. The Lorentzian and power fitting models are the ones obtained to fit our subjective web QoE results and are described by Eq. (3) and (4), respectively.

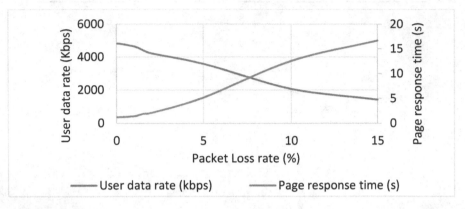

Fig. 10. Effect of the packet loss rate on the user data rate and the web page response time

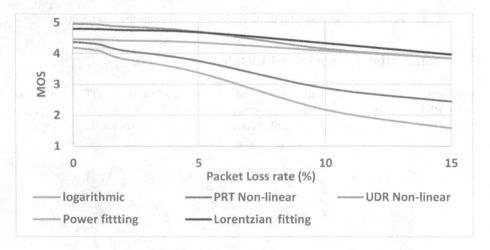

Fig. 11. Effect of the packet loss rate on the web QoE for various models

From Fig. 11 and 12, it can be seen that the UDR non-linear model is too optimistic while evaluating the web QoE whereas the PRT non-linear model is too conservative with the logarithmic curves (from Table 1) being the most conservative.

The missing link between the user data rate (UDR) and the page response time (PRT) based model is the effective page size, *ps* (in kB) of the downloaded page. Therefore, the Lorentzian fitting model described in Eq. (3) has been extended as

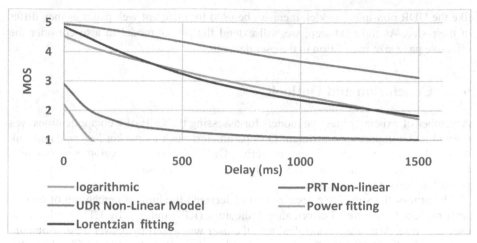

Fig. 12. Effect of the link delay rate on the web QoE for various models

specified in Eq. (6) and will be referred to as the "Final Proposed Model based on the Lorentzian function" (FPML):

$$MOS = 5 - \frac{500}{1 + \left(10.316 + \frac{2.841 \cdot r}{ps} \right)^2} \qquad (6)$$

The UDR non-linear model considers an average page size of 125 kB while the page sizes have increased over the years, being 312 kB in 2008 and 1114 kB in 2012 [21]. The web page (www.radiobremen.de/bremenvier) has on average an effective page size (downloaded over the network) of about 350 kB due to the Firefox browser cache settings. Therefore the subjective test results curve is much closer to the web QoE results for year 2008 obtained by the page size and the user data rate dependent Lorentzian fitting curve in Fig. 13. The power fitting model is also a good estimate but

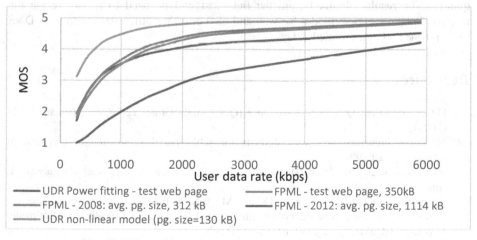

Fig. 13. Effect of user data rate and web page size on web QoE

like the UDR non-linear model, it cannot be used for different web pages as they differ in their size. As the next step, we will extend the power model to also consider the effective page size in addition to the user data rate.

6   Conclusion and Outlook

A number of existing objective models for assessing the QoE of web applications was studied and compared for different QoS parameters such as packet loss rate and link delay. To improve the existing objective QoE models or develop new models, different aspects related to web applications were identified and for validation subjective tests were carried out.

The aim of the subjective tests was to understand the human perception of quality with respect to the Key Performance Indicators (KPI) defined by ETSI such as the user data rate. After each controlled test, the user was asked to answer a questionnaire to ascertain the QoE as well as other related aspects. Based on the obtained results, different fitting (objective) QoE models were evaluated with an LTE scenario in an OPNET simulation. The model given in Eq. (6) that considers both user data rate and effective page size is proposed as the most suitable one to model web QoE objectively.

The knowledge gained from the lab tests will be used to roll out a larger campaign in the form of field tests that will be conducted using real networks based on various technologies e.g. xDSL, UMTS, HSPA, LTE, etc. The persons under field test install an app on their smartphone which measures different technical (QoS) parameters i.e., the connection quality as well as at which time different services are used and where the person is located while using the service. In this way, it can be identified whether the environment and context of the usage (e.g. at home, in the stadium, on the way, at the department store or at work) will affect which services are used and how they are rated in terms of QoE. After a completed service, the app presents a small questionnaire to the user to enquire the QoE rating. Thus the information about how the service quality is perceived by the user in the respective context and technical link quality. The results obtained from the field test will be used to further refine the proposed objective QoE model for web and also consider other aspects such as DNS lookup time and other related delays.

References

1. ITU-T definition: Quality of Experience (QoE) Study Group 12 Geneva, January 16-25 (2007)
2. ITU-T recommendation P.800: Methods for subjective determination of transmission quality (August 1996)
3. Akamai.com (2013), Akamai Homepage, http://www.akamai.com/ (last accessed: June 6, 2013)
4. Egger, S., Hossfeld, T., Schatz, R., Fiedler, M.: Waiting times in quality of experience for web based services. In: 2012 Fourth International Workshop on Quality of Multimedia Experience (QoMEX), July 5-7, pp. 86–96 (2012)

5. Fiedler, M.: EuroNGI Deliverable D. WP. JRA. 6.1. 1: State-of-the art with regards to user-perceived Quality of Service and quality feedback (May 2004), `http://eurongi.enst.fr/archive/127/JRA611.pdf` (last accessed: June 6, 2013)
6. Nielsen, J., Hackos, J.: Usability engineering, vol. 12518406. Academic press, Boston (1993)
7. Fiona Fui-Hoon, N.: A study on tolerable waiting time: how long are web users willing to wait? Behaviour & Information Technology 23(3), 153–163 (2004)
8. Jupiter Research Report: Retail Web Site Performance: Consumer Reaction to a Poor Online Shopping Experience (2006), `http://www.akamai.com/dl/reports/Site_Abandonment_Final_Report.pdf` (last accessed: June 6, 2013)
9. Akamai Reveals 2 Seconds as the New Threshold of Acceptability for eCommerce Web Page Response Times, Press Release (2009), `http://www.akamai.com/html/about/press/releases/2009/press_091409.html` (last accessed: June 6, 2013)
10. Battelle, J.: The Search: How Google and Its Rivals Rewrote the Rules of Business and Transformed Our Culture. Portfolio (2005), `http://perspectives.mvdirona.com/2009/10/31TheCostOfLatency.aspx` (last accessed: May 17, 2013)
11. Shaikh, J., Fiedler, M., Collange, D.: Quality of Experience from user and network perspectives. Annals of Telecommunications 65(1-2), 47–57 (2010)
12. Ameigeiras, P., Ramos-Munoz, J.J., Navarro-Ortiz, J., Mogensen, P., Lopez-Soler, J.M.: QoE oriented cross-layer design of a resource allocation algorithm in beyond 3G systems. Computer Communications 33(5), 571–582 (2010)
13. Johnson, N.L., Kotz, S., Balakrishnan, N.: Continuous Univariate Distributions, ch. 16, vol. 1. Wiley, New York (1994)
14. ITU-T, G.1030: Estimating end-to-end performance in IP networks for data applications (2005)
15. Ameigeiras, P., Ramos-Munoz, J.J., Navarro-Ortiz, J., Ramiro-Moreno, J., Lopez-Soler, J.M.: QoE Evaluation of Scheduling Algorithms for NRT Services in LTE. In: Proc. ICT-MobileSummit 2009, Santander, Spain (2009)
16. Meenan, P.: WebPagetest – Website Performance and Optimization Test, `http://www.webpagetest.org` (last accessed: June 6, 2013)
17. Huang, J., Xu, Q., Tiwana, Q., Mao, Z.M., Zhang, M., Bahl, P.: Anatomizing application performance differences on smartphones. In: Proc. ACM/USENIX Int. Conf. Mobile Systems, Applications, and Services (MobiSys). ACM, San Francisco (2010)
18. Mathworks: Curve Fitting Toolbox, `http://www.mathworks.de/products/datasheets/pdf/curve-fitting-toolbox.pdf` (last accessed: June 6, 2013)
19. Rawlings, J.O., Pantula, S.G., Dickey, D.A.: Applied regression analysis: a research tool. Springer (1998)
20. Hyndman, R.J., Koehler, A.B.: Another look at measures of forecast accuracy. International Journal of Forecasting 22(4), 679–688 (2006)
21. Average Web Page Size Triples Since (2008), `http://www.websiteoptimization.com/speed/tweak/average-web-page/` (last accessed: May 22, 2013)

Network Planning for Stochastic Traffic Demands

Phuong Nga Tran, Bharata Dwi Cahyanto, and Andreas Timm-Giel

Institute of Communication Networks
Hamburg-Harburg University of Technology, Hamburg, Germany
{phuong.tran,bharata.cahyanto,timm-giel}@tuhh.de

Abstract. Traffic in communication networks is not constant but fluctuates heavily, which makes the network planning task very challenging. Overestimating the traffic volume results in an expensive solution, while underestimating it leads to a poor Quality of Service (QoS) in the network.

In this paper, we propose a new approach to address the network planning problem under stochastic traffic demands. We first formulate the problem as a chance-constrained programming problem, in which the capacity constraints need to be satisfied in probabilistic sense. Since we do not assume a normal distribution for the traffic demands, the problem does not have *deterministic equivalent* and hence cannot be solved by the well-known techniques. A heuristic approach based on genetic algorithm is therefore proposed. The experiment results show that the proposed approach can significantly reduce the network costs compared to the peak-load-based approach, while still maintaining the robustness of the solution. This approach can be applied to different network types with different QoS requirements.

Keywords: Network planning, stochastic traffic demands, chance constrained programming, genetic algorithm.

1 Introduction

Network planning is an old but never outdated research topic in telecommunication networks. It is a very complex task because it has to resolve the conflict of interest between the network service provider, who wants to minimize the expenditure and the services users, who expect a good QoS. Accurate network planning is one of the crutial factors that ensure a business success for the network operators.

The classical network planning problem, assuming static traffic demands given by single trafic matrix, has been studied extensively for decades [1]. Different studies focused on different network technologies with different QoS requirements. But the general objective is to find a network with minimum cost, which can accomodate the given traffic demand. The common approach to solve this problem is to model it as Linear Programming (LP) problem and use some well-known optimization tools, e.g. CPLEX [2] to solve it. Besides, many researchers

D. Pesch et al. (Eds.): MONAMI 2013, LNICST 125, pp. 216–227, 2013.

have also proposed heuristic algorithms such as genetic algorithm, simulated annealing, local search, and etc, to solve the problem for large networks whose solution cannot be obtained from CPLEX within a reasonable time. Even though the above problem is already very complex, its solution can be inefficient. This is because the traffic is not deterministic but fluctuates heavily over time, as shown in Fig.1. If the traffic demand matrix covers the peak rate of the traffic demands, the network will be very costly due to the overestimated traffic volume. If the traffic demand matrix represents the mean rate, the resulted network may not be able to guarantee a certain QoS. Therefore, the traffic demands must be represented by so-called *effective rates*, which are between the peak rates and the mean rates. However, there is so far no effective way to determine these rates that can result in the most efficient network.

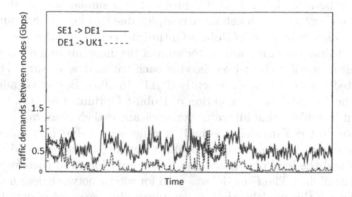

Fig. 1. Traffic fluctuation - Data was taken from GEANT project [3]

Assuming static traffic demands may be acceptable when the traffic characteristic is unknown to the operator. However, for a better network planning, one should carefully study the potential traffic behaviour and has some assumption on the stochastic traffic model. Moreover, once the network is already under operation and the traffic volume can be easily captured by measurement, re-optimizing (re-planning) the network should definitely take into account the stochastic behavior of the traffic. Nowadays, when the traditional networking infrastructure tends to migrate to the cloud networking, in which the network resourses can be easily accommodated on demand, the re-planning should be done frequently to optimize the expenditure as well as the network QoS. This motivates us to study the network planning problem for stochastic traffic demands.

2 Related Work

The network design problem under traffic uncertainty has attracted many researchers. Many methods have been proposed to handle the data uncertainty.

The first approach is to use Stochastic Programming [4]. In this approach, traffic uncertainty is captured by a finite number of matrice, each of which is assumed to occur with a certain probability. This is then modelled by a deterministic equivalent linear programming problem. Even though it is one of the earliest techniques to deal with uncertainty data, it is not very popular in telecommunications.

The second approach, a well-known method in communication network design, is Robust Optimization introduced by Soyster in 1973 [5]. Using this approach, no information of the probabilistic distribution of the traffic uncertainty is required. Instead, a solution is robust if it is feasible for all traffic volumes in the given uncertainty set. Robust Optimization can be applied differently in network design. In multi-hour network planning, the traffic fluctuation is modelled by multiple traffic matrice [6, 7]. The network is designed so that each traffic matrix can be accommodated non-simultaneously in installed capacities. This problem can be formulated as an LP problem in a similar way to the classical network planning, but it is much more complex due to a larger ammount of constraints. Another realization of Robust Optimization is to use the *hose model* [8]. The model defines upper bounds on the sum of the incoming and outgoing traffic flows for all network nodes while allowing each traffic flow to vary. This model has attracted a lot of attention recently [9–11]. In 2004, Bertsimas and Sim introduced the Γ-model as an extention of Robust Optimization [12]. In realistic scenarios, it is unlikely that all traffic demands are at their peak rate at the same time. Hence, in the Γ-model, a (small) non-negative value Γ is introduced to restrict the number of simultaneous peaks. Changing Γ relates to adjusting the robustness and the level of conservatism of the solutions and therefore provides additional flexibility. The Γ-model was used for robust network design in [13–16]. The weakness of this model is that its complexity increases exponentially with Γ due to a large combination of simultaneous peaks. Additionally, the choice of Γ is rather vague because it does not say much about the robustness of a solution although they are related.

The third approach is to use Chance-Constrained Programming (CCP) introduced by Charnes and Cooper in 1959 [17]. In CCP, the constraints must be maintained at a prescribed level of probability. In communication network planning, these are usually capacity constraints guaranteed at a certain probability, which is actually the overload probability of the links. Using the CCP, we must assume that the probability distribution of traffic demands is known. This is usually not the case of greenfield network planning. However, when a network already exists and re-optimizing is required, this information can be obtained from traffic measurement data. If the traffic follows a normal distribution, the CCP problem has a deterministic equivalent, and hence becomes an LP problem, which can be solved by optimization tools. If the traffic follows a log-normal distribution, the CCP problem can be approximated by a deterministic equivalent, which turns into an LP problem as well. In other cases, the problem is very hard. Our contribution in this work is a genetic algorithm to solve the network planning problem for stochastic traffic demands with arbitrary probability distribution modelled by Chance-Constrained Programming.

The rest of the paper is organized as follows. Section 3 presents the mathematical model of the problem using CCP. Section 4 introduces our proposed genetic algorithm. Section 5 discusses the performance of the algorithm and Section 6 concludes our work.

3   Problem Formulation

We consider the following network design problem. An undirected connected graph $G = (V, E)$ representing a potential network topology is given. On each link, capacity can be installed with a certain cost. The installed capacity is bounded by the available physical capacity of the link. A traffic demand between any two nodes is stochastic and is given by a (discrete) probability distribution function. Traffic demands are assumed to be statistically independent from each other. A coefficient ϵ is introduced as the QoS parameter. The task is to find a network with the minimal cost, in which the overload probability of each link is bounded by ϵ.

The problem can be mathematically presented using the following notations:

- $k \in K$ denotes a commodity representing a traffic demand.
- l denotes a link in the potential topology.
- $r \in R$ denotes a route conneting the source and destination nodes. A set of possible routes R connecting any two nodes is pre-computed.

Given Parameters

- T_k: traffic demand of the commodity k. Since the traffic demands are stochastic, T_k is a probability density function (PDF).
- C_l: available physical capacity of link l.
- c_l: cost of a bandwidth unit on link l.

Decision Variables

- Bandwidth assignment b_l: a positive real variable denoting the bandwidth allocated on link l
- Routing variable: $f_r^k = 1$ if the traffic of the commodity k is routed through route r. Otherwise, $f_r^k = 0$. We assume a single-path routing, hence f_r^k is a binary variable.

Constraints

- Routing constraint:

$$\sum_{r \in R} f_r^k = 1 \qquad \forall k \qquad (1)$$

Equation (1) ensures that every flow is routed through one of the pre-computed paths.

Assuming $N(N \leq K)$ traffic flows going through link l and T_k being the PDF of each traffic demand, the PDF of the aggregated traffic on link l, T^l, is the convolution of all flows and given as:

$$T^l = T_1 \otimes T_2 \otimes ... \otimes T_N \tag{2}$$

– Link overload probability constraint:

$$\int_0^{b_l} T^l(x)\, dx \geq 1 - \epsilon \qquad \forall l \tag{3}$$

Equation (3) guarantees that the traffic load on link l is smaller than or equal to its installed capacity b_l with the probability of $1 - \epsilon$. This equals to link overload probability smaller than ϵ. Equation (3) is equivalent to:

$$\prod_{k, f_l^k = 1} \int_0^{b_l} T_k(x)\, dx \geq 1 - \epsilon \qquad \forall l \tag{4}$$

– Physical capacity constraint:

$$b_l \leq C_l \qquad \forall l \tag{5}$$

Objective

$$\min \sum_l c_l \cdot b_l \tag{6}$$

The objective is simply to minimize the total network cost.

4   Genetic Algorithm

The mathematical model presented in the previous section is a non-linear optimization problem. In this section, we introduce a heuristic approach based on the genetic algorithm to solve it. Genetic algorithm uses the concepts of population genetics and evolution theory to optimize the *fitness* of a *population* of *individuals* through *mutation* and *crossover* of their *genes*. The advantage of the genetic algorithm is that it is able to explore a large solution space and hence to avoid local optima.

4.1   Encoding

A chromosome is encoded by a set of numbers $\{r_1, r_2, ..., r_k, ...r_K\}$ where r_p is a positive integer representing a route of commodity p. Each position k is related to a certain commodity and the corresponding traffic demand. A chromosome thus represents the routing solution for all demands on the network.

4.2   Forming a New Population

A new population is evolved by a mechanism to select and to form new individuals using genetic operators called *crossover* and *mutation*. Crossover produces new individuals that inherit genes from their parents while mutation enables offsprings to have different genes from their parents. Both of these genetic operators aim to produce some (hopefully) better individuals for the next generation (iteration). The bad performing individuals (according to the fitness parameter) from the previous iteration will be naturally removed and substituted by the new ones. In this work, each population is composed of 20 individuals. At each iteration, 20 new individuals will be generated.

4.3   Calculating the Solution Cost and Fitness Evaluation

The cost of a solution is the the total cost of capacities installed on all links to accommodate traffic using the routing solution represented by an encoded chromosome. From the chromosome, one knows which flows are going through each link. The PDFs of all traffic flows are convoluted to get the PDF of the aggregated traffic flow. After that, we can calculate the bandwidth needed on the link so that the overload probability is bounded by a given parameter ϵ. In this work, we assume a discrete PDF, which is represented by a finite vector, for the ease of the computation. If the PDFs of the traffic demands are given as continuous functions, they should be discretized for the convolution computation.

Fitness evaluation is to decide which chromosomes meet the expectation and can be carried to the next iteration. In this work, the fitness is reflected by the total cost of a solution. The current five best solutions (with lowest cost) are always chosen to the next step. The other solutions including the invalid solutions, are chosen with a certain probability. The reason to choose some bad solutions is to avoid the local optima.

4.4   Algorithm Framework

The algorithm is represented in details by the flowchart in Fig. 2 The algorithm starts with 20 initial individuals encoded into chromosomes as described in section IV.A. From this initial population, 20 child solutions are generated by crossover or mutation of random genes. The cost of these solutions (including the parent solutions) are calculated and evaluated. 20 solutions which qualify the fitness evaluation will be carried to the next iteration. The process is repeated until a termination condition is reached. The condition can be for example a pre-determined number of iterations or a certain number of iterations during which no better solution is found.

5   Performance Evaluation

To evaluate the performance of the proposed network planning algorithm, we carried out two experiments on a small 6-node network and the German 16-node network, shown in Fig.3. The genetic algorithm was implemented in C++.

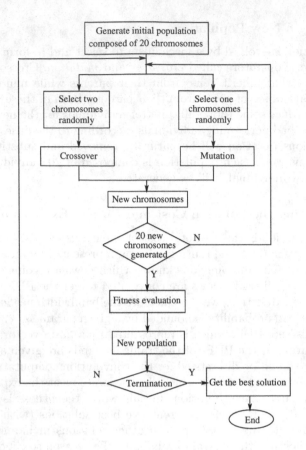

Fig. 2. Genetic algorithm framework

The traffic demands for the 6-node network are taken from GEANT project [3], while the traffic demands for the German network are taken from the DFN network provided at [18]. The traffic data was firstly extracted and its discrete PDF was constructed. We assumed that the cost of a bandwidth unit on each link is 1, so that the total cost is simply the sumation of the bandwidths. For the German network, 5 shortest paths were pre-calculated while for the 6-node network, all possible routes were considered.

5.1   Performance of Genetic Algorithm

In this work, the number of iterations in the genetic algorithm is set to 500 for the small network and 1000 for the big network. In practice, one can terminate the algorithm based on the quality of the solution, e.g. the objective function reaches a certain value or the best solution does not change over a certain number of iterations. Fig.4 and 5 show the evolution of the genetic algorithm over time (iterations) in two experiments. The red curve represents the best solution at each iteration while the blue one represents the average of the whole population.

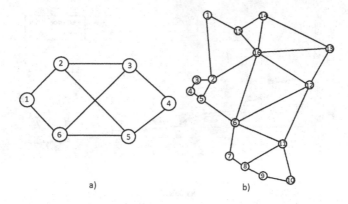

Fig. 3. Network topologies: a) 6-node network, b) German 16-node

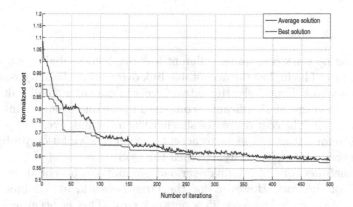

Fig. 4. Performance of genetic algorithm - 6-node network

The best solution always gets better or at least stays the same after each iteration, while the average solution can get worse. This is due to the fact that a bad solution can still be selected to the next iteration with a certain probability. This helps to avoid the local optima. As can be seen from the figures, the larger the network is, the more iterations are required to obtain a good solution. For the small network, from the iteration 250, the solution is improved very slowly and not much. For the German network, the solution still has potential to be improved at the iteration 1000. Therefore, it is difficult in practice to determine the number of iterations before terminating the algorithm. It is recommended to terminate the algorithm when the best solution does not change for a certain time.

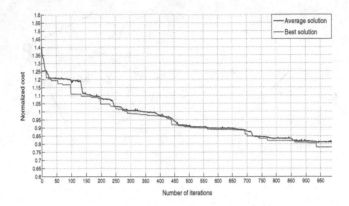

Fig. 5. Performance of genetic algorithm - German network

5.2 Network Cost

The resulting network cost under different link overload probability is shown in the Fig.6 and 7. The higher the acceptable link overload probability is, the lower is the network cost. Especially, the network cost in case of a small link violation probability can decrease significantly compared to the one when no link overload is tolerated at all. The cost decreases slowlier when the link overload probability is high. Therefore, it makes sense to accept a small link violation probability to reduce the cost while not sacrifying much the QoS.

In the small network, if 5% link overload proability is accepted, we can save about 45% of the cost. However, for the large network, at 5% link violation probability, we save only about 25% network cost. This is because in a large network, there are many more flows going through a link. The traffic loads on links tend to be averaged out, rather than heavily fluctuate. This avoids some extreme peak and hence the cost saving from a small violation probability is also reduced. This can be seen in the Fig.8 and 9.

Table 1. Comparison of statistical network planning with other approaches

	Peak-based	$\epsilon = 0\%$	Mean-based	$\epsilon = 5\%$
Normalized cost	1.24	1	0.45	0.53
Link overload prob.	0%	0%	18% - 25%	5%

Table 1 shows the comparison of the proposed statistical network planing method with mean-load-based and peak-load-based approach for the 6-node network. The solution for the mean-load-based and peak-load-based approaches are found by linear programming (CPLEX). Using the peak-load-based approach, the normalized network cost is 1.24 while using the proposed statistical planning method, the normalized cost is 1. In both cases, the link violation probability is

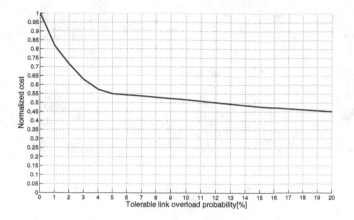

Fig. 6. Network cost vs. link overload probability - 6-node network

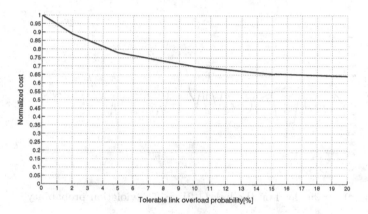

Fig. 7. Network cost vs. link overload probability - German network

0%. Using the mean-load-based approach, the cost is low (only 0.42) but the QoS is also very poor. The link overload probability ranges from 18%-25%. Accepting 5% of link overload probability results in a good compromise.

Another advantage of this proposed approach is that for different networks with different QoS requirements, one can simply adjust the link violation probability accordingly.

5.3   Aggregated Traffic on Links

Fig.8 and 9 shows the traffic load on a link in the 6-node network and the German network, respectively. In each figure, the red line indicates the bandwidth allocated on the link. As can be seen from the figure, the link overload probability is bounded by the predefined parameter $\epsilon = 5\%$. We can see that by accepting a small violation probability, the capacity needed on the link is reduced, especially for the small network.

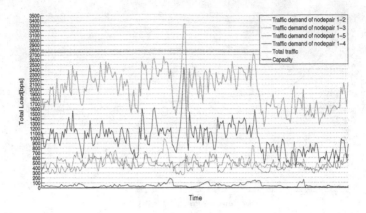

Fig. 8. Traffic load on the link (1-2) - $\leq 5\%$ violation probability

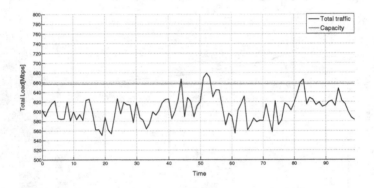

Fig. 9. Traffic load on the link (1-2) - $\leq 5\%$ violation probability

6   Conclusion

In this paper, we have proposed a new approach to solve the network planning problem under stochastic traffic demands using the genetic algorithm. The proposed method guarantees the network to carry stochastic traffic under a predefined link overload probability. The experiments showed that by accepting a small link overload probability, the network cost can be reduced significantly. Compared to the peak-load-based approach, the proposed method applied for $\epsilon = 0\%$ results in a clearly lower cost. Even though the algorithm cannot guarantee the optimal solution (due to the nature of the heuristic), it provides a relatively good solution. The limitation of this approach is that it guarantees the overload probability for each link only. In the future, we will develop an algorithm that can guarantee the overload probability for the end-to-end flows.

References

1. Bienstock, D., Chopra, S., Gnlk, O., Tsai, C.Y.: Minimum cost capacity installation for multicommodity network flows. Mathematical Programming 81, 177–199 (1998)
2. Ibm website, http://www-01.ibm.com/software/integration/optimization/cplex-optimizer/
3. Geant project, http://www.geant.net
4. Dantzig, G.B.: Linear programming under uncertainty. Management Science, 197–206 (1955)
5. Soyster, A.L.: Convex programming with set-inclusive constraints and applications to inexact linear programming. Operations Research 21, 1154–1157 (1973)
6. Pavon-Marino, P., Garcia-Manrubia, B., Aparicio-Pardo, R.: Multihour network planning based on domination between sets of traffic matrices. Computer Networks 55(3), 665–675 (2011)
7. Aparicio-Pardo, R., Skorin-Kapov, N., Pavon-Marino, P., GarciaManrubia, B.: (Non)-reconfigurable virtual topology design under multihour traffic in optical networks. IEEE/ACM Transactions on Networking 20(5), 1567–1580 (2012)
8. Duffield, N.G., Goyal, P., Greenberg, A.G., Mishra, P.P., Ramakrishnan, K.K., van der Merive, J.E.: A flexible model for resource management in virtual private networks. In: ACM SIGCOMM, Cambridge, USA, pp. 95–108 (September 1999)
9. Chekuri, C., Oriolo, G., Scutella, M.G., Shepherd, F.B.: Hardness of robust network design. Networks 50(1), 50–54 (2007)
10. Altin, A., Yaman, H., Pinar, M.C.: The robust network loading problem under polyhedral demand uncertainty: Formulation, polyhedral analysis, and computations. INFORMS Journal on Computing (2010)
11. Mattia, S.: The robust network loading problem with dynamic routing. Universita di Roma la Sapienza, Tech. Rep (2010)
12. Bertsimas, D., Sim, M.: The price of robustness. Operations Research, pp. 35–53 (2004)
13. Koster, A., Kutschka, M., Raack, C.: On the robustness of optimal network design. In: IEEE International Conference on Communications (ICC 2011), Kyoto, Japan (June 2011)
14. Poss, M., Raack, C.: Affine recourse for the robust network design problem: between static and dynamic routing. Zuse Institute Berlin, Tech. Rep (2011)
15. Belotti, P., Capone, A., Carello, G., Malucelli, F.: Multi-layer mpls network design: The impact of statistical multiplexing. Computer Networks 52(6), 1291–1307 (2008)
16. Altin, A., Amaldi, E., Belotti, P., Pinar, M.C.: Provisioning virtual private networks under traffic uncertainty. Networks 49(1), 100–155 (2007)
17. Charnes, A., Cooper, W.: Chance-constrained programming. Management Science, 73–79 (1959)
18. Dfn network, http://sndlib.zib.de

Software Enabled Future Internet – Challenges in Orchestrating the Future Internet

Alex Galis[1], Javier Rubio-Loyola[2], Stuart Clayman[1], Lefteris Mamatas[1],
Sławomir Kukliński[3], Joan Serrat[4], and Theodore Zahariadis[5]

[1] University College London, U.K.
[2] Cinvestav Tamaulipas, Mexico
[3] Orange Labs Poland
[4] Universitat Politècnica de Catalunya, Spain
[5] Synelixis, Greece
{a.galis,s.clayamn,l.mamatas}@ucl.ac.uk,
jrubio@tamps.cinvestav.mx, slawomir.kuklinski@orange.com,
serrat@tsc.upc.edu, zahariad@synelixis.com

Abstract. This position paper presents SoftINTERNET an initiative for a service-aware and management-aware network control infrastructure for heterogeneous networks (i.e., wired and wireless) that uses software driven features for the elaboration, development, and validation of networking concepts. The proposed infrastructure aims to optimally integrate the connectivity and management layers. It operates across multiple network environments and on top of private and public network clouds utilising fixed and mobile virtual resources, OpenFlow enabled network devices like switches and routers, and networks of Smart Objects. In this position paper, we discuss the motivation, architecture and research challenges for such a promising concept.

Keywords: Software Defined Networks, Software Enabled Networks, Virtualization, Orchestration.

1 Introduction

1.1 Background

In this paper we present an initiative to integrate heterogeneous networks, including wired/wireless networks and smart-objects, from both the service and management and control viewpoints, considering them as crucial aspects of Future Networks. The intention is to define a service-aware control and management architecture which provides a service infrastructure and an on-demand programmable network, along with dynamic and global resources, and self-management capabilities that are based on interoperable connectivity protocols and open interfaces.

The initiative presented in this paper is named SoftINTERNET (i.e., Software Enabled Networks Connecting and Orchestrating the future Internet of people, content, clouds [51], devices and things) [1]. SoftINTERNET aims to integrate, orchestrate, and map control enablers as embedded capabilities into Software-Driven

D. Pesch et al. (Eds.): MONAMI 2013, LNICST 125, pp. 228–244, 2013.

Network infrastructures, in order to make them service-aware and management-aware, as a natural evolution of the software-defined network initiatives (i.e., see section 2). The mapping of these enablers into virtual infrastructure and physical resources involves an aggregation of connectivity, computation and storage resources.

Our approach to this challenge is through the deployment of a flexible and programmable network infrastructure supporting software driven network features that can be instantiated on-demand. These instantiations will be addressing the changing service requirements and resource constraints, yet scalable across multiple services and multiple domains, that can maintain QoS for the end-users of a service, and that provide a level of isolation and security from one service to another.

SoftINTERNET targets and addresses requirements for Future Networks [55] including:

• Software Driven Networking – Future Networks should support the following design goals: Functional Programmability and Elasticity; Integrated Virtualisation of Connectivity, Storage and Processing Resources, including the limited resources in Smart Objects and mobile devices; personalized services and embedded In-Network Management. This we call 'Software Driven and Enabled Networks as a Service'.

• Interworking – Future Networks are represented by the interconnection, interoperation and orchestration of heterogeneous networks (i.e. fixed and mobile) that are sharing their virtualised resources. Processing, Storage and Communication Resources spanning over multiple network domains are being aggregated to provide services in a simple and pervasive manner.

• Service Provider Access – Future Networks should offer unrestrictive access to different service providers by supporting qualified access mechanisms to a set of network-embedded resource-facing services, and by providing scalable, personalized and self-managed inexpensive networking infrastructures on demand.

• Service Provisioning – Future Networks can support the complete lifecycle of complex services by combining existing elements in a new and creative ways that were often not efficiently interoperable before. QoS and security guarantees are pivotal for the management of the services' lifecycle.

This paper is organized as follows. Related work is presented in Section 1.2 which is followed by the motivation for the SoftINTERNET concept as presented in Section 2. The architectural model is presented in Section 3. Section 4 presents the research challenges of SoftINTERNET. Section 5 provides concluding remarks of this paper.

1.2   Related Work

The areas related to the SoftINTERNET concept are summarized in this Section. These areas include future Internet architectures, programmable networks, open networking, and infrastructure and mobile clouds.

1.2.1   Future Internet Architectures

Architectural changes of the Internet have been promoted by several initiatives. In USA, there are several significant initiatives. NeTS [4] (Networking Technology and Systems) was a program of the National Science Foundation (NSF) on networking research with the objectives of developing the technology advances required to build next generation networks and improve the understanding of large, complex and heterogeneous networks. NetSE [5] proposes a clean-state approach to properly meet new requirements in security, privacy and economic sustainability. GENI [6] (Global Environment for Network Innovations) is a virtual laboratory for network experimentation, based on a 40 Gbps real infrastructure. Stanford Clean Slate [7] proposes a disruptive approach by creating service platforms available to the research and user communities. In Europe, Future Internet initiatives mostly try to develop platforms to support services and applications by utilizing the current Internet infrastructure. G-Lab [8] (Design and experiment the network of the future, Germany), which is the German national platform for Future Internet studies, includes both research studies of Future Internet technologies and the design and setup of experimental facilities. GRIF [9] (Research Group for the Future Internet, France) and Internet del Futuro [10] (Spain) promote cooperation based on several application areas (e.g. health) and technology platforms. Moving towards modern content-aware networking, we can highlight DONA (Data-Oriented Network Architecture) [11] and TRIAD [12] approaches, where content providers can publish content and users request named data from the network.

In the clean-slate Future Internet design track and building on wireless and mobile background, the 4WARD project [13] proposes four main architecture pillars: network virtualization, in-network management, new path abstraction (Generic Path) and networking of information. The SAIL [14] project builds around the concepts of the network of information, cloud networking (for managing and controlling computing, storage and connectivity resources by automatically moving or scaling up or down the resources required by the applications and open connectivity services for providing efficient multi-path/multi-layer/multi-domain transport and routing.

Other projects working in the area of Future Internet include: a) NEBULA [15] with focus on secure and trustworthy cloud computing; b) eXressive Internet Architecture [16], with emphasis on an architecture that inherently supports communication between diverse entities, provides for intrinsic security and includes a pervasive minimal functionality that needs to be present in network nodes for functions like trust management, access to services, hosts and content, and interaction among users, ISPs and content providers; c) PURSUIT [17], which builds on the results of PSIRP [18] and aims at changing the routing and forwarding fabric of the global internetwork so as to operate entirely based on the notion of information according to the publish/subscribe communication model; d) FI-WARE [19], which is developing a platform providing all the necessary technologies to support Future Internet service delivery and provisioning; and e) AKARI Project [20] of Japan, which advocates the use of virtualization as the basis of the Internet architecture in the next generation [21], extending the idea of isolated virtual networks to (1) Transitive virtual networks - cooperation and/or communication between virtual networks, and (2) Overlaid virtual networks-one virtual network over the other.

1.2.2 Programmable Networks

Many projects use virtualization to support programmability [49], [52], [22]. The physical switch interfaces are abstracted and partitioned into so called switchlets, which allow a shared use of the physical switch resources. Different research projects address the virtualization of various network components and their programmability. From switches and links [23] to switchlets [22], active nodes [24] and routelets [25].

The dynamic deployment of new services includes the composition of complete network architectures as virtual networks [26], [27], [25]. Projects like Netscript [28] or Tempest [27] support the notion of Virtual Active Networks [26] over IP networks or virtual networks using safe partitioning over ATM respectively.

Motivated by concepts introduced in the RESERVOIR project [29], providing isolation between the physical infrastructure, and the virtual environment using an overlay network, our goal is to provide a managed network virtualization infrastructure that is based on the SoftINTERNET approach. Thus, instead of reproducing the control complexity and overhead associated with existing networks, we create an abstraction layer, based on a common network model, enabling multiple independent and isolated network applications run over a single physical network infrastructure, dealing with the network logical functionality and its control aspects.

1.2.3   Open Networking

Stanford University has developed a solution for Open Networking, with the aim to: (1) separate data and control planes and define a vendor agnostic API/protocol between the two; (2) design a logically centralized control plane with an open API for network applications and services and (3) virtualize the network infrastructure. The OpenFlow protocol [30] has been proposed for the communication between the network nodes and the centralized network controller, and the FlowVisor [31] framework has been proposed for resource virtualization in this context. The interest on the Open Networking approach and on the OpenFlow protocol is growing worldwide, and in March 2011 the Open Networking Foundation [32] was created with the aim to promote the Open Networking approach and to standardize the OpenFlow protocol.

Specifications of OpenFlow version 1.3.1 have been published in September 2012. Several manufacturers have already developed network nodes supporting OpenFlow, and several open source OpenFlow controllers are available (i.e. NOX [33], Beacon, Maestro, etc.). A lot of works in the area of OpenFlow are in place worldwide in order to extend its field of applications, from LAN to WLAN [34], and even core and GMPLS networks. In addition several EU FP7 projects are dealing with OpenFlow, like OFELIA [35], OpenLAB [36], SPARC [37] and with Open Networking in general SAIL [38]. The main objectives of these projects are to provide testing facilities based on the OpenFlow protocol, and to investigate and propose possible extensions to it in order to overcome its main limitations, in particular related to scalability. Moreover, the FI-WARE project [39] is taking into consideration the OpenFlow technology as a mean to provide open APIs to control and monitor networks and network nodes. Even if several OpenFlow controllers have already been proposed to control and manage open networks,(see NOX, Maestro, Beacon, etc.) there does not exist a clear reference architecture for them. SoftINTERNET aims to define a reference structure for an Open Network controller, able to support virtualization and programmability for this kind of networks.

1.2.4   Infrastructure and Mobile Clouds

Server virtualization technology commonly used in data centres and clouds raises new challenges for both the research and the industry community. In such environments, not only the number of network endpoints is significantly large compared to the physical network infrastructure (due to the fact that each physical server can host dozens of virtual servers), but these endpoints are dynamically created, terminated, and migrated from one physical server to another. One approach to provide data networking in a virtual environment, extending the physical network into the virtual server domain using L2 virtual switches such as Cisco Nexus 1000 or openVSwitch, may be based on the IEEE 802.1qbg [40] standard, in which virtual machines are considered as clients of the physical network. It has the limitation associated with the dynamic nature of such an environment, and the fact that typically it should serve more than one independent tenant. A recent approach to deal with these challenges is by creating an overlay network used to connect the virtual servers (see [41, 42, 43]). Following this approach, virtual networks are no longer considered as clients of the physical infrastructure, thus reducing the network complexity and the dependency between the virtual environment and the physical network infrastructure.

The research area of Mobile Cloud Computing (MCC) is relatively new and there is no consensus even for basic definitions yet. For example, Cisco defines the mobile cloud as mobile services and applications delivered from a centralized (and perhaps virtualized) data center to a mobile device such as a smartphone [44]. The Mobile Cloud Computing Forum [45] defines MCC as an infrastructure where both the data storage and the data processing happen outside of the mobile device. Alternatively, MCC is defined as a combination of mobile web and cloud computing [46][47][48].

2   Motivation for the SoftINTERNET Approach

The integration of the Internet, software technologies and traditional telecommunications and communication technologies, has been always a challenge for network and service operators, as far as service deployment and management [53], [54] is concerned. Different frameworks and architectural approaches have been proposed in the research literature and in commercial work. New approaches and technologies are causing a paradigm shift in the world of network architectures. The motivation behind this shift is the still-elusive goal of rapid and autonomous service creation, deployment, activation, and management, resulting from ever-changing customer and application requirements. Research and development activity in this area has clearly focused on the synergy of a number of concepts: programmable networks, network virtualization, self-managing networks, open interfaces and platforms, and increasing degrees of intelligence inside the network. The next generation of Software Defined Networks (SDN) needs to move from being merely *Defined* by software to be *Driven* by software and must be capable of supporting a multitude of providers of services that exploit an environment in which services are dynamically deployed and quickly adapted over a heterogeneous physical infrastructure, according to varying and sometimes conflicting customer requirements. The three key stages of this technological synergy for the main Software Driven Network concepts are depicted in Fig. 1.

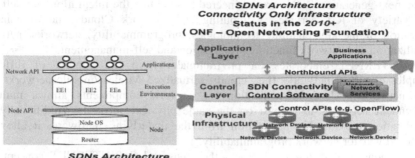

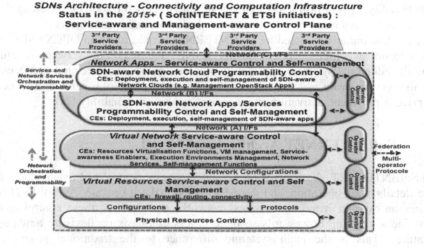

Fig. 1. SDN Evolution - Conceptual View

Programmability in network elements (switches, routers, and so forth) was introduced over a decade ago as the basis for rapid deployment and customization of new services (e.g. first architectural state of the SDN Conceptual View). Advances in programmable networks have been driven by the industry adoption of Open-Flow and a number of requirements that have given rise to a new business model of the same telecom business actors, and roles (e.g. *second architectural state of the SDN Conceptual View: Software-Defined Networks*). We are moving away from the "monolithic" approach where systems are vertically integrated toward a component-based approach, where systems are made of multiple components from different manufacturers, interacting with each other through open interfaces to form a service. The result is a truly open service platform representing a marketplace wherein services and service providers compete with each other, while customers may select and customize services according to their needs (e.g. *third architectural state of the SDN Conceptual View: Software Driven/Enabled Networks*).

The next generation SDNs are engineered to facilitate the integration and delivery of a variety of ICT services, Computing and Network Clouds and to enhance integration of the key enabling technologies: programmability, networks, network virtualization and network function virtualisation and self-management.

SoftINTERNET elaborates on programmability in the context of different examples of virtual networks (i.e., clouds, virtualized wireless/mobile networks and open networks). Using virtualization on network components allows multiple independent networks to coexist on the same physical substrate. Additionally, as virtualization provides an abstraction from the underlying hardware, it allows a simplified way for network programmability.

The fundamental difference between the envisaged SoftINTERNET concept and previous SDNs [50] is the switch to a connectivity and computation infrastructure which is both a service-aware and a management-aware network foundation, where the network elements have direct support for service lifecycle and built-in support for management functionality. This infrastructure utilizing shared virtualised resources, including those in wire, wireless and resource-constrained mobile devices and smart objects.

All these initiatives including SoftINTERNET would result in OPEX reduction for the telecom and cloud operators. SoftINTERNET focuses on the service orchestration and the additional systemic opportunity of additional revenue creation that is enabled by the service-aware and management-aware control plane (e.g. rapid and on-demand service deployment, activation, management and programmability [1]).

3   SoftINTERNET Architectural Model

In SoftINTERNET, the focus is on the service-aware control and management plane, the details of its operation, and the APIs which make it operate. As SoftINTERNET relies on existing wired and wireless networks and devices, these control elements provide a mapping downwards so there is less emphasis on devising new physical features. This is the main systemic difference to the traditional programmable networks and the recent activities on Network Function Virtualisation Network Functions Virtualisation (NFV) [56], Network Operating System and Network Orchestration, which are manly targeted to ONF validation. An important feature of the architecture is a cross-layer approach i.e. interfaces and mechanisms that enable control and exchange of information between different SoftINTERNET layers – this provides the ability to push requirements from one layer to the next in a configurable and dynamic way. The proposed functional decomposition simplifies the implementation that is driven by the envisioned functionality. It has to be noted that such an approach is completely different from that of OpenFlow which does not decompose network layers into functional blocks.

One key component of the SoftINTERNET architecture is the description of services provided by each layer using building blocks defined by an abstract model. SoftINTERNET does not intend to create new models, but rather to examine and reuse well-established ones, e.g. IETF ForCES, ONF's OpenFlow's switch model and YANG (NETCONF). Accordingly, SoftINTERNET will extend the chosen model to satisfy the requirements in order to depart from their current 'network function' view and get closer to the 'network service' view.

Composition of services using such a methodology will enable the SoftINTERNET architecture to have a very fine-grained degree of service programmability as well as to encompass any new future layer primitives. The ability to dynamically insert new layer primitives would be empowered to adapt to future needs. In essence the building-block approach will allow SoftINTERNET to define, deploy and manage, at runtime, new functionalities and services. These functionalities will be published from bottom-up, whereby each layer publishes to the upper layer the functions that it can provide and ultimately the user will be able to see which services are available. They would be able to be pushed from top-bottom, where the user can request one or more specific services which would then have to be created from existing infrastructure or instantiated at run-time and then published to the user.

The SoftINTERNET concept is developed according to the features mentioned in the third architectural state of the SDN Conceptual View (Fig. 1) based on a Software Driven/Enabled Networks approach. In opposite to SDN proposed by ONF SoftINTERNET is a systematic approach, The overall SoftINTERNET architecture is split into layers depicted in Fig. 2 according to the functionalities described hereafter.

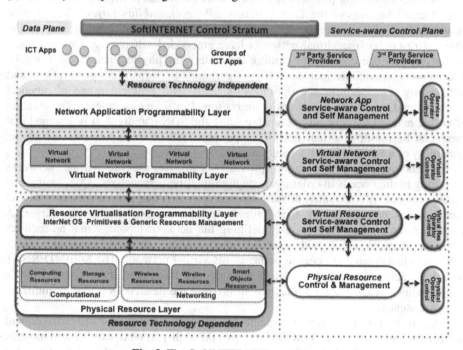

Fig. 2. The SoftINTERNET Architecture

The lowest layer, *Physical Resource Layer* role is to cope with heterogeneous environments. It has two main functions. It provides a uniform view (via virtualization) of different technological network and computational resources (a kind of resource abstraction) and it has intrinsic autonomic and programmable management of the resources, which provides a fast-reaction time for management operations and facilitates scalability of the SoftINTERNET solution in case of distributed management implementation. The Physical Resource Layer exposes some functions to other layers, for example there is monitoring and controlling of resources used by other layers. The monitoring information provides not only the information about the resource health and usage but also about the power consumption, which makes the SoftINTERNET approach energy efficiency ready. It is assumed that such 'physical resources' can be provided by multiple owners/operators across multiple domains. The deployment of the SoftINTERNET architecture will be in a form of additional control elements to the wired and mobile environments with adaptation to specific physical resources.

It is worth mentioning that Smart Objects are also part of the architecture. IoT and "Smart Objects" are expected to become active participants in information, social, industrial and business processes where they are enabled to interact with services and application and communicate among themselves and with the environment by exchanging data and information about the environment, while reacting autonomously to the "real/physical world" events and influencing it by running processes that trigger actions and create services with or without direct human intervention.

From the underlying physical resources, a set of virtual networks can be created using the mechanisms of the *Virtual Network Programmability Layer*. These virtual networks have different properties according to specific needs. As in case of the physical resources, the virtual networks have embedded self-managed mechanisms. Moreover, they can control and monitor the underlying physical resources. The self-management operations include self-configuration, performance optimization, and self-healing. The performance optimization deals with efficient usage of physical resources and cross virtual network optimizations (traffic management). The creation of virtual networks can be programmable using the SDN paradigm. It is assumed that there can be multiple virtual networks operators. All of these facilities aid in the scalability of a SoftINTERNET solution.

The end-users and application providers can use specific virtual networks according to their needs in order to create high-quality, personalized, QoS-aware, and secure services. It is assumed in the proposed approach that programmability of end user services is provided by the *Network Application Programmability Layer*. A simple example would be of a user defining the network topology that he requires from the network along with specific functionalities (firewall, transcoder, load-balancers) instantiated at specific points in his virtual network. The SoftINTERNET would be able to create this virtual network and instantiate the requested user's functionalities at the required locations to provide the desired QoS, e.g. minimizing network latency.

It has to be noted that the aforementioned programmability and self-management of different layers of SoftINTERNET requires the ability to send, execute and monitor the execution code and therefore the management operations should be extended appropriately. In order to do that we need an execution environment that can be centralized (for example OSGi [2]) or distributed.

The scalability of the proposed architecture is enabled by the scalability for the following architectural elements: virtualisation of all types of physical resources; the separate mechanisms and mappings of virtual resources to wire, wireless and smart objects networks; the control elements of the service-aware and management-aware control layer; the northern APIs as depicted in Fig. 1 and by the use of Virtual Machines for the programmability of the service and network components.

4   Research Challenges of the SoftINTERNET Approach

SoftINTERNET should cope with heterogeneous environments providing uniform view (virtualization) of different technological networks and computational resources. This functionality is a part of Physical Resource Layer. The research challenges to assess this view with special emphasis on the wireline, wireless and Smart Objects virtual control adaptation are graphically depicted in Fig. 3 and they are described hereafter.

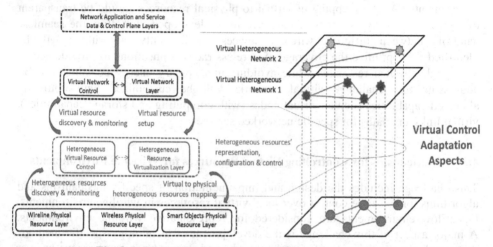

Fig. 3. SoftINTERNET's Virtual Control Adaptation Aspect

4.1   Mechanisms to Control Virtual Resources for Wireless Environments

This challenge refers to the necessary technology-dependent tactical actions and algorithms for run-time control over local virtual resources in wireless network environments using technology specific operations. This challenge addresses basic configuration functionalities including virtual resource creation, activation, adjustment and termination operations. Dedicated mechanisms and algorithms developed for on-the-fly manipulation of resources in dynamic environments with conflicting requirements according to up-to-date feedbacks from local network monitoring activities are also part of this challenge. These may include adaptive re-allocation of virtual resources according to changing network conditions or service demands. Additionally, this challenge deals with the critical nature of developing autonomous actions that provide network stability and optimizations in absence of higher-level control. This includes for example virtual resource remapping in case of resource scarcity that can be provided internally to the virtual network control. Additionally, the provisioning and utilization of the programmable resources are not to be limited to the network resources only, but also to storage and processing resources, to provide a complete set of programmable resources for the applications.

4.2   Mapping Virtual to Physical Resources for Wireless Environments

This challenge includes the design and implementation of specific mechanisms and algorithms for optimised mapping of virtual resources onto the physical resources in the wireless environment. Specific optimisation techniques will be developed for efficiently mapping between virtual resources and the physical network infrastructure. In this case of wireless infrastructures, certain characteristics and capabilities have to be considered, e.g. limited bandwidth, processing capabilities, storage, energy (battery), type of interfaces supported of the mobile nodes and mobility, conflicting requirements.. As the mapping of virtual to physical resources should be transparent to higher control layers, mechanisms have to be developed that allow the seamless hand-off between different wireless devices. Additionally, algorithms will be identified that optimize the coverage of wireless radio connections to provide access to enough physical resources while avoiding unnecessary energy consumption. By addressing this challenge virtual networks will be customized with optimally allocated capabilities such as virtual nodes (with computing and storage capabilities), virtual links and paths for specific networked services.

4.3   Mechanisms for Controlling Virtual Resources for Wireline Environments

This challenge includes the design and implementation of specific mechanisms and algorithms for run-time control over local virtual resources in wireline environments. OpenFlow environments are considered for representative wireline environments. A major aspect of this challenge is the development of technology-specific methods that enable the provisioning of virtual networks and storage/processing resources over OpenFlow substrate infrastructures. This includes the creation, configuration and tearing-down of virtual resource components, considering both networking and computational/storage resources, e.g. so that link bandwidth or network computation power can be adjusted on-the-fly based on conflicting requirements.. By using OpenFlow switch virtualization, networking resources can be re-allocated according to changing network conditions or service demands. Additionally, this challenge considers the development of autonomous actions that provide virtual network stability, performance and optimizations even in absence of higher-level control. These include e.g. virtual resource remapping in case of resource scarcity, increased resilience through transparent resource migration in case of hardware failure or energy saving using adaptive virtual resource consolidation.

4.4   Mapping Virtual to Physical Resources for Wireline Environments

This challenge includes the design and implementation of specific mechanisms and algorithms for optimised mapping of virtual resources onto the physical resources in wireline environments. Specific optimisation techniques will be developed for efficiently mapping between virtual resources and the physical network infrastructure. Such mapping will involve a wide variety of resources available from the underlying wireline network, including communication, computing and storage capabilities. The mapping will take into account the top-level service/operational requirements such as the demanded QoS requirement and resilience capability to be embedded into the resulting virtual network. By addressing this challenge virtual networks will be customized with optimally allocated capabilities such as virtual nodes (with computing and storage capabilities), virtual links and paths for specific networked services.

4.5   Mechanisms for Controlling Virtual Resources for Smart Objects

This challenge will identify and implement the mechanisms required for the discovery, registration and monitoring of virtual and physical resources, configuration and control (including reservation, isolation and release) of virtual resources, and creation of service components in smart objects environments. Taking into account the technology-agnostic requirements of the SoftINTERNET virtual network control layer, this challenge will identify the technology-dependent control mechanisms needed to meet these requirements.

The control mechanisms will not only be used at this layer/level but they will also need to expose information to the upper layers in order to allow management and control of virtual networks across more than one technology-specific physical domain. It will allow receiving triggers from the upper layers for setting up and tearing resources, as well as adding/removing functionalities and creating service components within the virtual networks which will be accommodated on virtual components residing on smart objects substrates. In this context, an abstract identification model needs to be defined to reference each smart object, as single element or part of a group, for all the control/configuration processes. To realize this, appropriate interfaces need to be defined.

Regarding the management and control of the smart object substrate, this challenge includes investigating relevant mechanisms both for substrates with integrated control and data planes (current practice) and for substrates with a Software Defined (e.g., OpenFlow-based) type of control. The latter approach, recently proposed in [3], is based on a clear separation between control and data forwarding. It has the potential to provide the necessary abstractions and to ease management needed for supporting multiple applications over smart object networks and results in better utilization of the physical infrastructure resources. With respect to this, this challenge deals with the adaptations that are required to support the Software Defined Networking concept on smart object virtual networks taking into account the limited capabilities of the nodes and focusing on the need to manage the control overhead.

4.6   Mapping Virtual to Physical Resources for Smart Objects

This challenge deals with the critical nature of developing the mechanisms and techniques needed to optimize the mapping of virtual resources on physical smart object resources. The objective is to continuously optimize the use of the physical resources (e.g. utilization, energy efficiency) as well as to provide self-organization and self-healing capabilities by appropriately (re)grouping virtual resources and mapping them accordingly to the best set of physical resources. This mapping should ensure that each operation made on a virtual device has to take effect on the physical object. In fact, all the operations allowed by SoftINTERNET on virtual instances of the smart objects should then be replicated in a tangible way on real objects. To achieve this each real object must exhibit a set of APIs that enable the interaction with the equivalent virtual object.

This challenge also develops functions for the setup and control of necessary physical object clusters to support, as an entity, virtual resource requirements in a performance and energy efficient manner. Furthermore, the mapping of virtual to physical resources will support different levels of in-network processing which are needed to provide the best trade-off between computational and networking-related energy consumption in energy-limited smart object environments.

The aforementioned operations should remain transparent to the upper layers, meaning that individual virtual networks should be agnostic to any reconfigurations taking place at the physical level and avoiding performance deterioration.

4.7   Energy Management and Optimisation

This challenge deals with the critical nature of developing the mechanisms for Energy- cognisant Internet including optimizing the energy consumption within the limits of a single network and/or a network of networks and /or network of Data Centres and Clouds, based on system virtualization plus the optimal distribution of VMs across the set of networks and servers and providing stabilization of the local networks following electricity demand-response loops.

In Fig. 4 below we have identified and outlined the new closed control loop functionality, which is applicable to energy saving technologies. Fig. 1 shows those logical functions, the information base, and their interactions.

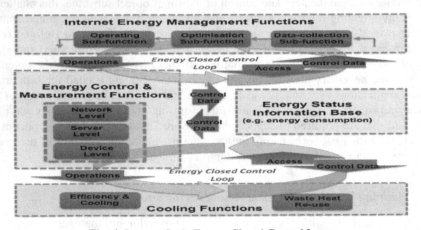

Fig. 4. Internet Scale Energy Closed Control Loops

4.8   Mature and Deployable Autonomic and Optimised Management Integrated feature and qualities

This challenge deals with the critical nature of developing the mechanisms and enablers and systems for autonomic management functions applied not only to the physical resources, but also virtual resources located inside the network. In addition, a unification of all autonomic functions should be realised to enable coordination, orchestration, governance and knowledge closed control loops as applied to all autonomic functions. In this approach the management and control functions would be distributed and located or hosted in or close to the managed network and service elements.

4.9 Scalable Programmable Delivery Infrastructures as Systems of Inter-Orchestration for Big Data and Service Networks

This challenge deals with the critical nature of developing the mechanisms for the transition from current systems designed around discrete and static pieces of uncorrelated silos of content centric information or silos of networks to systems which are more programmable with decentralized control of big data and service networks, incorporating technologies which enable associative orchestration and interactions, and which often leverage virtualisation technologies to provide the capabilities to enable those interactions. In order to integrate such delivery systems, as well as offer new systems to support enhanced composition and correlation - which is what systems of Inter-orchestration is all about, in the end appropriate virtual platform technologies will need to be deployed.

5   Concluding Remarks

This position paper discusses the motivation, architecture and research challenges for the next generation Software Defined Networks (SDN). The next generation of Software Defined Networks (SDN) needs to move from being merely Defined by software to be Driven and Enabled by software and must be capable of supporting a multitude of providers of services that exploit an environment in which services are dynamically deployed and quickly adapted over a heterogeneous physical infrastructure, according to varying and sometimes conflicting customer requirements.

This paper presents SoftINTERNET an initiative for a service-aware and management-aware network control infrastructure for heterogeneous networks that uses software driven features for the elaboration, development, and validation of networking concepts. The proposed infrastructure aims to optimally integrate the connectivity and management layers. It operates across multiple network environments and on top of private and public network clouds utilising fixed and mobile virtual resources, OpenFlow enabled network devices like switches and routers, and networks of Smart Objects.

Acknowledgments. The work for this article was partially supported by the European Union UniverSELF and Dolfin projects, by the project TEC2012-38574-C02-02 granted by the MEC Spanish Ministry and partially funded with FEDER funding.

References

[1] ETSI. Software-aware and Management-aware SDN" initiative initiated and lead by members of the SoftINTERNET consortium (e.g. 3rd ETSI Future Networks Workshop 9-11 April 2013 - http://www.etsi.org/news-events/news/617-2013-fnt-intro)

[2] OSGi Alliance, http://www.osgi.org/About/HomePage

[3] Luo, T., Tan, H.P., Quek, T.Q.S.: Sensor OpenFlow: Enabling Software-Defined Wireless Sensor Networks. IEEE Communications Letters 16(11), 1896–1899 (2012)

[4] National Science Foundation, Networking Technology and Systems, NeTS (2008), http://www.nsf.gov/pubs/2008/nsf08524/nsf08524.htm

[5] National Science Foundation. Network Science and Engineering (NetSE) (2010), http://www.nsf.gov/funding/pgm_summ.jsp?pims_id=503325

[6] BNN Technologies. GENI: Exploring networks of the future (2010), http://www.geni.net/

[7] Stanford Clean Slate, http://cleanslate.stanford.edu/

[8] G-Lab (2008), http://www.german-lab.de/home/

[9] Jutand, F.: National Future Internet Initiatives - GRIF (France) (2010), http://www.francenumerique2012.fr/

[10] AETIC, Internet del Futuro (2008), http://www.idi.aetic.es/esInternet/

[11] Koponen, T., et al.: A Data-Oriented Network Architecture. In: SIGCOMM 2007, New York, USA, pp. 181–192 (2007)

[12] Gritter, M., Cheriton, D.: TRIAD: A New Next-Generation Internet Architecture (2000), http://www-dsg.stanford.edu/triad,July

[13] EU FP7 4WARD project website, http://www.4ward-project.eu

[14] EU FP7 SAIL project website, http://www.sail-project.eu

[15] NSF FIA NEBULA project website, http://nebula.cis.upenn.edu

[16] NSF FIA eXpressive Internet Architecture project website, http://www.cs.cmu.edu/~xia

[17] EU FP7 PURSUIT project website, http://www.fp7-pursuit.eu

[18] EU FP7 PSIRP project website, http://www.psirp.org

[19] EU FP7 FI-WARE project website, http://www.fi-ware.eu

[20] AKARI Project website, http://akari-project.nict.go.jp/eng/index2.htm

[21] Harai, H.: AKARI Architecture Design Project in Japan (August 2008), http://akari-project.nict.go.jp/eng/document/asiafi-seminar-harai-080826.pdf; Wetherall, D., Tennenhouse, D.: The ACTIVE IP Options. In: Proc. of the 7th ACM SIGOPS European Workshop (September 1996)

[22] Merwe, V., Leslie, I.M.: "Switchlets and Dynamic Virtual ATM Networks. In: Proc Integrated Network Management V (May 1997)

[23] Chan, M.C., Huard, J.F., Lazar, A.A., Lim, K.S.: On Realizing a Broadband Kernel for Multimedia Networks. In: Ventre, G., Danthine, A., Domingo-Pascual, J. (eds.) COST-237 1996. LNCS, vol. 1185, pp. 56–74. Springer, Heidelberg (1996)

[24] Peterson, L.: NodeOS Interface Specification., Technical Report, Active Networks NodeOS Working Group (February 2, 1999)

[25] Campbell, A.T., De Meer, H.G., Kounavis, M.E., Miki, K., Vicente, J.B., Villela, D.: The Genesis Kernel: A Virtual Network Operating System for Spawning Network Architectures. In: Second International Conference on Open Architectures and Network Programming (OPENARCH), New York (1999)

[26] Da Silva, S., Florissi, D., Yemini, Y.: NetScript: A Language-Based Approach to Active Networks. Technical Report, Computer Science Dept., Columbia University (January 27, 1998)

[27] Merwe, V., Rooney, J.E., Leslie, S.: I.M.: Crosby, S.A.: The Tempest - A Practical Framework for Network Programmability. IEEE Network (November 1997)

[28] Yemini, Y., Da Silva, S.: Towards Programmable Networks. In: IFIP/IEEE International Workshop on Distributed Systems: Operations and Management, L'Aquila, Italy (October 1996)

[29] EU RESERVOIR project web site, http://62.149.240.97/

[30] McKeown et al: OpenFlow: enabling innovation in campus networks (March 2008)

[31] Sherwood, et al: FlowVisor: a network virtualization layer (October 2009)

[32] Open Networking Foundation web site, http://www.opennetworkingfoundation.org

[33] Gude et al.: NOX: towards an operating system for networks

[34] Yak, K.-K., et al.: OpenRoads: Empowering Research in Mobile Networks

[35] EU FP7 OFELIA project website, http://www.fp7-ofelia.eu

[36] EU FP7 OpenLab project web site, http://www.ict-openlab.eu

[37] EU FP7 SPARC project website, http://www.fp7-sparc.eu

[38] EU FP7 SAIL project website, http://www.sail-project.eu

[39] EU FP7 FI-WARE project web site, http://www.fi-ware.eu

[40] IEEE, 802.1Qbg – Edge Virtual Bridging, http://www.ieee802.org/1/pages/802.1bg.html

[41] Rochwerger, B., Breitgand, D., Epstein, A., Hadas, D., Loy, I., Nagin, K., Tordsson, J., Ragusa, C., Villari, M., Clayman, S., Levy, E., Maraschini, A., Massonet, P., Muñoz, H., Toffetti, G.: Reservoir - When One Cloud Is Not Enough. IEEE Computer 44(3), 44–51 (2011)

[42] Sridharan, M., Duda, K., Ganga, I., Greenberg, A., Lin, G., Pearson, M., Thaler, P., Tumuluri, C., Venkataramiah, N., Wang, Y.: NVGRE: Network Virtualisation using Generic Routing Encapsulation, IEFT Draft, http://tools.ietf.org/html/draft-sridharan-virtualization-nvgre-00

[43] Mahalingam, M., Dutt, D., Duda, K., Agarwal, P., Kreeger, L., Sridhar, T., Bursell, M., Wright, C.: VXLAN: A Framework for Overlaying Virtualised Layer 2 Networks over Layer 3 Networks., IETF Draft, http://tools.ietf.org/html/draft-mahalingam-dutt-dcops-vxlan-00

[44] http://www.cisco.com/web/about/ac79/docs/sp/Mobile_Cloud_Device.pdf

[45] http://www.mobilecloudcomputingforum.com/

[46] Christensen, J.H.: Using RESTful web-services and cloud computing to create next generation mobile applications. In: Proceedings of the 24th ACM SIGPLAN Conference Companion on Object Oriented Programming Systems Languages and Applications (OOPSLA), pp. 627–634 (October 2009)

[47] Liu, L., Moulic, R., Shea, D.: Cloud Service Portal for Mobile Device Management. In: Proceedings of IEEE 7th International Conference on e-Business Engineering (ICEBE), p. 474 (January 2011)

[48] Bonomi, F., et al.: Fog computing and its role in the internet of things. In: Proceedings of the First Edition of the MCC Workshop on Mobile Cloud Computing. ACM (2012)

[49] Galis, A., Denazis, S., Brou, C., Klein, C. (eds.): 'Programmable Networks for IP Service Deployment. Artech House Books (June 2004), http://www.artechhouse.com/Default.asp?Frame=Book.asp&Book=1-58053-745-6 ISBN 1-58053-745-6

[50] Rubio-Loyola, J., Galis, A., Astorga, A., Serrat, J., Lefevre, L., Fischer, A., Paler, A., de Meer, H.: Scalable Service Deployment on Software Defined Networks. IEEE Communications Magazine/ Network and Service Management Series (December 2011), http://dl.comsoc.org/ci1/ ISSN: 0163-6804

[51] Chapman, C., Emmerich, E., Marquez, F.G., Clayman, S., Galis, A.: Software Architecture Definition for On-demand Cloud Provisioning. Springer Journal on Cluster Computing (May 2011), http://www.editorialmanager.com/clus/, http://www.springerlink.com/content/m31np5112525167v, doi:10.1007/s10586-011-0152-0

[52] Galis, A., Plattner, B., Smith, J.M., Denazis, S., Moeller, E., Guo, H., Serrat, J., Laarhuis, J., Karetsos, G.T., Todd, C.: A flexible IP active networks architecture. In: Yasuda, H. (ed.) IWAN 2000. LNCS, vol. 1942, p. 1. Springer, Heidelberg (2000)

[53] Clayman, S., Clegg, R., Mamatas, L., Pavlou, G., Galis, A.: Monitoring, Aggregation and Filtering for Efficient Management of Virtual Networks. In: IEEE CNSM mini-conference 2011: 7th International Conference on Network and Service Management, Paris, France (October 2011), http://www.cnsm2011.org/, http://cnsm.loria.fr/

[54] Clegg, G., Clayman, R., Pavlou, S., Mamatas, G., Galis, L., On, A.: the Selection of management and monitoring nodes in dynamic networks, March 2012. IEEE Computer Society Press, Los Alamitos (2012), http://doi.ieeecomputersociety.org/10.1109/TC.2012.67

[55] Matsubara, D., Egawa, T., Nishinaga, N., Kafle, V.P., Shin, M.K., Galis, A.: Toward Future Networks: A Viewpoint from ITU-T. IEEE Communications Magazine 51(3), 112–118 (2013)

[56] Network Functions Virtualisation (NFV) – ETSI Industry Group started in (January 2013), http://portal.etsi.org/portal/server.pt/community/NFV/367&whitepaper&whitepaper, http://portal.etsi.org/NFV/NFV_White_Paper.pdf

Enabling Cloud Connectivity
Using SDN and NFV Technologies

Fariborz Derakhshan, Heidrun Grob-Lipski, Horst Roessler, Peter Schefczik,
and Michael Soellner

Bell Labs Germany
Alcatel-Lucent

Abstract. Cloud environments play an important role for network and
service providers. Cloud network providers require ubiquitous, broadband and minimum-delay connectivity from network providers. There
are different realizations of cloud connectivity based on the Software Defined Networking (SDN) and the Network Function Virtualization (NFV)
paradigm. In this paper we introduce a new concept based on the OConS
architecture developed within the SAIL FP7 project. Our advanced connectivity concept focuses on interdomain connectivity.

Keywords: Interdomain path computation, cloud resource
management, SDN, NFV, open connectivity, SAIL.

1 Introduction

Provisioning cloud services based on a platform of distributed data centers was
the emerging approach of the past years (Amazon EC2 [1], Google Cloud Platform [2]). By means of virtualization of storage and processing resources, and
more and more also network resources, the distributed cloud is able to provide infrastructure as a service for a wide range of applications. Two concepts
support service-oriented (virtual) connectivity in the cloud: Software Defined
Networking (SDN) and Network Function Virtualization (NFV). Based on these
concepts we show how cloud connectivity can be realized in a multi-domain
network of distributed clouds. The interdomain resource allocation described in
this paper provides an open connectivity service to cope with the complexity
of multi-domain networks, especially with regard to control, management and
algorithmic elasticity.

This paper is organized as follows: In section 2 we give an overview on
the current developments and problems concerning open connectivity concepts.
In section 3 we handle the provisioning of resources for cloud connectivity. In
section 4 we study the hierarchical and flat interdomain connection management.
Section 5 concludes the paper and gives a short outlook to future work.

2 Current Developments and Problems

The concept of Software-defined Networking (SDN) was formally defined in 2009
by Martin Casado but originated as far back as 2007 on work from him, Nick

D. Pesch et al. (Eds.): MONAMI 2013, LNICST 125, pp. 245–258, 2013.

McKeown and Scott Shenker. In 2011 SDN was taken up by IETF [3] and is nowadays brought forward by the Software-defined Networking Research Group (SDNRG) [4]. The second trend that is gaining more and more ground is called Network Function Virtualization (NFV) and is promoted by ETSI [5]. In the following we take a closer look at both technologies and clarify the relation between them and the current developments and the concerning problems.

SDN was originally conceived for a campus network usage and was later applied in data centers and is used today also between them. The SDN model is based on the split between the forwarding plane and the control plane. One goal of SDN is to allow applications to request services from the network which can automatically be deployed and monitored. Thus SDN is about bridging the gap between application and network.

In the past applications assumed bandwidth as free and abundant, but in todays networks bandwidth is a scarce resource and must be managed accordingly. Applications also could not impact the delay, availability and dynamicity of the network. SDN was conceived to allow applications to inform the network about their preferences such that it can configure the connectivity accordingly. On the other hand the network can also inform the applications about the changes of topology, bandwidth, delay etc. If the application is implemented to behave appropriately, an improved service is the result.

A prominent implementation that facilitates SDN is OpenFlow which was originally developed by the Stanford University. Today OpenFlow is being taken care of by the Open Networking Foundation [6]. However OpenFlow is not the only representative of an SDN implementation. With ForCES [7], General Switch Management Protocol (GSMP) [8], NetConf [9], and even the well known SNMP [10] there are more standard control technologies and interfaces that are able to configure the forwarding plane at least inside a single network node.

Another approach is the virtualization of network functions so that they can run on more or less general purpose hardware instead of dedicated hardware applied in telecommunication networks today. With the NFV approach operators have the possibility to implement their needed functions anywhere in the network. These functions include switching elements and routers, mobile network nodes, security equipment like firewalls and deep packet inspection appliances, as well as application layer solutions like session controllers, load balancers, content distribution networks, etc. Thereby NFV seeks to reuse existing virtualization mechanisms and is standardizing the interfaces between network elements. NFV is brought forward today by an ETSI ISG (Industry Specification Group).

It is to note that single network functions can also be virtualized and deployed without SDN. An SDN can also exist without NFV-based services. Thus, SDN and NFV are orthogonal technologies.

Network operators are not only interested to save equipment costs by applying NFV-based services on industry standard high volume servers, switches and storages, but also in the possibility to scale them arbitrarily. Furthermore operators need a management system that can orchestrate all the virtualized functions to offer optimized services. This latter goal was addressed in the Scalable and

Adaptive Internet Solutions (SAIL) Project [11] in the Open Connectivity Services (OConS) framework conceived to cope with the challenges posed by the Future Internet. OConS relieves the instantiation, launch and interconnection of functions by use of a specified orchestration procedure. With this OConS can even support challenging flash crowd situations as well as cloud networking and network of information scenarios [12].

SDN and NVF were conceived to enable an easy integration of new services and applications into the cloud. However there are some caveats with both technologies. The problem of SDN is that centralized SDN controllers are a bottleneck and represent a single point of failure. Moreover the performance of the software switch is an issue of concern, for example when it has to carry out complex rules or extensive header rewrites. The latter raises the need for expensive hardware counteracting the wish for a simple switch equipment. And, last but not least, for some applications where the rules in the switch are not preconfigurable additional delay must be taken into account when a logically central and physically distributed set of central controllers must be consulted for packets that a switch cannot handle on its own.

The problem with the NFV partly lies in the fact that the NFV software is more complex to build and harder to maintain due to its distribution onto several machines. Also the reliability of the service is not easily accomplished and depends on interconnectivity, link throughput and delay.

3   Provisioning Connectivity in the Cloud

In the age of social communities, web-based applications connect many social groups with many users via their shared and linked multi-media content like pictures, audio or video. New services built from combinations of such content sources can become popular in a very short time and need a dynamic and powerful infrastructure to be processed. In order to decouple the service growth from the available physical hardware basis, a cloud provider may be used to manage the virtual infrastructure.

The SAIL [11] project developed a model how a cloud provider that owns or contracts several distributed data centers can offer a system for service creation and deployment in a heterogeneous environment, i.e. dealing with several local cloud management systems, and interconnecting the local cloud domains [13].

Figure 1 gives a simplified view of the proposed interworking of cloud and network domains. At the cloud level the cloud provider will set up a distributed cloud manager to create and configure the storage and processing resources to be deployed as virtual machines (VMs, not shown in Figure 1) in the distributed data centers DCn.

Thinking about real implementations, the OpenStack [14] collection of open source technologies delivers a scalable cloud operating system. Initially the OpenStack project was announced in 2010 by Rackspace and NASA but today many players build on the OpenStack open source software initiative for building clouds. Over 150 companies gathered in the OpenStack collaboration and provide architectural input, contribute code, and/or integrate it into their business offerings.

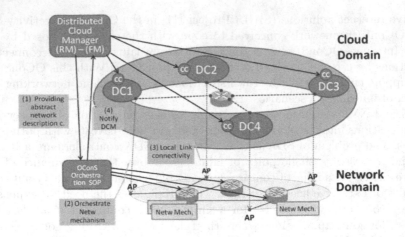

Fig. 1. Interworking of cloud and network domain functions

The OpenStack cloud operating system is able to control large pools of computing, storage, and networking resources. All these resources are managed through a so called dashboard which runs in a browser in a RESTful manner. The dashboard gives administrators and users the control needed to setup and monitor a complete service consisting of computing, storage and networking instances.

In order to set up an application network between the created VMs in the data centers, three steps are necessary as described in the approach of SAIL [15,16]:

- The first step is to transfer an application graph into a virtual network of communicating VMs.
- The second step is to connect the virtual VMs with the physical interfaces in the data centers which is typically done by support of a hypervisor respective the management tools that come with it (e.g. based on libvirt in an open source environment). This has to be managed in each data center by the local Cloud Controller (CC) in a coordinated way. To enhance this task, the SAIL project proposes to use the OCCI-based description technique OCNI [17], and provides the corresponding tools via the libNetVirt library [18,19].
- The third step is to connect the distributed data centers with dedicated managed networking resources, also across different network domains that guarantees a certain degree of end-to-end (i.e. DC to DC) QoS as required by the application network.

Typically the connectivity view between the distributed data centers at the cloud level is based on a "single router abstraction" for the network. The distributed cloud manager delegates the task of network and path deployment to the contracted network provider which first translates the single router network descriptions into potential subtasks to related network domains (and their providers) and then orchestrates the appropriate managed network services. At the attachment points between data center and network as well as between network domains, the corresponding dynamic protocol parameters have to be exchanged through a link negotiation protocol [13].

Within this approach, the current paper discusses a proposal for the architecture, protocols and algorithms for resource and path management across multiple network domains offering interconnectivity services to cloud providers.

4   Interdomain Connection Management

The effort for connection management can significantly increase due to the dynamics of the network resources, and due to the universality of users' (cloud providers', end-users', applications', etc.) resource demands and preferences. To relieve the intradomain network controller in our architecture the management of domain-external resources is delegated to an entity called interdomain DCU (Domain Control Unit). The interdomain DCU treats each connected domain as a single resource with specific attributes.

In [20] we introduced a network architecture with a DCU in each domain separating the data plane from the control plane and comprising most of the control plane mechanisms (i.e. path computing) into one single entity. The DCU clients in each network element deliver topological and resource information to the local DCU which then abstracts from the details of domain-internal topology and resource information to a global information, e.g. domain load state, such that detailed domain-specific topology and resource information is hidden towards the interdomain DCU. Detailed information about topology (e.g. addresses of the network entities) and resources remains in the local DCU.

There are already diverse path computation mechanisms that can be applied for the interdomain resource allocation. In this paper we describe enhanced concepts that utilize additional resource information to improve the efficiency of the interdomain connectivity management.

Generally, the connection management can be divided into three parts: The first part comprises the gathering of current network topology and resource information. We focus on delivering abstract resource information from each domain to the interdomain DCU and storing them in its Traffic Engineering Database (TED) together with a timestamp. This TED also stores network topology, operator policies and predefined interdomain paths. In section 4.4 we introduce a novel mechanism called PSCEH (Publish Subscribe with Configurable Event Handling) to increase the efficiency and quality of the information exchange. Resource information can be for example the load of computational resources, current storage capacity, link bandwidth, and network topology. The second part consists of path computation and connectivity configuration performed by the interdomain DCU based on the available topology and resource information. In the third part controllers' decisions are enforced on the respective network entities in order to realize the connectivity.

Some aspects of information retrieval and path calculation follow the ideas of interdomain PCE (Path Computation Entity) procedures, e.g. [21]. Based on the PCE concept the mechanisms described in this paper in sections 4.3 and 4.4 utilize additional resource information and interact tightly with the TED which further includes operator policies to improve the efficiency of the interdomain connectivity management.

4.1   Hierarchical Interdomain Connection Management

For hierarchical interdomain connection management the DCU of each domain registers at an interdomain DCU during network startup. The DCUs send a registration request to potential interdomain DCUs and receive an ACK from the responsible instance. Since the network structure is supposed to be quite static the mapping of the DCUs to the responsible interdomain DCU can be predefined by the network provider in order to reduce the discovery effort. During registration the operators deliver their policies to the interdomain DCU, which stores them in the TED together with the respective topology information.

Figure 2 shows the hierarchical interdomain connection management performed by the interdomain DCU to set up a path between the source domain S and the destination domain D.

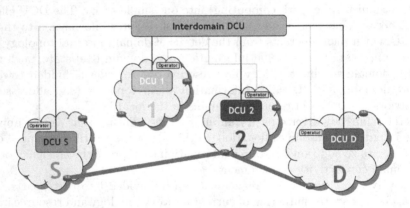

Fig. 2. Interdomain connection management by the interdomain DCU between a source domain S and a destination domain D via intermediate domains 1 and 2

When a request arrives at a local DCU, the DCU first checks whether the destination address of the request can be found in the topology information of the local TED. If the DCU cannot resolve the request, it forwards the request to its interdomain DCU. The interdomain DCU first sends a request to all of its DCUs in order to identify the domain containing the destination address. The DCUs then check whether the requested destination address is stored in their TEDs. The DCU which keeps the requested address in its TED responds to the interdomain DCU with an ACK. The information the local DCUs submit to the interdomain DCU is kept at minimum possible level to encapsulate the data only within elements where they are needed.

After the destination domain is identified, the interdomain DCU first retrieves the resource information from its TED to compute candidate paths from source to destination with respect to the constraints defined in the request. Constraints can be for example a minimum bandwidth, an application class like HD video, real-time video conferencing, user class, security level, etc.

If the resource information of some DCUs in the candidate paths is not up-to-date, i.e. the corresponding time stamp is too old, the interdomain DCU sends an explicit request to all concerned DCUs to retrieve the current resource state. Triggered by this request the respective DCUs perform a path computation within their domain to determine the current resource information. After receiving the resource state updates the interdomain DCU selects the optimum final solution among the candidate paths and informs the source DCU.

The hierarchical architecture however has two disadvantages. If the processing capacity of the interdomain DCU and the links towards the interdomain DCU are not dimensioned sufficiently (which can be very expensive) an overload situation might occur which in worst case can lead to an outage of the interdomain DCU and consequently of the complete interdomain connection management, if no duplicate interdomain DCU is available.

4.2 Peer-to-Peer Interdomain Connection Management

In order to cope with the disadvantages of the hierarchical interdomain connection management we define a flat architecture by transferring the interdomain DCU functionality into the DCUs. In this case unresolved resource requests are forwarded by the source DCU to all neighboring peer DCUs. For avoiding the flooding of the entire DCU network, it can be organized according to a spanning tree.

Like in the hierarchical architecture each DCU checks whether the requested destination address is stored in its TED. The DCU which keeps the destination address in its TED responds to the requesting DCU with an ACK. After the destination domain has been identified, the source DCU first retrieves the resource information from its TED to compute the candidate paths to the destination with respect to the constraints defined in the request.

If current resource information is needed, the source DCU triggers all DCUs of the candidate path to deliver current resource state updates. The source DCU then determines the optimum final solution. Figure 3 shows the flat peer-to-peer interconnection management architecture. In this example a path set up between a source domain S and a destination domain D is triggered by the DCU S.

In order to speed up the path computation process the source DCU can provoke each DCU on the candidate path to compute a local path and perform local flow establishment during the time when the source DCU itself does the same. This preconfiguration of the involved domains allows for immediate forwarding of the packets of the request.

The advantage of a flat architecture is the lack of a single point of failure, however its disadvantage is an increase of interdomain communication and more delay in responding to requests due to the absence of a central supervisor and

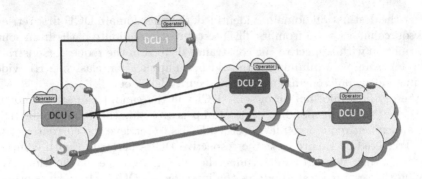

Fig. 3. Peer-to-peer interdomain connection management between a source domain S and a destination domain D via intermediate domains 1 and 2

database. Further, the transfer of the interdomain DCU intelligence into the DCUs makes the latter more complex and more expensive.

4.3 Multi-criteria Resource Management

For a rapid and adaptive path computation and for responding elastically to the requests of clients we introduce an algorithm for multi-criteria path computation to be applied by the interdomain DCU in a hierarchical architecture or by the source DCU in a flat architecture.

To cope with the complexity of the path computation the interdomain or the source DCU first considers the priorities of performance indicators (e.g. bandwidth, delay, etc.) as defined by the client through weights assigned to them. Given a set of n performance indicators with priorities $p_1, p_2, \cdots, p_n$ the DCU successively computes the paths satisfying the defined optimization criteria with respect to the corresponding indicators in decreasing order of importance. After sorting the indicators in descending order of their priorities the algorithm starts the computation of the optimum solutions $\{S_1\}$ with respect to the first indicator and a predefined default solution tolerance $t_{1,0}$. In case that no solution is found, the algorithm checks whether the acceptable tolerance limit is already reached or not. If not, it increases the tolerance and restarts the computation of solutions. Otherwise, if no more tolerance is acceptable, it returns an empty solution set $\{\emptyset\}$.

In case that a solution set $\{S_1\}$ is found, the algorithm continues the procedure with the next parameter only if it exists and has a non-negligible priority ($p_{i+1} \sim p_i$) that justifies the computation effort. In this case the algorithm searches the solutions $\{S_2\}$ within the previously found solution set $\{S_1\}$ that satisfied the criteria concerning the first indicator. If no solution is found the algorithm tries again to relax the solution constraints (increase the tolerance t_2) first with respect to the current less important indicator, and then successively, if still no solution is found, with respect to the previous more important indicators. In case that multiple solutions are found the final solution is randomly chosen among them. Figure 4 depicts a schematic flow chart of the algorithm.

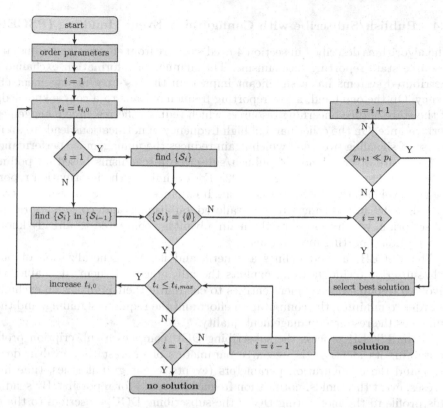

Fig. 4. Multi-criteria path computation starts with the performance indicator with the highest priority p_i and with a predefined initial solution tolerance $t_{i,0}$. It only proceeds to the next indicator if its priority p_{i+1} is non-negligible. In case of an empty solution set $\{\emptyset\}$ the algorithm tries to expand the tolerance interval of solutions and restarts the optimization. The process stops when an exit event occurs.

The priorities of indicators are predefined by the clients according their needs. The less the number of indicators and the larger the tolerances, the less the computational effort, but also the lower the quality of solutions. To increase the efficiency of the process, each solution can be tagged with a time stamp and stored in the TED such that a new computation of solutions is only started if the already available solution has become obsolete. The expiration conditions can be dynamically defined by the controller. However, a re-computation can also be triggered proactively to improve the quality of available solutions. The new solution can then be offered to the requester without its explicit request.

The described mechanism can be enhanced to estimate the resource demand of arriving requests in advance by applying statistical and probabilistic methods on the current network resource state.

4.4   Publish/Subscribe with Configurable Event Handling (PSCEH)

The algorithms described in section 4 need support from efficient and adjustable resource state reporting mechanisms. The manner of information exchange in distributed systems has a significant impact on the resource management efficiency. On the one hand, a low reporting frequency leads to a coarse knowledge of the state of the concerning resources which reduces the resource management performance. On the other hand, a high frequency of notifications leads to an increase of signaling overhead which again reduces the management performance.

There are diverse kinds of publish/subscribe mechanisms based on polling, pulling, pushing or advertising, e.g. [22]. For optimizing the information reporting we developed the PSCEH mechanism. It enhances the basic publish/subscribe paradigm by introducing provider-tailored publishing and consumer-oriented subscription, which represents the main advantage compared to already known information reporting mechanisms.

The PSCEH method defines a generic and flexible generalization of publish/subscribe techniques and exploits the advantages of them. It enables the involved resource management entities to customize their information exchange in order to minimize the computation effort and the required signaling, and thus enhances the resource management quality.

In the PSCEH process the subscribing DCU compiles a subscription profile containing its identity, the resource parameters of interest (bandwidth, delay, etc.) and the configuration parameters (events, event granularities, time hystereses, event thresholds, notification frequencies, etc.) for reporting. By sending this profile to the monitoring DCUs the subscribing DCU subscribes to the reports of them. The parameters in the profile may be defined as optional or mandatory. In case that an event as defined in the profile occurs, the concerning DCUs send a notification to the subscribing DCU.

Figure 5 shows an example of the PSCEH in a hierarchical environment with exchange of subscription and notification messages between interdomain DCU as subscriber and DCUs as publishers. If the interdomain DCU needs the resource information of the DCUs 1, 2 and D, it compiles a subscription profile as described above and sends it to them. Thus, whenever an event of interest occurs, the DCUs notify the subscribing interdomain DCU according to its subscription profile.

Figure 6 shows an example of the PSCEH in a flat peer-to-peer environment with exchange of subscription and notification messages between peer DCUs. In this case, if the DCU S needs the resource state information of DCUs 1, 2 and D, it compiles a subscription as above and sends it to them. The rest of the process is the same as described above.

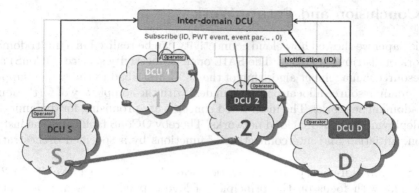

Fig. 5. PSCEH supporting hierarchical interdomain connection management

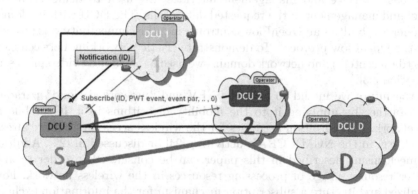

Fig. 6. PSCEH supporting peer-to-peer interdomain connection management

The subscribing DCU has the possibility to redefine the parameters of the reporting by updating the corresponding entries in the profile. This way, the PSCEH mechanism allows the DCUs to adapt not only the notification frequency but also the measurement parameters and the reporting events to their actual needs and privacy requirements.

Further, the PSCEH allows for collecting resource information prior to the arrival of resource requests such that the DCUs are relieved from time consuming message exchange. This depicts a non-trivial advantage in time-critical stress phases with short inter-arrival times of requests. By decoupling the information exchange from the time-critical decision phase the PSCEH enables the DCUs to apply more complex resource management and optimization algorithms with sophisticated and customized preprocessing of resource information.

For relieving the DCUs in the central architecture from interdomain path computation the interdomain DCU has to be protected by redundancy mechanisms to prevent any inoperability.

5   Conclusion and Future Work

In this paper we showed how cloud connectivity can be realized in a multi-domain network of distributed clouds. The SAIL open connectivity service (OConS) and the resource management algorithm of the DCU described in this paper support interdomain resource allocation that can deal with the complexity of forthcoming multi-domain networks. The introduced concepts are promising for dynamic service deployment in future cloud networks. Thereby OConS facilitates the instantiation, initiatian and interconnection of functions by a specified orchestration procedure.

A first proof-of-concept demonstration was shown at the FuNeMS 2012 in Berlin [20] with focus on the principles of load-dependent resource allocation between application, cloud management (CloNe) and network (OConS). Thereby a web-based service and management interface was used to demonstrate the control and management of the requested data paths. The DCU with its domain controller was built as an OpenFlow controller and the connectivity was provided using the OpenFlow protocol. To demonstrate elastic networking between cloud nodes (data centers) and network domains we used a distributed video processing application [23].

In the future we intend to take the NFV and "networked cloud" paradigm a step further by applying it to the mobility algorithms in a 4G mobile access network. Virtualization activities for the wireless access system are already studied, e.g. in the NGMN CRAN activities [24] or discussed in [25]. Additionally, mechanisms described in this paper can be considered in order to allow a better resource usage of processing resources in the wireless network. For a centralized architecture a subscription mechanism for the information exchange described in section 4.4 can be applied whereas for a decentralized architecture an information retrieval triggered by broadcast messages is more advantageous. Furthermore, it will enable a more efficient (physical processing) resource utilization allowing for either energy saving gains or additional processing headroom for next-generation features in wireless networks as already envisaged in the LTE-Advanced specifications.

Acknowledgments. This work has been partially funded by the European Commission under grant FP7-ICT-2009-5-257448-SAIL. We would like to thank our colleagues in the SAIL project for the many fruitful discussions.

Abbreviations

ACK	Acknowledgement
D	Destination
DC	Data Center
DCU	Domain Control Unit
I-DCU	Interdomain DCU
NFV	Network Function Virtualization
OCCI	Open Cloud Computing Interface
OCNI	Open Cloud Networking Interface
OConS	Open Connectivity Services
PCE	Path Computation Entity
PSCEH	Publish Subscribe with Configurable Event Handling
S	Source
SAIL	Scalable and Adaptive Internet Solutions
SDN	Software-Defined Networking
TED	Traffic Engineering Database
VM	Virtual Machine

References

1. Amazon Elastic Computer Cloud (Amazon EC2), aws.amazon.com/ec2
2. Google Cloud Platform, cloud.google.com
3. Bird of a feather session on Software-defined Networking (SDN), IETF-82, Taipei (November 17, 2011), tools.ietf.org/agenda/82/sdn.html
4. Software-defined Networking Research Group (SDNRG) of the IRTF, trac.tools.ietf.org/group/irtf/trac/wiki/sdnrg
5. Network Functions Virtualization Introductory White Paper. SDN and OpenFlow World Congress, Darmstadt, Germany October 22-24 (2012), portal.etsi.org/NFV/NFV_White_Paper.pdf
6. Open Networking Foundation, http://www.opennetworking.org
7. Doria, A., Hadi Salim, J., Haas, R., Khosravi, H., Wang, W., Dong, L., Gopal, R., Halpern, J.: "Forwarding and Control Element Separation (ForCES) Protocol Specification", IETF RFC 5810 (March 2010)
8. Doria, A., Hellstrand, F., Sundell, K., Worster, T.: General Switch Management Protocol (GSMP). V3, IETF RFC 3292 (June 2002)
9. Enns, R., Bjorklund, M., Schoenwaelder, J., Bierman, A.: Network Configuration Protocol (NETCONF). IETF RFC 6241 (June 2011)
10. Case, J., Harrington, D., Presuhn, R., Wijnen, B.: Message Processing and Dispatching for the Simple Network Management Protocol (SNMP). IETF RFC 3412 (December 2002)
11. The SAIL Consortium, http://www.sail-project.eu
12. Ferreira, L.S., et al.: Open Connectivity Services for the Future Internet. In: IEEE Wireless Communications and Networking Conference (WCNC2013), Shanghai (April 2013)

13. SAIL, Refined CloNe Architecture, Deliverable FP7-ICT-2009-5-257448-SAIL/D.D.3, SAIL project (October 2012), www.sail-project.eu
14. OpenStack Cloud Software, www.openstack.org
15. SAIL, Applications for Connectivity Services and Evaluation, Deliverable FP7-ICT-2009-5-257448-SAIL/D.C.4, SAIL project (February 2013), http://www.sail-project.eu
16. Puthalath, H., Soares, J., Melander, B., Sefidcon, A., Carapinha, J., Melo, M.: Negotiating On-demand Connectivity Between Clouds and Wide Area Networks. In: IEEE CloudNet 2012, Paris, France (November 2012)
17. PyONCI, github.com/danieltt/PyOCNI
18. libNetVirt, github.com/danieltt/libnetvirt
19. Turull, D., Hidell, M., Sjdin, P.: Using libNetVirt to Control the Virtual Network. IEEE CloudNet 2012, Paris, France (November 2012)
20. Derakhshan, F., Grob-Lipski, H., Roessler, H., Schefczik, P., Soellner, M.: On Converged Multi-domain Management of Connectivity in Heterogeneous Networks. In: Future Networks & Mobile Summit 2012 Berlin, Germany, July 04-06 (2012)
21. Vasseur, J.P., Zhang, R., Bitar, N., Le Roux, J.L.: Backward-recursive PCE-based Computation of Shortest Constrained Inter-domain Traffic Engineering Label Switched Paths. IETF RFC 5441 (April 2009)
22. Esposito, C.: A Tutorial on Reliability in Publish/Subscribe Services. In: DEBS 2012, Berlin, Germany (2012)
23. SAIL, Demonstrator for Connectivity Services. Deliverable FP7-ICT-2009-5-257448-SAIL/D.C.5, SAIL project (February 2013), http://www.sail-project.eu
24. NGMN Alliance, Projects, www.ngmn.org/de/workprogramme/wpoverview.html
25. Haberland, B., Derakhshan, F., Grob-Lipski, H., Klotsche, R., Rehm, W., Schefczik, P., Soellner, M.: Radio Base Stations in the Cloud. Bell Labs Technical Journal 18(1), 129–152 (2013)

Information Model for Managing Autonomic Functions in Future Networks

Makis Stamatelatos[1], Imen Grida Ben Yahia[2], Pierre Peloso[3], Beatriz Fuentes[4],
Kostas Tsagkaris[5], and Alex Kaloxylos[1]

[1] National and Kapodistrian University of Athens, Panepistimiopolis, Ilissia, 15784, Athens
{makiss,agk}@di.uoa.gr
[2] France Telecom, 78 Olivier de Serres, 75015, Paris
imen.gridabenyahia@orange.com
[3] Alcatel-Lucent Bell Labs, Site de Villarceaux, 91620, Nozay (France)
pierre.peloso@alcatel-lucent.com
[4] Telefónica I+D, Distrito C, Ronda de la Comunicación s/n, 28050 Madrid
fuentes@tid.es
[5] University of Piraeus, 80 Karaoli & Dimitriou, 18532, Piraeus
ktsagk@unipi.gr

Abstract. Future Internet (FI), a dynamic and complex environment, imposes management requirements, complexity and volume of data which can hardly be handled by traditional management schemes. Autonomic network and service management can be a powerful vision; a promising solution paving the way towards fully autonomic systems provides a three-level management approach and develops Information Modelling extensions for semantic continuity. This paper aims at proposing an Information Model for abstracting autonomic mechanisms for network management tasks and convincing on the relevance of using/extending standardized information models for system specification.

Keywords: Information Model, Autonomic Communications, Network Management, Future Networks.

1   Introduction

Operators today are facing large scale issues: they serve hundreds of millions of customers and mass of customization; they rely on thousands of different network elements with proprietary implementations; they spend M-euros for the adaptation and integration of Network Elements (NEs), Element Management Systems (EMSs) and Network Management Systems (NMSs); they need to handle thousands of alarms per day in each medium-size Network Operating Centre. In this sense, Operators are seeking for advanced management solutions implementing self-* functions to handle complexity, alleviating integration issues, reducing both CAPEX and OPEX and minimising Time-to-Market of new services.

Autonomic network management is expected to solve these issues, but this adoption is yet far from being generalized. That is why in UniverSelf project [1],

D. Pesch et al. (Eds.): MONAMI 2013, LNICST 125, pp. 259–272, 2013.
© Institute for Computer Sciences, Social Informatics and Telecommunications Engineering 2013

which has the goal to foster the conditions for such an adoption, the paradigm shifted from autonomic network management to management of autonomic functions which are themselves managing the network. To achieve such a result, a novel Unified Management Framework (UMF) has been specified. Hence, the UMF revolve around autonomic functions which embody intelligence into network entities (physical or virtualized). The set of specifications imposed to these autonomic functions define what is hereafter named Network Empowering Mechanisms (NEMs). UMF also defines a set of core functions, operations and mechanisms for the proper governance, coordination and knowledge exchange among the NEMs.

The design of an Information Model able to support the management operations of thousands of vendor-specific NEMs, becomes of utmost importance. This Information Model needs to support the seamless integration with existing management systems.

The aim of this paper is to propose subsets of Information Model for autonomic functions (NEMs) based on the TM Forum's Information Framework (SID) [2]. The extensions of the SID model were designed to achieve the specification of UMF interfaces and cover the NEMs structure and lifecycle of NEMs, actions and information manipulated by NEMs, as well as the policies driving the NEM behaviour. The rest of the paper is organized as follows. Section 2 presents the UMF and essential information flows. Section 3 presents the information modelling within the UMF framework whilst Section 4 details the UMF Information Model following SID patterns. Section 5 presents the usage of the UMF Information Model in deriving object-level information items utilised during the NEMs lifecycle.

2   UMF-Framework for Autonomic Mechanisms

UMF has been designed based on FI autonomic networks requirements and encompasses a set of functionalities resolving manifold networking problems. UMF primal objective is to enable trustworthy integration (plug-and-play) and interworking of NEMs within the operator's management ecosystem. The successful deployment of NEMs necessitates their governance/administration, their orchestration/coordination and corresponding information and knowledge sharing. These demands steered to introduction of the concept of UMF core (Fig. 1), which consists of three functional blocks: Governance (GOV), Knowledge (KNOW) and Coordination (COORD). UMF follows a three level approach; UMF manages NEMs which, in turn, manage and optimise network resources and services (Fig. 1).

NEMs specifications details that a NEM is designed as a piece of software implementing an algorithm forming a control loop that can be deployed in a (part of a) network to enhance/simplify its control and management (e.g. take over some operations). An intrinsic capability of a NEM is to be deployable and interoperable in an UMF context (e.g. an UMF compliant network).

The GOV block provides interfaces and functions for the Operators to deploy, pilot, control and track progress of NEMs in a unified way, including fusion of business goals and respective translation to NEM-policies thus realising the policy-continuum [3]; the COORD block provides tools for identifying and avoiding conflicts among autonomic functions (as realized by NEMs) and ensure stability and performance when several NEMs are concurrently working; the KNOW provides tools to make NEMs find, formulate and share relevant information and knowledge towards enabling or improving their operation.

Fig. 1 illustrates also the key information flows among UMF blocks as well as between the UMF and the NEMs. Operator's business goals and services description form the key input for GOV block which provides policies to the other UMF blocks. COORD sends the "Call-for-GOV" notification, in cases a problem needs direct invocation of GOV mechanisms; KNOW provides (i) COORD with information enabling NEM coordination, (e.g. NEM objective, type, etc) as well as network-level knowledge, and (ii) GOV with aggregated knowledge and performance measurements targeting policy evaluation (i.e. whether and in what extent the policies communicated by GOV have achieved the intended improvement on the network performance). Moreover, UMF supports certain interactions with NEMs, such as NEMs registration to the UMF core blocks; GOV communicates the NEM mandate (a "turn-on" command); COORD communicates the NEM Control Policy whilst KNOW communicates Information Exchange Policy (for knowledge production and sharing).

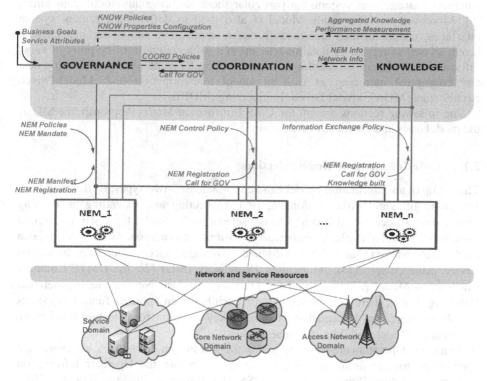

Fig. 1. UMF: 3-level management and information flows.

The need for an Information Model to formalize the interactions between NEMs and the UMF core and address interoperability among different NEM developers is apparent. Information Model enables semantic interoperability among management systems (e.g. EMS, NMS, etc.) which are being managed in a unified way by the UMF and in turn manage network and service resources through NEMs' deployment.

3   Information Modelling

An Information Model provides a system conceptualisation; several definitions have been provided by standardization fora and initiatives. According to IETF, an Information Model is *"an abstraction and representation of the entities in a managed environment including definition of their properties, operations and relationships. It is independent of any specific type of repository, software usage, platform, or access protocol."* [4]. TMF states that *"an Information Model is a representation of business concepts, their characteristics and relationships, described in an implementation independent manner"* [2]. In 3GPP *"Information Model denotes an abstract, formal representation of entity types, including their properties and relationships, the operations that can be performed on them, and related rules and constrains."* [5].

The presented (and other) definitions conclude on conceptualisation and formality. Within UMF, Information Model is considered as an enabler for convergence/unification of management systems. It is applicable to legacy and emerging management systems, in particular those featuring autonomic capabilities [6]. Moreover, an Information Model is also used to define management system interfaces, communication interfaces between application and upper management layers as well as repository data models. From a software engineering point of view, Information Model is an enabler for software development, ontology development and conceptual reasoning as well as model transformation (e.g. Model-Driven Architecture (MDA), Model-Driven Engineering (MDE)).

The following sections present the UMF Information Model Approach, the SID as the model basis and the identified extensions.

3.1   UMF Information Model Selection

The set up of an Information Model can be of – at least – two types; (i) defining from scratch to fill gaps within a domain; or (ii) selecting and extending an existing Information Model. When it comes to the selection of a model for UMF, the second approach has been applied. Particularly, various Information Models have been established and are in use in Telco's domain, covering service, resource, customer and device management: TMF Information Framework (SID) [2], the DMTF Common Information Model (CIM) [7] and the Directory Enabled Network next generation (DEN-ng) [8][9]; therefore, the second approach has been applied. Table 1 compares the above mentioned Information Models. A key criterion for selecting a reference Information Model for UMF is standardisation.

Typically, Operators are involved within the TM Forum Frameworx in general and specifically for the definition of the SID in use within the Operator Information System (Operations Support System, OSS and Business Support Systems, BSS). Moreover, SID covers various management domains (e.g. customer, resources, services, and partnerships) whilst it also defines a set of common business entities, specifically policy domain modelling including policy architecture, policy specification, and policy management. These are key elements to UMF objectives in particular managing autonomic functions through the GOV block, and the reasons to take SID as a basis for the UMF Information Model.

Table 1. Information Model Comparison

Comparison Features	CIM	SID	DEN-ng
Software patterns	No	Some	Many
Compatibility to OMG [14]	No[1]	Yes	Yes
Standardized	No	Yes	No
Link with business	Not clear	Yes[2]	Yes[3]
Context model	No	No	Yes[4]
Finite state machine/dynamic diagrams	No	No	Yes[5]

3.2   UMF Information Model Basis and Extensions

The approach for establishing the UMF Information Model and extending the SID starts with the identification of concepts defining and characterising the exchanged information items within UMF and between the UMF core blocks and the NEMs. A mapping was made to SID equivalent concepts followed by either semantic alignment to SID concepts or elaborating on extensions following the "SID usage Guide" and the "SID patterns" [2]. Iterations ensured consistency within the identified concepts.

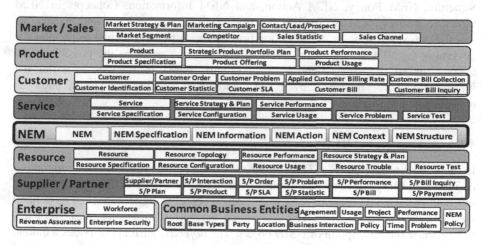

Fig. 2. Proposed NEM layer in SID ABEs

The resulted SID extensions are mainly related to the NEM concept. For example, for service and resource performance, service class or service profile we reuse existing concepts from the SID. With the deployment of UMF and NEM, there is a need to model the NEM data and information that Operators need to be aware of for

---

[1] It has its own Meta-Object Facility (MOF).

[2] Part of global Business Process Framework (ETOM), Application Framework (TAM) and Information Framework (IF).

[3] Policy continuum for translating business goals to low-level configuration actions.

[4] To apply policies with respect to the context of resource, service and customer.

[5] To describe the state/behaviour of a managed entity.

communication with these NEMs, switch them on/off, customize their actions and configurations, etc. The NEM is a new managed entity that Operators need to handle; in this sense, we propose extending the SID layers with new NEM layer (Fig. 2) containing specific ABEs (Aggregation Business Entities, a group of entities belonging to a common domain).

Apart from basing the UMF Information Model on the SID, we also adopted the DEN-ng context diagram [10] and then tried to reuse it as we considered it mandatory for managing autonomic entities. In fact, from the literature one can see the potential and adequacy of DEN-ng to manage autonomic mechanisms; albeit the fact that DEN-ng has not been standardised or even open sourced so far, is still a crucial issue.

4   UMF Information Model

The proposed Information Model components aim at conceptualising NEMs as autonomic functions and potentially incorporating them within SID framework. Following initial modelling attempt [13] UML diagrams have been elaborated following SID modelling approach for proposing the main concepts: the NEM Structure, NEM Policy, NEM Action, and NEM Information. Concepts in NEM Structure abstract NEM as provided functionality, software package, and manager of specific network resources. NEM Policy provides specification related to policies for governing the NEM's behaviour. NEM Action diagram specifies the possible NEM actions (linked to management actions). Finally, NEM Information specifies the information items managed by NEMs and their relation to specification of management information.

4.1   Extensions to SID

In the SID root diagram (Fig. 3) the *RootEntity* class defines the attributes common to define/select SID entities related to service, resources and policies. The *commonName* attribute enables SID users to refer to a specific object using terminology as defined by application-specific needs. The *description* attribute (optional) enables SID users to customize the description of a SID object. The *objectID* attribute provides a unique identity to each entity. The abstract class *Entity* extends the *RootEntity* class and represents those entities playing a business function .

An abstract class *NEM* extends the class *Entity* (Fig. 3). NEM captures functionality related to management of network resources and services which is part of the Operator's mission. This is captured by the "*manages*" association showing the link to the set of *Managed Entity* (i.e. a resource or a service) managed by a given NEM. The *NEMpolicy* defines the policies applicable to a given NEM and extends the SID policy class, whilst the *NEMStates* capture the state of a NEM (section 5.2).

Following the SID specification pattern, *NEMSpecification* and *NEMPolicy Specification* classes have been defined for the *NEM* and *NEMPolicy* classes respectively. The specification classes describe the invariant part/information of the entity, which enables the construction of an entity.

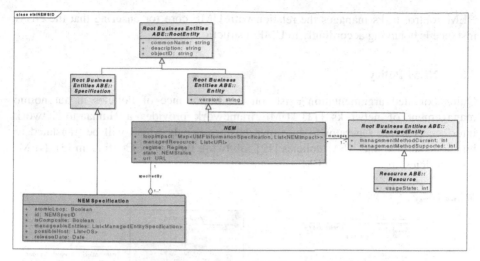

Fig. 3. NEM linked to TMF-SID root diagram

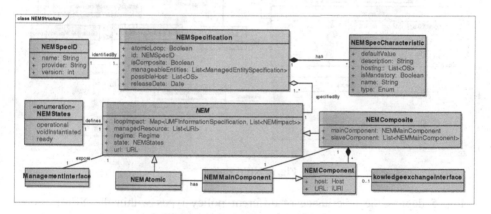

Fig. 4. NEM Structure

4.2   NEM Structure

Fig. 4 represents the structure of *NEM* which is specified by attributes grouped in a *NEMSpecification* which is *identifiedBy* the *NEMSpecID* allowing a unique identification of the "NEM class" in the catalogue. The *NEMSpecID* regroups three (3) attributes, namely, *name*, *provider* and *version*. A NEM exposes a management interface enabling UMF control over NEM.

A NEM can be either *NEMAtomic* or *NEMComposite*. An atomic NEM has centralized software running on a single machine, while a composite NEM has distributed software running on multiple machines. This is slightly different from the SID pattern as the *NEMComposite* is not composed of multiple NEMs but of multiple *NEMComponents*, and a *NEMAtomic* is composed of a single *NEMComponent* which may expose a *KnowledgeExchangeInterface*. The *NEMMainComponent* handles the

NEM control tasks manages the relation with UMF core for ensuring that the NEM instance is behaving accordingly to UMF instructions.

4.3   NEM Policy

Quite extended argumentation exists on the importance of Policies in autonomic management of networks [11]. UMF framework provides a Human-to-Network interface enabling Operator to fuse own business goals which will be translated to business, service and NEM policies [12] following the Policy Continuum [3]. NEM-level policies are targeting NEM management.

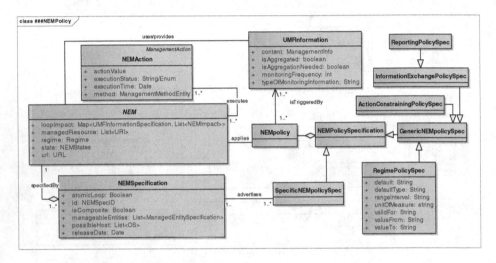

Fig. 5. NEM Policy

Fig. 5 depicts the inheritance of different policy types within the NEMs scope following the inheritance of SID *PolicySpecification* . Different policy types have been specified applicable to NEMs inheriting from *NEMPolicy* class. *GenericNEMpolicySpec* specifies the *GenericNEMPolicy* abstract class representing policy types applicable to any NEM; the format is defined by the UMF specification.

RegimePolicySpec specifies the *RegimePolicy* communicated to NEMs by COORD for setting the frequency and the modalities at which the NEM autonomic loop is invoked (e.g. "run once every 10 min", "run continuously", "run now only once", "run when such X condition is true", etc.).

ActionConstrainingPolicies (specified by the *ActionConstrainingPolicySpec*) are issued by COORD to constraint a NEM instance possible actions, aiming for example, at avoiding conflicts among NEM instances and can either disable specific NEM actions, or suspend the enforcement of the planned action to a validation by COORD or constrain the range in which a parameter can be set. *InformationExchangePolicies* (specified by *InformationExchangePolicySpec*) are issued by KNOW for organizing the information exchange, as for example, when a NEM share information needed by another NEM; KNOW is to organize a subscription between these NEMs. *ReportingPolicies* are specific *InformationExchangePolicies* issued by GOV to set the rules of information reporting from the NEM to GOV. *SpecificNEMPolicies* (specified by *SpecificNEMPolicySpec*) are tailored to NEM behaviour and objectives. In traffic engineering, for example, such policy sets whether NEM targets energy saving or congestion avoidance.

4.4   NEM Action

NEM actions include management, configuration and optimization actions to be applied by a NEM instance to network resources or services, driven by respective policies, as presented in section 4.3. Fig. 6 depicts the inheritance of Actions: *NEMActions* are executed by *NEMs* onto *ManagedEntities* (i.e. resources or services).

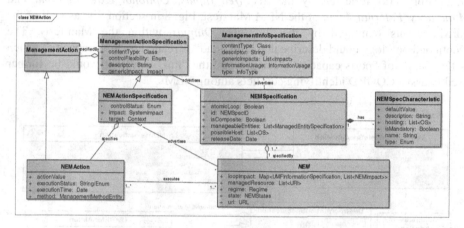

Fig. 6. NEM Action

Three levels of NEM actions specifications are depicted. *ManagementAction Specification* corresponds to the nature of the action, e.g. "switch on/off a router's port" and is used to build catalogues of actions e.g. the list of the nature of all the actions performed by a given NEM, which corresponds to the *Possible_Actions* field of the NEM Manifest (section 5.1,Fig. 8). A NEM-agnostic catalogue should be also used to complete an ontology describing the relations among the network elements. This ontology could describe, for example, that "switching on/off a port" is changing "link capacity" if "port" is "composing" the "link".

NEMActionSpecification designates the action, e.g. "Switch on/off the port 12 of router 1.1.1.1" and is used to build catalogues such as the indexation in COORD of NEMs actions for conflict identification. *NEMActionSpecification* extends the *ManagementActionSpecification* with the *context* attribute (in the above example the designation of the port 12 of the router 1.1.1.1) taken from DEN-ng [10].

NEMAction represents the action actually performed by the NEM and contains the *actionValue*, which in the above example can be either "On" or "Off". The

NEMActionSpecification describes (with its *controlStatus* attribute) the allowed control of the action, while the *ManagementActionSpecification* describes (with its *controlFlexibility* attribute) the allowed control of this kind of action (this property only depends on the flexibility offered by the NEM designer at implementation time).

4.5   NEM Information

Fig. 7 depicts the inheritance of NEM Information. *UMFInformation* objects are exchanged among UMF blocks as well as between UMF blocks and NEMs. Fig. 7depicts three levels regarding information.

ManagementInfoSpecification correspond to the nature of the information, e.g. "link load" and is used to build information catalogues. Such class can capture the information types acquired by a given NEM class which can be "optional" or "mandatory" (as reflected by the *Acquired_Inputs, Optional_External_Input* and *Mandatory_External_Input* of the NEM Manifest, Fig. 8 in section 5.1) as well as the NEM outputs (captured by the *Available_Outputs* within the Manifest). The mentioned ontology could describe that "link load" is related to "link capacity" which is the "sum" of "ports capacity" "composing" the "link" whilst it would be further used to assist COORD identifying conflicts among NEMs.

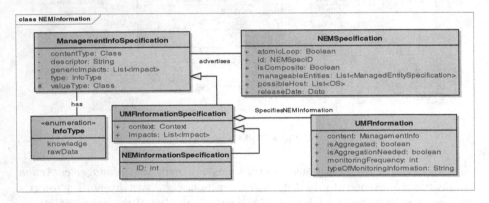

Fig. 7. NEM Information

UMFInformationSpecification designates the information, e.g. "The link load between router 1.1.1.1 and router 2.2.2.2" for building catalogues, e.g. the indexation in KNOW of all NEMs' available outputs for the identifying knowledge source when organizing knowledge exchange with other UMF entities, and the indexation in COORD of NEMs' inputs for identifying NEM conflicts. *UMFInformationSpecification* extends the *ManagementInfoSpecification* with the *context* attribute (in the above example the designation of the link: router 1.1.1.1 to 2.2.2.2), taken from DEN-ng extensions.

UMFInformation represents the information actually exchanged through a Knowledge Exchange. To this aim, KNOW takes in charge its organization, which will be materialized by an *InformationExchangePolicy* (Fig. 5). *UMFInformation* inherits from *ManagementInformation* (from SID) specified by an *UMFInformation Specification* and enriched with a *context* (in order to know that the "load" which is "70%" is actually referring to the "link" between "router 1.1.1.1" and "router 2.2.2.2".). The actual value is of any sub-class of *ManagementInformation* (in SID). The *ManagementInformationSpecification* and the *contentType* which sub-class *ManagementInfo* will be used to describe the value of the *UMFInformation*.

5   Information Model in Action

In the following paragraphs a case for the utilisation of the UMF Information Model is presented. Initially, the derivation of object level information is provided; in turn, the usage of those objects in the NEM lifecycle is described.

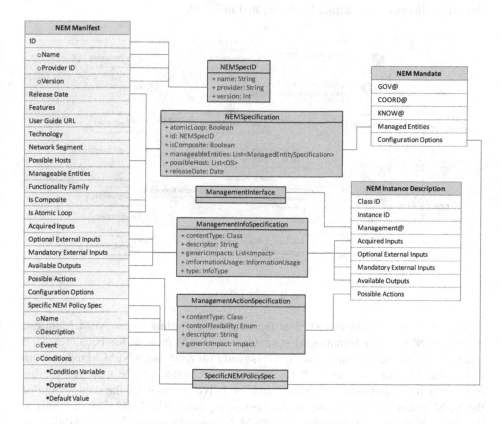

Fig. 8. Derivation of NEM Manifest, NEM Mandate and NEM Instance Description

5.1   Derivation of Object-Level Entities

A NEM class is described by a machine-readable **Manifest**, providing object-level information (e.g. managed network elements, NEM class identification, etc.) for the

Operator to deploy the NEM in its infrastructure. A **NEM Mandate** is issued by GOV to a NEM instance as a set of instructions identifying the NEM instance settings and the network elements, resources, and services assigned to this NEM instance. NEM Mandate provides the needed information for exchanges with all UMF blocks. A **NEM Instance Description** is issued by the NEM during its registration to the UMF system and details information monitored and actions taken by the NEM instance. Fig. 8 presents the derivation of the NEM Manifest, the NEM Mandate and the NEM Instance Description from the UMF Information Model.

5.2   Information Model in NEM Lifecycle

This section presents the NEM lifecycle and the interactions between a NEM and the UMF using the derived objects (i.e. Manifest, Mandate, and Instance Description). The NEM lifecycle can be traced as illustrated in Fig. 9.

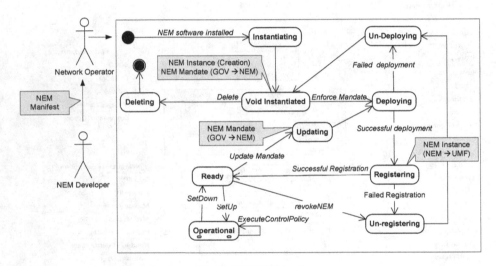

Fig. 9. NEM Lifecycle

The Operator deploys the NEM at the network according to the NEM Manifest, setting the NEM to the Instantiating state. Once the NEM instance has been created, it reaches the Void Instantiated state, and it is ready for receiving a NEM Mandate from GOV. The Mandate determines the network resources that will be managed by this instance and its configuration options, and its delivery completes the deployment of the NEM instance (which passes to the Deploying state). The NEM then proceeds to the Registering state by providing the NEM Instance Description to the UMF core blocks; NEM reaches then the Ready state and, providing no conflicts have been identified by COORD, will move to the Operational state following a Setup command from GOV . In this state the NEM instance is operational and works under the control of COORD block. The Updating trans-state is reached every time an updated NEM Mandate is received from GOV, which forces the NEM instance to get back to

Deploying. On reception of a *revokeNEM* message from GOV, the NEM instance reaches the Void Instantiated through the Un-registering and Un-Deploying states whilst on reception of a Delete message from GOV the NEM instance will disappear from the UMF system.

6   Conclusions

Autonomic mechanisms are cornerstones of the next generation of Telco's management approaches. However, to reach large deployment and efficient management of those mechanisms, Operators need specific key enablers. UMF Information Model for autonomic functions abstracts and represents what Operators need to know in order to deploy, configure and activate efficiently autonomic mechanisms.

In UniverSelf project we consider autonomic mechanisms as managed entities and define the main data and information that enable Operators govern, coordinate and develop knowledge about them. Deploying autonomic mechanisms without Information Model will lead to "vendor-specific" and proprietary implementations which will increase the integration issues and prevent adoption. Operators are investing in information model set up in TMForum or in 3GPP, as well as the harmonization between both efforts. It is mandatory that the data exchange, interfaces of Autonomic mechanisms follow these standards bodies. In this paper we selected the Information Framework (SID) in order to be compliant to Operators choices and to reduce integration costs and we proposed a set of classes and concepts towards defining the needed concepts for the management of autonomic functions.

The proposed models have been developed following SID patterns; this means that related semantics can be incorporated in the models in an automated way. This way, as reported in [15] a set of benefits can be gained, regarding implementation challenges as tools can work with the patterns through the transformation, ultimately pulling implementation code from a library written by experts and inserting it into the final application and/or system.

Acknowledgment. The research leading to these results has been performed within the UniverSelf project [1] and received funding from the European Community's Seventh Framework Programme FP7/2007-2013) under grant agreement n° 257513.

References

1. The UniverSelf Project, http://www.univerself-project.eu
2. The TMForum Information Framework (SID), GB922_SID_Rel_13-0_Addenda_Files, http://www.tmforum.org/InformationFramework/1684/home.html
3. Davy, S., Jennings, B., Strassner, J.: The policy continuum—Policy authoring and conflict analysis. Computer Communications 31, 2981–2995 (2008)
4. The Internet Engineering Task Force, IETF, RFC 3198, Terminology for Policy-Based Management

5. 3GPP, TS 32.181, User Data Convergence (UDC), Framework for Model Handling and Management
6. Wong, A.K.Y., Ray, P., Parameswaran, N., Strassner, J.: Ontology mapping for the interoperability problem in network management. Journal on Selected Areas in Communications 23(10), 2058–2068 (2005)
7. The Common Information Model (CIM) Specification, http://www.dmtf.org/standards/cim/cim_spec_v22
8. Strassner, J.: DEN-ng: achieving business-driven network management In: IEEE Network Operations and Management Symposium (NOMS), pp. 753–766 (2002)
9. Strassner, J., Hong, J.W.-K., Kyo, K.: A framework for modelling and reasoning about network management resources and services to support information reuse. In: IEEE International Conference on Information Reuse & Integration (IRI 2009), pp. 85–90 (2009)
10. Strassner, J., et al.: The Design of a New Context-Aware Policy Model for Autonomic Networking. In: International Conference on Autonomic Computing, ICAC (2008)
11. Strassner, J.: Policy-based Network Management: Solutions for the Next Generation. Morgan-Kaufman Publishers (2003) ISBN 1-55-859-1
12. Galani, A., Tsagkaris, K., Demestichas, P., Nguengang, G., Grida Ben Yahia, I., Stamatelatos, M., Kosmatos, E., Kaloxylos, A., Ciavaglia, L.: Core functional and network empower mechanisms of an operator-driven framework for unifying autonomic network and service management. In: 17th IEEE International Workshop on Computer-Aided Modeling Analysis and Design of Communication Links and Networks, CAMAD (2012)
13. Ben Yahia, I.G., et al.: Which Information Model for Autonomic Mechanisms Framework. Presentation at 3rd ETSI Workshop on Future Network Technologies (2013)
14. Object Management Group, http://www.omg.org
15. Strassner, J., et al.: The Design of a New Policy Model to Support Ontology-Driven Reasoning for Autonomic Networking. In: Latin American Network Operations and Management Symposium, LANOMS (2007)

DICE: A Novel Platform to Support Massively Distributed Clouds

Anna Förster[1], Koojana Kuladinithi[2],
Andreas Timm-Giel[3], Carmelita Görg[2], and Silvia Giordano[1]

[1] University of Applied Sciences of Southern Switzerland
[2] University of Bremen, Germany
[3] Hamburg University of Technology

Abstract. Massively distributed clouds (MDC) have a huge potential in serving novel applications and services in many situations. Mainly, they are able to provide communication without the use of an infrastructure and to guarantee full data and user anonymity. However, their implementation is not trivial and requires innovation in many different fields, such as opportunistic communications, big data management and security. In this paper, we present our first design of a MDC supporting architecture, called DICE: Distributed Infrastructureless Cloud sErvices. We present our main application scenario and focus on implementation challenges and early results.

1   Introduction

Recently, the idea of massively distributed clouds (MDC) has emerged, where services are provided in a completely distributed and infrastructureless manner. Many applications, e.g. environmental monitoring, participatory sensing, or social networking, can be much better served by a such a paradigm, where users do not need to use or pay for an infrastructure. Instead, they can leverage the direct communication between devices in their proximity to exchange localized data.

The main novel properties of MDC are a decentralised architecture with infrastructureless communications and data anonymity, which would indeed change the existing understanding of cloud services and their markets. Its realisation relies on innovation in opportunistic and heterogeneous communications, security and privacy, big data management, and energy management. These make the implementation of an MDC a challenging task. Furthermore, real users and their behaviour need to be incorporated very really in the implementation process, as they cannot be simulated satisfactorily.

On the other side, implementation of MDCs has been hindered also by prejudices in the area of wireless communications, where the prevailing opinion is that only a stable and highly available infrastructure can guarantee a particular level of service. However, even the best infrastructure cannot guarantee the timely and local availability of data itself, such as touristic information or environmental properties. Such data is mostly gathered by end users and needs to be

D. Pesch et al. (Eds.): MONAMI 2013, LNICST 125, pp. 273–286, 2013.

inserted by them into the data cloud to be useful. However, current practice does not allow to do this in a cost-free and user-friendly manner, thus data quality suffers. On the other hand, opportunistic communications require people and devices to cooperatively exchange data and to be geographically close to each other. This is typically seen as a limitation, as it possibly delays the propagation of data. However, our own preliminary study on the impact of device density on data propagation in a purely opportunistic environment [2] has shown that even low country-wise population densities can support fast data propagation.

Motivated by these early results and by the high interest shown in the community [1,2] we have decided to proceed with a prototype implementation of an architecture, able to support MDCs, called DICE (Distributed Infrastructure-less Cloud sErvices). In the rest of this paper, we first present and discuss some related efforts in Section 2, before presenting our main application scenario in Section 3. Section 4 gives an overview of the DICE architecture, which is under active development. Then we discuss possible usage and business models for our envisioned services in Section 5. Finally, we summarise our next steps and conclude the paper in Section 6.

2   Motivation and Related Efforts

The motivation of our work is many-fold. It is mainly based on the general user dissatisfaction with existing cloud and mobile services, their usability, functionality and privacy preservation. There are three main arguments, which we discuss here: *service accessibility*, *service usability* and *user privacy*.

2.1   Service Accessibility

Currently cloud services are in theory accessible by anyone at zero cost. However, reality looks differently. A clear requirement to use any of these services is to have Internet connection. However, Internet penetration rates worldwide were still only 34.3% in 2012[3]. Even in the most "connected" continent, North America, the penetration rate was 78.6% – thus, at the best case, only two third of the population has access to these services. In the worst case, in Africa, only 15.6% can leverage them.

We can already see some interesting approaches of providing Internet connection to remote areas, such as Google's Loon Project[4]. The main idea is to launch Internet Balloons over rural areas, which connect to satellites to provide Internet connection. However, such projects are not cost-efficient and do not scale well.

Another challenge are the services themselves. Metropolitan areas tend to have more and more sophisticated services for their citizens than rural areas. Low-population regions are simply not attractive from the business point of view.

---

[1] http://www.smartsantander.eu

[2] http://citi-sense.nilu.no

[3] Source: www.internetworldstats.com/stats.htm

[4] http://www.google.com/loon/

Thus, the gap between urban and rural areas becomes even larger, sharpening also other problems such as health, employment, etc.

Moreover, provision of cloud services seems to be restricted mostly to large industrial players. Independent developers, startup companies, charity organisations and academia have little chances to provide services because of their high support costs. Standard support for cloud services, such as identification and security applications, data management, etc, are costly. This problem has been already partially addressed by the OpenStack initiative[5], which provides such services to developers free of charge. While this is an important step, the service and infrastructural support remain a stumbling block.

2.2 Service Usability

Existing cloud and mobile applications and services typically concentrate on one particular application scenario, such as place rating, message exchange, data storage, etc. Some of the most prominent examples are listed and compared in Table 1, such as Facebook, Twitter, Foursquare, Dropbox, etc. A very simple example is provided by state-of-the-art everyday communications and the "share" buttons, e.g. to share something on Facebook, Twitter or Wordpress. There, sharing a particular piece of information is simple and at the same time complex: it is simple to push the button, but then you need to decide which of all available services to use, maybe you need to authenticate yourself again, to write a small comment, etc. This broad spectrum of various social networks is

Table 1. Comparison between existing web and cloud services and the envisioned Massively Distributed Heterogeneous Clouds.

Service/ Application	Network Connectivity		Architecture		Communication			Anonymity /Privacy	Geographic Relevance		Usage	
	Infra-structure	No Infr.	Centr.	Distr.	Single User	Mult. Users	Any User		Global	Local	Passive	Active
Social networks (Twitter, Facebook)	X		X		(X)	X	(X)	none	X		(X)	X
News Feed (RSS)	X		X			X		hidden from other users	X			X
Streaming (Youtube)	X		X			(X)	X	hidden from other users	X			X
Community-based webpages (Tripadvisor, Foursquare)	X		X				X	partial	X	X	X	X
Event or Tourist Information (LongLake Festival Lugano)	X		X				X	hidden from other users	X	X		
Participatory Sensing (Bikenet)	X		X				X	hidden from other users	X			X
Cloud Storage (Dropbox)	X		X		X	X		none	X			X
Cloud Services (Googledocs)	X		X		X	X		none	X			X
MDC (DICE)		X		X			X	anonymous	X	X	X	X

[5] http://www.openstack.org

a very good example of the rather bad usability of current mobile services and their high complexity.

Another example is the broad spectrum of locally available services and applications. Nowadays, every festival and every event in any city provides its users with its own mobile application. However, before such an app becomes useful, it needs to be found and installed. Many disappoint with bad user interface, with missing language settings or with outdated or missing information. In every city, there is currently a myriad of these services and applications and it is impossible even for locals to find and use them all. For tourists, who would profit most from such services, they are impossible to find. Namely, they face also the language and cost challenges: information about services is mostly defined in the local language and the cost for searching for them online is very high because of roaming charges.

2.3   User Privacy

Another challenge is user privacy in these services. Here, we differentiate between *passive* and *active* usage of services. If an application or service has a purely informative characteristic, like an event or tourist service, the user is *passive*, as she never inserts any information. However, even if the user is only asked to rank or review a particular item, like a hotel or a restaurant, she becomes an *active* user. In the first case, user privacy or anonymity does not play a significant role. However, also here the complete privacy of the user is violated, as it is known that she uses a particular application. In the second case, user privacy has a significant role, as she gives away personal data.

In our Table 1, none of the presented services or application offer complete data or user privacy. In all cases, the privacy is supported by state-of-the-art authentication and encoding mechanisms, but these do not *guarantee* that the data cannot be viewed by a third party, legally or illegally.

The only solution to this problem is to offer complete anonymity to the users. *This is different from post-anonymization of their data for presentation purposes, as it requires that their personal data or any description of the data (e.g. location and time of acquisition) is never stored nor propagated through the network..* To the best of our knowledge, this service is not offered by any current service or application. This can be seen also in Table 1, where we also compare existing services and applications to our novel MDC approach.

3   Application Scenario

There exist already many different applications and systems targeted to environmental monitoring. However, they tend to concentrate on one particular issue or topic: e.g. on air pollution, on restaurant rating, etc. We refer to all these applications as *environmental awareness applications*. These applications refer to any kind of simple or complex data, related to our environment. However, in our scenario, we do not limit in any way the kind of data users can gather or exchange. Instead, users are completely free to gather any data:

- Environmental properties, such as noise levels, humidity, temperature, air pollution, or crowdness.
- Environmental ratings, such as a dark street you should avoid, a romantic place for a picnic, or a great street with many restaurants.
- Problems, such as broken street lamps, or trash in the park.

By using such an application, the users will create and leverage a generally better awareness about their environment. They insert this information into the "cloud" and can retrieve it from there. Depending on their needs or interests, they will be able to view instantaneously important information.

3.1   Requirements Analysis

This application scenario exhibits some important **requirements** in order to be truly useful and safe at the same time:

1. **Data heterogeneity:** The cloud must be able to handle any kind of data, without any restrictions in size or type.
2. **Data anonymity:** In order to guarantee safe exchange of data and thus true user security, the data must be completely anonymous.
3. **Scalability:** The cloud must be able to handle very big data.
4. **Low support and usage cost:** To facilitate usefulness, the cloud service must be free of charge for users and very low cost to providers and supporters.

Especially points 2 and 4 are new to cloud services and generally to mobile applications. While current solutions attempt to guarantee user safety with complex and expensive encryption and identification algorithms, we turn to a new perspective: anonymous data. State of the art security mechanisms have one trivial, but crucial disadvantage: they rely on storing user data somewhere. Thus, at least in theory, the possibility to access this data is always present, be it by mistake or on purpose. This problem is often described also as the "friendly, but curious cloud".

With our requirements of data anonymity, the application will become much more lightweight and will in fact guarantee user safety. Provided that data is never associated with any user, it is impossible to break the privacy of the users, on purpose or mistake.

Another requirement worth discussing is the last one, low support and usage cost. This is typically not or only weakly considered in research-oriented applications. Furthermore, it is usually assumed, that cloud and generally mobile applications are low-cost by default. This is not necessarily true, as practice shows. For example, while an application like FourSquare is free of charge, its usage is very expensive in roaming areas. On the other side, such environmental awareness applications are most useful for people out of their comfort zone, i.e. outside their country of residence. Consequently, the usefulness of our application is only provided when usage and support cost are always close to zero.

3.2 MDC Paradigm

The requirements analysis above clearly shows that this application scenario is perfectly suited for the Massively Distributed Cloud (MDC) paradigm, described in [1] and previous sections. MDC not only fulfils all requirements of our application scenario, but also exceeds them. Mainly and most importantly, it fully supports at the maximum possible level the following three:

- Full data and user anonymity
- Complete infrastructural independence
- Zero usage cost

MDC is completely distributed and each device runs its own instantiation of the MDC platform. The so called "cloud nodes" can be any communication-enabled devices: smartphones, sensor nodes, but also more powerful nodes such as laptops or tablets. Depending on their location and available resources, we differentiate between **mobile** against **static** and **fully functional** against **low capability** cloud nodes. While end users typically carry their devices with them (fully functional mobile nodes), special points of interest can be equipped with fully functional, but static cloud nodes. There is no functional difference between these mobile and static nodes. The difference arises rather from their availability at a particular location, thus providing service guarantee. For example, the city counsel office or the train station might decide to fix a MDC-enabled device to make sure that data is always available at a particular location.

Low capability devices are crucial to MDC and its properties. Current Wireless Sensor Network (WSN) installations are under-utilized, running typically a single, simple data gathering application. While a single node has severely restricted resources, a sensor network can have more significant freely available distributed resources. Thus, individual resource-restricted nodes can act as normal MDC nodes, but can also organize into groups and coordinate to manage the available data together. These sensor networks are typically static, but there are also some mobile examples (e.g. sensors installed on buses or trains).

In the next section we will discuss our architectural design called Distributed Infrastructureless Cloud sErvices (DICE) to support such an environmental awareness application, using the MDC approach.

4 DICE Architecture

Figure 1 offers a high level overview of the envisioned DICE architecture. This highlights our first implementation attempt to realise the MDC paradigm. The DICE architecture differentiates between the main cloud platform with its provided services and applications running on top. In contrast to typical middleware solutions, the main DICE platform can also be run stand-alone and provides the user with a simple interface to select sensor sources and to share them. Thus, users may decide to contribute without leveraging the results themselves. This includes especially sensor nodes, where the sensor nodes themselves are not interested in the data, but provide data and resources to the rest of the cloud.

DICE applications run on top of the platform and provide means of processing various sensor data and representing them in a meaningful way to the user. For example, air pollution data can be represented as a map and combined with pedestrian navigation systems. However, also high-level data can be handled, such as problems in the city, where the problem and the required intervention are represented on a map or on a list.

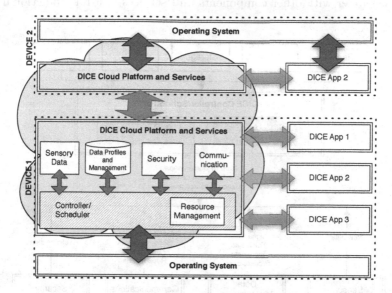

Fig. 1. General DICE Architecture

The main DICE services include data acquisition and management, opportunistic heterogeneous communications, security and resource management. The latter, complemented with a controller and scheduler, builds the central DICE component. It provides resource access to all other services and is crucial to resource-restricted devices such as smartphone or sensor nodes.

4.1 Scheduler and Resource Management

Even with modern smartphones, resource management is an important and crucial task. DICE requires massive data exchange and sensor data acquisition. Thus, a scheduler is used to allow access to different resources and components of the system, such as communication, data storage, sensor data access, etc. The scheduler is combined with a smart resource manager, which learns the behavior of the device (either its user or the applications running on it) to optimally use its free resources.

Therefore, the scheduler monitors and manages the available resources in a very flexible way. It requires a sophisticated interface to all other DICE services, such as communication or data management, and gives them access to resources or hinders them from using resources. An example is newly available data at a cloud node: the data management service must signal this to the scheduler, who will evaluate the available resources and either allow or disallow the data management to communicate the new data to the cloud neighbors. The functionalities of the scheduler are implemented with state of the art scheduling techniques, complemented with machine-learning techniques for monitoring and prediction of available resources at individual cloud nodes. Figure 2 shows the interaction of the scheduler with other components and services in a fully functional cloud node.

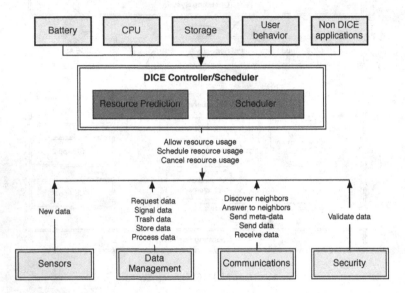

Fig. 2. Overview of the DICE Scheduler/Controller

4.2 Data Acquisition and Management

The data management service of DICE is envisioned to be a highly flexible and smart component, able to identify new data, to aggregate it with existing data, and to identify old or irrelevant data. The main implementation specific requirements are:

- Opportunistic data exchange and management: DICE requires data to be stored throughout the network, and accessible at different points in opportunistic and distributed manner.
- Guarantee the anonymity of data by merging it with existing data and thus loosing any hints to the original source.
- Manage the available resources and compress the available data: For example, while fully functional nodes like smartphones can probably hold a large amount of data, low capability nodes cannot and probably need to organize into clusters to enable meaningful data storage.
- Prepare the data for presentation to the user, e.g. in form of maps or lists of latest data.

In order to fulfill the above requirements in **Data Acquisition and Management** in DICE, we consider the following approaches.

- Use of geo-spatial data stamps and hash-codes: These techniques are used in order to avoid data duplicates while preserving the full anonymity of data. Thus, traditional meta-data, such as creator address, is not necessary to recognise duplicate data.
- Use of smart clustering algorithms: moving the data to the right place where it should be accessed, replicating the data so that it is not lost in case of failure, etc. Furthermore, local organization and role assignment will be considered in order to cope with the resource restrictions on low capability nodes. For example, a single node can take over the role of an access node for several of its neighbors. The same node can also serve as a communication gateway to smartphone and other low capability cloud nodes.
- Novel data distribution and aggregation techniques: Some cloud nodes act as on-the-fly aggregation points (very different from standard aggregation). Therefore, we consider decentralized aggregation protocols to establish communication to these nodes, to continuously update that data, and to decide when to offload data. The gossip-based approaches that have been successfully applied to peer-to-peer systems [3] are adapted to work in opportunistic and distributed manner [4].

4.3 Heterogeneous Opportunistic Communications

Our objective is to develop a radically different communication paradigm than existing networking approaches have: dedicated endpoints (source/sink) do not exist, data is not forwarded, but aggregated and an omnipresent distributed knowledge base is created. This consists of mainly 2 components of (1) the neighbourhood management and (2) the selective transmission of information to neighbours (e.g., it has to be decided, which information is to be sent at which time to which neighbors). For the **neighborhood management** the following requirements are being considered:

- The communication technology is heterogeneous: e.g. WiFi Direct, Bluetooth and NFC for smartphones and IEEE 802.15.4 and Bluetooth for WSNs.
- Most devices are battery powered, therefore energy efficiency is an important requirement.
- Support of cecurity, privacy and anonymity schemes of the higher layers.

The second component of **selective transmission of information** is designed based on some ideas on caching and forwarding strategies from Information Centric Networking (ICN) [5] based architectures. Once the neighbors are discovered, one-hop data communications between neighbors are initiated. We focus on the content that parties need to exchange instead of the hosts on which the content resides. The content itself is named and this is ideally suited for the DICE neighborhood as the participants' focus in this environment is simply the

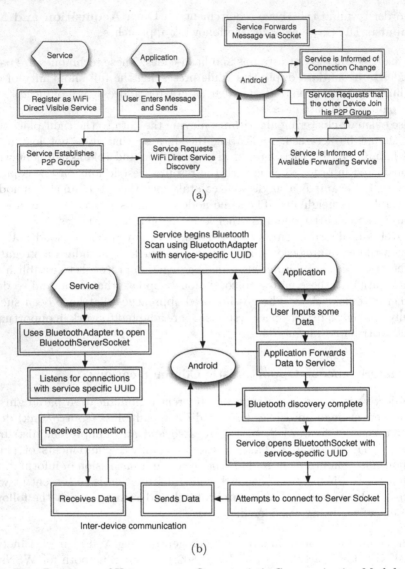

Fig. 3. First Prototype of Heterogeneous Opportunistic Communication Module using WiFi Direct and Bluetooth

information itself. The information is disseminated in a distributed environment to support the selection of suitable neighbors based on the amount or quality of available data in the nodes (instead of the distance to the sink) [6].

Figure 3(a) and 3(b) show our first prototype implementation of **Heterogeneous Opportunistic Communication** module on the Android platform. The WiFi Direct and Bluetooth communication technologies are used in the initial implementation. We use extremely simple forwarding protocol. When a device wants to send a message, or receives a message it hasn't seen before, it will simply forward the message to all of its peers who have also installed the DICE service. The WiFi Direct operates in infrastructure mode, which affords it a number of advantages over ad-hoc mode.

As shown in Figure 3(a), the Android **WifiP2pManager** class provides a number of relatively simple functions for identifying and connecting with peers. Once a connection has been established, **WifiP2pInfo** object provides the necessary information to open a socket with the group owner. Although WiFi Direct requires Android API level 14, legacy devices can still connect to an existing WiFi Direct network as if it were a regular access point. This may allow us to extend the app to support older devices in the future. The BluetoothAdapter is the primary object used in Android's Bluetooth API. It represents the device's physical Bluetooth Adapter, and enables device discovery, changing bluetooth visibility, and accepting connections. As shown in figure 3(b), upon the completion of Bluetooth discovery, Android provides us with a list of BluetoothDevices, which allows us to open a BluetoothSocket to connect with a remote device.

The current implementation will be extended to support the following features of **Heterogeneous Opportunistic Communication** of DICE.

- Develop a reliable neighbor discovery protocol: neighboring participants in a DICE environment across heterogeneous network technologies (WiFi Direct, Bluetooth, NFC) need to be identified, updates of the neighborhood need to be detected with minimum signalling. Therefore different modes need to be supported, e.g., push/pull. This means DICE nodes can announce their presence as well as they can probe their environment to retrieve information.
- Develop a smart broadcasting scheme making use of the wireless broadcast advantage for information distribution.
- Develop algorithms to predict the quality of a link to a neighbour in means of link stability and link quality, but also in relation to the amount and quality of available data.
- Develop methods (gateway concepts) to communicate between neighbors with heterogeneous link layer technologies, e.g. connect sensor nodes with IEEE 802.15.4 to smartphones with WiFi access.
- Develop an efficient data link-layer protocol: the signalling overhead needs to be kept to a minimum to optimize performance and energy-efficiency, still the reliability of the transmission between neighbors needs to be maintained.
- Develop schemes supporting the information security realized in the the higher layers: e.g., encryption on link layer, link-layer protection against modification
- Support anonymity of data already in link-layer: this needs to be considered together with higher layers functions, but it needs to be ensured that link layer protocols do not contradict higher layer anonymity of data.
- Develop a smart forwarding protocol: The features such as named based information dissemination, caching at different points and transmitting of the information, specially in a distributed environment should be considered.

4.4   Data Security and Safety

The DICE collects and propagates data from several users. This data consists of the primary data on the one hand, but also of derived data. The protection of this information must be assured by trustful handling without being too restrictive, as the usage of this (derived) information is the key to having handy and useful applications. However, the innovative concept of anonymous, infrastructureless data transfer and storage in DICE leads to new security threats:

- How to ensure no users are acting purely selfishly and only consuming data from the DICE instead of also contributing and forwarding?
- How to prevent an application or any third party from manipulating the data used by other applications in order to distort the data base? As there is no global server the data that is sent by devices nearby cannot be validated and must therefore be trusted.
- How to guarantee anonymity on the one hand and prevent abuse of the system on the other hand?

Though we do not focus on implementing very sophisticated security features for the first prototype, we will concentrate on lightweight (in term of memory and CPU usage) protocols and energy efficient implementations. Particular attention will be given to design interoperability between devices with very different capabilities, thus the need to support negotiations between different cryptographic and security parameters. Our first prototype implementation will be open to possible trade-offs between degree of security and system efficiency.

5   Application Ecosystem

In the previous section we have presented the implementation design of our DICE architecture. However, its usage and the possible business models behind it are as important as its functionality or performance. In summary, DICE is and will be implemented as an open-source community effort, so that everybody can take advantage of it everywhere. Any other business model for the main supporting architecture is unthinkable because of the targeted applications. However, DICE provides only the platform, not the data and not the user-oriented applications. At the same time, we assume that data emerges from usage: i.e. if you want to use a DICE service, you need to also produce/sense data. Thus, the remaining question is which kind of applications DICE is able to support and what are their underlying business models. We differentiate between:

End-user simple applications. These applications are end-user oriented and visualise or generally consume directly the data provided by other users. For example, a map representation of the noise levels around the current location of a user or a list representation of the closest vegetarian restaurants. The shared properties are simple visualization/representation in a map/list/table and simple processing of the available data by summarising, averaging, etc.

These applications are simple to implement. However, different users have different tastes and preferences for how a particular piece of data should be represented. For example, some people prefer generally using a map, some prefer using a list. Additionally, while the processing of the data is trivial, there are also billions of possibilities how to combine it. For example, Alice might want to see all vegetarian or biological restaurants around but also all Jazz bars, but Bob might be interested in all non-Asian grill restaurants.

Thus, the solution is to provide the users directly with the possibility to "implement" their data consumption applications in a building-block style. There, several visualisation options are provided together with a free selection of data filters. Not only that the user will be able to customise their own applications, they will also be able to exchange the applications themselves through the DICE platform. This will further motivate end users to participate in the process and increase the attractiveness of the platform, keeping it at zero costs for the users. The building-block style application programming will be part of the open-source community effort, to make sure again that the service can reach all citizens.

Sophisticated or specialised applications. Some applications will require a more sophisticated data mining processing behind the scenes than simple data presentation. For example, all reports arriving from citizens about their environment, such as broken street lamps, need to carefully recognised to make it more comfortable to the end users. For example, a typical report would be "broken street lamp!" or "flowers need some more water here!". These reports will have a geospatial timestamp to localise the problem, but no tags nor meta data. Thus, the application running on the smartphone of the gardening brigade in the city needs to filter all messages relevant to it, irrespective of the language or the exact wording they use. This will require a sophisticated data mining approach.

However, also other usages are possible, such as using DICE as the main traditional-style communication platform in case of emergencies of disasters. In this case, a specialised application is needed to serve the needs of fire brigades, police or volunteers. Thus, such applications become the task of professional programmers and data mining experts, who can sell their products to local authorities, industries or organisations, who need more complex data processing or non-standard solutions.

Advertisements. Another possible usage of the DICE platform is to launch advertisements or other paid information to local users. For example, a small shop in the city centre might decide to send a 20% coupon to all users around to draw their attention and to come in. The payment option makes it possible to keep the advertisement for a longer time near the shop or to give it priority when propagated within the DICE platform.

The above examples show in how many different ways such a platform can be used and how many novel business models can arise form it especially for small, medium and startup businesses. Similarly to the app boom in all currently available app stores, DICE is able to generate a whole new ecosystem of applications and services at extremely low cost for end users.

6   Conclusion and Outlook

In this paper, we have discussed a feasible implementation design for a new approach to cloud computing, called the Massively Distributed Cloud (MDC). The DICE architecture is completely independent from communication infrastructures and instead uses direct communications between devices to exchange relevant data. Services in this cloud are also distributed, where users are able to define their very own requirements. The DICE architecture presented here is under active development for the Android platform.

As future work, both simulative and theoretical analysis will be done to evaluate DICE platform and its services. The objective is to do a requirement analysis (in terms of requirements in communication and networking, resource management, security, data management, etc) to investigate how the proposed architecture can be adapted and scalable in different application scenarios. Further, our implementation work should be extended for heterogenous platforms (Android, IoS, WSN, etc) and devices (smart phones, tablets, sensors, etc). Last but not least, we will launch a real user pilot study to evaluate the social attractiveness of this novel paradigm and better meet user requirements and expectations.

Acknowledgements. We would like to thank our European colleagues and friends, Amy L. Murphy from FBK Trento, Italy; Alberto Montresor from the University of Trento, Italy; Axel Wegner from TuTech Innovation GmbH; Frank Bittner, Ulfert Nehmiz and Mehmet Kus from Otaris Interactive Services, Germany; Mischa Dohler from WorldSensing Inc., Spain and Oliver Gerstheimer from chilli mind GmbH, Germany. The presented vision in this paper has been the result of fruitful and interesting discussions with these people. Further, we thank Isaac Supeene for the implementation work done in communication module during his stay at the University of Bremen as an exchange student.

References

1. Förster, A., Kuladinithi, K., Timm-Giel, A., Görg, C., Giordano, S.: Towards the massively distributed cloud. Under submission (2013)
2. Garg, K., Giordano, S., Förster, A.: A study to understand the impact of node density on data dissemination time in opportunistic networks (in under review, 2013)
3. Jelasity, M., Montresor, A., Babaoglu, O.: Gossip-based aggregation in large dynamic networks. ACM Trans. Comput. Syst. 23(1), 219–252 (2005)
4. Guerrieri, A., Carreras, I., De Pellegrini, F., Montresor, A., Miorandi, D.: Distributed estimation of global parameters in delay-tolerant networks. Computer Communications 33(13) (August 2010)
5. Jacobson, V., Smetters, D.K., Thornton, J.D., Plass, M.F., Briggs, N.H., Braynard, R.L.: Networking named content. In: Proceedings of the 5th International Conference on Emerging Networking Experiments and Technologies, CoNEXT 2009, pp. 1–12 (2009)
6. Wenning, B., Lukosius, A., TimmGiel, A., Görg, C., Tomic, S.: Opportunistic distance-aware routing in multi-sink mobile wireless sensor networks. In: Proceedings of the ICT-MobileSummit (2008)

Author Index